Taking Religious Pluralism Seriously

Taking Religious Pluralism Seriously

Spiritual Politics on America's Sacred Ground

Edited by

Barbara A. McGraw
and Jo Renee Formicola

Baylor University Press
Waco, Texas USA

Book Design by Gryphon Graphics
Cover Design: Pamela Poll

Portions of chapter 12 are reprinted from *The Protestant Presence in Twentieth-
Century America: Religion and Political Culture* by Phillip E. Hammond. Used with
permission by the State University of New York Press ©1992 State University of
New York. All Rights Reserved.

Library of Congress Cataloging-in-Publication Data

Taking religious pluralism seriously : spiritual politics on America's
    sacred ground / edited by Barbara A. McGraw and Jo Renee
    Formicola.
      p. cm.
    Includes bibliographical references (p.   ) and index.
    ISBN 1-932792-33-3 (pbk. : alk. paper)
    1. Religion and politics--United States. 2. United States--Religion.
    3. Religious pluralism--United States.   I. McGraw, Barbara A.
    II. Formicola, Jo Renee, 1941-   .
    BL2525.T35 2005
    201'.5'0973--dc22
                                                          2005021035

Printed in the United States of America on acid-free paper

To Robert S. Ellwood, whose emphathy with the world's many peoples and faiths continues to move and inspire me and generations of other admirers.
—Barbara

To my husband, Allan, who makes me believe that I can accomplish anything.
—Jo Renee

Contents

Foreword

What does it mean to take religious pluralism seriously? What does it mean to take religious freedom seriously? And how are these two related? This is the set of questions out of which this volume has arisen. They are certainly among the most significant issues in America's new and ever-evolving identity crisis. *Who are we*, we who have launched our ship of state with the words, "We the people of the United States of America"? In the past forty years, since the passage of the Immigration Act in 1965, newcomers have come to America from all over the world, bringing with them the religious traditions of the world. We are now not only Protestants, Catholics, and Jews; we are Hindus and Muslims, Jains, and Sikhs, Buddhists and Zoroastrians, practitioners of Santeria and Wicca. And many of us, some 12 percent according to one poll, are not part of any religious tradition at all.[1] But we are all Americans. Discerning what that means, taking our religious diversity seriously, and bringing the best we have to the creation of a common society—this certainly constitutes one of the most significant challenges the United States has to face today.

To recognize the significance of this challenge, we must see clearly that America's religious diversity is a concomitant of our commitment to religious freedom. They go together. In the beginning, of course, many of those who came to these shores from Europe sought freedom for themselves without imagining that religious freedom should become the basis for a society that would include those who differed from them. In the colonial period there were settlements like the Massachusetts Bay Colony where the Puritan tradition was "established" and where Catholics, Quakers, and Jews were not welcome to stay more than a few days. At the same time, there were opponents like Roger Williams, who rejected such a civil establishment of religion and insisted on toleration and freedom of conscience. His opposition to the Puritan establishment was based on his religious conviction that an established state religion claimed for human institutions the judgments that are God's alone. Indeed, religious faith cannot be coerced by the state, but requires "soul freedom." That very freedom of the soul, of conscience, is suffocated by making religion subject to the dictates of civil authorities. His argument for government free of religious intrusion was, essentially, a theological argument rendered in the service of civil society.

In the course of America's history and formation, there have been many people, like Roger Williams, who have made essentially civic arguments out of religious conviction. From his time to ours, people of deep religious faith have been among the strongest supporters of a public sphere of government that neither intrudes upon religious faith nor is intruded upon by religious institutions. Our civic debates and our religious debates are both important and are both public, but they are distinct and they draw on distinct sources of authority.

There is no question that many of the founders were Christians, but they were determined to create a civic space that would not be dominated by their own faith or any other. Time and again in debates about religious establishment, the likes of Jefferson and Madison argued against state support for religion, and they did so out of religious conviction. They were not "secular," a term that would be an inaccurate anachronism. They were guided by deep religious sensibilities to make a civic argument for a secular state. In his 1785 "Memorial and Remonstrance," Madison argued that the State is not a competent judge of religious truth and has no business interfering in matters of religion. "Whilst we assert for ourselves a freedom to embrace, to profess, and to observe the religion which we believe to be of divine origin, we cannot deny an equal freedom to those whose minds have not yet yielded to the evidence which has convinced us."[2]

For Madison and for many of the founders, the argument for the nonestablishment of religion was theologically grounded. It was certainly not an argument between believers and unbelievers, or between religion and what we now call "secularism." Rather, both sides grounded their views in fundamentally religious affirmations: In standing for religious freedom—even freedom from any form of religion—we honor the very freedom ordained by God. The 1786 Act for Establishing Religious Freedom in Virginia, which became a model for the constitutional approach to the matter, insists "that our civil rights have no dependence on our religious opinions" and resolves that "no man shall be compelled to frequent or support any religious worship, place or ministry whatsoever . . . nor shall otherwise suffer on account of his religious opinions or belief; but that all men shall be free to profess and by argument to maintain, their opinion in matters of religion."[3]

Those who affirmed the Bill of Rights in 1791, with the powerful First Amendment, "Congress shall make no law respecting an establishment of religion or prohibiting the free exercise thereof," could not have fully imagined the religious diversity of America today with our Muslim, Buddhist, Jain, and Hindu citizens. But they did affirm that fundamental principle with a view to the question of religious diversity. Indeed, in the two-year debate over religious freedom in Virginia, Jefferson had argued that the Virginia Act "meant to comprehend, within the mantle of its protection, the Jew and the Gentile, the Christian and the Mahometan, the Hindoo and infidel of every denomination."[4]

In the more than two centuries since then, the sturdy principles of free exercise of religion and the nonestablishment of religion have stood the test of time. America's religious diversity has broadened to include substantial and increasingly vocal groups like those Jefferson only imagined. Religious freedom is, to be sure, the fountainhead of this diversity. And, of course, America's secular humanist traditions are also a product of the freedom of conscience built into the constitutional foundations. Freedom of religion is also freedom *from* religion of any sort. Jefferson's intention in Virginia, as he put it, was to protect not just the variety of believers, but the many forms of nonbelievers, the "infidels" of every faith.

The changes to the American religious landscape that have come with the enactment of the 1965 Immigration Act have caught many people quite by surprise. This new era transformed U.S. immigration policy from one that favored European immigrants to one that welcomed peoples from all over the world. It is no coincidence that this legislation was drafted in the same era that produced the Civil Rights Act of 1964. Congress was able to recognize that the elimination of discrimination on the basis of race or religion required that we look broadly at institutionalized forms of discrimination, including our immigration policy. Thus, in the past forty years, the face of America has become increasingly multicultural and more religiously pluralistic than anyone might have imagined even a century ago when European immigrants passed the Statue of Liberty on their way to Ellis Island. Immigrants from China, India, the Middle East, Indonesia, South America, and elsewhere arrive in America to make new lives, and they bring their unique cultural identities and religious beliefs and practices to cities and towns all across America.

Religious pluralism is a challenge of faith for each and every religious tradition, raising the question of how we as people of faith understand and relate to neighbors of other faiths. Our religious traditions are not all the same, although there is much common ground. Religious difference can be threatening, and attitudes toward the religious other can be fraught with demeaning stereotypes. The past decades have seen the emergence of hundreds of new kinds of interfaith initiatives across America—interfaith blood drives and Habitat for Humanity projects; interfaith discussions on domestic violence, urban violence, and war; interfaith community worship services at Thanksgiving and on Martin Luther King, Jr. Day. Developing a public forum for the discussion of moral issues that are rooted in conscience and religious faith is a significant part of what Barbara McGraw refers to as the Conscientious Public Forum. These are conversations and encounters that are critical to the moral health of our society.

Our new religious diversity is also a challenge for our civic lives and for our discussion as citizens. Here, the presence of minority religious communities is clarifying to the polarization that has taken place around the proper role of religion in public life. If we view these issues from the standpoint of an American Buddhist or Muslim, the religious right vs. secular left polarization, which Barbara McGraw sees as having dominated our thinking, becomes almost irrelevant. This is the gift that religious minorities bring at times when we have been mesmerized by the clamor of the culture wars. They provide both sides with an alternative view that points to the basic issues of religious freedom and the nonestablishment of religion. Many Muslim, Hindu, and Buddhist communities find the freedom of religion in America to be the very ground that supports the flourishing of their faith. Others find it a relief to be in a country where freedom includes the freedom of conscience not to participate in any religious community at all.

A new conceptualization of American identity will certainly have to take account of the changing face of the American people. Even at a time when the emergence of a confident "Christian America" movement is evident, the facts of our American "we" give us a different picture. Muslim Americans have a "Ballot Box Barbeque" in Dallas, and in Houston, they join the caucus process to elect delegates to our national party conventions. Sikh Americans litigate for their rights when facing workplace discrimination on account of their turbans. A Buddhist astronaut died on the *Challenger* and a Hindu astronaut on the *Columbia*. This more complex view of ourselves will require not only the Conscientious Public Forum that enables us to engage one another in and through the distinctive religious or moral language of our conscience. It will also necessitate what McGraw calls the Civic Public Forum that engages our best energies in and through the public language, the bridging language, of our Constitution.

Creating a multireligious, democratic nation requires continued engagement with each other in multiple arenas. The distinction McGraw makes between these two forums of engagement—the religious or conscientious and the civic—is a very significant one. When a Muslim community is blocked from purchasing a property in Palos Heights in suburban Chicago, the public forum can become both heated and muddled. Religious ignorance, prejudice, fear, and privilege can and did come into play. These issues are critical, and the arena for these discussions should be a public interfaith forum. Indeed, a judge in this case recommended a series of interfaith encounters as one approach to resolving the dispute. But matters of law, equal treatment, equal access, and civil rights also come into play. These issues are critical also, and the arena for these discussions should be city council meetings, planning board meetings, and, if necessary, courts of law. There are not only religious issues at stake in many such disputes, but critical constitutional issues. All public forums are, in one sense, local. It is in each local community that the struggle to regain what McGraw calls "America's Sacred Ground" will take place.

Barbara McGraw here and in her previous book, *Rediscovering America's Sacred Ground*, has underlined how important it will be to look to the past in order to find our future. There she finds that the founding fathers took account of a much greater religious diversity than current debates would lead us to believe. She locates America's fundamental identity not in religious traditions that were prominent at the founding, but in freedom of conscience and the principles that frame freedom's expression, which she refers to as "America's Sacred Ground." As McGraw points out, however, freedom of conscience involves more than freedom to worship. Rather, she argues, the founders envisioned a nation engaged in what Jefferson referred to as "free argument and debate," drawing on a variety of perspectives, including religious perspectives. It is important that we be able to distinguish, however, between what are essentially theological debates in which we look for evidence and support to scriptures and resources of our own religious or ethical tradition, and civic debates in which we look for evidence and support to our shared constitutional covenants of citizenship.

America's Sacred Ground provides terminology that makes that distinction clear: the Conscientious Public Forum and the Civic Public Forum. The distinction is important to understand. Our theologies, our religious histories, and the resources of our individual conscience will remain distinctive and particular. They are the bearers of some of our deepest differences. In the ethical conversations that stem from our theological convictions, we will not expect to reach consensus, but we will better understand the issues, we will appreciate our very real differences, and we will even seek to persuade one another of our views. But our civic conversation must ground us not in our particular and different faith traditions, but in the constitutional principles that bring us together and that protect every one of us, even those with whom we disagree most vehemently. Here, as McGraw sees it, our public discourse cannot be a debate between overarching worldviews vying for dominance, but must be a dialogue that takes place on the undergirding common ground of citizenship.

Like McGraw, I believe that the challenge of America's new and wider pluralism is not that it requires a break with the past, but rather that it spurs us to claim for a new and more complex age the principles of religious freedom that shaped our nation. The challenge is now to make good on the promise of religious freedom, so basic to the very idea and image of America from the very beginning. Pluralism is much more than the simple fact of diversity. Pluralism is not a given, but an achievement. It is engaging that diversity in the creation of a common society. Now, as then, the task is to engage in the common tasks of civil society people who do not share a single history or a single religious tradition. How can we do this when we are all coming from so many different directions and are without a common language? McGraw shows us that a common language can be derived from the political framework, principles, and purpose of the nation set down by the founders— America's Sacred Ground.

In this volume, McGraw and her collaborators engage in a conversation that began at sessions of the American Political Science Association and the American Academy of Religion on the subject of "America's Sacred Ground." Coming from diverse religious and humanist perspectives, they address the differences between the two kinds of public forums: the Conscientious Public Forum and the Civic Public Forum. Their different perspectives and their distinctive voices interrupt the "religious right/secular left" polarization with a much more complex multireligious conversation. They try out the language and framework of America's Sacred Ground and reaffirm, in a new key, the principles on which the nation stands. Not unexpectedly, they do not all agree, but they demonstrate how the wisdom and perspectives of their religious traditions would participate in both the Conscientious Public Forum and the Civic Public Forum. They give us a glimpse in this conversation of why it is so important to take religious pluralism seriously.

Creating a vibrant multireligious democracy in which difference is a strength rather than a liability is not only America's challenge, but an issue for nations throughout the world today—from Malaysia and Indonesia to Germany and France. How can we create an environment that is safe both for interreligious conversations and civic conversations? How can we productively engage our deepest differences in the creation of a common society? And these are not only national issues as nations come to grips with major demographic shifts and multiple new religious currents, but they are also international issues, as national and nongovernmental actors attempt to work together on issues too large for any to solve alone. *Taking Religious Pluralism Seriously* shows us a way to reach across boundaries of difference, while remaining rooted in fundamental and common principles. There could be no more important work today.

Diana L. Eck
Professor of Comparative Religion and Indian Studies
Frederic Wertham Professor of Law and Director,
The Pluralism Project, Psychiatry in Society, Harvard University

[1] The Barna Group, General Religious Beliefs Survey, 2002. http://www.barna.org/FlexPage.aspx?Page=Topic&TopicID=2

[2] James Madison, "Memorial and Remonstrance," *Letters and Other Writings of James Madison* (Philadelphia: 1867), I:162ff.

[3] "An Act for Establishing Religious Liberty," in *The Life of Thomas Jefferson in Three Volumes*, ed. Henry A. Randall (New York: Derby & Jackson, 1858), 31–48.

[4] Cited in Barbara A. McGraw, *Amicus Curiae Brief, Elk Grove Unified School District et al. v. Newdow*, Case No. 1624, 13 February 2004, 18. See also Susan Jacoby, *Freethinkers: A History of American Secularism* (New York: Henry Holt, 2004), 19; and Barbara A. McGraw, *Rediscovering America's Sacred Ground: Public Religion and Pursuit of the Good in a Pluralistic America* (Albany: State University of New York Press, 2003), 82–84.

Preface

Barbara A. McGraw and Jo Renee Formicola met quite by serendipity at the American Political Science Association Meeting in Philadelphia in 2003. McGraw, from California, and Formicola, from New Jersey, had never crossed paths before, but sat down next to each other at a panel discussion on faith-based initiatives. After the panel presentations and the discussion among the participants that followed, McGraw and Formicola turned toward each other and began to talk about their similar concerns—the role of religion in American public life and the policy process, religious pluralism, and some of the current challenges to both religion and government.

McGraw's book, *Rediscovering America's Sacred Ground*, had just been published, and Formicola also had recently published *Faith-Based Initiatives and the Bush Administration* with two other colleagues. Animated conversation soon led to an exchange of perspectives about religious pluralism in America. Both scholars expressed a desire for religion, in all its manifestations, to participate in public discourse in a way that would nevertheless preserve the separation of church and state. As their conversation continued, it became apparent to them that expanding the discourse about the role of religion in public life could make a significant contribution to public policy debates. Consequently, Formicola suggested that they work together on such a project and use McGraw's moral and political framework for public discourse from *Rediscovering America's Sacred Ground*, which welcomes religion as a participant in a context that preserves freedom of conscience and its expression for everyone. When McGraw and Formicola returned to their respective educational institutions, they put together an invitation to participate and began contacting potential contributors—religious studies and political science scholars who could speak from the perspectives of a number of religious orientations represented in America.

McGraw and Formicola submitted panel proposals to the American Political Science Association and the American Academy of Religion for their annual meetings in September and November the following year. In the meantime, they developed a book proposal for the project, and the religious studies and political science scholars who had signed on to the project began drafting chapters. The APSA and AAR panels sparked further interest and debate, and McGraw and Formicola returned to their respective educational institutions to finalize their own chapters and edit the remainder. This book is the result.

Each of the contributors of the chapters is both a scholar and a practitioner of his or her religious tradition. Speaking from the perspectives of Judaism, Confucianism, Catholicism, Eco-Spirituality, Mormonism, Islam, Black Churches, Hinduism, the Baptist Church, Buddhism, and Unsecular Humanism, the chapters address current public debates about religion and values through McGraw's framework for debate, which she refers to as "America's Sacred Ground."

Barbara McGraw begins this book by introducing the reader to "America's Sacred Ground," its two-tiered Public Forum (the Civic Public Forum and the Conscientious Public Forum), and the principles that guide it. In so doing, she shows how the American system embraces pluralism, while not devolving into moral relativism, and how religious people, acting responsibly in accordance with the principles of the two-tiered Public Forum, can contribute to public debate while not undermining the system makes an open discourse from a variety of perspectives possible.

Kenneth Wald responds in his chapter that Jews have developed two political ethics over their four-thousand-year history. These two ethics have "led them to embrace either theocracy or a hostility to any religiously based claims in the public square," both of which align with what McGraw has critiqued as top-down overarching worldview approaches to government. Nonetheless, Wald believes that Jews may be especially situated today to provide a "middle way" that comports with America's Sacred Ground.

Thomas Selover provides a Confucian perspective to analyze some of America's current problems. He points out the growth in numbers of Asians and the influence of their religious traditions, including Confucian values, in the United States. His chapter speaks about Confucian civic virtues and their special emphasis on the linkage between the personal, social, and cosmic realms. He shows how Confucianism can provide an enriched perspective on the principles of America's Sacred Ground.

Jo Renee Formicola contends that the Catholic Church is playing two conflicting roles today in American public life. One is as the protector of the unborn, the poor, and the vulnerable; the other is as defender of its own interests, particularly in the matter of clerical sexual abuse. She contends that this inconsistent behavior has created "both a moral and a political dilemma for its leadership and laity," making it more difficult for Catholicism to play a meaningful role in building the good society on America's Sacred Ground.

Stephen Woolpert examines the "dynamic and creative connection between spiritual and environmental concerns." He does this by exploring the politically and spiritually influential eco-spiritualist, His Holiness the Dalai Lama. Woolpert's chapter looks at the Dalai Lama's "ecological praxis and shows how in certain ways, it amplifies the principles illustrated in America's Sacred Ground."

John Pottenger looks at the "gap between the moral teachings of the Church of Latter Day Saints, the cultural relativism of American society," and the government's involvement in "private social relations." His chapter gives a unique perspective on how the LDS Church "works to protect its identity and defend its sense of community by supporting religious liberty and focusing on issues related to the family." In so doing, Pottenger illustrates the ways in which such issues can be addressed within the context of America's Sacred Ground's two-tiered Public Forum, while at the same time exhibiting a tension with it.

Muqtedar Khan adds a distinct voice to this book. He comments on three unique groups among Muslims in America, and shows how each is attempting to advance religious and social notions of Islam within American public life. Further, he discusses how the tragedy of 9/11 exaggerated and traumatized the Muslim potential to participate in helping to create a greater American society. Nevertheless, he shows how one group came to embrace America's Sacred Ground and has come to prominence amongst Muslims in America, in large part because of 9/11.

James Lance Taylor gives new insight into the African American Christian experience in America. He begins with a discussion of the nature of Black religious involvement in the Civic and Conscientious Public Forums, then explains the origins of the Black spiritual cosmos and its relationship to America's Sacred Ground, and ends by showing various Black religious responses to American public life. His chapter discusses the dual role of Black religion—as both an opiate and a liberator of its people in American history.

Anantanand Rambachan maintains that the relationship between Hinduism in America and America's Sacred Ground is uniquely symbiotic. He points out on the one hand that the wisdom of Hinduism's essentially pluralistic theological vision, based on the inherent worth of the human being as the embodiment of the infinite divine spirit (brahman), complements and supports America's Sacred Ground. He suggests on the other hand that the encounter may have the effect of reforming and moving Hinduism more swiftly to affirming those indispensable elements of its worldview that are consistent with the principles of freedom, equal justice, and dignity.

Derek Davis looks at the change in the Baptist tradition of support for religious liberty. He maintains that the historic commitment to separation of church and state has been diminished "dramatically" due to the prevailing belief that America needs moral reform, and that it must come "through increased government advancement of religion." He opposes the notion that the only way to stem the tide of moral decline is by loosening constitutional religious prohibitions and urges a return to the Baptist witness for religious liberty, which he argues "staked out" America's Sacred Ground before John Locke and the American founders.

Rita Gross gives a Buddhist response to how religious groups can contribute positively to public life. She maintains that it is critical for religious groups "to renounce exclusive truth claims regarding verbal and symbolic accounts of religion" in the Civic and Conscientious Public Forums, so that a cooperative exchange of ideas that seeks understanding can take place. Significantly, she enriches the discussion about the meaning and scope of the two Public Forums of America's Sacred Ground by analogizing them to the Buddhist doctrine that "form is emptiness; emptiness is form."

David Machacek and Phillip Hammond identify two changes in the Civic Public Forum. The first is that the language of rights has become the language of public moral discourse; the second is that the courts, as the arbiters of constitutional values, have replaced the sovereignty of churches in the public square in such matters. While some have accused the courts of creating an antireligious, amoral form of secularism, Machacek and Hammond argue that the Supreme Court's moral stance is humanistic, but "decidedly" unsecular in that it is actually "reaffirming, if not rediscovering" America's Sacred Ground.

All of these responses are indicative of how important it is to move beyond the current "religious right/secular left" impasse by opening the public discourse to a broad spectrum of views. The chapters of this book enrich that discourse, as they provide various ways of thinking about faith and freedom in the context of contributing to a conversation about building a good society. Rather than pressing competing belief systems, the chapters show how issues can be addressed from various perspectives, while nevertheless preserving the essential "sacred ground" of the nation, which is what makes the participation of everyone possible in the first place. In so doing, the chapters contribute to a conversation that can help America regain its footing on America's Sacred Ground.

The editors wish to thank all those who helped in the completion of this book. Among those are Allison Formicola and Jeffrey Humby, who helped with many of the technological problems that emerged during the writing process. Special thanks goes to Kristin Weis, whose help on the citations and bibliography in this volume was invaluable.

We are also indebted to Carey C. Newman, director, Baylor University Press, whose enthusiasm for this project was an inspiration to both of us, and Diane Smith, the production editor, who expedited the schedule for publication, which the editors have appreciated. We are also especially pleased with the cover for this book and wish to thank Pamela Poll for its colorful and striking design.

The editors also wish to thank the American Political Science Association and the American Academy of Religion for the opportunity to exchange ideas for this book at the annual conferences of those organizations in 2004. In this regard, Barbara A. McGraw expresses her gratitude to the Saint Mary's College of California Faculty Development Committee for providing the financing that made it possible for her to attend these and other such events, and Jo Renee Formicola wishes to thank the College of Arts and Sciences at Seton Hall University for funding her trips to the American Political Science Association meetings in 2003 and 2004, making this project possible.

Lastly, Barbara A. McGraw would like to thank her husband, Patrick M. McCollum, who gave up his wife to her office "in the back" for many, many weeks, and who, as usual, held the home and everything else together in the meantime, and Formicola thanks her husband in her dedication of this project to him.

Barbara A. McGraw
Jo Renee Formicola
March 2005

Chapter 1

Introduction to America's Sacred Ground

Barbara A. McGraw

> Literary talents may be prostituted and the powers of
> genius debased to subserve the purposes of ambition or
> avarice; but the feelings of the heart will dictate the lan-
> guage of truth, and the simplicity of her accents will pro-
> claim the infamy of those, who betray the rights of the
> people, under the specious, and popular pretence of jus-
> tice, consolidation, and dignity.
>   —Elbridge Gerry, *Observations on the New Constitution*
>   *and the Federal and State Conventions* (1788)[1]

REFRAMING THE DEBATE

Today the debate about the role of religion in American public life, and its
role in shaping American values, is mired in a clash between the religious
right and the secular left—the extremes of each vying for dominance. The
strident polemical rhetoric that characterizes the debate polarizes the nation

and undermines the potential for the many other voices of America's pluralistic society to be heard. The current polarization in the popular political discourse of the nation into these two main camps not only divides the nation's people, but also obscures the fundamental structures and principles that make the whole conversation possible in the first place. The result is confusion about the very structures and principles that ultimately serve liberty and equal justice, as well as the whole purpose of the American experiment: the pursuit of the good society.

This confusion is occurring because the debate between the two sides has emerged as a contest between two opposing worldviews—the winner being the side that receives the most votes and therefore gains power over the other. It is no wonder, then, that inflammatory rhetoric is everywhere in the political discourse as each side uses whatever means are available, even including (in some cases) outright dissemination of misinformation, to sway public opinion. The main problem with this situation is that each side, in effect, is assuming there are no rules other than those that make up the procedures by which decisions are made—that is, there are no principles to ground the system itself. Therefore, the idea prevails that the majority rules regardless of the result. Seeing no grounding principles, the secular left and religious right rush to fill the void.

On the one hand, the secular left takes the view that the nation should adhere to a strict interpretation of the doctrine of separation of church and state. The idea is that if the public square is purged of religious influences, and therefore religious views and values are not imposed on others through the instrumentalities of the state, then America will safely preserve liberty and justice for all. The problem with this approach is that history has shown time and again that the secularization of government and society does not necessarily serve those goals. The former Soviet Union was a secular state, and it devolved into a totalitarian regime. Saddam Hussein's Baathist government in Iraq was secular, yet it too was a brutal regime. Clearly, secularism is not the panacea that the secular left believes it is.[2]

On the other hand, the religious right takes the view that public opinion should be swayed to produce a majority in favor of infusing government with Christian, or some say Judeo-Christian, values. The right argues that these are the values on which the nation originally was founded, even though they are not specifically referenced in the Declaration of Independence or the Constitution. The idea is that all governments require a religious worldview to provide the values that hold societies together—and America is no different. The Christian right contends that the Christian tradition has legitimacy as the moral basis of the United States because it is the primary religion of the West, and therefore it is in large part what informed the American founders.

Here, too, history has shown that infusing the state with a particular religious moral worldview, even someone's particular version of Christianity, does not necessarily serve liberty and equal justice. Everyone is amply familiar with the horrors of the Inquisition in Europe, the abuses of John Calvin's Geneva, and the persecutions of the theocracies of colonial America—including the Massachusetts Bay Colony, whose Puritan founders left England's persecution of them only to persecute others in their New World home. Furthermore, Adolf Hitler originally justified persecution of the Jews on the basis of Christian tradition.[3] Clearly, the imposition of a particular interpretation of Christian values onto other Christians and non-Christians through the instrumentalities of the state is not the panacea that the religious right believes it is.

In this author's view, liberty and equal justice will not be served by winning favor with the people and convincing a majority to vote for one side or the other. Nor will liberty and equal justice be served by packing the courts with judges who adhere to one view or the other. Moreover, the problem will not be solved by a mediated compromise across the boundaries of the two camps. The problem will be resolved only if Americans rediscover the founding fathers' fundamental framework, principles, and purpose underlying the American political system.

The founders' idea was to create a space for the many voices of American society to be heard by establishing a political system that preserves the peoples' civil rights, particularly the rights of conscience and expression. These are necessary not only to protect America's minorities (including religious minorities), from discrimination, but also to expand all Americans' opportunities to glean insights from each other, in the hope that together they would advance their understanding of how America can fully realize its promise. That is, although the founders did not fully realize in their own time the ideal to which they appealed, the political system they established was based on a fundamental framework and set of principles that, if fully implemented, would provide maximum liberty for all within a moral context that would serve as the means for building the good society from the ground up. This author refers to that framework and its principles and purpose as "America's Sacred Ground."

Unfortunately, what is occurring in the debate today is undermining America's Sacred Ground. First, the dominant participants, that is, the religious right and secular left, have become entrenched. The result is the reification of circumscribed positions and narrow reasoning, which has led to a standoff with little hope of either side or anyone else circumventing the impasse. Second, the standoff itself has led to a glorification of the battle— the "culture war"—with the media taking sides and the goal being victory of one side over the other, rather than pursuit of the good for the nation as a whole. This is why it is important, even critical, for the debate to engage a much broader spectrum of participants across America's pluralistic society.

Some contend that the engagement of those in the many minority religions with those in the majority is not warranted because those minority faiths include only a small percentage of the American people. However, American history has shown that it is generally those from the margins of society who rise up and reinvigorate the principles of the nation, taking American ever closer to the ideal of liberty and justice for all. Further, the wisdom from the world's religions in America in conversation with American ideals no doubt will contribute to public discourse in new ways, and in so doing, will help to open up the now entrenched debate. Moreover, while it can certainly be said that the vast majority of America's people are Christian, what is often forgotten in the debate today is that Christianity itself is not monolithic. Christianity is wonderfully diverse, and that diversity brings a whole spectrum of pluralistic perspectives to the conversation as well. To ignore this is to ignore the ongoing discourse within Christianity itself, which is rich with insights and possibilities for moving public debate beyond its current impasse toward a greater understanding of the principles underlying the nation.

This book attempts to bring together some of the many voices of America's pluralistic society, representing several Christian perspectives (Catholic, Mormon, Baptist, Black churches), as well as Judaism, Islam, Buddhism, Hinduism, Eclectic Eco-Spirituality, Confucianism, and Humanism, to address issues in the contemporary public debate in America today while engaging the framework, principles, and purpose of America's Sacred Ground. In so doing the hope is to show how a more open discourse on critical issues of the day can be conducted without undermining the fundamental structures and values of the nation, and also how each religious perspective can contribute to the rediscovery of America's Sacred Ground.

The rediscovery of America's Sacred Ground in public discourse, however, will not provide "common ground" in the sense that it necessarily directs a particular outcome in the resolution of the issues of the day. What it can do is provide a common language, structure, and values for the debate that is consonant with the original intentions of the American founders. In so doing, America's Sacred Ground can provide moral clarity that facilitates a much broader discussion than occurs today. That way Americans can work together toward reasoned compromise, while not compromising America's Sacred Ground in the process. Then the American people may just fulfill the founders' hope "that America would be fertile enough for the good to take root, grow, and flourish in a lively, free, and open forum for debate about religion and morality—not by force, but by choice."[4]

Before turning to the various religious perspectives in the other chapters in this book, it will be necessary for the reader to become familiar with the fundamental framework, principles, and language of America's Sacred Ground. What follows, then, is an introduction to America's Sacred Ground. Those interested in more in-depth philosophical and historical support for the ideas presented here are referred to this author's previous publication, *Rediscovering America's Sacred Ground: Public Religion and Pursuit of the Good in a Pluralistic America* (SUNY Press, 2003), to which many of the contributing authors of *Taking Religious Pluralism Seriously* also refer.

BUILDING THE GOOD SOCIETY FROM THE GROUND UP

In order to rediscover America's Sacred Ground, it is helpful to explore, at least briefly in this venue, a significant aspect of the theory of government that was prevalent in Europe before the establishment of the United States. This is the theory of government that was rejected by John Locke in works that were central inspirations to the American founders a century later.[5] That rejected approach was based on traditional Christian political theory. It was a religious justification for government that developed from the doctrine of original sin.[6] Its central premise was this: People are inherently sinful, and so government is necessary to restrain the sinful nature of human beings. In other words, the role of the state is to keep people uniformly "in line," in accordance with the doctrines of the authorities—that is, not sinning.

This approach requires that government and religious organizations be close allies. The churches seek government's involvement for an effective means to enforce church doctrine regarding sin, and government uses the sanction of the church to justify its punishments. Under this system the state is an instrument of religion and religion is an instrument of the state. Government dominates the people by establishing a uniform moral order, which is promoted by exercise of the coercive power of the state. That is, it is a top-down overarching moral worldview *enforced* by the state. Examples of top-down overarching systems around the world include classical Hinduism, which generated the caste system as an expression of *dharma* (the moral order) as a reflection of *rita* (the divine order); medieval Catholicism and the Holy Roman Empire; the Church of England and the seventeenth-century British Crown (which John Locke opposed); Neo-Confucianism and the eleventh and twelfth century Song Dynasty in China; and, today, Islam and Saudi Arabia.[7] (Figure A on the following page provides a visual representation of this "top-down" type of system.)

In European history, those who promoted this top-down system of government believed it provided the best way to ensure that society would be peaceful and good. But John Locke's immediate experience of his own society, and his review of societies throughout history, proved to him that this approach did not result in a society that could be thought of as good.[8] Rather, that approach resulted in terrible wars, religious conflict and strife, the torture and hanging of heretics, and the corruption of both religion and government.[9] Moreover, coercion of the people made no sense to Locke, because that would make them heretics to their own convictions.[10] It was clear to Locke that what a top-down overarching worldview system produced in practice was far from the peaceful society that uniformity promised. Consequently,

FIGURE A

"Top-Down Overarching Worldview"
Approach to Government

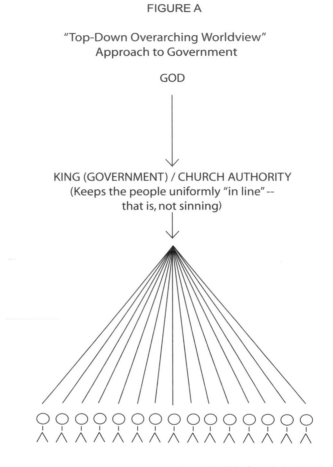

GOD

KING (GOVERNMENT) / CHURCH AUTHORITY
(Keeps the people uniformly "in line" --
that is, not sinning)

©2003 Barbara A. McGraw

John Locke, contrary to his earlier writings,[11] developed an approach that rejected the doctrine of original sin as a basis for government and the whole political system derived from it.[12]

Although there are recent dissenters,[13] the prevailing view of Locke in the academy has been that Locke was a "secular"[14] philosopher who rejected religion and whose political philosophy promoted a religion-free public square. However, that assessment is fundamentally flawed. Locke did not reject religion. Instead, he shifted to a different religious idea based on a very simple theology: there is God, and God communicates *with the people*. Consequently, Locke advocated the view that God's relationship and communication are not with the elites of religious institutions and the state, who then coerce the people to conform to their interpretation of God's will. Instead, God's relationship and communication are with each individual human being—

through conscience. The idea is that God comes to conscience through revelation, spiritual or other insight, and through nature and reason.[15] This is why freedom of conscience must be preserved: so that the people can listen for and hear the voice of God and participate in society according to that call.

In other words, according to Locke's political theology, one of the main functions of government is to preserve God's relationship with the people by establishing a government that does not involve the domination of the people by the state—or by the churches through the instrumentalities or sanction of the state.[16] Rather, Locke's idea was that government should be formed by the people and for the people to preserve the people's natural, inalienable rights, especially freedom of conscience and its expression.[17]

But the question for those who held to the top-down overarching worldview approach to government was this: How is the good society going to come about, if the state and the churches are not working together to tell people what is right and then enforcing their idea of right? It was Locke's view that, because history had shown that a peaceful and good society did not result from top-down governmental coercion, the only way it would even be possible for a good society to come about would be to set up a political system that preserves the liberty of each individual to discern through his and her own conscience what is pleasing to God. Then, as individuals of conscience freely express themselves from the perspective conscience gives them, they work together to create the good society from the ground up. In other words, Locke devised a political system that limits the authority of state and church elites and instead relies on the goodwill of the people to act in accordance with conscience in the public forum and work together to seek the true and the good. As John Locke said:

> For truth certainly would do well enough, if she were once left to shift for herself. She seldom has received, and I fear never will receive, much assistance from the power of great men, to whom she is but rarely known, and more rarely welcome. She is not taught by laws, nor has she any need of force to procure her entrance into the minds of men. Errors indeed prevail by the assistance of foreign and borrowed succours, but if truth makes not her way into the understanding by her own light, she will be but the weaker for any borrowed force violence can add to her.[18]

That is, in such a system, God works through the people as they engage in a great conversation about religion, morality, and the general welfare. In so doing, they build the good society by establishing a government based on the "social contract" of the people.[19] Beyond this, however, the people are free to form associations or "spontaneous societies."[20] These associations are authentic because their members participate voluntarily.[21] Moreover, because the people involved are free to express conscience without governmental interference, but with governmental protection from severe punishment (e.g., physical harm) by others, the people are more likely to live by the courage of their convictions. Consequently, these associations or societies, what this author refers to as "communities of conscience," benefit from the exercise of the moral agency of their members. (Figure B provides a visual representation of this "ground-up" type of system.)

FIGURE B.

"Ground-Up" Approach to Government

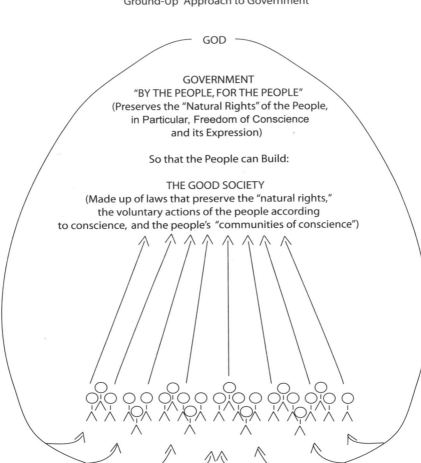

©2003 Barbara A. McGraw

The founding fathers adopted John Locke's fundamental ideas. They took Locke's theory, his political theology, and put it into practice. They set up a government by the people and for the people, and they acknowledged freedom of conscience and the right to express conscience as the primary rights of the people. They understood that not only were these rights to be protected for the private benefit of individual people, but that a government by and for the people was to serve as the *means* to the good society.[22] The founders expressed Locke's philosophy in the Declaration of Independence and preserved the inalienable rights of conscience and expression in the First Amendment to the U.S. Constitution and in the constitutions and declarations of rights of the states.[23] For this reason, elsewhere this author has referred to John Locke as the "prophet of America."[24]

These Lockean fundamentals, adopted and put into practice by the American founders, are what constitute America's Sacred Ground, which underlies the founding documents of the nation. In sum, America's Sacred Ground is: (a) a political theology based on God's relationship with each and every human being, which gives rise to (b) the inalienable right to freedom of conscience, which is freely expressed in (c) a context, that is, the "Public Forum" where (d) the people can fulfill the purpose of the system—to build the good society from the ground up.

FIGURE C

"America's Sacred Ground" consists of:
•   A political theology, based on God's relationship with each and every human being,which gives rise to
•   the inalienable right to freedom of conscience, which is freely expressed in
•   a context, that is, the "Public Forum," where
•   the people can fulfill the purpose of the system—to build the good society from the ground up.

©2003 Barbara A. McGraw

IN PURSUIT OF A GOOD SOCIETY THAT IS FREE FOR *ALL*, NOT A STRUCTURELESS, AMORAL "FREE-FOR-ALL"

Aiming for the True and the Good

The founders agreed with Locke that a top-down overarching worldview approach to government does not produce a peaceful, good society. That approach results in the corruption of political processes and oppression of the people as various elites vie for dominance.[25] This is why liberty of the people is at the core of the founders' ground-up approach to government. But the founders never intended freedom of conscience and its expression to be only for each individual's own self-interested benefit. Rather, the Public Forum, within which conscience is expressed, was to provide a moral and political context that ensures that the people have the political ability and opportunity to build the good society.

Consequently, the founders did not establish a system that would be merely a "free-for-all" with no moral grounding, which would amount to a battle for dominance. Rather, the political system set out in the founding documents of the nation has a basic framework that is grounded in moral principles that stand behind those founding documents. These, in turn, provide the greatest chance for America to fulfill its intended purpose—a society that is free for *all*, while aiming for the true and the good.[26]

The First Core Principle: Freedom of Conscience and Its Expression

The framework and principles of the Public Forum of the American political system begin, of course, with liberty—specifically, freedom of conscience and its expression. This derives from the natural law in the "state of nature" where the people have "free will," and consequently the people's actions are not predetermined by God.

The American founders, and John Locke before them, understood that a political system that values freedom in search of the true and the good requires a free and open Public Forum for debate, conversation, and action—where ideas can be exchanged and actions can be taken and witnessed. In this way, the overall goal of building the good society from the ground up is served by providing the maximum opportunity for good ideas to be considered and put into practice by the people.

At the time of the founding of the United States, of course, certain states limited who would be permitted to serve in government. However, no such limit ever existed at the federal level and, at the state level, such limitations generally were drawn narrowly and eventually were totally eliminated.[27] Even when such limitations existed, there were still admonitions in the state constitutions and declarations of rights that the people's full freedom of conscience and expression otherwise were to be ensured by the state.[28] This approach makes sense because, if conscience and its expression are the *means* to the good society, then it follows that the founders could not have intended expressions of conscience to be suppressed in the Public Forum. In fact, this is *what freedom is for*. All expressions are to be welcome in the Public Forum—including, or perhaps even especially, religious expression.

Yet today many argue that the founders did not intend the Public Forum to be open to the myriad perspectives that can be found in contemporary American society. On the one hand, strict secularists argue that the doctrine of separation of church and state eschews religious expression in the Public Forum.[29] On the other hand, those in the religious right contend that religious expression is appropriate for the Public Forum, but that the founders could not have anticipated the vastly diverse religious landscape of today's America. They argue, therefore, that the impact of those diverse perspectives should be limited in public debate. The founders' own time consisted only of various sects of Protestants and perhaps a few Catholics and Jews, they contend. Hence, they argue, it was only Christian or Judeo-Christian perspectives that the founders would have wanted as contributions in public debate because those perspectives were embedded in the culture at the time of the founding and therefore were assumed by the founders. Consequently, these "traditional" faiths should hold sway in the Public Forum.

However, the founders did not eschew religion in public life, as the secularists contend, nor did they limit religious public expression to Christian or Judeo-Christian viewpoints. Instead, freedom of conscience was extended to everyone. While it is true that the vast majority of the population was then (as it is today) Christian, the American founders still took others into consideration when they wrote the constitutions of the United States and the individual states.

As far back as John Locke's 1690 *Letter Concerning Toleration*, a most influential document for the American founders, Locke argued in favor of civil rights for every sort of religious people. He not only included those in the most controversial Protestant sects of his day, but also Catholics, Jews, Muslims (Mahometans), Native Americans, and pagans.[30] In this regard, Locke maintained:

> [I]f solemn assemblies, observations of festivals, public worship be permitted to any one sort of professors [i.e., religious people], all these things ought to be permitted to the Presbyterians, Independents, Anabaptists, Arminians, Quakers, and others, with the same liberty. Nay, if we may openly speak the truth, and as becomes one man to another, neither pagan, nor Mahometan, nor Jew ought to be excluded from the civil rights of the commonwealth because of his religion.[31]

He even contended that those practicing "idolatry, superstition, and heresy," as well as "heathens" should have their civil rights.[32]

The founding fathers followed John Locke's lead, but went even further. Richard Henry Lee expressly acknowledged broad pluralism when he advocated for religious freedom, stating: "I fully agree with the Presbyterians, that true freedom embraces the Mahomitan [Muslim] and the Gentoo [Hindu] as well as the Christian religion."[33] In his "Notes on Religion," Thomas Jefferson echoed John Locke specifically when Jefferson stated: "Shall we suffer a Pagan to deal with us and not suffer him to pray to his god? . . . It is the refusing *toleration* to those of different opinion which has produced all the bustles and wars on account of religion."[34] In addition, Jefferson held that religious freedom should extend well beyond familiar and established Christian sects, and he noted that his view was held widely by others when the Virginia Act for Religious Freedom was being debated:

> The insertion [of Jesus Christ in the preamble] was rejected by the great majority, in proof that they meant to comprehend, within the mantle of its protection, the Jew and the Gentile, the Christian and the Mohammedan, the Hindoo *and the Infidel of every denomination.*"[35]

Also, the founders' many references to God were so varied that one can reasonably conclude that the founders meant to convey a message of inclusiveness that goes well beyond Judeo-Christian conceptions of "God," even beyond a conception of God as necessarily having to be *a* god.[36] The founders used such names as "Supreme Governor of the Universe," "Governor of the Universe," and "the Universal Sovereign."[37] The Declaration of Independence uses the phrase "Nature's God," which should be read as meaning "the God of Reason."[38] In addition to that phrase, it uses the terms "Creator," "Supreme Judge of the world," and "Divine Providence." Furthermore, Jefferson specifically acknowledged that those whose concept of "God" includes many gods nevertheless have the right to freedom of conscience: "[I]t does me no injury for my neighbor to say there are twenty gods or no God."[39] As regards Benjamin Franklin's perspective on the matter, one of his biographers has noted:

> At one point [Benjamin Franklin] expressed a belief in a single supreme God who supervised a number of lesser gods, one of whom had created our world; and he dreamed up an elaborate ritual for a private deistic religious service of his own to take the place of what went on in churches.[40]

The most that can be said is that whomever or whatever the founders meant by use of the word "God" or their other names for the Divine, their understanding was that it created the world and is capable of communicating truth and good to individual human beings. That is, it in some way provides human beings with conscience. Therefore, whether or not the founders identified as being Christian,[41] the founders sought to be much more inclusive than is generally acknowledged, knowingly framing a Constitution that would permit "Jews Turks & infidels"[42] and "Pagans, Deists, and Mahometans,"[43] to be president of the United States.

Moreover, the founders expressly included atheists. Locke had argued that freedom of conscience should not be permitted to atheists "because the denial of God threatens the '[p]romises, covenants, and oaths, which are the bonds of human society' and 'undermine[s] and destroy[s] all religion' and so 'can have no pretence of religion whereupon to challenge the privilege of toleration.' "[44] However, the founders did not limit freedom of conscience only to those who profess a belief in God.[45] As Jefferson said in his "Notes on Religion," "Locke denies tolerance to those . . . who deny the existence of a god . . . it was a great thing to go so far . . . but where he stopped short we may go on."[46]

Clearly, the founders contemplated a future pluralistic society beyond that of their own. Moreover, freedom of conscience was not mere "toleration" or limited to freedom of worship, but was intended to include all as participants in a great conversation.[47] Perhaps Richard Henry Lee put it best when he said in 1787, "It is true, we are not disposed to differ much, at present, about religion; but when we are making a constitution, it is to be hoped, for ages and millions yet unborn. . . ."[48]

Obviously, the founders were aware of many more diverse religious orientations than the participants in today's religious right/secular left debate would lead the public to believe. Therefore, although there were dissenters at the time,[49] the eventual political system established by the founders took account of people of all religious persuasions. Consequently, not only is religion to play an important role in the American system, but people of all faiths and no faith have full freedom of conscience and expression so that they can participate in a great conversation in the free and open Public Forum in pursuit of the true and the good.

The Second Core Principle: Equal Dignity

The American founders also understood that a political system that values freedom in search of the true and the good must provide a legal context for the actions of the people—in order to serve liberty. Otherwise, there would be no basis on which to settle disputes that arise when the liberty of one person impacts the liberty of another. The result would be, as Locke put it, a "state of war" where everyone resorts to the exercise of power—through either collective group or individual action. The most powerful would rise to the top and consolidate power—and then proclaim themselves worthy. These would then dominate and erroneously label that domination "liberty," while undermining the liberty and expression of everyone else.[50] Such a system would be the antithesis of the system that Locke envisioned and the founders established.

Thus, freedom is not a principle that can stand alone, because when it does, it holds the seed to its own destruction. Rather, in order for freedom to prevail to the fullest extent possible for *all*, it must be balanced by its counterpart—the equal dignity of every human being. That is, every person is inherently worthy. Whatever their particular talents, abilities, or afflictions, they are the children of their Creator.[51]

Locke argued, therefore, that there must be an impartial judge of disputes—a legal system that is formed by the people to hold in place a context, the Public Forum, for freedom of conscience and its expression, while at the same time recognizing the equal dignity of every person. This is Locke's "social contract," on which the founders based the American system, where the people bargain away to the state their right to take the law into their own hands in exchange for the state's preservation of the freedom and equal dignity of the people—their inherent inalienable rights. Only when the state fails to fulfill that function do the people have the right to rebel and reestablish a political/legal system that does preserve their natural rights.

The Two-Tiered Public Forum of America's Sacred Ground

In order to provide maximum liberty of the people, the American political system requires government to be limited in its function. At the same time, government is necessary in order to ensure that the equal dignity of every person is respected, and therefore one person's or group's expression of liberty does not result in the limitation or demise of the liberty of others. Further, if the whole purpose of the American system is to build the good society from the ground up through the speech and action of a free people, then the Public Forum must provide maximum opportunity for the great conversation about the true and the good to prevail. In effect, then the two core principles together require drawing a line between those matters that are in the purview of the government and those matters that are in the purview of the consciences and expressions of the people.

To accomplish these goals, the American system as conceived by the American founders has, in effect, two tiers, each of which has grounding principles. This author refers to the first tier—the realm for legitimate governmental action and the forum for public debate about the extents and limits of legitimate governmental action—as the "Civic Public Forum" and the second tier—the realm of public duties that are not the subjet of governmental action and the forum for debate about the meaning and scope of those duties—as the "Conscientious Public Forum."

The "Civic Public Forum" and Its Principles: "No Harm" and "Consistency/No Hypocrisy"

The Civic Public Forum is guided by two basic principles—that is, two fundamental laws, both of which serve the two core principles of freedom and equal dignity. The first is the law of "no harm." This is the principle that no one may harm another in his "life, health, liberty or possessions."[52] Therefore, the people enjoy liberty in their beliefs and activities—unless, in the case of activities, there is harm to another.[53] The second principle is the law of "consistency/no hypocrisy," a reversed Golden Rule: Do not do unto others what you would not want done unto you.[54] That is, there should be equal justice. To deny to others what we do not deny ourselves would be profound hypocrisy, which Locke and the founders held to be of the greatest offense to reason and God because it is in utter discord with the natural law of equal dignity.[55] Thus, the Civic Public Forum has a religious and moral ground in that it is framed by principles that, in turn, serve the core principles of freedom and equal dignity based on the natural law.

Consequently, the religious right's argument that the United States is not wholly "secular," as strict secularists claim, is correct. However, the religious right's view that the government should foster *all* Judeo-Christian moral values in society is fundamentally flawed. Only those moral values that are compatible with the Civic Public Forum principles are legitimate contributions in the Civic Public Forum for law and governmental enforcement.

One may certainly point out that the core principles and the laws of the Civic Public Forum owe a debt to a particular theological and philosophical thread in the Christian tradition, just as another may argue that another thread of the Christian tradition has at times promoted top-down overarching worldview dominance. But, in any event, to the degree that the values and practices of a particular version of Christianity go beyond the scope of the Civic Public Forum, they are not legitimate bases for governmental action.

In fact, the American founders were very clear that they did not want church authorities to impose their will on the people and thus thwart the American system—the system that makes possible a society of free people who can aim for the true and the good and build the good society from the ground up.[56] It is important to emphasize, however, that, in order to build the good society, the founders did contemplate that religious *people* would participate publicly from the perspective of conscience, including religious conscience, while respecting the core principles and the two laws. In fact, the founders themselves participated in this way. For example, in his "Bill for Establishing Religious Freedom" (1779), Thomas Jefferson made religious arguments in the Civic Public Forum:

> Almighty God hath created the mind free, and manifested his supreme will that free it shall remain by making it altogether insusceptible of restraint; that all attempts to influence it by temporal punishments, or burthens, or by civil incapacitations, tend only to beget habits of hypocrisy and meanness, and are a departure from *the plan of the holy author of our religion*. . . .[57]

Furthermore, religious voices have been raised in defense of the two core principles and the two laws of the Civic Public Forum throughout American history. For example, the Quakers, in effect, appealed to the principles of the Civic Public Forum when they actively participated in the Civic Public Forum in the years leading up to the Civil War, and before, as advocates for the abolition of slavery. Also, in the mid-nineteenth century, Elizabeth Cady Stanton and Phoebe Palmer of the "holiness" movement, which was a Christian evangelical movement, argued in favor of women's rights, again appealing, in effect, to the principles of the Civic Public Forum.[58] And Martin

Luther King Jr.'s many sermons advocating for African Americans' civil rights used religious imagery and were significant contributions to the Civic Public Forum debate. As a matter of fact, religion in defense of the oppressed is especially appropriate in the Civic Public Forum because "the oppressed hold a special place for America's Sacred Ground, as they did for Locke, because they guide America to an ever-unfolding understanding of the depth of the sacred civil rights. . . ."[59]

It is clear, therefore, that the strict secularists' argument that religion and morality are not proper matters for public debate is flawed. This strict secularist view that religion should be something that people keep hidden, in private, out of the view of others, is based on a fundamental misunderstanding of how the American system works and a misconception about the purpose of the nation. In fact, John Locke and the American founders expressly contemplated a "public" place for religion.[60] This has to be so because, if it were true that religious voices did not belong in public, then the whole purpose of the American system—to build the good society from the ground up in accordance with conscience—would be thwarted.

Still, the secularists' view is correct that religion cannot legitimately dictate law and public policy beyond the limits of the Civic Public Forum. As they note, for example, while Jefferson invoked religion in favor of public policy, he also rejected the notion that any civil or ecclesiastical "legislators and rulers" have any legitimate authority over "the faith of others," and said that the imposition of "their own opinions and modes of thinking" has "established and maintained false religions over the greatest part of the world and through all time. . . ."[61] That is why the political system established by the founders requires that government's role is to be limited to preserving freedom and equal dignity by enforcing the "no harm" and "consistency/no hypocrisy" laws of the Civic Public Forum, whether it is influenced by religious or secular ideas, and to providing for the general welfare of the people in a manner that is consistent with those principles.

As shown below, religious and moral expressions that go beyond the scope of the Civic Public Forum are legitimate public expressions as well. However, they belong in the second tier of the Public Forum.

The "Conscientious Public Forum" and Its Principles: "Raising Consciousness" and "Participation"

In light of the immediately preceding discussion, one might conclude that all matters not legitimately in the purview of governmental action are "private" concerns. However, such a conclusion, if put into practice, would undermine a critical component of America's Sacred Ground.

Government's limited role certainly leaves much to individual conscience and the "communities of conscience" that individuals create. However, a system that requires little of the people through the coercive force of governmental action requires much of the people in terms of their individual and collective duties to their fellow human beings and society as a whole. Yet Americans are so focused on "rights" that they have forgotten that rights imply duties—public duties that, if not exercised, undermine the whole purpose of the nation to as great a degree as would failure to adhere to the two laws of the Civic Public Forum. These are duties of the "Conscientious Public Forum." The Conscientious Public Forum does not involve the coercive force of government, and therefore it is the forum for persuasion and voluntary acceptance.

Like the Civic Public Forum, the Conscientious Public Forum is guided by two basic principles—in this case, two fundamental moral duties. In fact, the two duties of the Conscientious Public Forum are corollaries of the right to freedom of conscience and its expression, which are protected by law and governmental action in the Civic Public Forum.

Recall that the reason for freedom of conscience and its expression is so that God (however conceived by the people) can enter the Public Forum through the people from the ground up. It follows, then, that in order for a political system to fulfill that goal, the people's first duty is to move beyond their own wants and desires, and to broaden their sights—that is, to raise consciousness to God, the universal, the whole collective (however understood, whether religiously or not), so that they can reflect and discern what it is that promotes the good for everyone within the context of the two-tiered Public Forum of America's Sacred Ground.[62]

It also follows further that, to fulfill the system's goal, the people's second duty is to do one's best to contribute, within the context of the two-tiered Public Forum of America's Sacred Ground, to the development of the good society. That is, the people must fulfill their duty to raise their hearts and minds to the ultimate—God, Universal Reason (i.e., "nature's God"), Universal Compassion, the Divine (however conceived)—and discern what conscience directs, and then express conscience in speech and action with honesty and respect for others in the two-tiered Public Forum of America's Sacred Ground. Otherwise, the system cannot fulfill its intended purpose: to make a better world. Consequently, raising conscience and participating in the two-tiered Public Forum are not merely private endeavors, but also are public responsibilities. As this author has written elsewhere:

> Thus, freedom of conscience was not preserved [by the founders] as a kind of benign right for the private benefit of individual people. Rather, the expression of the free consciences of the people in the Public Forum was deemed to be central to the entire American enterprise because it was to be not only an end for individuals, but the *means* to a good society. That is, while freedom of conscience is private and voluntary (Madison)[63] and thus "solely between man and his God" (Jefferson),[64] *freedom's function is to promote the public, as well as the private, good.*[65]

Hence, the duty to participate calls for the people to bring into public conversation in both tiers of the Public Forum insights gleaned from raising conscience, and to listen to the views of others for understanding "so that conscience is informed and the good can be revealed."[66]

Consequently, when some who identify with the religious right or the secular left refuse to listen to the views of others, they necessarily cannot be informed participants in the public conversation and cannot fulfill the founders' vision for how the good society may be achieved. Rather, in order to be a full participant, one must submit one's views to others so that they can be explored, and one must make sincere attempts to discover what might be valuable about others' perspectives, including unfamiliar or even contrary perspectives. That is, the system that the founders envisioned contemplates a free people exchanging ideas and seeking understanding in a cooperative effort in the search for the true and the good.

Most important, however, Americans are duty bound to educate themselves, their children, and their communities about America's Sacred Ground—the political theology, freedom of conscience and its expression, the two-tiered Public Forum framework, the principles of the Public Forum, and its overall purpose—to build the good society from the ground up. Only then can the people be bulwarks against those who seek to establish the top-down overarching worldview approach to government that Locke

FIGURE D

THE FRAMEWORK AND PRINCIPLES
OF THE TWO-TIERED PUBLIC FORUM

The Core Principles — Freedom and Equal Dignity

1. *The Civic Public Forum*
   a. The Law of No Harm
      No one may harm another in his/her life, liberty, or property.
   b. The Law of Consistency/No Hypocrisy
      No one may deny to others what one is not willing to deny oneself.
2. *The Conscientious Public Forum*
   a. The Duty to Discern What Conscience Directs
      By raising conscience to God, the Universal, etc.
   b. The Duty to Participate in the Public Forum in Accordance with Conscience
      By speech, action, and by listening to others' views, all with honesty and respect for others.

©2003 Barbara A. McGraw

and the founders rejected. And only then can a system that values liberty nevertheless aim for the true and the good.

This is not to say, of course, that there will not be disagreements about the meaning and scope of the principles of the Public Forum, and this is not to say that America's Sacred Ground's political theology must be *believed*. It is simply that America's Sacred Ground is the foundation that makes the whole debate about religion and morality possible—even the debate about the extents and limits of America's Sacred Ground itself. That is, America's Sacred Ground cannot be denied without risking the very thing that has made all debates possible in the first place.

Fulfilling the Duty to Participate Requires Moral Virtue

The Civic and Conscientious Public Forums provide only the basic principles that frame a political system that values liberty and the contributions of the people from the ground up. Consequently, in order that liberty does not devolve into licentiousness, the people's duty to participate requires people to promote a moral vision for society that goes beyond what government can accomplish. For most, this includes the formation of "communities of conscience," including religious communities, or at least an exploration of personal virtue, which may include eclectic spirituality drawing from many religious and philosophical sources. In fact, the development of moral virtue well beyond the bare principles of the two-tiered Public Forum of America's Sacred Ground is in large part what freedom is *for*.

It follows, then, that America's Sacred Ground relies in large part on the goodwill of the people. The people's freedom is limited only by matters within the purview of governmental action in the Civic Public Forum, which ensures that both tiers of the Public Forum are free and open for everyone. Consequently, in order for the system to fulfill its intended purpose (to build the good society), the people have a duty to exercise their freedom responsibly with a view toward what is conducive to creating the good society—within the limits of the Civic Public Forum and its two laws. This is because freedom is not for one's individual happiness, but *for the happiness of everyone*.

A system that is free for *all*, and not an amoral "free-for-all," requires that the people strive to be virtuous and live virtuous lives, within a system that makes everyone's pursuit of virtue possible. As James Madison said, "To suppose that any form of government will secure liberty or happiness without any virtue in the people is a chimerical idea."[67] That is, it is *an illusion*. Hence, it is *because* the government is not involved from the top down in the moral ordering of people's lives that the people have a moral duty to order their own lives. This is why, as John Adams said, "Our constitution was made only for a moral and religious people. It is wholly inadequate to the government of any other."[68] As this author has said elsewhere:

If enough of us do not [fulfill] the conscientious moral principles, then we will end up proving our founders wrong: a society of free individuals does not promote the good—not even the good as separately conceived by society's various constituents; it promotes a licentious society where individuals have no regard for their nation and its future, only themselves. When that happens—when we have lost sight of what freedom was for—we will surely be in danger of losing the liberties that the founders and all of our forbears fought so hard to give to "ages and millions yet unborn."[69]

RENOUNCING THE DEBATE'S FALSE DICHOTOMY AND FALSE CHOICE

When America's Sacred Ground is rediscovered, it becomes clear that the current public discourse is itself framed in a way that actually is in the process of undermining the framework, principles, and purpose of the nation. In large part, America's Sacred Ground has been put at risk by a debate involving a false dichotomy that presents a false choice.

The "Two-Sided" Debate vs. an Open Public Conversation

The public discussion is framed as a debate between two "sides." That is, the metaphor of public "debate," to which the founders referred,[70] has become distorted. Today, it connotes a trial of sorts, based on a legal model, where each "side" presents its case in stark contrast to the other. Pursuant to this model, the people's primary exercise of freedom is to serve, in effect, as judge and jury, and vote—thereby choosing the winner of the debate.

But a debate that involves the sort of truncated, unrelenting position-taking, exemplified by stonewalling and obstructionism, that occurs today is not what the founders, or Locke before them, had in mind. Rather, the system they envisioned contemplates a free people, empowered to be and do good according to conscience, whose exercise of liberty goes well beyond voting. As shown earlier in this chapter, in order for the system to fulfill its intended purpose, the people are to participate in a great conversation in the two-tiered Public Forum by *exchanging* ideas and seeking *understanding* in a *cooperative* effort in search of the true and the good. This does not involve only two "sides," nor does it involve a "winner-takes-all" power struggle for the most votes.

The False Dichotomy of the Current Debate

The two sides in the debate today present a false religious/secular dichotomy. The prevailing narrative in the media and politics elevates the religious right and secular left in public discourse, giving those two sides, in effect, the whole stage. Not only does this effectively eliminate a platform for the myriad other contributions that could be made, but the religious/secular dichotomy itself is an utterly erroneous way to think about the system that was established by the American founders. This mistake is the reason that neither side can make sense of the fact that the founders made numerous references to God, while at the same time expressed reservations about religion. But the founders' references and reservations are not in conflict; they only appear to be so from the perspective of the debate because neither side of the religious/secular dichotomy has embraced America's Sacred Ground.

As shown above, there *is* a religious basis to the nation, founded in John Locke's political theology, which was adopted by the American founders. It was based on God's relationship with the people, who then build the good society from the ground up according to conscience imbued with God (however conceived by the people). That is why the founders made references to God.

But, as also shown above, this does not imply, as the far religious right contends, that the religious right's particular version of Christianity or the Judeo-Christian tradition is a valid dictate for the political/legal direction of the nation. Rather, the founders distrusted religion when it is aligned with government in violation of the Civic Public Forum principles, and thus tends toward an overarching worldview to be imposed on the people from the top down. Consequently, the founders intended to separate church and state.

This does not imply, however, that the Public Forum is to be devoid of religious expression. What the separation of church and state doctrine means in the American context, in light of the political theology underlying the nation, is this: Freedom of conscience and its expression are to be preserved for everyone, while the government is to stay out of religion otherwise, so that the people can raise consciousness to the Divine (however conceived) and bring conscience into the two-tiered Public Forum in a conversation about how to build the good society from the ground up. That is, the founding fathers had religious reasons for separation of church and state.

Consequently, those in the far religious right make a fundamentally erroneous claim when they contend that the United States is a Christian (or Judeo-Christian) nation. The American founders could not have meant to make Christianity the basis for the nation because then, just as now, there were numerous versions of Christianity. Some Christianities have ideologies that are compatible with parts of America's Sacred Ground and some do not.[71] And all Christianities have beliefs, values, and practices that go well beyond the framework, principles, and purpose of America's Sacred Ground.[72] That is why the choice of any one of them would be a return to the top-down overarching worldview approach to a political system that the founders *repudiated*.

Secularists also make an erroneous claim when they attempt to eliminate Christians' or others' participation in public life on the basis that they are "religious" perspectives. In fact, secularists' rejection of religion as a valid subject and contributor in the Public Forum, in an attempt to create a "neutral" public square that is devoid of religion, is its own version of a top-down overarching worldview.

The founders' concept of the separation of church and state is not about eliminating religious participation in public life, but is about eliminating the power of any particular religion—or any other ideology—to dominate the people through the instrumentalities of the state. That is, if America's Sacred Ground is to be preserved in the face of attempted top-down overarching worldview power grabs in the debate today (by either the religious right or the secular left), then it is incumbent on Americans to recognize that the dichotomy that matters is not religion vs. secularity, but *domination vs. liberty*.

The False Dichotomy's False Choice

The false dichotomy is problematic for yet another reason. On the one hand, the religious right takes the view that "God" is America's foundation and concludes that the Christian (or Judeo-Christian) tradition is, therefore, the moral foundation of the nation. This moral absolutist view is necessary, they contend, otherwise America would be subject to a free-floating moral relativism and stand for nothing. On the other hand, strict secularists eschew moral absolutism in favor of what amounts to a morally relative approach. In their view, taking a particular moral stance would limit the give-and-take exchange among many multicultural perspectives that can lead to practical solutions to the nation's problems. Thus, the religious right/secular left dichotomy presents itself as a choice between moral absolutism and moral relativism. This is, however, a false choice.

Although in some sense the founders held that the nation is grounded in God, one cannot conclude from this that the founders adopted a particular religious tradition for the nation. That is, the founders' references to God and religion do not support the claim that they chose a Christian or Judeo-Christian absolutist moral foundation for the nation. Yet it does not follow from this that there is *no* moral foundation to the nation, as strict secular relativists contend.

The moral relativists' assumption is that a "free-for-all" discourse with no grounding principles is a more open discourse, one that is more welcoming to the myriad views in America's pluralistic society. But this assumption is misplaced. If the stated position of strict moral relativists actually were adopted, it would be highly likely to result in the demise of the give-and-take exchange they value. The reason is that there no doubt would be competing forces, each with no greater claim than another, that would vie for dominance. With no grounding principles, there would be nothing to prevent one or another top-down overarching worldview to emerge as dominant. When domination would be achieved, freedom and its expression would be lost.

Such dominance would be the antithesis of the give-and-take approach that the moral relativists desire. Obviously, this is not what the moral relativist has in mind.

In fact, the moral relativists' own internal logic is inconsistent because it actually is based on a moral value—the value that it is *good* for all voices to be heard—and therefore the supposed relativism is not really relative. The conclusion is clear: Secular moral relativists are in fact assuming unwittingly a moral, legal, and political foundation, with grounding principles, that makes the discourse of myriad multicultural views possible.

Consequently, neither moral absolutism nor moral relativism is valid. Rather, the choice between the "all" of Christian (or Judeo-Christian) absolutism and the "nothing" of moral relativism, both of which risk top-down dominance, has obscured the fundamental framework, principles, and purpose of the nation, which makes the discourse of myriad multicultural views possible. That was the founders' choice; it is America's Sacred Ground.

America's Sacred Ground does not establish an absolute moral vision, which is what the secular left fears and therefore vehemently opposes, but it also does not abandon society to the nihilistic void of moral relativism, which is what the religious right fears and therefore vehemently opposes. Rather, it provides a fundamental political structure that frames the public debate for maximum participation by everyone in America's pluralistic society, while also providing basic principles that serve as "ground rules." *This* is the system that values pluralism—not the structureless and foundationless moral relativity of the strict secularists, and not the system of absolute values of the religious right. This is a system that is free for *all* and not a "free-for-all" because it is grounded in the principles of America's Sacred Ground.

CONCLUSION

There is considerable discussion today about American values. However, there does not seem to be much agreement about what those values are. Instead, there is division in the nation over many serious issues: the right to die with dignity, the right to life/abortion rights, the death penalty, the definition of marriage, the role of the government in helping the poor, and more. As important as these issues are, their resolution is not the main problem in the debate, regardless of how crucial those issues are to those who argue about them in public and to those on whose behalf those arguments are made. The main problem is that the debate itself is being conducted in a manner that is undermining the foundations of the nation.

There is a growing assumption in the media and politics, and among the people in general, that public debate involves competing worldviews, each vying for dominance. Then whoever gets the most votes wins the debate— the prize being the power and the right to impose an overarching top-down worldview on the people as a whole. That is, once power is gained, domination is legitimate. In other words, there is nothing sacred at the core of the nation that is not subject to majority opinion. But the truth is that there *is* a foundation to the nation, the foundation that holds in place the whole conversation to begin with—the system that makes it possible for the people to build the good society from the ground up.

America's moral and political framework not only provides a forum for the participation of many diverse people in America's pluralistic society, but is itself founded on the fundamental value that it is good for *all* voices to be heard. In fact, when one looks back to the founding of the nation, one finds not a strict adherence to a particular worldview, as was found in previous approaches to government throughout history. Rather, one finds a fundamental belief that an open discourse from a variety of perspectives would be more likely to lead to the true and the good than one that limits participation. If the discourse remains grounded in America's moral and political framework, new approaches and perspectives challenge those that have become entrenched, and when they do, they contribute to the continued revitalization of and progression toward America's democratic ideals.

Advances that have fulfilled that promise have been made throughout American history, for example, the abolition of slavery, the recognition of women's rights in the law, civil rights legislation, and laws to protect the disabled. Such advances have not been made by changing the underlying structure and principles of the nation, *but by appealing directly to them*. At times this has required an amendment to the Constitution because the nation's sacred ground is not the Constitution itself, but is the religious and moral ground on which it stands. As John Dickenson wrote in 1788:

> [A] constitution is the organization of the contributed rights in society. Government is the exercise of them. It is intended for the benefit of the governed; of course [it] can have no just powers but what conduce to that end: and the awfulness of the trust is demonstrated in this—that it is founded on the nature of man, that is, on the will of his Maker, and is therefore sacred. It is an offence against Heaven, to violate that trust.[73]

It is clear that the founders (and John Locke before them) held that our inalienable rights have a Divine origin. It does not follow from this, however, that the founders intended anyone's particular conception of God to frame those rights. Rather, freedom of conscience and its expression in a great inclusive conversation were held to be the means to the true and the good. Thus, even at a time when the founders did not give full effect to the import of the Bill of Rights in the legal system they established in that they failed to abolish slavery and did not accord women equal rights, among other things, the founders nevertheless embraced pluralism, expressly acknowledging that the United States embraces many people of many different faiths—some vastly different than those found in the familiar cultures of the West.

Pluralism does not equate to moral relativism, however, as some in the contemporary debate fear. Rather, the valuing of pluralism requires a moral foundation, the moral foundation that holds that it is good to welcome all religio-cultural expressions in the free and open Public Forum—the moral foundation that, together with its supporting framework and ultimate purpose, has been referred to here as America's Sacred Ground. This is the foundation that holds that the state may not sanction the infringement of the inalienable rights of its minorities, even in the face of a powerful and vocal majority (in support of the core value of liberty), and this is the foundation that holds that no one may deny to others, through the instrumentalities of the state, what one is not willing to deny oneself (in support of the core value of equal dignity). In sum, therefore, it could be said that the unifying principle of America's Sacred Ground is pluralism itself.

It follows from all that has preceded that the U.S. Supreme Court is not the ultimate moral referent of the nation; its decisions can be critiqued on the basis of whether or not they are in accord with America's Sacred Ground. That is, the Constitution is a document that should be interpreted by reference to its underlying framework, principles, and purpose and not by reference to whatever majoritarian interests hold sway at any one time, whether religious or secular. Those who argued against the ratification of the Constitution when it did not include a Bill of Rights had it right, and those who argued that it was not necessary to include a Bill of Rights in the Constitution had it wrong. The Bill of Rights is the embodiment of the moral heart of the whole political system. While the Bill of Rights is not the nation's "sacred ground," it is the first building block of a people committed to liberty and equal justice *for all*.

Thus, America's Sacred Ground is not liberal or conservative; nor does it entail purely secular or purely religious ideas. Rather, America's Sacred Ground is what frames America's identity—not as it is, but as it should continually strive to be.

> [A]s we dig deeply to find the roots of our identity . . . what it is that joins all of the multifarious beauty of the diversity of our people and the plurality of our beliefs—we discover that our identity is not found in a vision of the many made one. We are not a people with one appearance, one history, one culture, one religion. Ours is a people that is much more beautiful because we are not defined by ethnicity, national origin, common perspective, appearance, or anything else like that. We are defined by a vision of the many *as* one, all standing on America's Sacred Ground—all striving in a free and open forum for debate and action, where truth can "shift for herself," for what we believe will make a better world. And if, and only if, the Public Forum is free and open, and conscience is expressed, . . . can it be said, as it was said in 1788, that "[t]he voice of the people is . . . the voice of God."[74]

Chapter 2

American Jews and the Public Role of Religion

Kenneth D. Wald

INTRODUCTION

In her clarion call to reorient American thinking about the public role of religion, Barbara McGraw urges the nation to rediscover its Lockean roots.[1] Locke's emphasis on the sovereignty of individual conscience provided the intellectual basis for what she calls America's Sacred Ground, the view that a good society results only when citizens are endowed with "freedom to be and do good according to one's conscience."[2] For Locke, this was a profoundly religious understanding because God provided humans with a moral instinct that enabled them to discern justice.

Americans have strayed from this primal understanding of the place of religion in a well-ordered society, McGraw argues, due to the development of two destructive perspectives. Theocracy, the belief that public law should be subordinate to church doctrine, violates the cardinal principle of individual sovereignty by harnessing the coercive power of the state, achieving moral order by imposition rather than the free choice of individual citizens. Despite the best of intentions, history teaches that the imposition of an authoritative worldview by the state will "ultimately lead to oppression through dominance, which, in turn, results in uprisings by those who are oppressed. . . ."[3]

She is equally if not more critical of what she calls secularism, a doctrine defined by the belief that religious claims have no legitimate place in the public sphere.[4] In banishing religion from public debate, secularists ape theocrats by utilizing law to silence particular voices in political discourse. In the name of preserving civic peace, she charges, the secular left would effectively impose one overarching worldview, committing precisely the same sin attributed to theocrats. Both theocrats and secularists ignore Locke's admonition that individuals must be allowed freely to form and pursue their God-given conscience in public deliberation.

What insights or traditions do American Jews bring to the vexing question about the proper public role of religion? Does Judaism offer anything of value to the effort to reclaim the Sacred Ground envisioned by the founders? Is it possible to find a theological warrant for a multitiered public discourse in which religiously inspired positions have a legitimate and constructive role by delving into the Judaic tradition? No doubt, in a tradition as old and rich as Judaism, there are intellectual resources that could sustain such a perspective. Yet the author is compelled to argue a more negative position. Jewish political thought cleaves comfortably to either theocracy or secularism, precisely the positions that McGraw regards as inconsistent with the concept of America's Sacred Ground. Hence the author sees Jews in general as unlikely recruits in the effort to move the discourse back to what McGraw identifies as first principles.

This chapter argues that because of their history, Jews have tended to embrace either a theocratic or a secular position toward religiously based claims in the public square. The theocratic position is normatively hostile to the ideas that underlie America's Sacred Ground, and the secular one, more common in the United States, subscribes to a *weltanschauung* that responds with concern and hostility to any religiously based claims in the public square. The author stresses that these are not the only positions that can be argued legitimately from within the Jewish tradition, but rather that they are the dominant perspectives that one is likely to encounter when reconnoitering contemporary Jewish political thought. Accordingly, advocates of McGraw's return to first principles will need to develop a compelling case that the Lockean norm better safeguards Jewish needs than the two positions that have tended to attract most Jewish support. This does not mean the situation is hopeless. Although they have not developed a strong theological argument about the proper role of religion in a liberal state, American Jews as individuals have no problem understanding their own political behavior from a perspective that seems quite consistent with the spirit of America's Sacred Ground. This self-understanding, partial and imperfect though it is, offers some important pointers that may help to reconstruct the Lockean understanding that McGraw found embedded in American constitutional thought.

This chapter begins by discussing the development of political thinking in Judaism. Such an argument may seem peculiar to those who assume as a matter of course that all great religious traditions confront political conflicts and develop a doctrinal understanding about political norms. But much as it was once believed that the Biblical prohibition on graven images prevented the development of Jewish visual art, some scholars have imagined that the lack of autonomy in the Jewish community for most of its four thousand years similarly inhibited the development of a political ethic. Once this conception is dispelled, the chapter considers how the Jewish experience has encouraged a tendency to embrace either theocracy or secularism. The final section contemplates a "middle way" and in so doing exploits the curious tendency of contemporary American Jews to both worry about the "intrusion" of religion in politics and, paradoxically, to understand their own political thinking as grounded in Judaic tradition.

THE POLITICAL IN JUDAISM

> To speak of Jewish political theory as one might speak of western or Christian political theory, is to sharply dramatize how forlorn and unattended it is.
> —Bernard Susser[5]

Scholars have engaged in a lively debate about whether or not Judaism can be understood as a political religion in any meaningful sense. The doubts arise because Jewish theology developed and was codified during periods when the Jewish community enjoyed almost no agency. For most of their history, Jews were a subject people lacking sovereignty and autonomy. Accordingly, while Judaism developed a rich and comprehensive legal code to govern internal community life, many observers assert that the Judaic tradition did not extend to broad questions about forms of governance or other political essentials. One finds in this tradition little overt exploration of such foundational Western political questions as the meaning of justice, the bounds of freedom, or the nature of the state.[6] These questions were seldom explored simply because they had little relevance to a *diaspora* people characterized by powerlessness and almost completely dependent on the sufferance of non-Jewish rulers.

The lack of concrete political doctrine became apparent in the 1930s and 1940s when Jews began to debate the shape of government for what would become the first modern Jewish state in Palestine. At hearings convened by the British, several rabbis urged the authorities to consult the great legal code of medieval Judaism, the *Shulhan Arukh*, for guidance about the best system of governance for Israel. The influential Orthodox critic Yeshayahu Leibowitz thought such an approach completely wrongheaded because it assumed too much of the law. He raised retrospectively a series of rhetorical questions for advocates of a "Torah state":

> What do you mean by a state according to the Torah, and what will its legal system be? Will this be a democratic state, in which political authority derives ultimately from the people who confer it upon their leadership, or will it be a state in which political authority flows down from the apex of a political pyramid? Will office holders be elected or appointed, and by whom? Will this be a state that maintains an army and weaponry and includes the conduct of war, when necessary, among its legitimate functions, or will it be a neutral and pacifist state that does not acknowledge war at all as an instrument of policy? Will the economy of the state be based on private enterprise, each person doing as he pleased with his own property, with production based on the institutions of hired labor, or will it be a socialist or communist economy?[7]

Such questions were beyond the purview of the law, Leibowitz opined, because they had never been considered by the sages. Hence the law "does not and could not deal with even one of the political and social questions of an independent Jewish society in the present, since none of these questions were relevant"[8] in the environments where the law was codified.

It is important to point out here that Jewish law has the capacity to address the kinds of questions that arise in contemporary civilization, but that unlike systematic political theory, Judaism approaches and frames such issues in the context of its experience. As communal autonomy was largely delimited to settling disputes among members, so the law was focused on the task of conflict resolution in a close-knit ghettoized setting. By contrast to the discursive style of Western political theory, Jewish political thought was carried along by a "contextual, idiographic, juridically concrete discourse that rarely departs from the life-world in which it is embodied."[9] In this world, Susser continues, "Abstractions are boiled down to legally manageable particulars, universals apprehended in their specific representations and theory condensed into operational dicta."[10] His style was not thought to be conducive to the architectonic thinking recognized as political philosophy in the West.

Against this view, Daniel Elazar argued long and hard during his distinguished career that Jews had developed a polity with a distinctive political culture that addressed a broad range of overarching questions.[11] Moreover, he maintained, Judaism contributed significantly to the foundation of Western democratic tradition by promoting the concept of covenantal thinking. When they regained sovereignty after the establishment of the State of Israel in 1948, he argued, Jews could draw on this tradition to help them shape the new state according to Jewish principles. The reconstitution of a sovereign Jewish state and Elazar's call for research on the Jewish political tradition created a subfield of Jewish political studies. It featured individual studies about the political dimensions of Judaism[12] as well as collaborative work about

Jewish approaches to governance and political life.[13] Some political scientists have drawn on various approaches in their discipline to mine the political lode in Jewish experience.[14]

As in many debates that begin with polar positions, time has softened the edges of the conflict between those who consider Judaism apolitical (in the Western sense) and scholars like Elazar who regard it as quintessentially political. This synthesis accepts that traditional Jewish political thinking appeared narrow and focused solely on pressing matters of internal governance, with little regard for first principles and even less of what Michael Walzer has described as "high politics."

Yet the seemingly idiosyncratic conditions that produced such narrow thinking had larger implications for governance in general. For example, pondering the puzzle of how Israel managed to create and sustain a democratic political system in an environment that surely encouraged the development of a garrison state, Allen Dowty turned to the practices of self-government in the nineteenth-century Eastern European Jewish communities.[15]

In exercising the limited sovereignty allowed them by czarist officials, these communities developed such important norms as the legitimacy of dissent, competition for positions of authority, the development of organizations intended to promote particular points of view, and other precursors of democracy. These practices were never formalized as theological principles or developed as a systematic approach to governance. These *shtetls* never became democratic polities as the term has come to mean in the West. Nonetheless, Dowty argues, the habits and orientations they promoted were important building blocks of a democratic worldview. Because the majority of the Zionist leaders emerged from that milieu, the ideas about governance within them eventually spread to Jewish organizations and to the pre-state Jewish community in Palestine. This contributed significantly to a readiness for democracy in the new Jewish state.[16] If theology did not address issues of governance head on, the living tradition surely confronted them.

The creation of the State of Israel in 1948 provided the first opportunity for Jewish self-government on a societal level since the collapse of the ancient Jewish commonwealth. Although Israel's founders adopted many symbols of the tradition and often drew on its religious language for justification and legitimation, the design of state institutions appeared to owe much more to Western models and assumptions and even more to the example of Great Britain. While the proclamation of independence declared that Israel would be "a Jewish and democratic state," the former seemed more a tacit recognition of the religious identity of the population than a clear source of guidance about how to practice public life in the new nation. The special accommodations made to preserve the Jewish character of the state were governed by necessity rather than preference and produced a type of nonliberal democracy that some have described as "ethnic democracy."[17] Nonetheless, the earlier models of governance in the religious tradition continued to function as a source of political culture.

Even granting Elazar's larger argument, however, we are left with the reality that the political culture embedded in Judaism is unlikely to advance the cause of reconstituting discourse on religion and state along the lines advocated by McGraw. Indeed, the political forms advocated in the Judaic tradition are almost a perfect illustration of the perspectives that McGraw holds responsible for profaning America's Sacred Ground.

THEOCRACY

> A Jewish state is, by definition, one in which religion plays a public role and is accorded public status.
> —Charles Liebman[18]

To religious Jews, the Hebrew Bible is national history. As such, the stories it tells are not necessarily understood allegorically but are considered blueprints for living a good life. That the forms of government in the Bible do not meet contemporary standards for democratic governance has not dissuaded some traditionalists of their value as a means of ordering human life. Indeed, democracy—understood critically to incorporate popular consent and the kinds of conscientious individualism emphasized in *Rediscovering America's Sacred Ground*—is highly problematic from the traditional Judaic perspective.[19]

The central defining event in the development of Judaic civilization was the covenant between God and Moses on behalf of the Jewish people. The Jews were freed from Egyptian slavery, Martin Sicker argues, not merely to achieve self-realization but rather to become the People of God. "The purpose of the Exodus," he writes, "was to transfer the Israelites from servitude to Pharaoh to servitude to God."[20] By accepting the "yoke" of the covenant, the Jewish people undertook to fulfill their obligations to God as revealed in divine writ.

As piety has traditionally been understood in Judaism, it is less a matter of theology or faith, and much more a matter of adherence to the law shown by performing deeds of loving-kindness.[21] A religious Jew is enjoined to follow *halacha*, a term drawn from the root for motion and perhaps best understood as "The Way." As the term suggests, Jewish law is not an individuated code that prescribes private behavior for Jews but rather an encompassing guide about how life is to be lived as a community. Following the law is not an end in itself but rather a way of fulfilling the obligations to God that are implicit in the covenant. In this way of understanding religious obligation, Judaism is much closer to Islam than to Christianity, a religion commonly defined by right belief.

In Judaism, as explicated by Maimonides during the classic period of Jewish history, there is no sense of the independence of civil from religious law.[22] There can be none in principle because civil law is considered implicit in religious law. The two modes of law are compatible in practice only to the extent that civil law does not contravene religious obligation. The distinction between the two forms of law points to a fundamental difference between civil law rooted in liberal democracy and law as understood from the perspective of Judaic civilization. Liberal societies operate on the model of the sovereign individual exercising choice with free and open competition of ideas in the political market. In McGraw's formulation, the nonbeliever who rejects God is as entitled to participate in public debate and decision making to the same degree as the most pious believer. Traditional Judaism regards God as the source of law, which can never be determined by mere numbers. Those who transgress the laws are heretics who cannot reasonably be allowed to participate in collective decision making.

In two respects, it is difficult to reconcile the norms of traditional Judaic governance with the Lockean standard embraced by McGraw. McGraw insists, first, that a political system that honors America's Sacred Ground cannot accept the top-down imposition by the state of an overarching value system because such imposition undercuts the God-given sovereignty of individuals. As she argues, "individual freedom of conscience is the core American civil right."[23] Yet the traditional Judaic model of governance assumes precisely such a top-down standard as the basis of law. The choice was made for the Jewish people collectively when they affirmed the Mosaic covenant, and subsequent generations are bound by that agreement no less than the people who first made it. As such, acceptance of the covenant with all that entails is a condition of citizenship.

Furthermore, McGraw makes a central distinction between the religious beliefs of individuals, which are not to be debarred from public deliberation, and the corporate rights of churches, which have no legitimate standing in political debate. This distinction stems from Locke's theological belief "that God's concern is not with society or any group but with *each individual* whose duty it is to do what is in accord with independent conscience imbued with God."[24] As she goes on to argue, Locke understood "authentic religion" as a matter of individual conscience based on direct communication from God, having little to do with "the traditions and customs of institutionalized religion."[25] This perspective only makes sense in a context which distinguishes between the organizational and ideational forms of religion—i.e., believers and their churches—or between religion as belief vs. religion as community.[26] But *halacha* rejects this distinction, mandating the conditions of community that must exist in order for individuals to perform the *mitzvot* commanded by the Torah. Judaism is the religion practiced by the Jewish people, not individual Jews. In this conception, the failure to honor the law has consequences for the entire Jewish people, not just the offender. While *halacha* is a matter for interpretation, the right to offer authoritative interpretation is effectively limited to religious elites who derive their status from institutional standing. Hence if Jewish religious values are deemed legitimate elements in public debate, it follows that corporate Judaism is necessarily involved in setting the parameters of public life. That clearly violates McGraw's insistence that religious institutions not be privileged in the conduct of public life.[27]

The interpretation proffered here would not find universal consent among students of Judaic tradition, and others have advanced normative models that find ways to respect the autonomy of the civil sphere. In fact, one of Israel's most influential modern thinkers, Yeshayahu Leibowitz, argued passionately for recognizing two kingdoms and urged religious authorities to foreswear political activism precisely because such matters were beyond their competence. Others have maintained that the kind of theocracy common in rabbinic literature is qualitatively different from the conventional use of the term in contemporary theory and that Judaic traditions are quite compatible with democratic governance. In practice, whatever the political messages embedded in the Judaic tradition, the State of Israel has enjoyed a robust democratic system for more than half a century. Notwithstanding such realities, however, the theocratic position still enjoys normative status among interpreters of Judaic tradition who demand a "Torah state."

This debate has principally concerned the type of governance that Jews should create in their own state. What of Jews who live elsewhere? Perhaps *halacha* can be adapted to the situation of the majority of the world's Jews who live outside Israel, especially to those who reside in societies with liberal democracies. But this author doubts that the sages and commentators who developed and codified *halacha* in the Middle Ages could even have imagined societies such as the United States where Judaism was ensured religious equality and Jews were granted full citizenship without regard to religious affiliation. However, among the most traditionalist segments of the Orthodox population, the views attributed to Torah should still be followed irrespective of time and place. Believers residing in open societies are encouraged to live apart in their own insular communities where they implement the mandates of the tradition to the extent allowed by law.[28] While they may participate in democratic politics as a means of securing community interests, they do not reject the principle of theocracy and continue, where possible, to govern themselves under its dictates. It is thus unlikely that the traditionalists will devote much energy to challenging the normative ideal of theocracy even as they negotiate a political environment where theocracy is not a realistic option.

SECULARISM: THE BACKGROUND

> Jewish opposition to public religion rested on the assump-
> tion that religion meant Christianity.
>
> —Naomi Cohen[29]

For most contemporary Jews, especially in the United States, dim memories of theocracy have given way to the kind of secularism that McGraw considers inimical to America's Sacred Ground. To understand the contemporary American Jewish attraction to secularism, it is necessary to remember the thousands of years of history that preceded the Jewish arrival in the United States. For centuries after the expulsion from Jerusalem, Jews were essentially homeless, finding refuge in various places but never fundamentally secure from arbitrary attacks or expulsion. The masses of Jews were consigned to miserable conditions in ghettos or remote settlements. This treatment was no accident but a conscious policy of Christian authorities who wished to enforce religious uniformity in medieval Europe and could cite the degraded condition of Jews—their poverty, powerlessness and social isolation—as the inevitable fate of heretics and nonbelievers.[30]

There was an explicit political dimension to this powerlessness. When the classic Judaic position was codified in the Middle Ages, European Jews lived primarily as aliens in monarchies which fused religion and state. As non-Christians under this regime, Jews did not enjoy the rights of citizenship. Individual Jews might occasionally attain positions of influence or honor as "court Jews," but the status was always at the sufferance of a non-Jewish authority and favor could be withdrawn at the whim of a fickle ruler. The lesson that Jews seemed to have learned is that a state defined by religion was a state that excluded them from the full protection of the law.

With the rise of modernity and the spread of the liberal conception of citizenship as a right, however, Jews encountered a fundamentally new situation, the opportunity to participate as full citizens in the public life of liberal democracies.[31] In countries where theocracy was not an option, most Jews adapted in practice to the new realities. In time this led to a widespread tendency to assume that Judaism was not merely compatible with liberal democracy but essentially demanded it. Jews embraced the liberal or egalitarian state with a fervor that few other people displayed. In particular, Jews often became the staunchest opponents of religious expression in the public square.

When asked about the most important guarantee of religious freedom in the United States, most Americans would undoubtedly refer to the famous religion clauses in the First Amendment. These provisions, which both bar state support for religion and state interference with religious practice, are justly celebrated for their contribution to the flourishing of religious diversity in the United States. And yet, for Jews, the First Amendment is *not* the most significant part of the Constitution. If they were aware of it, most American Jews would probably point instead to an obscure clause of Article VI that ends with the ringing declaration, "no religious test shall ever be required as a qualification to any office or public trust under the United States." This provision, seldom invoked in litigation, has nonetheless been the key to Jewish political inclusion in the United States. Section 3 of Article VI marks the first occasion when a Christian society offered full and unfettered citizenship to its Jewish residents and placed that guarantee in a foundational document. Although test oaths of various kinds remained on the books in a number of states, the federal ban was an important signal that citizenship in the United States was not in any way contingent on religious affiliation.[32] Jews, Muslims, and nonbelievers, the groups that had always failed the religious tests at the state level, would not be denied a role in the governance of the United States.[33]

Jewish society flowered in the United States because the institutional conditions interacted with a broader ideology that rejected ascriptive characteristics as a legitimate bar to social advance. As Herbert McCloskey and other students of the American ethos have discovered, American culture is permeated by the assumption that individuals should have free reign to succeed to the limit of their possibilities.[34] This does not deny the very real barriers that long kept various minorities and women out of the competition for success—slavery and segregation, various forms of discrimination, and other such practices. But for Jews as a whole, even with the reality of discrimination and the limits on upward mobility, the opportunities for success were still more apparent in the United States than in any other society where Jews resided in large numbers. Little wonder that America became the "Golden Land" in the eyes of Jewish migrants from around the globe or, as the last Lubavitcher rebbe, Menachem Mendel Schneersohn, frequently described it, "the Kingdom of Kindness."

THE JEWISH EMBRACE OF SEPARATIONISM

The Jewish embrace of what some scholars have called, not entirely approvingly, the separationist faith, stems from the belief that the constitutional wall between government and religion facilitated Jews' success in the United States. Little wonder that Jews have cherished Washington's famous reply to the letter of goodwill sent upon his inauguration by the Hebrew Congregation in Newport, Rhode Island. Washington expressed great satisfaction that "the Children of the Stock of Abraham" enjoyed full equality in America as a matter of natural right rather than mere toleration granted "by the indulgence of one class of people." When Washington described toleration as a flimsy foundation that could be withdrawn at whim, Jews could heartily affirm his view based on their tenuous status under European monarchs. Rather, citizenship was precious, something that could not be revoked and something that Jews, like other Americans, were entitled to by virtue of their status as human beings.

As the Jewish community adjusted to its situation in the United States and gradually acquired the social capital to engage in collective political action, it became the key player in the campaign to deny religion a privileged position in the public sphere. The labeling of these groups as "defense organizations" underlines how the drive to keep religion out of the public realm was deeply entangled with a sense of Jewish insecurity about the community's place in a predominantly Christian society. During the 1950s and 1960s, lawyers from the American Jewish Committee and American Jewish Congress filed and argued many of the cases that defined the reach of the religion clauses of the First Amendment.[35] The nonsectarian groups that collaborated on lawsuits, such as the American Civil Liberties Union, were also heavily supported by Jewish members and activists. While the plaintiffs on whose behalf the cases were fought came mostly from other sectarian religious traditions, these organizations nonetheless used such cases to restrict state endorsement or support of religion in any way. More recently, virtually every initiative to shape public policy by reference to religious values is perceived by Jews as an "incursion" into forbidden territory. Thus Jewish defense organizations continue to fight efforts to restore state-supported prayer to public schools, to fund private religious education with tuition tax credits, and to turn over state functions to sectarian organizations under the rubric of faith-based funding.

This concern permeates the mass political culture of American Jewry. In study after study, Jews stand out from other religious groups and from people with similar levels of education by their staunch commitment to a separationist understanding of the First Amendment.[36] Apart from expressions of sentiment recorded by opinion surveys, this strong orientation also influences vote choice. In the presidential elections of 1992, 1996, 2000, and 2004, Jews favored the Democratic presidential nominee by margins of better than three to one, a lopsidedness that recalls the astonishing support enjoyed by Roosevelt and Truman a half century earlier. These patterns have been surprising because of sustained Republican efforts to attract Jews to the GOP standard by trumpeting the party's support for Israel. Jews have largely resisted these efforts because of concern about the emergence of evangelical Protestants as the most loyal constituency and the driving force in the leadership of the Republican Party. Notwithstanding efforts by Republican religious conservatives to anchor themselves in an inclusive "Judeo-Christian" heritage or to appeal to generic "people of faith," many Jews associate evangelicals with the drive to create a Christian America. This perception, not altogether unfounded,[37] alarms such Jews because it appears to threaten their hard-won status and undermine their security.

One might argue that the Jewish position is entirely consistent with McGraw's understanding of America's Sacred Ground because it challenges practices that seem to grant public favor to Christian religious practices and institutions. McGraw herself makes a sharp distinction between privileging religious *institutions* in any way—something that is clearly antithetical to the Lockean understanding—and discouraging religious *expression* in political debate. If the goal of Jewish defense organizations was simply to deny privilege to Christian religious institutions, then it would be consistent with her understanding of the proper limits on religion in a liberal society.

But the attack on granting favor to religious institutions is usually couched in the broader secularist terms that McGraw rejects. Reflecting their constituency, Jewish defense organizations often find problematic the very tendency to incorporate religious and theological perspectives in public discussion. When a Jewish vice presidential nominee called in 2000 for a greater public role for religious values, his harshest critics came from the world of Jewish communal services. They argued that encouraging religious expression in political debate would inevitably open the way for significant incursions over and through the sacred wall of separation. Better to encourage a language of universalism, they believed, than to incorporate particularism of any form—even their own—in the language of political debate. When it comes to public discourse in liberal democracy, the predominant Jewish political culture exemplifies the secularist mentality that forecloses the possibility of a return to Lockean roots that are fundamental to America's Sacred Ground.

EMERGING TRENDS

Characterizing American Jews as separationists clearly overstates the degree of consensus in the community. The two most traditionalist streams within American Jewry, the Modern Orthodox and Ultra-Orthodox, have parted company with their coreligionists on some questions about religion and state. Their defense organizations look much more kindly than Conservative, Reform, and Reconstructionist Jews on various initiatives that permit or encourage greater religious expression in the public square. In briefs filed with the Supreme Court and in public statements, they have come out in favor of faith-based social service programs, state-funded scholarships for religious education, and school choice programs—all opposed by mainstream Jewish organizations.

Several Jewish scholars have developed a critique of the separationist perspective, calling for Jews to welcome a more public role for religion in the public square. The principal advocates for what this author calls the dissenting position have come from the ranks of American conservatism and have been active in the effort to draw Jews closer to positions associated with the

Republican Party. Will Herberg was the first influential voice in this campaign, but it became a broader effort with the emergence of Jewish neo-conservatism in the 1970s.[38] Irving Kristol, Milton Himmelfarb, Murray Friedman, and others used the pages of *Commentary* as a vehicle for challenging Jewish faith in the separationist doctrine.

Although these efforts marked a move away from secularism, a development that ought to be celebrated by advocates of McGraw's position, the dissenters ended up at the other extreme that McGraw criticizes. The Jewish critics of separationism sometimes argue from self-interest, that is, that Jews will benefit directly from some of the programs advocated by theocrats. They argue, for example, that public funding for pervasively sectarian schools through tuition tax credits, textbook purchases, and vouchers dovetails nicely with efforts to build Jewish day schools, a priority in the community's effort to combat assimilation and assure long-term survival. At base, however, the dissenters make a broader argument about the kind of society that promotes the welfare of the Jews. Noting that Jews are a minority, a tiny minority at that, the critics of separationism maintain that religious minorities are more likely to be respected in a society that values religion than in a state that confines it rigidly to the private sphere. As Dalin recently summarized this position, "American moral and political culture uninformed by religious beliefs and institutions undermined the position of Jews and Judaism and the health of a democratic society."[39] Hence, it was argued, Jews should welcome practices such as voluntary prayer in public schools or invocations at graduation ceremonies despite the compulsion they entail.

Whether or not the critics of separationism have a case, their arguments fail to respect McGraw's insistence that policies involving government's coercive power should not advance the religious interests of any particular group over another. When one goes beyond the rhetoric to the specific policy prescriptions that are supported by the Jewish dissenters, one discovers practices that do just that—defending the "under God" phrase in the Pledge of Allegiance or, say, restricting marriage rites to heterosexual couples. Both policies clearly impose religious ends that are not freely chosen by individuals. Indeed, the policy prescriptions of the dissenters resemble the imposed top-down overarching worldview that is a hallmark of theocratic thinking. The Jewish critics have thrown out the separationist baby only to wade in the theocratic bathwater. Neither comports with McGraw's prescription for the proper ordering of religion and state.

A MIDDLE WAY?

This chapter has argued rather gloomily that the Judaic political tradition does not offer much hope for McGraw's vision of an America that properly relates religion and politics. The dominant strands of Jewish thinking about the subject tend instead to exemplify the competing poles that McGraw holds responsible for undermining the Lockean vision inherent in America's Sacred Ground as the foundation of the Constitution. The author recognizes the possibility that other observers will explore the tradition and find elements that are closer to McGraw's preferred position, but believes they will also have to argue against the understandings that have prevailed in Jewish thinking about this subject.

While these problems are no doubt related to particular aspects of Judaism, they may also affect other faiths that resemble Judaism in its communalism. Scholars have long noted an important link between liberal thought and Protestantism: both traditions are most comfortable in reasoning about individuals and uncomfortable when thinking about groups. Classical liberalism is often accused of treating citizens as deracinated individuals who have no claims on society except as individuals. In much the same manner, Protestantism traditionally defined itself a collection of individuals who voluntarily accepted certain doctrines. Given Locke's status as both a seminal liberal thinker and a staunch Protestant individualist, it is not surprising that these assumptions are central to the argument of *Rediscovering America's Sacred Ground*. Many other religious traditions take a more communal approach that treats religion primarily as a group phenomenon. Such traditions, like Judaism, may struggle with the liberal individualism that pervades McGraw's reasoning precisely because they assert a communal perspective that speaks of group rights and obligations. Thus, McGraw has to reconcile her vision with traditions that operate from very different core assumptions about the meaning of religion.

So is there no way that Judaism can contribute positively to McGraw's campaign for the reconstruction of America's Sacred Ground on Lockean terms? If one looks beyond the language of the Judaic tradition and the contemporary advocates of secularism, there is compelling evidence that the operating style of American Jews in politics—what they do rather than what they say—exemplifies the behavior that McGraw celebrates and could profitably be held up as a normative model for society as a whole. As noted at the outset of this chapter, Jewish political thought often departs stylistically from what is recognized as political thinking in the Western tradition. Where the latter is broad and rests on abstract moral principles, Jewish thinking on politics, like *halacha* in general, tends to be inductive—narrowly and closely drawn from the experience of the Jewish people rather than from abstractions.[40] In that spirit, it is entirely appropriate to consider how American Jews have managed to articulate what they consider distinctively Jewish political perspectives while simultaneously refusing to accept the legitimacy of faith-based political argumentation in the public square.

American Jews, a predominantly liberal political group, have no trouble thinking about their *own* ideological commitments in a religious way. Since the beginning of empirical research on Jewish political liberalism, scholars have reported that Jews regard their social agenda as an expression of Jewish religious thinking. In his classic study *The Political Behavior of American Jews*, Lawrence Fuchs argued that Jewish liberalism indeed drew on such core Jewish religious values as *tzedakah* (charity) and the characteristic Jewish embrace of education and internationalism.[41] He noted that Jewish calls for social reform in the early twentieth century reflected a tradition that rejected both asceticism and otherworldliness and bore a strong affinity with the prophetic tradition of the Hebrew Bible. In a variety of surveys, Jews define a "good Jew" as somebody who pursues social justice and equality, assigning lesser priority to traditional markers such as ritual observance or commitment to Israel. In the eyes of many members of the community, political liberalism is nothing less than applied Judaism.

Whether this assumption is correct or not—and many critics believe it either misstates or incompletely expresses Jewish belief—it nonetheless demonstrates a way of thinking that is compatible with McGraw's argument about the American Sacred Ground. That is, Jews draw their political convictions from religious thinking. As liberals, they would deny the legitimacy of imposing a sacred canopy, an overarching worldview, on a democratic nation and be nervous about the overt connection between political positions and theology. Yet the idea that their own political views are thought to be grounded in religious conviction does not seem to trouble them much.

Perhaps the key is the *manner* in which this linkage is forged. Consider the prayer for the United States that is part of the Sabbath liturgy in conservative Judaism:

> We ask your blessings for our country, for its government, for its leader and advisors, and for all who exercise just and rightful authority. Teach them insights of Your Torah, that they may administer all affairs of state fairly, that peace and security, happiness and prosperity, justice and freedom may forever abide in our midst.[42]

Notice what is missing. The careful language encourages political elites only to draw on the wisdom of the tradition when they exercise public authority. Conspicuously absent is any call for political leaders to convert to Judaism, to establish Judaism as a state creed, or even to demand that the Ten Commandments be enshrined as public policy. Rather than stating that this or that political position represents God's preference, the logic is that Judaism contains deep truths about human behavior that, if kept in mind by policymakers, will produce a more humane, generous, peaceful, and just state for Jews and non-Jews alike. The prayer treats Judaism as a resource that could be drawn upon to build a better society. The appeal is to God, but the Divine is asked to make an impact on society through communication with the individual consciences of the authorities.

Such an approach is entirely consistent with how *halacha* itself was formulated. The Talmud, the collected oral commentaries on the Torah, contains reports of debates among the sages and scholars. While Torah was accepted as binding authority, the very idea of fixed religious truth was challenged by this mode of presentation. By arguing and debating the meaning of the law, treating the text as provisionally and incompletely understood, the great authorities established a model that encourages the search for new and better interpretation. A famous debate between Hillel and Shammai was said to have been "resolved" by a heavenly voice declaring, "Both these and those are the words of the living God, but the *halakhah* follows the opinions of the House of Hillel." This left open the possibility that the contemporary judgment in favor of Hillel would one day be reversed. Little wonder that Jews call for humility in discerning God's will in political life.

One might simply dismiss this as the inevitable strategic perspective of a religious minority with no hope of converting society to its position. But even if this kind of careful and limited role for religion in public affairs grows out of the Jewish experience, it would not hurt if all Americans thought of themselves as members of persecuted religious minorities. Under such circumstances, they would foreswear efforts to insist that American society impose a specific religious code in favor of a more constrained call for religious values in the public square.

This approach is quite different from what passes for religious rhetoric in contemporary public debate. At its worst—which is often how it is manifested—such discourse is reduced to the crude formulation that this or that policy or practice is the "moral" or "Christian" way and that alternatives are accordingly immoral or unchristian.[43] Once shocking, such language has become commonplace. Confident they know "what would Jesus do" in any situation, contemporary theocrats have transformed a call for reflection into a list of divine mandates. This amounts to claiming that "God is on our side." The Jewish approach discerned here takes a more nuanced position, recognizing the difficulty of extracting political guidance from religious tradition and counseling modesty about drawing direct connections between theology and public policy. However, it appears that it is the same kind of careful ground-up (rather than top-down) use of religion that McGraw regards as a constructive affirmation of Lockean principles.

Jews would probably be more comfortable with calls to encourage religiously based political deliberations if members of other major religious traditions in the United States drew on prominent minority voices in their own communities. Protestantism offers the neo-Orthodox vision of the late Reinhold Niebuhr, who reminded Christians that Original Sin applied to them as well as to The Other.[44] Niebuhr counseled Christians to recognize the possibility that their interpretations of God's will had less to do with divine inspiration than with self-interest. It was hard work to figure out what God meant in political affairs, and such claims should be cloaked in modesty. Hence, they should be extremely cautious about asserting any political position as more Christian than another. Similarly, if they wanted to speak constructively about politics to their Jewish fellow citizens, Roman Catholics could profitably rediscover the late John Courtney Murray.[45] Acutely aware that Catholics were a numerical minority in a predominantly Protestant society, Murray argued that the church should avoid trying to force Catholic political solutions on society lest the opponents of those positions use their numerical supremacy to force Catholics to live with Protestant policies. The "Catholic Peace" required forbearance rather than zealotry.

Despite texts and culture that suggest otherwise, Judaism as a living tradition offers potential resources to bolster America's Sacred Ground. That said, as long as calls to incorporate religious thinking in public discourse are interpreted by Jews as a mandate for granting Christian values pride of place, there is little prospect that Jews will embrace the call for a return to first principles. Their history reminds Jews that God talk in the public square is often a prelude to their expulsion from the political community.

Chapter 3

Confucianism on America's Sacred Ground

Thomas Selover

INTRODUCTION

Among the religious and cultural traditions that have found a home on America's Sacred Ground, Confucianism is one of the most difficult to spot.[1] Overt manifestations of Confucian spirituality are hard to come by, even in East Asian countries. Like the spring rain that soaks into the ground and disappears, Confucianism is elusive yet productive. Still, Confucianism is present here and has the potential to make important contributions to the Public Forums on America's Sacred Ground, both on the level of supporting and reinforcing the civic virtues required by the framework and on the level of specific policy questions with which many are currently wrestling.

Unlike the other religious and cultural traditions represented in this book, Confucianism, for the most part, has not taken an organized institutional form. In traditional East Asian societies, extended families and patrimonial states (Weber) have been the major carriers and arenas of Confucian practice. Thus, in the Confucian case, there is little possibility of misconstruing "religion" in the Free Exercise clause as referring primarily to religious institutions, for the core Confucian religious institution is the Confucian-influenced family itself.

Therefore, it is relevant at the outset to ask, "Who are Confucians, on America's Sacred Ground?" To ask the question another way, "To whom and for whom do the resources of the Confucian moral, spiritual, and cultural tradition speak?" Self-identified Confucians are a rare breed in any part of the world, but Confucian sensibilities may come more naturally to those from East Asian cultural backgrounds, and are often taken for granted. Confucians in America, then, are a diffuse community composed mainly of East Asian immigrants and their descendants, as well as those of any ethnic background who have found persuasive power in the writings of Confucius or his eloquent latter-day disciples, even those whose life course has been influenced by a particularly profound fortune cookie. At the other end of the spectrum from diffuse to deliberate, there are strongly Confucian aspects in the Unification movement led by Rev. Sun Myung Moon, originating in Korea and a relative newcomer to the American religious scene. Thus, Unificationists can also be considered Confucian, in that they participate in many cultural patterns and assumptions evincing a Confucian heritage. In short, for purposes of this discussion, anyone for whom some Confucian ideas make sense as ways of thinking about common human life, and about how to develop goodness in society on America's Sacred Ground, may be deemed, notwithstanding other affiliations, an honorary Confucian.

In addressing the question of religious pluralism, it is helpful to bear in mind the possibility, even likelihood, that a person may hold or ascribe to multiple religious or cultural identities. As W. C. Smith has demonstrated, the problematizing of such manifold participation is a modern Western phenomenon that has spread relatively recently to other parts of the world.[2] This is not to say that there are no logical incompatibilities among religious traditions, but rather that such incompatibilities do not prevent (historically, have not prevented) persons from finding meaning and significance through the resources of more than one tradition. Thus, in practical terms, there may be multiple and even conflicting religious and philosophical warrants competing in the Conscientious Public Forum on behalf of the same policy initiatives in the Civic Public Forum, and multiple warrants may be persuasive to the same person.

It must be noted, however, that virtually any religious or philosophical perspective worth its salt could be considered what Barbara McGraw calls an "overarching worldview."[3] All the historic religious traditions claim an authority beyond the consensus of individual consciences, and the Confucian tradition is no exception. The Confucian tradition was originally "top-down" in both the philosophical and sociological senses. Yet, such was also true of the more limited religious plurality of the founding period of the United States. The successful maintenance of America's Sacred Ground, therefore, does not depend on watering down those "absolute value" commitments, but only on moderating how they are understood to contribute to the proximate good of a jointly constructed society pursued in the freedom of conscience.

An ancient Chinese teaching, quoted by a leading Confucian philosopher known as Mencius, offers that "Heaven sees as our people see, heaven hears as our people hear."[4] Mencius cites the passage to indicate that the "Mandate of Heaven" for political leadership is revealed through the response of the people, a point that will be discussed further below. As used in this article, the phrase also includes the Confucian understanding of the ground of personal conscience. The "Heavenly pattern" corresponds in many ways to natural law as understood by America's founders; it is that which makes America's Sacred Ground possible.[5]

Like other religious and cultural traditions, Confucian thought has within it assumptions about the nature of the world, and therefore about the proper way of living in the world. The resources of the tradition powerfully address three interlocking or intersecting realms of human activity and development: the personal or individual, the communal or social, and the ecological or cosmic. On the individual level, the emphasis is on conscience, understood primarily in terms of responsibilities rather than rights. On the level of human community, there are two distinctively Confucian emphases—the family as the arena of the most "inalienable" relational ties, and "government by virtue" as the link between personal and public. On the level of ecology, Confucian thought expects human sensitivity to be expanded to sympathetic appreciation and responsible co-creativity in the world of myriad beings. Each of these Confucian principles is modified somewhat in being transplanted to America's Sacred Ground, but by the same token, each has a contribution to make in enhancing a common understanding of the format and foundations of that Ground. In what follows, these "realms" are discussed in turn, followed by specific applications to issues of common concern in our society at present.

CONSCIENCE AT THE CORE

The emphasis on the centrality of individual conscience in the underpinnings of America's Sacred Ground resonates strongly with deeply held Confucian beliefs and experiential wisdom. The English word "conscience" corresponds to the Chinese *liangxin* (pronounced "lyangshin"), literally the originally good heart-and-mind, or originally good thinking and feeling.[6] Confucians are confident that conscience is both the voice of Heaven within the individual and the surest guide to right-making action. Indeed, over time in the Confucian tradition, Heaven came to be located practically as the Heavenly principle or pattern (*tianli*) in the core of human being. That is, the heavenly pattern is to be found primarily by investigating one's own mind and body, and immediate relationships.

This Confucian understanding of conscience as the presence of "Heaven's pattern" within each person has a threefold significance. First, it means that each individual, in the core of his or her being, has a reliable guide for action. Moral knowledge, in the words of the later Confucian philosopher Wang Yangming, leads directly to moral action; indeed, genuine knowledge and action cannot be separated.[7] The key issue, then, is discovering genuine moral knowledge through discernment.[8] Wang's point about "extending" such knowledge and discernment through action dovetails nicely with the principle in the Conscientious Public Forum of "raising conscience to God, the universal (reason, compassion, etc.), the Divine." In Confucian terms, "raising our conscience to God" means aligning the experiential, individual conscience with divine or heavenly principles. There is a duty of discernment—the responsibility to discern and apply what conscience directs.

Second, the recognition of the universal presence of conscience as moral intuition, in oneself and others, in opponents as well as supporters, is a fundamental element in the Confucian "creed of commonality." While Confucians do not necessarily expect a common creed affirmed by all to emerge, they do uphold a creed of commonality, namely that humans are more alike than different, sharing a basic humanity that provides for mutual sensitivity and understanding. Beyond all differences of articulation or experience, Confucians affirm that there is something fundamentally human and valuable shared by all, and that people can relate with one another on the foundation of this commonality in the midst of human variety and diversity. The Confucian dictum to "honor the moral nature" (cun de xing) includes both in oneself and in others.[9] This is just the sort of commitment to common humanity that can effectively support the "no hypocrisy" principle of America's Civic Public Forum.

Third, though, the universal presence of conscience is not sufficient for a good life or a good society; conscience must be nurtured. While most later Confucians share Mencius's faith in the ultimate goodness of human nature (xing),[10] they recognize that the "sprouts of goodness" are often overwhelmed by societal circumstances. Moreover, the caution of another early Confucian philosopher, Xunzi (pronounced "shun-ze"), that there are unruly tendencies in human nature that have to be controlled and educated, is also relevant to American society. Xunzi held that the most important and effective way of controlling those unruly, antisocial tendencies was not through extensive dependence on penal law, rewards and punishments, but rather through nurturing a public sense of propriety and civic ritual. The inborn conscience alone is not sufficient; it must be nurtured and stimulated through proper education, especially in a person's formative years, if it is to function as a reliable guide in adulthood. Such an education system is necessary on a continual basis, if the moral foundations of culture are to be successfully practiced, handed down, and preserved. From a Confucian point of view, this is no less true of the moral foundations of America's Sacred Ground.

In a well-known passage from the *Analects*, Confucius remarks that there is a key point or thread that links together and unifies his teaching about conscientious human life. His disciple Zengzi elaborated that the key axis was along the lines of investing one's heart-and-mind (*zhong*, doing one's best) and moral empathy (*shu*, literally, "likening-to-oneself").[11] As it happens, the Conscientious Public Forum requires these same two virtues as the "unifying thread" of Confucius to make unity among the many (*e pluribus unum*), namely conscientious engagement coupled with empathetic sensitivity and perspicacious judgment.

Describing the process of "likening to oneself," Confucius elaborated a fundamental principle of conduct: What you yourself do not want, do not impose on others.[12] Thus, Locke's principle of a "reverse Golden Rule"[13] has deep roots in Confucian soil, going back at least to the time of Confucius and his followers. Indeed, given the fascination of seventeenth-century intellectuals in Europe with Chinese culture, this Confucian provenance may be the remote source for Locke himself, by way of the Jesuit translators of classical Chinese texts and the Enlightenment thinkers for whom China was an example of humane civilization.[14] Thus, Confucius, the East Asian "teacher of myriad generations," may well have been the first one to articulate a core principle of America's Sacred Ground.

FAMILY AND MORAL COMMUNITY

Among the major philosophical and religious traditions of the world, Confucian thought is noteworthy for its attention to human-relatedness, with special emphasis on family relations. From a Confucian perspective, humans are not first and foremost individuals, who then form relationships among each other. Rather, human beings "become human" (or learn to be human) in and through primary relationships. This ancient insight is corroborated by much modern social psychology and cultural anthropology.

In traditional Confucian sources, the primary human ties are outlined in a set of "five relations" (*wulun*). In a modernized and gender-inclusive form, the Confucian "five relations" are: parent and child, elder and younger siblings, husband and wife, person-in-charge and subordinates (i.e., "workplace relations"), and friend to friend. These five relations are understood dynamically rather than statically, in the context of a lifelong process of learning to be human. Among the five, the three family-based relations have held primary importance. From a traditional Confucian point of view, this primacy is grounded in the nature of reality itself. However, the emergence and maintenance of ordered familial relationships in Confucian-based cultures can be regarded as a long-term achievement, rather than as simply "doing what comes naturally."

On the downside, the five-relations pattern led to rigidity in family structures in East Asian countries and thus to modern critiques of the Confucian family, critiques of which self-reflective contemporary Confucians are well aware.[15] The husband-and-wife relationship, for example, was characterized by the problematic notion of "distinction of functions" (*bie*). However generously this "distinction" is interpreted, it cannot be denied that historically it signified a serious limitation on the range of human growth and development, particularly for women.[16] A current alternative model of character and family development, known as the "four great realms of heart" or "four spheres of love," helps overcome this rigidity while still incorporating some of the strengths of Confucian forms. This model places primary emphasis on the content of family relations, on mutuality rather than hierarchy, though still with a sense of order. The four spheres or realms of love are the children's sphere, siblings' sphere, spouses' sphere, and parents' sphere.[17]

The "four spheres of love" model distinguishes the child's sphere from the parental sphere, thereby focusing on the process of developmental growth in loving capacity. In later life, the child's sphere is not outgrown but rather enhanced by development in other spheres. The development of parental love and concern for one's children sheds new light and warmth of understanding upon one's relation with one's own parents, even after they have passed from the scene, retrieving primordial experiences that may have been lost to conscious memory. Part of the wonder and excitement of the spousal sexual relationship is the possibility for new life to be engendered; in turn, one of the most deeply mutual manifestations of a couple's spousal love is in parenting. Paternity and maternity themselves entail primary responsibility for the life, nurturing, and well-being of the next generation.[18]

In this context, the traditional Confucian desideratum of "honoring the moral nature" in oneself and others can be extended to "honoring the moral nature of the family," especially because moral quality (*de*) is understood to be nurtured and even passed down through family. These primordial family ties provide central orientation to the rights and responsibilities of being human. A Confucian-style family-based approach to rights and responsibilities can thus strengthen and nuance the Lockean rights discourse that has been so powerfully influential around the world and has assisted in the overcoming of human suffering in many countries.[19]

The family is constituted by bonds of affection and mutual obligation that make claims upon the individual human conscience. Families are not voluntary associations among individuals; they are mandated communities of biological ties and mutual responsibilities. Our conscience and consciousness are nurtured and shaped by parents, siblings, relatives, and other significant figures, and only in that context does our ability to "act conscientiously" develop. Among other things, families function to nurture future good citizens. Thus, Confucian sensibilities offer a critique of Lockean individualism to the extent that it fails to take with sufficient seriousness the place of family, particularly intergenerational family, in the unwritten "constitution" of human flourishing.[20]

On the other hand, if those primordial ties do not in fact exert substantial pull on the consciences of individuals, there is little hope of remedying the situation by relying on state enforcement. The burgeoning caseload of bitter and high-stakes divorce and other family-law cases in the United States simply corroborates Xunzi's view, that education and ritual practice, not reliance on law codes, is the key to preserving family and society. The vital point for Confucian sensibility is that the fully reflective conscience will recognize primordial ties, especially family ties, as primary obligations.

GOVERNING BY VIRTUE:
THE CIVIC AND THE CONSCIENTIOUS

Confucianism as a way of life and thought is much concerned with the public square, with the kind of leadership and government that is conducive to human flourishing. A major theme of Confucian reflection, past and present, has to do with the nature of a good society and its government. The principle that "Heaven sees as our people see" was originally articulated in this context. But in traditional Confucian societies there was little formal way for "our people" to express their viewpoint and response, short of public protests or armed rebellion.[21] The traditional assumption was that Heaven is benevolent and intends or "mandates" benevolent government by an appropriately virtuous ruling house. As long as that lineage maintained its "virtue" (de), it could continue to receive Heaven's favor; when it failed, it would be replaced by a "change of Mandate" (geming, the modern Chinese word for "revolution").

The term de, translated here as "virtue," has the connotation of "moral power," "moral sway," or "moral charisma"; it is a potency or field of force, the natural response to which, in the political arena, is homage. In the earliest layers of meaning, de was an almost magnetic power on the part of the sage or holy leader, which drew the respect and awe of followers. Governing by virtue, then, means reigning by the sway of virtuosity, rather than relying on coercive force; it is the Confucian ideal of a good society, believed to have been realized in high antiquity. Thus, Confucian "governing by virtue" (de zhi) has traditionally been articulated in terms of the personal virtue of rulers. The political vocation of the Confucian cultural elite was always to try to "moralize" the conduct of those in leadership positions. Confucian officials often took it upon themselves to present local grievances to the imperial court. In this sense, Confucian officials were supposed to be proto-representatives of the people, not chosen by them but taking the people's well-being as their own. Based on the benevolent intent of Heaven, such a government was supposed to be "for" the people, though not "of" or "by" them.

From an American viewpoint, this Confucian task may appear as a futile exercise, at best. Americans are suspicious of such political claims to benevolence in high places, placing much more faith in the virtues of the political system itself than in the virtue of any particular leader. In America, people are less concerned with the personal morality of elected leaders (though it can become an issue), or even their qualifications for office, than with the integrity of the system by which they are chosen and under which they serve. The point of America's Sacred Ground is that the system of government itself is a locus of virtue (*de*). Though there may be some concern about the personal virtue of presidents and other elected leaders, the primary loyalty in American political culture is to the system, including such notions as "checks and balances." Civic education in America celebrates these systemic virtues above and beyond the personalities who happen to occupy leadership positions. In addition, the lore of the founding fathers presents them as virtuous precisely in their roles as shapers of the system. Their major contribution was in framing a system of government to be the locus of *de*, a virtuous system that commands the loyalty, respect, and even awe of its citizens.[22]

In Confucian terms, there are two aspects of *de* in the American system. To say "Sacred Ground" is to identify the agreed-upon foundation and basic principles of the republic as having the sacred and powerful quality associated with virtue. At the same time, for the system to function effectively, there must also be diffuse virtue on the part of citizens. Connected with reflections on conscience, this virtue can be understood both as inborn and inalienable, and as requiring consistent nurture. This dual aspect of virtue is cognate with the concept of "radiating radiant virtue" (*ming ming de*) in the "Great Learning," a classic Confucian text that has widely influenced East Asian thinking.

Manifestly, any system of "governing by virtue" that is based upon the commonality of *de* will require numerous "schools of virtue" for the continuous training of free, responsible citizens. This task of education for political virtue cannot be the domain of public schools alone, because schools do not reach the adult population in any great numbers. Historically, it has been religious organizations that have provided "schools of virtue," including political virtue. The requisite aspect of such training is not a matter of imparting worldviews, but of nurturing conscientious consciousness that leads to appropriate action.[23]

Confucius said, "To see what is right and not do it shows a lack of courage."[24] On the question of how to develop courage, Confucius refers to the importance of a "sense of shame." This Confucian sense of shame is not mere personal embarrassment, like finding in public that one's socks do not match, nor is it only a matter of personal propriety. The sense of shame is akin to righteous indignation, and connotes a feeling of responsibility for the state of affairs. It is a public-oriented virtue that inspires action for the public good. It is in this sense that Confucius said, "Knowing shame is akin to courage," including political courage.[25] In the American system, too, people have not outgrown the need for a sense of shame.

Though it originated in a top-down monarchical society, the Confucian perspective on government by virtue can make an important contribution to appreciating the duties, and beyond that the spirituality, of public service in a complex republic. The diffuse sense of *de* can today serve as an appropriate philosophical warrant for participatory democracy. By the same token, Confucian thought on governing by virtue is enriched by the experience of America's Sacred Ground, in ways that may be exportable to the homelands of Confucianism.[26]

CONTINUITY OF ECOLOGICAL COMMUNITY

The third intersecting sphere of human activity envisioned in Confucian sources is the cosmic or ecological sphere. As the tradition developed, the theme of "continuity of being" or consanguinity with the "myriad beings" (*wanwu*) came to occupy a prominent place in Confucian reflection. This sphere was given classic expression in the "Western Inscription" of Zhang Zai (1020–1077):

> Heaven is my father and Earth is my mother, and even such a small creature as I finds an intimate place in their midst. Therefore that which extends throughout the universe I regard as my body and that which directs the universe I consider as my nature. All people are my brothers and sisters, and all things are my companions.[27]

The practical consequences of this inspirational statement are only now being developed in Confucian thought, but surely some kind of ecological stewardship is implied in the ideal of "forming one body with Heaven, earth, and the myriad beings." Confucian sensibilities can thus contribute to resolving the ecological issues that are urgent for both tiers of the Public Forum.

Contemporary Confucians such as Tu Wei-ming are rightly critical of unqualified acceptance of the "Enlightenment project" in that it has entailed a Faustian attitude of conquest toward the environment, which we now realize is partly responsible for the ecological crisis.[28] Conversely, the question of the culpability or innocence of various religious perspectives in this looming crisis is asked with rising urgency. Harvard's Center for the Study of World Religions has been publishing a series of books on religion and ecology, including one on Confucianism.[29] The main theme of that volume is an exploration of the ways that "unity with Heaven, earth and the myriad beings" can provide not only guidelines but also motivation for ecological responsibility. Likewise, the Unificationist pledge of "living for the sake of others" should be understood as encompassing responsible action with respect to the "myriad beings."[30]

In a sense, Confucianism adds yet another set of warrants for the path of restraint and responsible use that we increasingly recognize as the way we must tread. Whatever the shortcomings of the Kyoto Accords, for example, the United States cannot abstain, morally or practically, from the conscientious search for ways to alter the present trajectory of economic enlargement. Nor can it, without grave hypocrisy, celebrate the American Conscientious Public Forum while ignoring the duty to participate responsibly in the emergent world public forum, which has been inspired in part by the example of America's Sacred Ground.

ISSUES

There are a number of specific areas of public debate to which Confucian resources can offer a conscientious contribution. Two are briefly touched on here: the distinction between the Civic and Conscientious Forums in terms of law and litigation, and the vexing question of same-sex relationships in terms of marriage and civil law.

The Role of Litigation

According to the lore of Confucius, he traveled from one regional principality to another, seeking a local ruler willing to put his teachings into practice; this pattern became a frequent theme in the biographies of later Confucians as well. Mencius apparently traveled with a large retinue of followers, seeking to persuade those in power to his point of view and policy emphases. The book that bears his name contains records of several dialogues and debates between Mencius and his rivals. When someone commented disapprovingly that Mencius seemed to be fond of disputation, he replied that he did not relish debate, but that he was forced to it by necessity due to the prevalence of incorrect ways of thinking and doing.[31] There is thus a Confucian imperative for participation in public debate. The general implication is that all citizens have a duty to enter the fray, the earnest debates in the Conscientious Public Forum, rather than sitting on the sidelines and decrying the direction that opinion is taking.

Parallel to the responsibility for entering the Conscientious Public Forum is the aspiration for limiting the reach or domain of the Civic Public Forum, in terms of laws and legal cases. When Confucius was asked about his ability in hearing litigation, he replied that he was no better than others at doing so, but emphasized the desirability of not having cases in the first place. Confucius's teaching that the goal should be having few cases contributed to an emphasis on family or village elders resolving disputes before they became entangled with government processes. The basic Confucian sources were written long before law and law-making were considered as arenas for public participation. The traditional Confucian sense of positive law is based on the assumption that law-making is the prerogative of the ruling minority, often exercised narrowly for their own benefit. Thus, Confucians express concern that the domain of law not be overly extended at the expense of informal case-by-case arrangements, which are felt to be more humane and more just. Consequently, from a Confucian point of view, the unchecked growth of litigation in our society, as in predatory divorce, personal injury, or malpractice cases, is indicative of a breakdown in the social fabric of consensus and a failure to provide for alternative means of settling civil disputes peaceably.

Taken together, these two points indicate that the distinction between the Conscientious and Civic Public Forums ought to be clarified and strengthened. In practice, a limitation on use of the legal system for adjudication of civil clashes, returning to less litigious procedures for resolving disputes, would be more conducive to a good society than our current bloated court system. The use of the courts to make and enforce policy against the prevailing consensus in the Conscientious Public Forum would be viewed from a Confucian perspective as a weakening and even violation of that Forum. Instead, possibilities for mediation, with the Civic Public Forum yielding space for the positive impact of participants in the Conscientious Public Forum, ought to be explored. Through de-privatization of the debates within it, the Conscientious Public Forum can address many injustices more effectively, fairly, and immediately than the Civic Public Forum, in a way that does not undermine future debate. Thus, the Confucian persuasion encourages civilian participation in public square debates, while also supporting a limitation of reliance upon laws, courts and litigation.

Same-sex Relations and the Definition of Marriage

A thorny issue in the Conscientious Public Forum that has policy implications in the Civic Public Forum is the divisive debate over same-sex relations and the legal, moral, and religious definition of marriage. From a Confucian point of view, the religious or moral definition is primary, and the natural tendency of Confucian thinkers is to seek for a guiding principle in Heaven's pattern (tianli). One of the Confucian scriptural resources for understanding Heaven's pattern, the "Great Commentary" of the Book of Changes, makes a cosmological statement that can be applied to couples: "One yin, one yang is the Dao."[32] The Dao, the way and proper pattern of human life, is fulfilled in the unity of yin and yang, female and male, wife and husband. In terms of Confucian cosmology, the conjugal relationship of husband and wife is not only one of the five primordial ties of human relatedness, but integral to the realization of Heaven's pattern. Thus, from a Confucian point of view, legal codes, to the extent that they are necessary at all, are secondary and ought to reflect that primary basis.

Confucians on America's Sacred Ground must recognize, however, that such an argument from cosmology belongs solely to the Conscientious Public Forum, in which competing moral intuitions vie for support, and individuals wrestle conscientiously with such questions in the public square. Since this volume appears in that square, a Confucian case can appropriately be made, and its implications for the Civic Public Forum delineated. Confucians "prize harmony" (he wei gui) quite highly; they enter reluctantly into conflict, and seek to restore harmony as soon as possible. They may be more inclined to compromise than to crusade. But the Confucian wisdom is that just seeking "harmony" for its own sake, apart from a system of ritual and propriety, will not work.[33] Certain times and issues call for disputation.

Reminiscent of Xunzi's point about the necessity of continuous education in propriety, Anthony Guerra has documented the "Herculean efforts" of the Christian church over many centuries to achieve the religious/civic synthesis we call marriage in Western civilization.[34] For Confucians who come to share in this civilization, it would be counterintuitive and potentially deeply disturbing for marriage (between bride and groom) as a social institution to be given up or further compromised. From a Confucian point of view, parenting, including biological parentage, is one of human life's most rewarding possibilities, both personally and in terms of its contribution to the benefit of society, as well as to fulfilling Heaven's pattern. Thus, there is a special excellence (another meaning of de) envisioned in the loving, procreative couple that ought to be honored.

Mencius taught that "not to have progeny" was the most serious kind of unfilialness. While having grandchildren cannot be considered a right in the same way as life or liberty, the basic Confucian presupposition of human relatedness implies that duties and responsibilities flow from those primary relations. In heart, if not in law, there is some manner of claim on the part of older generations on the actions and choices of younger generations. On this level, one could even talk of the reciprocal rights of ancestors and descendants, of lineage and progeny. Of course, those "rights" cannot be legislated; they can only be advocated in the Conscientious Public Forum. But the unfamiliarity of such a notion as "family rights" should alert us to the philosophical and procedural limitations of Lockean individualism.[35]

The mandate of the Civic Public Forum is to respect and safeguard the inherent dignity of each human being, with his and her conscientious discernment. All individuals qua individuals are to be treated equally under the law, but the domain of law has its proper limits. In terms of civic benefits, such as in health care or taxation policy, the principle of Consistency/No Hypocrisy in the Civic Public Forum pertains: not to deny to others what one is not willing to deny to oneself. If such benefits are available for specific purposes, they must be available fairly.[36] It is worth noting, however, that the principle of "not denying to others what one is unwilling to deny to oneself" is two-edged: self-denial is one of the cardinal principles of many religious teachings, including Confucian ones, and deserves to be considered in the public debate over sexual expressions of all kinds.[37]

The whole issue of "rights to benefits" has skewed a much more fundamental and consequential debate. The core issue cannot be about individual rights at all, for there can be no right to marry envisioned by a Forum based simply on protecting individuals from harm. Nor is it about discrimination in the legal sense of that term. It is about discernment, and that means it belongs to the Conscientious Public Forum. In principle, the legal marriage certificate is not a license to cohabit but a civil ratification of a union that has taken place on other grounds, moral and spiritual. By its charter, the Civic Public Forum is not qualified to adjudicate those grounds. To change the legal definition of marriage by judicial fiat is to usurp the proper sphere of authority of the Conscientious Public Forum in ways that could be considered unconstitutional. Confucians cannot but protest such infringement of the Conscientious Public Forum and its attendant harms. A Confucian sense of shame is activated, and so a call to action is in order. As McGraw states, "to fail to condemn, when condemnation is in order, is *a failure to exercise the full force of one's freedom.*"[38]

Furthermore, the other main principle of the Civic Public Forum, the "Law of No Harm," translates into the Hippocratic principle, "first of all, do no harm," when applied to judicial and other governmental action. There is a serious possibility that rhetorical regularization of same-sex relations would dangerously destabilize the already challenged family culture. From a Confucian point of view, support of family and child-raising is eminently in the long-term interest of the state, and that would seem to be the only justification for the Civic Public Forum to be involved in marriage at all. In the order of human achievements outlined in the "Great Learning," "regulating the family" (*qijia*) comes before and is prerequisite to "ordering the state" (*zhiguo*). By extrapolation, the state that undermines the family is undoing its own foundation. Rather than rendering incoherent the legal definition of marriage, both legislators and the judiciary ought to tread with utmost care here, and reassess precisely what is the Civic Public Forum interest in marriage in the first place. If that interest is in the protection of the life and liberty of children and the institution of parenthood, then policy must follow that interest, which will guide whatever legal or constitutional steps are to be taken.

Surely, this is an issue on which feelings run deep, because much is at stake for nearly everyone. In closing, two points can be added. First, it is arguable that stability and fidelity in a same-sex relationship deserve some form of recognition. If so, that would be the task of the various constituencies of the Conscientious Public Forum to develop, and they may do so in different ways and to differing degrees. Second, the Confucian aspiration of fulfilling Heaven's pattern through marriage (one *yin*, one *yang*) is an achievement concept. It is an excellence to be striven for and an accomplishment to be celebrated, not a requirement to be imposed. It is freely available yet costly to achieve, a vocation that entails a special blessing. Advocacy for it in the Conscientious Public Forum requires new sensitivities and new ceremonies for new times.

CONCLUSION

The dominion of conscience in human life that is envisioned on America's Sacred Ground is well-supported by the confidence of Mencius and his successors in a natural (Heaven-endowed) goodness and moral discernment in each human being. But Xunzi's analysis is also germane; conscience cannot fulfill its role without nurture, support, and inspirational examples. Therefore, the educational mission of the Conscientious Public Forum and its participants is crucial to the long-term success of America's Sacred Ground in advancing toward the good society. That mission is a plural one: the many religious traditions and communities together serve to stimulate the conscientious consciousness of all citizens. For this reason, Confucians along with others can recognize the growth of various religious communities and their influence among the people as a positive development for the common good.

The Confucian five relations, and the four spheres or realms of love, signify that each person's humanity is realized through primal relationships, especially in the family. Though frequently taken for granted, this network or matrix of human relatedness actually forms the womb in which human character grows over the course of a lifetime. At the core of these realms of love, there is a special place for the blessing that is called "marriage" as a model of Heaven's pattern. Thus, "honoring the moral nature" of the family implies both personal commitment to realization of an ideal and public recognition of relational excellence (de). These familial relationships are naturally extended to encompass the wider human community, in ordered patterns of affection and mutual respect.[39]

The Confucian aspiration for virtuous governing finds in America's Sacred Ground a congenial "place" to develop further. "Heaven sees as our people see" resonates exceptionally well with the sentiment expressed in the *Essex Result* (1778), "[t]he voice of the people is . . . the voice of God."[40] The American democratic system of government is also to be honored as a locus of virtue (de), not least because it recognizes that the state is not the final author, arbiter, or advocate of the true and the good for which conscience longs. Moreover, the Heaven that "sees" is not simply the sum total or weighted average of the viewpoints of "our people." For each individual, the question to ask is the converse: "Do I see as Heaven sees?" This is a challenging question of the limits and possibilities of moral intuition and insight. The great Confucian thinkers and activists have believed it possible to have that kind of moral insight, and they strove to embody it through reflective meditation, affective sensitivity, and appropriate action. This Confucian hope resonates with Locke's faith, that God (however understood, and that dimly) gives revelation to individuals. Indeed, some such revelation would seem to be prerequisite to the good society for which all jointly strive.

The corollary of "Heaven sees as our people see" is that we the people endeavor to see as Heaven sees. It is this civilization's responsibility, that each and all govern themselves according to what is perceived to be Heaven's pattern, God's revelation, as well as to advocate and work for the realization of that pattern, in the two-tiered Public Forum of America's Sacred Ground. In this process, while rhetorically assuming a top-down model of the good society, American Confucians and Unificationists, like American Tibetan Buddhists, can be joyful and effective participants in building a good society from the ground up. Ultimately, the Confucian ideal is expressed as *Tian ren he yi*, the harmonious unity of Heaven and human. That, too, is an achievement, one being worked on from both sides.

Chapter 4

Catholicism and Pluralism: A Continuing Dilemma for the Twenty-First Century

Jo Renee Formicola

INTRODUCTION

The Catholic Church today is playing two conflicting roles in American public life, that is, in the Conscientious and Civic Public Forums as described by Barbara McGraw in her book, *Rediscovering America's Sacred Ground*. In the Conscientious Public Forum, the church works to persuade others of its moral positions by acting openly to protect the unborn, to speak as the voice of the voiceless, and to contribute to the moral debate over life issues. In the Civic Public Forum, the Church also seeks to influence others, but in this arena it does so by articulating ethical public policy choices and by becoming involved politically to effect changes in the law, particularly with regard to the issue of abortion. Recently, however, the church has resisted state authority and rejected many aspects of the law in the Civic Public Forum, specifically in the matter of clerical sexual abuse.

This chapter, then, argues that the church's inconsistent behavior in the Civic Public Forum has created both a moral and a political dilemma for its leadership and laity in the Civic Public Forum as well as in the Conscientious Public Forum. The first section of this chapter uses the election of 2004 to illustrate how the Catholic bishops justified and demanded moral coherence or spiritual consistency from the presidential candidates as a way to demonstrate their commitment to Catholic values in the Conscientious Public Forum. The second part, however, contrasts how the Catholic bishops themselves acted questionably in the matter of clerical sexual abuse in the Civic Public Forum. This chapter maintains that the bishops' inconsistent behavior has unwittingly limited their own credibility in both the Conscientious and Civic Public Forums. It also shows that such hierarchical behavior has made it more difficult for Catholicism to play a meaningful role in building the good society from the ground up within the context of America's Sacred Ground and the confines of the principle of separation of church and state.

This dilemma is based on a two-thousand-year history and an institutional structure that Catholics believe can be traced directly to Jesus' appointment of St. Peter as head of His church, one that reflects a hierarchical, divinely driven leadership that McGraw refers to as an "overarching worldview." Exclusivity and prerogatives have characterized Church history since A.D. 379, when Christianity became the official religion of the Roman Empire. From that vantage point the church leadership filled the economic, social, and charitable voids that occurred after the barbarian invasions of Western Europe. As a result, the church advanced its spiritual, and by default its political mission, always claiming that it pursued this expanded role in order to gain and maintain the maximum freedom of the church to carry out Christ's mandate: to save his followers. From its very inception, then, the church was a hierarchical, autocratic institution. Religious tolerance and/or pluralism were never part of the church's essence or ethos. In fact, it was just the opposite: the Catholic Church was, from its earliest history, a dominant, separate, controlling, divine institutional force within an evolving secular, political, and economic world. Within this system, the individual was respected as a creature of God, as well as a person in need of spiritual guidance, capable of earning salvation by doing the good works prescribed by the church.

By the Middle Ages, these ideas were paramount in church thinking, justifying its administration of the largest existent bureaucracy in Western Europe. Bishops oversaw the building of local churches, made clerical appointments, managed church fees, and developed a code of canon law.[1] The church was so powerful that by A.D. 800, Pope Leo III was able to crown Charlemagne as Holy Roman Emperor, creating a political system whereby pontiffs legitimized sovereign rulers and thus became part of a dual leadership scheme that lasted for the next six centuries.

After the Renaissance, however, the rise of nation-states, liberal democracy, and capitalism began to dissipate the political and economic power of the church. Weakened by the Protestant Reformation as well, the church continued to demand prerogatives and ecclesiastical privileges in Western Europe while denying them to other religious groups.

RELIGIOUS PLURALISM, CATHOLICISM, AND EXPEDIENCY

A Defense of Separation

With the discovery of America along with Catholic emigration to the colonies, the church gained another opportunity to extend its sacred mission: the salvation of souls. But to do this, the church needed to assure its existence in fact and in law as well as its freedom to carry out its spiritual obligation. Without being granted religious privileges, however, the Catholic leadership reacted to religious pluralism throughout American history in four different ways: by justifying religious separation, by using religious pluralism for social assimilation, by attempting to create an accommodation with the government, and by playing a role in policy advocacy. In other words, Catholicism in America has grappled with the notions and consequences of religious pluralism, ideas that it has embraced only pragmatically, and still accepts only for expediency.

Up to the nineteenth century, Catholics evolved into a separate and suspect immigrant minority. Their loyalty to foreign popes, obedience to autocratic bishops, and membership in a church that opposed most American ideals—such as liberalism, capitalism, and individualism—made them unwelcome participants in the American mainstream. Official American Catholicism responded to the principle of separation of church and state by social, educational, and political separation, often resulting in clashes with Protestants as well as the government on public policies that dealt with schools, religious practice, and social matters. Catholics remained aloof and practiced a "coercive intolerance toward non-Catholic religious expression,"[2] because the church taught its adherents that other religions were in error and thus undeserving of the rights that the church demanded for itself.

After the Civil War, American society embraced a new type of patriotism, "nativism." This intensified emphasis on all things American resulted in Catholics being forced even further into religious and ethnic ghettos under the protection of the church.[3] The Blaine Amendment, introduced in 1894, effectively cut off all state and federal funding for all religious—read "Catholic"—education in the United States. The hierarchy responded by preserving the Old World languages and culture, by erecting a comprehensive educational system for its adherents, and by providing the religious and social environment that the Catholic immigrant population had left behind.

A Means to Assimilation

By the turn of the twentieth century, however, the Catholic response to pluralism began to change. The growing immigration and soaring birth rate accounted for a jump in the Catholic population from approximately 10 million in 1900 to 20 million in 1930,[4] fueling Protestant fears that Catholics could challenge the American doctrine of separation of church and state. The hierarchy, began to recognize that the significant jump in population could be used to leverage its religious and social demands. They established organizations such as the American Federation of Catholic Societies to protect their religious interests, and the National Catholic Welfare Conference to issue policy statements and position papers about church concerns. Both actions exacerbated non-Catholic suspicions about their religious adversaries.

The bishops even went further and began to use religious pluralism as a means to bring about the social and political assimilation of their adherents. This movement became apparent as they mounted judicial challenges to the First Amendment that essentially gave the church wide latitude in moral as well as political matters. For example, in 1925, the Supreme Court upheld the right of Catholic parents to educate their children in their faith in *Pierce v. Society of Sisters*.[5] Soon thereafter, Catholic schools received government funding for textbooks, as allowed in *Cochran v. Louisiana State Board of Education*.[6] By 1930, over 2.5 million Catholic children were being educated in parochial elementary schools,[7] creating an alternative educational system within the *de facto* Protestant, public one.

The candidacy of Catholic Governor Alfred E. Smith of New York for the presidency in 1928 also provided an opportunity for Catholics to define themselves in terms of American values, to prove their loyalty to the government, and to become players in the U.S. political arena. Vilified for supporting "rum and Romanism," Smith was also accused of holding Catholic views that denied religious liberty, favored a fusion of church and state, and envisioned the church as "sovereign . . . over the state."[8] Although he denied the charges,[9] questions of the Catholic understanding of religious pluralism were central to the election of 1928 and reflected the importance and divisiveness of the principle in American society.

The Catholic laity, shunned by the mainstream of American society, felt a need to be accepted and to prove its patriotism. World War II became the critical turning point in their assimilation. Catholic charitable institutions gained credibility by their relief efforts. They were on the ground with humanitarian assistance long before any other government or private agency.[10] Further, the Vatican, which had lost clergy, schools, hospitals, and churches to the Communists during the war, promised to excommunicate anyone subscribing to Marxist ideology. As a result, some Catholics in the United States thought it wise to support the purpose of the McCarthy hearings[11] after the war, creating the impression that Catholicism should be equated with anticommunism, and in turn, Americanism.[12]

A Means to Accommodation

During the post war period, concerns over parochial education changed, thus adding to the general assimilation of the growing Catholic population.

The bishops intensified their judicial challenges for the public funding of religious schools, and in 1947 gained the right to receive public monies for the transportation of their students to parochial schools in *Everson v. Board of Education*.[13] The bishops' litigation also laid the groundwork for future federal and state jurisprudence that protected Catholic schools and their students from religious discrimination. The courts shifted their emphasis in Catholic educational challenges from one based on religious establishment concerns to one based on the creation of a zone of "child benefits" for all students.[14] Now the Catholic bishops entered a third phase in their reaction to religious pluralism: they were beginning to understand pluralism as a potential means to political accommodation, particularly as it was being applied through the courts to church institutions.

As a natural consequence, John Courtney Murray, S.J., the eminent Jesuit theologian, began to revisit traditional Catholic church-state theory after World War II, attempting to reconcile past religious demands for prerogatives with American expectations for religious pluralism. Murray argued that church-state theory, as well as Catholic theology, must be understood as evolutionary and subject to historical and political variables.[15] Although these were radical notions at the time, Murray reasoned that the church had to adapt its past, inviolable principles of ecclesiastical rights and privileges to the political contingencies of time and place in America.[16]

Besides recognizing the need for Catholic adaptation, the Jesuit argued that the central problems of religious pluralism in America were its implementation, which he referred to as an "exercise in civic virtue," and its solution, which he viewed as "an exercise in political intelligence."[17] To Murray, such difficulties could be overcome only within the confines of a "doctrine," one that he believed to be embodied in the First Amendment. To him the constitutional right that established religious pluralism in America existed in a state of continual development—one that required constant articulation, elaboration, discussion, and questioning.

Murray recognized the two clauses of the First Amendment as "cardinal elements"[18] of the American consensus for nonestablishment and religious freedom, as articles of peace or a transcendental means to attain a common good—that is, personal salvation. Because of this, he argued that the acceptance of the First Amendment as a framework for peace elevated it beyond a mere vehicle for social expediency and, thus, created a "moral norm"[19] and a collective moral obligation for Catholics.[20]

These ideas became crucial to Vatican II, a general council called by Pope John XXIII for the purpose of church renewal from 1962 to 1965. Murray was brought to the gathering, having made ethical, theological, and political claims for religious freedom in the past.[21] His arguments influenced the writing and passage of the *Declaration on Religious Liberty* (*Dignitatis Humanae*) in which the church officially declared that individuals have the right to religious freedom, a liberty that should be guaranteed constitutionally by governments as a civil right.[22]

Concomitantly, the Vatican gathering also addressed the question of the relationship of the church to the state. It altered its former stance on privilege, clarified its rights within the context of the times, and reconsidered its spiritual responsibilities. Vatican II maintained that the church was not identified with any political community, but that it should be allowed to preach its faith "and to pass moral judgments even in matters relating to politics, whenever the fundamental rights of man or the salvation of souls requires it."[23] As a result of Vatican II, then, the church officially recognized religious pluralism. It changed its long-held opinion that Catholicism is the only true religion; it recognized the right of all religions to exist and express themselves; and promised to respect and to participate in global movements aimed toward tolerance, sensitivity, and the recognition of the relevance of all religions.

The church's new political stance in effect validated the reality of American Catholic political behavior. In 1960, the aberrant candidacy and election of John Kennedy to the presidency caused the Catholic notion of religious pluralism to radicalize from a means to assimilation and to accommodation into a justification for Catholic politicians to distance themselves from the church in the Civic Public Forum. This created a dilemma for the church leadership because Kennedy, like his predecessor Al Smith, had to deal with the issue of religious pluralism when he ran for office. Questions about his loyalty to the Catholic Church versus his responsibilities to the entire public as a government official were challenged in a divisive West Virginia primary. This led Kennedy to respond to concerned Protestant clergymen in Houston that he subscribed to the principle of separation of church and state as an absolute political principle. He declared, "I will make my decisions . . . in accordance with what my conscience tells me is in the national interest, and without regard to outside religious pressure or dictate."[24]

Kennedy's speech set the tone for the rest of his campaign and justified the election of an independent Catholic for the presidency. It also highlighted the growing schism between the leadership and the laity over the future power of the church to influence political thinking and behavior in both the Conscientious and Civic Public Forums.

A Justification for Policy Advocacy

The Catholic bishops had been actively involved judicially on matters of religious exercise and discrimination from the early twentieth century, and by the 1960s, they increasingly began to file *amicus* briefs on First Amendment issues. The bishops were stunned, therefore, when the Supreme Court handed down its decision in *Roe v. Wade* in 1973. The Catholic hierarchy had adopted a pastoral approach,[25] rather than a judicial one, during the growing challenges for privacy rights at the time. Opting against filing an *amicus* brief at the jurisdictional level of litigation in *Roe v. Wade*, the bishops chose to let the matter be argued by others: the state, nonsectarian interest groups, and private individuals. The bishops did not even file an *amicus* brief at the merit stage, and claimed that for "strategic reasons [they] elected not to file an independent brief, but to participate in the development of the argument of the National Right to Life Committee.[26]

In hindsight, the bishops clearly made a judicial blunder by not filing in *Roe*. Perhaps too certain of the church's moral and legal claims against abortion, or simply convinced that the matter was more than a "Catholic issue," they assumed that the question could be handled by a coalition of lay litigants. However, the unexpected holding in *Roe* revealed that their reliance on non-sectarian interest groups was unwise and unacceptable. It became imperative that the bishops (as well as the Vatican) make the church's moral views known in the Civic Public Forum, and promote them in both the legislature and the courts in the future. Thus, it came as no surprise that a Catholic offensive against pro-choice policies would begin in the United States and become the basis for a unified political strategy to advance the church's theological belief in human dignity. From that point on, pluralism became a vehicle by which the bishops would politically impact public policy.

In the decades that followed, the church actively began to champion pro-life causes in terms of human rights, social justice, and economic development, particularly in Third World countries. With the accession of John Paul II to the papacy in 1978, the Vatican moved quickly to implement its nascent policy of "ostpolitik," that is, outreach, to Eastern Europe. It enlarged its diplomatic relations with over 190 states,[27] supported Solidarity in Poland, and was credited by some with the fall of communism. John Paul even co-opted the twin concepts of democracy and capitalism, advocating a "third way," or Christian means, to advance both political and economic freedom. Based on the teachings of Jesus Christ, the pontiff advocated the church's traditional social teaching as a tangential part of its spiritual mission to save souls. The Vatican, as an institutional actor, then increasingly began to understand and accept the necessity of being part of the democratic political process, but in a new way, so that the church could accomplish its spiritual goals within a new, world order.

THE RAMIFICATIONS OF PLURALISM
IN THE CONSCIENTIOUS AND CIVIC PUBLIC FORUMS:
STILL A CATHOLIC DILEMMA

The Vatican and the American Catholic bishops have changed and affected religious and political thinking radically in the United States since *Roe v. Wade* and the subsequent leadership of John Paul II and Benedict XVI. As recently as 2002, the Congregation for the Doctrine of the Faith, the church's office of dogmatic orthodoxy, headed up by, then, Joseph Cardinal Ratzinger, the current pontiff, issued a document entitled *The Participation of Catholics in Political Life*. It discusses the contemporary church view of the nature of religious pluralism, the obligations of lawmakers and citizens with regard to religious toleration, and the new understanding of role of the church in the political process.[28] In short, the church has now set down guidelines for Catholic politicians and Catholic citizens that will have a major impact on the dynamic interplay between the Conscientious and Civic Public Forums.

The document begins by stressing the point that "the life of a democracy could not be productive without the active, responsible, and generous involvement of everyone,"[29] and encourages Catholics to play a vital role in their own governance. But as far as the Conscientious Public Forum is concerned, the document defines religious pluralism in terms of both moral and ethical principles. It maintains that religious pluralism must be grounded in the true understanding of the human person, based on the right to life, and committed to the individual's personal need and right to practice moral coherence. Thus, the church recognizes that Catholics, as citizens, have the opportunity in the Civic Public Forum to "infuse the temporal order with Christian values;" the obligation to respect the nature, right, and autonomy of government; and the need to cooperate with other citizens.[30] At this point, though, the document falls into what McGraw calls the relativism/absolutism divide in the discourse. Because it holds that Catholic citizens must either reject a conception of religious pluralism that reflects moral relativism or do nothing, the Vatican holds that either action could be "injurious" to democracy, which should be based on a "solid foundation of non-negotiable ethical principles . . . the underpinning of life in society."[31]

To the church, this approach requires that everyone recognize the nature, needs, and destiny of the human being—that is, the centrality of the person as the context of the purpose of government. Thus, governments are expected to recognize first that everyone is made in the image and likeness of God, and that, therefore, each person has both a spiritual and a temporal dimension. As a result, the individual has equal dignity and worth before God, and the ability to transform him/herself into a better human being. The church translates this theological belief, known as *imago dei*, into political principles by recognizing the value of the individual as the basis for inalienable rights, the law, and the need in a democracy to secure equality, life, liberty, and social justice for all. These views are generally in alignment with America's Sacred Ground. However, a conflict occurs when those political principles are interpreted one way by American courts and legislative bodies in the Civic Public Forum and another way by the church with regard to "who" is the "individual," "human person," or "human being" to whom these principles apply. Most critically then, from the church's perspective, the recognition of the spiritual/temporal duality of the person also requires a moral, ethical commitment of the government to protect the right to life. The church would maintain, therefore, that it is justified to expect that legislatures, as well as every Catholic citizen, would promote pro-life policies that apply to the unborn at the point of conception with as much vigor as the born. The Vatican has said:

> [I]t must be noted that a well-formed Christian conscience does not permit one to vote for a political program or an individual law which contradicts the fundamental contents of faith and morals. In the face of *fundamental and inalienable ethical demands,* Christians must recognize that what is at stake is the essence of the moral law, which concerns the integral good of the human person.[32]

According to *The Participation of Catholics in Political Life,* the use of the church's traditional social teachings is the way to educate the consciences of the faithful, particularly those involved in political life so that they will promote human dignity and the common good. The Vatican considers such a demand on citizens and politicians, in particular, as the only way for them to be *morally coherent,* or spiritually unified, within their religious and secular lives. That is, there can be no difference between the moral views expressed in the Conscientious Public Forum and political views expressed in the Civic Public Forum. The church considers an individual's conscience to be one and indivisible and, thus, it rejects a dual moral code for private and political behavior. Indeed, the church argues that to deny one's moral convictions would be a "form of intolerant secularism"[33] that could lead to a "Catholic cultural *diaspora*"[34]—that is, a capitulation to values that would compromise one's opportunity to build a culture based on Catholic religious tradition. Consequently, the Vatican maintains in its 2002 political document that to scatter and squander Catholic values would limit the church's ability to influence government policies or structures that could help those striving "towards eternal life."[35]

The role of the church in this political context, however, is a limited one: to provide moral judgment on temporal matters,[36] to oppose repression, and to support those authentic institutions that allow for a maximum of citizen participation protected by the law.[37] All of this is motivated and justified by the church's responsibility to enhance the dignity of the person, and to enable the church to carry out its spiritual mission—to save souls.

This official Vatican discussion of politics is noteworthy and an official shift in Catholic thinking, but one that the United States Conference of Catholic Bishops[38] has championed since *Roe v. Wade.* The organization issued a statement as recently as September 2003 entitled *Faithful Citizenship: A Catholic Call to Political Responsibility,* to discuss the contemporary role of the Catholic citizen and the church in advancing moral priorities for public life in the United States.

The bishops maintained that the Catholic contribution to the advancement of the good society lies in its consistent moral stance, its commitment to those in need, and its sense of community within the larger social and political infrastructure, even though Catholics represent many different views. As a result, the hierarchy has called on the faithful to use Catholic social teachings and the moral/ethical guidelines on which they are based to explore and affect all facets of the public debate.

The bishops believe that policy discussions should revolve around questions of the life and dignity of the person, the importance of the family, and community participation. Other issues should include concerns about the needs of the poor and vulnerable, the dignity of work and the rights of workers, solidarity with those in need, and an involvement for God's creation, the earth.

The American Catholic bishops contend that these themes could be translated politically by raising specific policy questions and examining the stances of those involved in seeking political office. The *Faithful Citizenship* document raised ten questions to help focus the choices of voters for the elections of 2004. Specifying Catholic concerns, the hierarchy believes that answers should have been based on civic and political decisions viewed through the "eyes of faith" and designed to "bring . . . moral convictions into public life."[39] Topics range from questions of how to build a more just, secure, and peaceful world to how best to protect human life and dignity. In short, the bishops maintained that the church's role in this quest is to "enrich the political process" as it "affirm[s] genuine pluralism."[40] Thus, church leaders believe that they have, and continue to have, the obligation to educate Catholics on the moral dimension of public life and to share Catholic teachings with others so that all may form their own consciences in the light of their faith.

MORAL COHERENCE ACROSS THE CONSCIENTIOUS AND CIVIC PUBLIC FORUMS

Since the end of World War II, three forces have impelled the Catholic Church toward an acceptance of religious pluralism. One has been the pull of its adherents into the American mainstream with its promise of opportunities for advancement, assimilation, and accommodation, along with the challenges of life in a diverse society. A second has been the drive for church renewal after Vatican II, and the recognition of religious freedom as a civil right championed by Catholics in both a religious and political context. The third has been the increased activism of the hierarchy, alarmed by *Roe v. Wade* and energized by its need to play a vital role in the political process to advance human dignity. At the beginning of the twenty-first century, then, lay Catholics and their church leaders worked to become significant players in the American political process to advance their religious agenda in the public arena.

This has occurred even though Catholics have traditionally cast their ballots as individuals rather than as a voting bloc, and even though the bishops are only allowed by civil law to speak out on issues rather than on partisan political candidates.[41] In response, the church has historically proposed nonpartisan political approaches based on ethics and theological principles, specifically the centrality of the dignity of the human being, the right to life, and the need for moral coherence when advocating particular policy stands. All church positions on public policies and explanations of candidates' views flow from these three considerations. The role of the church and its leadership, then, is to communicate these notions to the faithful, to work to infuse them into the political debate, and to provide more moral choices in the public policy debate.

What does guarded support for religious pluralism mean for the American Catholic relationship with the U.S. government as the church attempts to use moral persuasion in both the Conscientious Public Forum and the Civic Public Forum? The answer lies with the *a priori* assumption that the state will protect the freedom of the church to carry out its salvific mission. Secure in its existence and purpose, then, both the Catholic laity and its leadership are able to take voluntary action on matters of morality free from government coercion. In the Conscientious Public Forum, according to McGraw, Catholics have two moral duties: first, to raise consciences to God, universals, and reason; and second, to participate in the public debate while listening to others' views in accord with their consciences. The means by which Catholics participate in the Conscientious Public Forum are through preaching, education, monitoring issues, working in religious coalitions, and capacity building. The church speaks, for example, as the voice of the voiceless on policies dealing with homelessness, health care, crime, and poverty through litigation, lobbying, demonstrations, and press conferences. In short, the church takes on the role of a special-interest group to affect public opinion and public policy aimed toward the common good.

Can Catholic candidates always translate the church's moral views in the Conscientious Public Forum into political stands in the Civic Public Forum? The election of 2004 can serve as a case study. It illustrates the difficulty of being morally coherent as a layperson, the complexity of enforcing such a stance by the U.S. Catholic bishops, and how the church's demand for spiritual consistency portends a different, potential reply to religious pluralism in the future.

The matter of how to interact with Catholics seeking public office was slated to be studied as part of a hierarchical task force under Theodore Cardinal McCarrick of Washington, D.C. in the fall of 2004. The bishops' committee was to study and report on how to adapt the earlier Vatican document,

Participation of Catholics in Political Life, as it applies to the American democratic, pluralistic context. It was expected that a report would be prepared
and issued after the 2004 election, but the assembled members of the hierarchy at their biannual meeting in June jumped the gun and reported several
points ahead of time from an interim report. Their statement entitled
Catholics in Political Life[42] served to remind both the faithful and the general
public that the hierarchy intends to play a key role in defining the parameters of voting choices in U.S. elections.

In their document, the bishops emphasized their "duty to teach about
human life and dignity, marriage and the family, war and peace, the needs of
the poor and the demands of justice."[43] Their pastoral responsibility, to educate others about the sacredness of human life, remains rooted in the theological belief that a soul is infused at the moment of conception, and
therefore the killing of an unborn child is "always intrinsically evil and can
never be justified."[44] As a result, the bishops argued that the legal system
cooperates in evil when it fails to protect life, and that "politicians have an
obligation to work toward correcting morally defective laws lest they be
guilty of cooperating in evil and in sinning against the common good."[45]

The bishops have always believed that they must educate, persuade, act,
and maintain communications with public officials who make such decisions. In 1981, they forcefully defended Catholicism's right to seek political
goals in the United States. "The right of religious organizations, of varying
views, to speak must be defended by all who understand the meaning of religious liberty and the social role of religion,"[46] they said. Spearheading a campaign for social justice during the Reagan administration, the bishops
advocated a halt to the arms race, a ban on abortion, and more aid for the
poor. The bishops, indeed, reached a high-water policy mark by issuing two
major pastoral letters[47] on the economy and the challenge of peace in the
early 1980s.

While they were able to enrich the public debate on both issues, they
simultaneously made aggressive demands for dogmatic adherence to pro-life
policy that often adversely affected Catholic politicians after *Roe v. Wade*. For
example, in 1984, when Geraldine Ferraro, a Catholic, became the Democratic nominee for vice president, signed a letter circulated by her Catholic
House colleagues, she maintained that there was a diversity of Catholic opinion on abortion. She was severely reprimanded and threatened with excom-
munication by then-John Cardinal O'Connor of New York, who accused her
of misrepresenting the Catholic position. He questioned how Catholics could
vote for such a candidate. Coming to her defense, then-Governor Mario
Cuomo of New York, in a speech at Notre Dame, argued that there were no
church teachings that required Catholic candidates to spread their beliefs in
the political arena, nor that there were any encyclicals or catechism that laid
out a political strategy for them to follow on such matters. Instead, he
lamented that "the Catholic trying to make moral and prudent judgments in

the political realm must discern which, if any, of the actions one could take would be best."[48]

What Cuomo detected was the new *political* position of the bishops: "making judgments about translating Catholic teaching into public policy, not about the moral validity of the teachings."[49] Indeed, the church was arguing that the Conscientious Public Forum positions of the Catholic politicians should be aligned with church doctrine and should also be the positions of such politicians in Civic Public Forum. Defending themselves, the bishops answered Cuomo and issued a carefully honed position statement which pointed out that the Catholic Church leadership was constitutionally committed to the separation of church and state, but that it could not support "the separation of religious and moral values from public life."[50] In an attempt at reconciliation, the hierarchy also admitted that there was much "room for dialogue about what constitutes effective, workable responses"[51] to the public policy solutions to the matter of abortion.

Since then, the Catholic leadership has been cautious in its criticism of Catholic politicians. However, a small number of conservative bishops reverted to form as John Kerry, a Catholic, made his bid for the presidency in 2004. They threatened punitive action, specifically the denial of the sacrament of Holy Communion, as a way to stifle the opinion of Kerry and other Catholic politicians who hold public attitudes that differ from the religious views of the church.

The refusal of the sacrament rests with individual bishops who have authority under established canonical and pastoral principles, and consequently there were different judgments among the bishops as to what to do. In Colorado, Bishop Michael J. Sheridan said that he would deny Communion to Catholic politicians and voters "until they have recanted their positions and been reconciled with God and the Church in the Sacrament of Penance."[52] In New Jersey, threats by Archbishop Robert Meyers resulted in then-Governor James McGreevy announcing that he would abstain from taking Communion. In other places, such as Missouri, Nebraska, and Colorado, Catholic politicians, including Senator John Kerry, were put on notice to reexamine their consciences before taking Communion,[53] in short, to figure out a way to reconcile church teachings with their political consciences.

Kerry, who followed three other Catholic candidates in his pursuit of the highest national office, opted to reject the hierarchy's call for spiritual and political unity, ignored the admonitions of the bishops, and took a pluralistic approach to major social issues. The Democratic nominee for president claimed to oppose abortion morally, but to support the right to choice and privacy for each woman politically. That is, he distinguished his political stance in the Civic Public Forum from his moral stance in the Conscientious Public Forum. Thus, while he essentially interpreted the question of abortion as a matter of his personal conscience, he had earlier translated his moral views politically by voting against the Partial Birth Abortion Law and the

Unborn Victims of Violence Act (2004). He had also opposed the Defense of Marriage Act (1996) while in Congress and promised, during his campaign, to end limits on stem-cell research if elected.[54] His views on all these issues are in conflict with Catholic social teachings and, according to some of the bishops, indicate a lack of moral coherence between his required conscientious views and his civic stances. Moderate bishops, reportedly, opposed the playing of the Communion card, but nevertheless remained silent.[55]

Indeed, the Vatican itself holds that a dual personal and political ethical code is unacceptable,[56] and therefore Vatican officials, including the former Pope, John Paul II, were reportedly "dismayed"[57] by the apparent discord among the bishops. They wanted to meet with the American bishops' task force before it began its work on the question of the denial of Communion in the fall of 2004, but that meeting was short-circuited by the conservative bishops who forced an airing of the issue before the national elections.

Capitalizing on the Vatican's support for moral coherence, and a desire to win more of the Catholic vote, President Bush campaigned conservatively on a variety of moral matters, particularly abortion, gay marriage, and stem-cell research. His personal conscience was reflected in his political appeal to "a culture of life," which he emphasized by signing the Partial Birth Abortion Ban and the Unborn Victims of Violence Act. He pointed to his attempts to defend the traditional religious notion of marriage and to limit government research on new stem-cell lines. In contrast to Kerry, the president embraced moral coherence on such issues and reached out to Catholics. He appealed to his own base and also was able to offer an alternative to conscience-conflicted Catholics. Further, on his trip to Rome during the campaign, and in an attempt to provide a united hierarchical front, President Bush even asked the Vatican secretary of state to pressure the American bishops to speak out about more political issues, including same-sex marriage. The president sought greater activism from the Catholic hierarchy in the United States, and in turn promised John Paul II, the pope at the time, to be more aggressive in his approaches to the cultural issues that they shared.[58] The pontiff praised President Bush for his promotion of moral values and his concern for international terrorism.[59] And, even though the former pope opposed the U.S. war in Iraq, President Bush was able to demonstrate his moral coherence with regard to abortion, stem-cell research and gay marriage, thus enabling him to cast a shadow over the spiritual consistency of his adversary. Even when prominent Catholic politicians like Senator Ted Kennedy[60] took the offensive with regard to the bishops' denial of Communion to John Kerry, their efforts appeared to be too little too late.

The pressure on Catholic politicians to take positions in the Civic Public Forum consistent with Catholic doctrine has evolved from differences in cultural values and religious loyalty in the past to stances on public policies, such as abortion, that impinge on moral and political issues today.[61] The bishops' demands on politicians in the Civic Public Forum have also changed from one of silent acceptance, as in the cases of Smith and Kennedy, to demands for moral coherence from Ferraro, and most recently from Kerry. In 2004, there were members of the hierarchy who wanted to punish Kerry, and as a result, Catholic candidates have now come full circle on the issue of abortion in the Civic Public Forum. They are being put into a position where they have to choose between hierarchical demands for dogmatic beliefs and pluralistic values. What is strange is that Kerry came up against a candidate who is not a Catholic, who did show moral coherence on the abortion issue, who stole the Catholic moral agenda on that matter, and who won the presidency. What will this mean for other Catholics who must deal with the question of abortion in the future?

The two-tiered Public Forum and the respective principles of each provide fertile ground for a debate on the abortion issue from both religious and nonreligious perspectives. However, when interpretations of the fundamental rights of man and to whom they apply is at stake, that debate is bound to be a contentious one. That is certainly so when the debate involves so volatile an issue as to whom the right to life applies. This is an especially difficult issue for those, such as Catholics, whose religious teaching conflicts with the view of America's courts and legislatures about the meaning and scope of human dignity. An issue such as abortion may be treated as a matter of freedom of conscience by a Catholic public figure, and thus fall within the Conscience Public Forum. However, it may also be interpreted as a civic/policy matter by the church leadership and thus be considered as an issue to be pursued in the Civic Public Forum. No surprise, then, that it leaves open the possibility of a clash of views. The view of the unborn as one who has a soul from the moment of conception, who is, therefore, "the other" and thus deserving of judicial and legal protections for the right to life is in contradistinction to the legal view that the unborn, at least at the early fetal stage, is not yet a human being, and therefore does not require such protections.

Abortion is one issue, then, that straddles both forums, but because the role of the Catholic Church is to persuade and to attempt to infuse moral principles into the public debate in both the Conscientious and Civic Public Forums, its own leadership and credibility must be above reproach in order to be effective. Thus, the demand of the hierarchy for moral coherence by candidates across the boundary between the Conscientious and Civic Public Forum is difficult to reconcile with the bishops' own lack of moral coherence, namely in the matter of clerical sexual abuse. Participation in the Conscientious Public Forum and the Civic Public Forum depends on it. And as a consequence, demands for ecclesiastical privilege and theological dominance will continually be challenged by the government, the laity, and other citizens if the Catholic bishops hope to be able to persuade and infuse Catholic moral principles into the public debate.

RESISTING THE AUTHORITY OF GOVERNMENT
IN THE CIVIC PUBLIC FORUM

The current Catholic crisis over the clerical abuse scandal[62] in the United States better illustrates the role that religious groups can or must play in the Civic Public Forum. It also illustrates how religious pluralism can hinder the creation of the good society if one group seeks special treatment and refuses to adhere to the principles of America's Sacred Ground while preserving the separation of church and state. In this arena, religious groups must accept the underlying principles of liberty and equal justice that emerge from the free will and equal dignity of the individual. Thus, the law of no harm to others and the law of consistency must apply to all. Religious groups must adhere to the law and obey state authority in this forum in order to advance the common good and to have credibility on moral issues in both the Civic and Conscientious Public Forums.

The crisis that has today overshadowed the Catholic Church in America has been fomenting since 1982, when public accusations of sexual misconduct against Father Gilbert Gauthes came to light in Lafayette, Louisiana. At that time, the U.S. Catholic Bishops' organization called for uniform, but nonbinding, guidelines to deal with clerical sexual abuse, particularly pedophilia. They included removing an offender priest from his assignment, referring him for medical evaluation, dealing promptly with the victim and his/her family, protecting the "confidentiality of the claim," and complying with the legal obligation to make appropriate information available to legal authorities.[63] By 1985, the matter was being studied systematically by the bishops' legal staff.

Three years later, the Vatican became involved. Discussions occurred between the American bishops and high-ranking officials in Rome where they tried to evaluate the ramifications of clerical sexual abuse within the context of canon law. By 1992, the United States Conference of Catholic Bishops (USCCB) officially instituted its earlier guidelines to deal with the abuse, and established a Joint Study Commission between representatives of the American bishops and leaders in the Vatican to deal with the problem. Finally in 1993, John Paul II admitted publicly that lawsuits against members of the clergy in the United States had reached a staggering $400 million,[64] and as the abuse scandals spread to Ireland, Germany, Canada, Australia, Britain, France, Mexico, and Poland, the pontiff made a formal apology to the victims. In 2001, the pope issued two documents on clerical sexual abuse. One dealt with pedophilia and defined it as one of the "graver offenses" against church law. The second charged the Vatican office of orthodoxy, the Congregation for the Doctrine of the Faith led at the time by the now-current pope, Benedict XVI, to establish guidelines as to how to deal with the abuse. The bishops were told from Rome that if "even a hint" of pedophilia existed, they were to "open an investigation and inform" Rome, but to be silent about the matter.[65]

Both John Paul II and the bishops originally attempted to protect the church's right to punish the clergy, not simply for the sin of sexual abuse, but also for the crime of pedophilia. That is, the Catholic leadership perceived its authority as total: both religious and civil with regard to the punishment of predator priests. The heart of the matter is one of power, and the bishops at their annual meeting in June 2002 drafted two documents to clarify the church's authority. One document is entitled *The Charter for the Protection of Children*, and a second document incorporated into it is known as *The Essential Norms for Diocesan/Eparchial Policies Dealing with Allegations of Sexual Abuse of Minors by Priests, Deacons, or Other Church Personnel*.

The *Charter* adopted a policy of outreach to the victims/survivors of clerical sexual abuse and offered them a sense of solidarity and concern. The bishops also agreed to put mechanisms in place to investigate allegations, to make the allegations public, and to report such incidents to public authorities. They held that valid complaints against members of the clergy would result in dismissal from their ministerial duties, and would require medical and psychological evaluation. They set up vehicles for accountability and assistance to dioceses, established safe environment programs, conducted better screening for candidates for the priesthood, and provided for better communications in cases of reassignments.

What the bishops minimized, however, was how to deal with the crime of clerical sexual abuse. They agreed to report allegations of pedophilia to civil authorities and to follow a zero-tolerance policy for the future, but the Vatican opposed these actions. Essentially, the Holy See was concerned with three main church interests: the need to protect the due process and appeals rights of priests; statutes of limitations on clerical sexual abuse; and the definition of the crime itself. In the end, it was clear, however, that Rome intended to control the process of prosecuting priests. It wanted to be able to review all cases and then return them to their appropriate dioceses for action. It expected to give the same penalties to priests who had committed crimes in the past, regardless of when the abuse occurred, and it reserved the right to define sexual abuse as a violation of the sixth commandment, rather than as a felony in civil law. Consequently, the bishops were careful to protect the clergy and the church leadership, citing exceptions to those policies in *The Essential Norms* where allegations were "canonically privileged."[66] At the same time, accused priests were encouraged to engage both civil and canonical counsel.

Even further, one-third or about fifteen thousand American Catholic priests who are members of "orders,"[67] and who are answerable to leaders other than bishops, have been supported in their abbots' and provincials' demands for exclusion from civil prosecution by the church. Under the aegis of the Institutions of Consecrated Life at the Vatican, the Conference of Major Superiors of Men, who represent the leaders of most orders, announced that they favor closely supervising abusive priests rather than expelling them from their ranks.[68] This flies in the face of the legal responsibility of civil authorities to protect society, to assure that no harm will come to its citizens, and that those who do violate the law will be treated consistently within the judicial system.

Thus a major church-state clash between the Catholic Church and civil authorities regarding the identification, treatment, and punishment of accused clerical sexual offenders is in the process of escalating in the United States. It is fueled, on the one hand, by state and local demands for information, often backed up by subpoenas, on the past management of predator personnel, as well as civil requirements for the oversight of future clerical assignments. This has been occurring throughout the United States. In Long Island, New York, twenty priests were brought before a grand jury in Rockville Center for clerical sexual abuse, but not indicted because religious authorities did not have the legal responsibility to report such acts to civil officials.[69] In Arizona, Bishop Thomas O'Brien of Phoenix confessed to having transferred predator priests to places where they could again victimize children. In exchange for immunity, he agreed to give up his authority to deal with such issues in the future and allowed comprehensive state oversight of the diocese in that area. In New Hampshire, Bishop John McCormack of Manchester acknowledged to state officials that there was evidence to show that his Diocese was responsible for child endangerment in the past. Part of the settlement between the church and the state allowed the Attorney General's office to audit church records for five years in order to assure that this would not happen again. It also required the Bishop's office to provide information on the diocese's past handling of sexual abuse allegations. In Boston, fifty-three subpoenas were issued to compel the testimony of archdiocesan officials concerning Bernard Cardinal Law's oversight, transfer, and treatment of clerical personnel. Over eleven thousand administrative documents were made available to the public.[70]

As a consequence, the Catholic Church has been subject to numerous civil prosecutions and penalties for protecting and, in many cases, reassigning known pedophile priests to different parishes. These public lawsuits have resulted in huge payments for the hiearchy's cover-up of crimes. In February 2004, a study commissioned by a National Review Board of the Catholic laity reported that over $573 million had been paid to settle over ten thousand claims brought against 4,392 clergymen, a number that has risen subsequently.[71] Since then, the Diocese of Boston has paid another $85 million dollar claim to victims of clerical sexual abuse,[72] and the Christian Brothers, a Catholic religious order, has reportedly settled a $6.3 million judgment on three former students who were sexually abused by clerical faculty members.[73] As the scandal continues to unfold, other dioceses will increase the payments and enlarge the process of reaching settlements with abuse victims. In Orange County, California, the diocese has paid at least $100 million to eighty-seven plaintiffs, and it is estimated that nine hundred additional allegations still await resolution.[74] In Dallas, a jury awarded plaintiffs $200 million, but the plaintiffs accepted only $30 million in order to save the diocese from bankruptcy.[75] Other dioceses have simply sold off many of their major land holdings to settle lawsuits, while some such as Tuscon, Arizona, and Portland, Oregon, have already declared bankruptcy, and still many others, like Spokane, Washington, are currently teetering on the verge of financial ruin. It is safe to say that as allegations and civil claims continue to escalate, the financial cost of Catholic clerical sexual abuse will only continue to climb, leaving the church in a monetary disaster.

Civil suits have even been augmented by criminal proceedings in Massachusetts. Former Springfield Bishop Thomas Dupre was charged with two counts of child rape, but kept from prosecution only by the state's statute of limitations. Although he was the first practicing clergyman to be indicted in that state, it is possible that many other states will pursue clerical sexual abusers in the same way. Growing state demands for prosecutions have been countered, however, by uneven responses among the hierarchy, and a lack of cooperation by several bishops, namely in New York and Los Angeles.

As a result, the clerical sexual abuse scandal has the potential to tip the scales of the church-state balance that has developed in the United States over the course of its history and to alienate the church membership as well. In the past, the church has been able to conduct its affairs without restriction, with canon lawyers managing matters of bankruptcy, embezzlement, and financial issues, while bishops handled personnel matters. But now the notion of what constitutes "internal matters" has become a source of contention. Where is the line between protecting priests, reporting their crimes, and protecting children? How should the Civic Public Forum law of no harm to others apply in this situation? Where is the line between administration and accountability? Where does pastoral responsibility end and civic duty start? How does the Civic Public Forum law of consistency apply to victims as well as to their abusers? The answers to these questions have a direct bearing on the laity as citizens, on the bishops as leaders, and on Catholicism within the context of U.S. religious pluralism. Those who see a major social, religious, and political crisis developing are aware that the clerical abuse scandal has the potential to test the laity's loyalty to its church, the bishops' credibility in moral leadership, and the church's dynamic relationship with civil authority in the long term.

The Catholic laity has pressured the church in the United States, insisting on the implementation of the laws of no harm and consistency for all among those who have suffered as a result of clerical sexual abuse. Within the church's traditional hierarchical structure, which has historically been controlled autocratically, the American bishops have, for the first time, consulted with the laity on how to resolve the sexual crisis. Never before having been allowed the individual right to interpret religious dogma, or the Bible, Catholics have had no experience in church decision making as elders, members of a fellowship, or participants in governing boards. But the sexual abuse crisis has resulted in a first: the establishment of a National Review Board, appointed by the bishops and composed of laypersons, to look into the scope and nature of the scandal. The Board engaged John Jay College to collect empirical data, and as a consequence has made formerly privileged information available to all church adherents and the general public, as well as provided a number of meaningful suggestions to assure that such events could never happen again. The bishops' attempt at transparency was a start toward the inclusion of the laity into the decision-making processes of the church and concluded with the Board making recommendations for further changes in church administration. These recommendations called for better screening and oversight of seminarians, increased sensitivity to responding to allegations of abuse, and greater accountability of church leaders. The Board also recommended increased participation by the faithful, improved interaction with civil authorities, consistent ecclesiastical reporting of allegations to civil authorities, and an "equitable resolution of all civil claims to restore trust and leadership in the Church."[76]

Further, the laity has been radicalized and activated by the clerical abuse scandal in the church, thus providing the first internal challenge to the authority of the bishops. One such group is the Survivors Network of those Abused by Priests (SNAP). Its purpose is to reach out to victims, build mechanisms for healing, bring justice to the perpetrators of sexual abuse, and to hold the church accountable for the crimes of its clergy and nuns. One of SNAP's main ways to do this is by providing the news media with reliable information. David Clohessy, SNAP's executive director, has characterized the relationship of the organization with the bishops by saying it "is not what it could be" but that its relationship with the laity "has never been better."[77] Another organization dedicated to similar goals is the Voice of the Faithful. Founded in Boston when the scandal broke, VOTF was established to support the survivors of sexual abuse, to support priests of integrity, and to promote structural change in the governance and administration of the church. Challenging the very foundations of Catholic leadership, one of VOTF's supporters, Rev. Donald Cozzins, claimed that the organization was on the verge of "unraveling the last feudal system in the West."[78] The latest figures show VOTF as having about thirty thousand members and two hundred affiliates across the United States, as well as a budget that topped $687,000 at the end of the fiscal year 2003.[79]

Both organizations have been very effective. They awakened and informed the laity about the suppression of information, as well as the mismanagement and the cover-up of predator priests. They have provided support to the victims and they have used their strength to push the National Review Board to bring pressure to bear on the church leadership to implement the *Charter* and the *Essential Norms* that the bishops' organization passed in 2002. These organizations do not intend to go away or to be dismissed by the church hierarchy. In short, they intend to hold the church accountable to the Civic Public Forum laws of no harm and consistency by using the court of public opinion to provide justice for the victims of clerical sexual abuse.

How the clerical sexual abuse scandal is resolved will also have a major effect on the leadership, management, and the future credibility of the bishops in both the Conscience and Civic Public Forums. Recently, resistance to the release of personnel files by the president of the United States Conference of Catholic Bishops, Bishop Wilton D. Gregory, regarding an alleged predator priest in his diocese pitted the church's demand for confidentiality against the right of an alleged victim to resolve a claim of molestation. The conflict resulted in a contempt ruling by the civil court against the diocese, an order to release the files by the bishop, and a judgment to pay a two-thousand dollar fine and court costs.[80] Clearly, the continued lack of understanding and unwillingness on the part of the Catholic leadership to deal with the criminal and civil ramifications of clerical sexual abuse within the confines of state authority has compromised its moral legitimacy in the Conscience and Civic Public Forums. Many bishops still do not understand that the crisis is like a festering sore that requires continual attention to bring about healing. After the issuance of the report by the National Review Board, Bishop Wilton Gregory declared that the abuse scandal had ended. *The New York Times* reported that he "declared with an emphatic finality in a news conference that the bishops had faced the problem, come clean, and swept the church of abusers."[81]

The short shrift given to such a seminal crisis of leadership only serves to dilute the bishops' role to infuse ethical and moral issues into the public debate in America in the Civic and Conscientious Forums. Consequently, their role will necessarily be questioned, as well as the church's claim to be the voice of the voiceless, as the protector of the unborn and a contributor to ethically grounded public policy choices. This will be a natural consequence if the leadership itself does not adhere to the laws that protect children and others from predator priests. They must follow the Civic Public Forum principles of no harm to others and consistency for all, or find themselves legally as well as morally suspect within the American political and legal infrastructure. Thus, the ability to advance policy stances on matters such as abortion, gay marriage, and stem-cell research will depend in great part on how the church deals with the authority of the government in the area of pedophilia and other types of sexual abuse.

A further stumbling block, however, is the Vatican and its traditional views of the nature of man and the role of government. In the past, Pope John Paul II was theologically committed to the belief that priests who are guilty of the sin of sexual abuse can admit guilt, seek forgiveness, pursue treatment, repent and change. In his thinking, reconciliation and repentance were critical to divine forgiveness and the personal reintegration of offender priests into the spiritual community. On the other hand, John Paul II believed that such absolution is within the purview of the church and part of its spiritual mission to save souls. This theological belief also fuels the church's insistence on its right and responsibility to prosecute and punish its clergy for the crime of sexual abuse as well, a matter that it has dealt with exclusively throughout its history.[82] Consequently, the Vatican has challenged U.S. civil authority in sexual abuse cases on a variety of issues, maintaining its right to forgive sin as well as to punish clerical crimes. It has vehemently opposed certain parts of the U.S. bishops' responses to the punishment of priests in *The Charter to Protect Children* as mentioned previously. This has been done particularly with regard to the punishment of those in "orders," situations where statutes of limitations have run out, the appeals process, and the definition of abuse.

The Vatican's attempt to frame the resolution of the scandal within the context of both the religious and political power of the papacy has compromised Catholic church-state relations in America and now provides a jurisdictional challenge to Benedict XVI as he begins his pontificate. It is important, therefore, to remember that it is this new pope who previously dealt with all of the allegations of clerical sexual abuse in his position as the former head of the Office of the Doctrine of the Faith, and who is probably the most knowledgeable about the scope and ramifications of the scandal. While the hearings of accused priests are secret, and their numbers are held in confidence, Benedict XVI has already shown his concern for the victims of clerical sexual abuse by attempting to reopen the case of Rev. Marcial Maciel Degollado, the Mexican founder of the Legonnaires of Christ. That said however, the Degollado case has yet to be resolved, and it should not be expected that a complete turnaround in Vatican policy will likely occur on all the complex and conflicting church-issues that have arisen from the scandal.

CONCLUSION

It is now possible to understand how and why the church embraced four expedient responses to religious pluralism throughout American history. These responses made it possible to (1) justify religious separation, (2) bring about social assimilation, (3) pursue political accommodation, and (4) play a role in policy advocacy. As a result, the church has been able to function in a meaningful way in the Conscientious Public Forum by persuasion, by infusing its moral principles into the conscientious public debate, and in the Civic Public Forum by enlarging policy choices. In addition, in the Civic Public Forum, the church has been able to help create the good society by its compliance with the law, as well as by challenging the law where it believes that church authority is compromised. All of this remains in jeopardy today, however, in light of the clerical sexual abuse crisis, even with a new pope directing its disposition.

During its earliest history and up to World War I, the Catholic hierarchy feared religious pluralism and responded by setting up its own separate hospitals, orphanages, and schools, thus limiting social and political involvement of Catholics. After World War I and the growth in the Catholic population in the United States, bishops understood that religious pluralism could serve to bring about the social and political assimilation of Catholics into the American mainstream. The U.S. bishops built on their new acceptance as a viable part of American society and pushed judicially for state accommodation to their religious freedom needs after World War II. However, after 1973 and the loss of the pro-life battle in *Roe v. Wade*, pluralism became the vehicle to justify hierarchical involvement in the public policy process in the Civic Public Forum.

Now, the circle is complete. The national candidacy of John Kerry illustrates how the Catholic bishops have returned to the idea of separatism by demanding moral coherence and dogmatic obedience within a political context in the Civic Public Forum. Thus, it is possible to conclude that the current Catholic hierarchical response to religious pluralism has been stricter and more demanding in the Civic Public Forum, and will most likely continue to be so into the future.

What does this mean for Catholic politicians as they pursue political office? They will be expected to take political stands that represent the view of their Church, particularly since "values" became a critical focus of the campaign of 2004. In a sense, the Catholic bishops' demands for moral coherence across the boundary of the Civic and Conscientious Public Forums laid the groundwork for, and reflected the actions of, other conservative religious groups within America today. After the successful result of a values-oriented political campaign by President Bush, it can be expected that the bishops' demands in the Conscientious Forum will continue and that they will expect greater moral coherence by Catholics in the Conscientious and Civic Public Forums in the future.

In the end, however, the church must reconsider how it communicates with Catholic politicians and how it should implement its values-oriented agenda. Punishments or threats of sanctions cannot serve as the means to keep politicians in line or to change their political commitments. Instead, the church must find a way to incorporate its ecumenical thinking and bring its assumed policy role to bear on broad discussions of the meanings of human dignity and freedom for all. In short, the Catholic bishops must play a major role in translating theological principles into broader political stands without infringing on the beliefs of others. Only then can they hope to infuse the political process with transcendental values that will enrich and enlarge the public debate in America, and perhaps even the meaning and scope of America's Sacred Ground itself.

Even more importantly, the demand for greater church control in the Civic Public Forum with regard to legal authority has created a major conflict in that the church has been sending the message "Do as I say, but not as I do." This has been the perception among Catholics and non-Catholics alike regarding the bishops in the matter of clerical sexual abuse. They want to determine the canonical requirements of clerical behavior as well as the legal processes by which predatory priestly actions will be resolved in the civic forum. Thus, the church's challenge to the authority of the state, its resistance to providing information, and lack of willingness to submit to the law are seminal to the church-state relationship in America. In short, the Catholic Church wants to determine its own jurisdiction within the Civic Public Forum, a principle that it has fought to maintain throughout its history.

There have always been, and will continue to be, concerns within institutional circles that a loss of church control over the punishment of clergy could lead to the government appointment of church personnel, as well as the administration of seminaries and other church charitable institutions. This occurred most recently in Germany under the Nazis and in Eastern Europe under the Communists, and currently characterizes the situation in China and Cuba under their atheistic regimes. The church as a two-thousand-year-old, international organization measures the clerical sexual abuse scandal in terms of its spiritual interests, history, and management responsibilities to maintain a universal and geopolitical church.

However, the state must recognize its responsibility to all its citizens, especially children. Thus, although the bishops will continue to resist where they believe they must, the authority of the state must supersede church prerogatives in order to assure that no harm comes to its citizens and that the responsible individuals will be held accountable. These measures will continue to be the standards by which both will operate and try to cooperate in the Civic Public Forum.

The church's stance, nevertheless, compromises its ability to make moral demands of Catholics in the Conscientious Public Forum. It undermines its moral authority to make a credible contribution to Civic Public Forum debates about law and public policy and to make moral demands of Catholic politicians and the laity. The church cannot require its adherents to be more moral than the moral leadership itself, nor can it demand moral coherence if the church itself is inconsistent in its own moral behavior. It cannot expect that its credibility will be accepted and respected if the clergy itself is untrustworthy. Only a credible hierarchy willing and able to deal with its own internal problems can hope to lead its adherents to their spiritual destiny and provide the moral leadership necessary to create the good society from the ground up within the framework of America's Sacred Ground. Clearly, it is only this type of model that makes possible the participation of the church and other religious voices in the Public Forum, while preserving the separation of church and state.

Chapter 5

Greening America's Sacred Ground: Eco-Spirituality and Environmental Politics

Stephen Woolpert

INTRODUCTION

Evidence is growing that the United States is on the threshold of an ecological crisis. Apart from an occasional energy shortage, it is not the kind of crisis that most Americans feel dramatically in their everyday lives, but it is measurable in terms of demographic dislocations, threats to health and safety, loss of biodiversity, and climate change worldwide.[1] The crux of the dilemma is that "the upward growth curve that characterizes consumer habits and technological development in modern cultures cannot be reconciled with the downward curve in the viability of natural systems."[2] The coupling of population growth with increasing affluence and technology is affecting in a comprehensive manner the entire complex of life systems on earth.

Most religious organizations in the United States have issued formal declarations calling for environmental stewardship as expressions of their faiths. However, as McGraw reminds us, America's Sacred Ground endorses the individual's right to put the dictates of conscience ahead of religious authority. The freedom to do so results from the direct relationship between the individual and the sacred order. One contemporary expression of this

87

centrifugal religious tendency is that significant numbers of environmentalists who see nature as a source of spiritual inspiration and enchantment,
including this author, are not members of an organized faith community.

Many spiritual ecologists reject the spirit-nature dualism that has been
engrained in Christian thought. While pleased that America's religious institutions are more actively addressing environmental problems, they prefer an
ecumenical spirituality that helps individuals feel more deeply connected to
God's presence in the natural world. Through the practice of prayer and
meditation, spiritual ecologists have sought to develop and strengthen a personal connection with a God of their understanding. They see each part of
nature—all creatures as well as the underlying processes and relations among
them—as precious to God, so that to honor God, humans must honor the
creation that God loves. Many spiritual environmentalists draw upon an
eclectic array of sources, including goddess-based ecofeminism, pantheistic
Native American cosmologies, and certain non-Western religious traditions,
most notably Buddhism.[3]

McGraw argues that the purpose of the American political order is to realize the public good by promoting pluralistic expressions of conscience, both
secular and religious, about the social order, including voices from outside
the mainstream. But while public environmental fora welcome participation
by mainstream religious organizations, nonsectarian eco-spiritual outlooks
are treated as largely irrelevant. Many people are indifferent or even hostile
to political expressions of environmental concern grounded in unorthodox
forms of spirituality. They are apt to imagine a self-righteous zealot dispens-
ing guilt, or a New Ager whose politics consists only of hanging crystals and
participating in the Harmonic Convergence. Similarly, environmental policy
making in the Civic Public Forum typically recognizes no valid aim beyond
human life itself. The idea that public expressions of concern for the natural
world can or should reflect a transcendent dimension of existence seems
unrelated to the pragmatic concerns of most environmental policy makers.

Yet spiritually grounded environmental activists illustrate the dynamic
interaction between political and spiritual endeavors that is needed for
America's Sacred Ground to function. They seek to change not only the political world but also their own ego identity. Their engagement in environmental politics is rooted in a transcendent ultimate vision that seeks both
environmental sustainability and a personal transformation from ego identification to ego disidentification. Nontheistic spiritual traditions depict this as
a transformation from "self" to "no self." In theistic traditions it is a transformation from "my will be done" to "Thy will be done." In either case it
amounts to a radical decentering of the ego in relation to a transcendent
realm.

This shift in identity constitutes a spiritual awakening, or in the Lockean
terms of America's Sacred Ground, enlightenment. Positive and negative
feedback loops from spiritually grounded political engagement, then modi-

fies the activist's worldview and self-concept, which in turn leads to further political choices; thus the cycle is repeated. This dialectical understanding of eco-spiritual praxis illuminates the crux of America's Sacred Ground by enlarging the purpose of environmental activism to encompass the liberation of the human spirit, while simultaneously expanding the concept of spiritual practice to encompass environmental activism in the Conscientious and Civic Public Forums.

In the present chapter, the dynamic and creative connection between spiritual and environmental concerns is illustrated by exploring one of the few politically influential proponents of eco-spirituality, His Holiness the Dalai Lama. He does not speak for all spiritually motivated environmentalists, for there are important differences among deep ecologists, ecofeminists, and others. But because His Holiness does lead an established, although minor, faith community of Tibetan Buddhists, the Dalai Lama's thought is representative in general terms of the contributions that nonsectarian eco-spirituality makes to the civic discourse over environmental problems. His approach to environmental issues is consonant with what Aldous Huxley calls "the perennial philosophy,"[4] or the common core of the world's great spiritual traditions.

This chapter first explores the Dalai Lama's ecological praxis and then shows how it exemplifies, and in certain ways amplifies, the fundamental laws and duties set forth in America's Sacred Ground.

HUMAN FULFILLMENT AND HARMONY WITH THE NATURAL WORLD

The Dalai Lama's distinctive contribution to civic engagement on environmental issues is what this author terms "ecological thinking," that is, integrative thinking about how things fit together, about patterns and contexts, and about human solidarity with the living world. His approach places environmental issues in larger contexts and portrays them in more dynamic terms. He underscores the ways in which individuals are members of a larger social and biotic community, and therefore leads all to consider environmental problems to be at least partly their own. This approach to environmental issues is exemplified by three central components of the Dalai Lama's ethical framework, each of which is consonant with America's Sacred Ground.

Holism: All Is One

Conventional politics all too often deals with conflict in a polarizing way. It tends to accentuate and exaggerate opposing tendencies. McGraw, for example, describes the false dichotomy that characterizes the current debate over the role of religion in public life. Adversarial legal proceedings, winner-take-all elections, and negative advertising are other notable examples of this tendency. However, all accounts of spiritual enlightenment emphasize non-duality. As one disidentifies from the ego, polar opposites merge into an undivided wholeness. This does not mean that political conflicts are avoided or glossed over. Rather, Spiritual Enlightenment leads to embracing conflicts and transcending opposition in order to bring about a fruitful synthesis.

This ontological unity is at the center of the Dalai Lama's approach to environmental problems. He emphasizes relationships and interlinkages. His way of thinking is grounded in holism rather than reductionism, that is, in the consideration of an issue, a topic, or a problem in its larger context. Contrary to the hierarchical nature of most environmental discourse, with humans at the top of the chain of being, the preeminent metaphor in ecological thought is the web of life or the circle of life. Humans are not seen as above or apart from the natural world.

The Dalai Lama's holistic worldview is congruent with the scientific understanding of environmental phenomena. The current scientific cosmology pictures an evolutionary universe that consists of nested systems-within-systems. Like the world's great spiritual traditions, it depicts the universe more like a developing embryo or organism than a machine. Matter is now viewed more as a process than as a thing. The Newtonian ontology of discrete entities that are outside of each other, and that exist independently in different regions of space and time, has been superseded by one characterized by patterns of interrelationship among complex dynamic systems. The entire universe, from the infinitesimal to the infinite, is unfolding through systems of spontaneous self-organization that are inextricably interconnected and interdependent.

The Dalai Lama calls this new cosmology one of the most promising developments in modern science, and he locates his ethical theory within a corresponding worldview. In Buddhist thought it is termed "dependent origination" or "dependent co-arising."

> [W]e cannot finally separate out any phenomena from the context of other phenomena. We can only really speak in terms of relationships . . . I find the concept of dependent origination (in Tibetan, *ten del*) . . . to be particularly helpful. According to this, we can understand how things and events come to be in three different ways. At the first level, the principle of cause and effect whereby all things and events arise in dependence on a complex web of interrelated causes and conditions is invoked. . . . On the second level, *ten del* can be understood in terms of the mutual dependence which exists between parts and whole. Without parts, there can be no whole; without a whole, the concept of parts makes no sense. . . . On the third level, all phenomena can be understood to be dependently originated because, when we analyze them, we find that, ultimately, they lack independent identity.[5]

No entity is isolated from this underlying nexus. Reciprocity and interdependence are therefore inescapable. He draws important ethical consequences from this ecological worldview:

> We begin to see that the universe we inhabit can be understood in terms of a living organism where each cell works in balanced cooperation with every other cell to sustain the whole. If, then, just one of these cells is harmed, as when disease strikes, that balance is harmed and there is danger to the whole. This, in turn, suggests that our individual well-being is intimately connected both with that of all others and with the environment within which we live. It also becomes apparent that our every action, our every deed, word, and thought, no matter how slight or inconsequential it may seem, has an implication not only for ourselves but for all others too. . . . It challenges us to see things and events less in terms of black and white and more in terms of a complex interlinking of relationships, which are hard to pin down. And it makes it difficult to speak in terms of absolutes.[6]

This ecological way of thinking about environmental problems sees the "stuff" of living systems as dynamic patterns of interaction, rather than as physical building blocks. Phenomena are systematically connected in both time and space. Thinking of the living world this way draws attention to its emergent, global properties—those properties that could not be predicted simply from knowledge of its component parts. Living systems are complex networks of interdependent patterns and processes, in which the environment of each organism consists partly of other organisms, and vice versa.

The Dalai Lama's eco-spirituality focuses on coherent wholes rather than fragments; he is concerned with relationships more than objects, with processes more than structures, and with networks more than hierarchies.[7] The metaphor of the web conveys a sense of the symbiotic relationship of all living things, with the human playing an integral but not a preemptive role. The boundaries between self and other, between human and nonhuman, and between life and nonlife are not absolute or impermeable.

Awakening: Form Follows Consciousness

A second common motif in spiritual thought is the primacy of human consciousness. The world's spiritual traditions generally accept that form follows consciousness: "As within, so without." An enlightened consciousness, awakened through spiritual practices such as prayer, meditation, and religious rituals, is the *sine qua non* of efforts to bring about a fundamentally better world.

The Dalai Lama asserts that the principle characteristic of genuine happiness is inner peace. One basic prerequisite for inner peace is the attitude with which humans relate to external circumstances—that is, an attitude that lacks attachment to temporary pleasure and material comfort, but that embodies compassion and lovingkindness toward others.

Of course, no approach to political participation can maintain the solipsism that the inner world of consciousness is entirely a matter of private experience. Even the most sublime spiritual experience is filtered through one's social and linguistic environment. But the reverse is equally true: political reality cannot be severed from its roots in human consciousness. For eco-spiritual activists, achieving a sustainable world requires an inside-out approach: the symptoms of environmental decline are external, but the fundamental causes are in the mind.

The Dalai Lama places this dialectical dynamic between the inner and outer worlds within the context of dependent origination; actions and their consequences cannot be understood except in the context of one's thoughts and intentions, and vice versa:

> If we take consciousness itself as the object of our investigation, although we tend to think of it in terms of something intrinsic and unchangeable, we find that it, too, is better understood in terms of dependent origination. This is because apart from individual perceptual, cognitive, and emotional experiences, it is difficult to posit an independently existing entity. Rather, consciousness is more like a construct which arises out of a spectrum of complex events.[8]

The primacy of spiritual awakening should not be misconstrued to mean that consciousness raising is sufficient in and of itself to achieve progress toward the common good. No amount of inner work can cause environmental problems to disappear by themselves. Prayer and meditation are no substitutes for concrete action. In the words of the Dalai Lama,

> [I]t is through achieving our aim by means of effort and self-sacrifice, through considering both the short-term benefit to us and the long-term effects on others' happiness, and sacrificing the former for the latter, that we attain the happiness which is characterized by peace and by genuine satisfaction.[9]

Biophilia: Loving-Kindness toward All Sentient Beings

The etymology of the word *ecology* refers to the study of "home." At the core of all forms of eco-spirituality lie expressions of affinity for our natural home, for which E. O. Wilson has coined the term "biophilia."[10] It is no coincidence that spiritual communities are often centered in sites of natural beauty. Prayer and contemplation tend to evoke an aesthetic appreciation of the created world. William Blake could "see the world in a grain of sand and eternity in an hour." He was pointing to a sense of the wholeness of things which has been eroded by the development of the modern world view. This dimension of eco-spiritual thought views the world as sacred, mysterious, and wondrous. It affirms that which is sublime and transcendent in nature.

All ecologically sustainable cultures have framed their understanding of plants, animals, and natural cycles as part of a coherent spiritual universe. Nature archetypes are commonplace in their ceremonies, rituals, and habits. These mythological figures, such as the Earth Mother, Gaia, the Green Man, and Pan, convey the fecundity, earthiness, and power of the natural world.[11] People have always oriented themselves by establishing direct and personal relationships to the places where they live and work. Until the past century, with its dramatic changes in communication and transportation, culture was very much a local phenomenon. Language, diet, clothing, architecture, and religion have traditionally been intimately related to particular locales.

Many Americans, however, think of culture as something set apart from the natural world. And no wonder: They interact almost exclusively with other humans and with human technologies. Economic and cultural globalization honors no community boundaries, human or natural. Communication technology now allows people to live increasingly in mediated worlds and disembodied, virtual realities. Consequently, their sense of place is fractured; they feel disconnected from where they live.[12]

This disenchantment with and alienation from nature robs it of any subjectivity. Nature is fundamentally an object rather than a subject, an "it" rather than a "thou." Culture has become "displaced"; people spend a great deal of time going somewhere else, in cars or in airplanes. Most of their belongings are supplied from unknown places; their wastes are shipped away and consigned elsewhere, also unknown. The feedback loops between individuals' actions and their consequences in the natural world have become disrupted.

Biophilia, by contrast, restores a sense of intimacy with nature. This understanding that all beings are intricately interconnected in a complex web of life animates the Dalai Lama's ecologically based praxis. He says, "The Earth, our Mother, is telling us to behave."[13]

ECO-SPIRITUALITY AND AMERICA'S SACRED GROUND

There are four ways in which the themes outlined above illustrate the general principles of America's Sacred Ground. First, eco-spirituality is congruent with the fundamental Lockean commitment to pluralism. It honors personal conscience over ecclesiastical authority. The Dalai Lama, for example, is well known for his tolerance of other religious traditions, actively encouraging people to celebrate their own faiths rather than convert to Buddhism. He argues that the fruits of love and compassion are the same for all religions, and that the promotion of these qualities is the main purpose of their teachings. For him the commitment to spiritual qualities such as compassion, love, patience, tolerance, and a sense of responsibility provides a natural, universal basis on which to ground ethics, independently of one's commitment to a particular religious creed.

Second, ontological wholeness is implicit in the overall structure of America's Sacred Ground, with its repudiation of hierarchy and either/or politics. Like eco-spirituality, America's Sacred Ground refutes the false dichotomies between the individual and community and between the human and nonhuman. All are interdependent. Personal happiness is inextricable from the well-being of the human and nonhuman world. Individual liberty is *for* the common good—in this case, the development of sustainable communities.

Third, eco-spiritual praxis reflects the political theology of America's Sacred Ground by affirming the nature of humans as spiritual beings and the existence of the human soul: a higher self that is not reducible to the ego. For the Dalai Lama, this is the self that attains happiness through acts of loving-kindness: "Spirituality I take to be concerned with those qualities of the human spirit—such as love, compassion, patience, tolerance, forgiveness, contentment, a sense of responsibility, a sense of harmony—which bring happiness to both self and others."[14]

In today's environmental discourse, proponents of such a view are often parodied as naïve optimists who ignore the human capacity for evil. The Dalai Lama refutes such a reading, however. Indeed he explains at length his understanding of the sources of greed, resentment, and aggression. Nonetheless, he does so in a way that is devoid of overarching religious doctrines or worldviews. He eschews the language of evil, sin, and righteous indignation. Instead he premises his argument on the assertion that the fulfillment of the human spirit is attained through kinship with all life.

Fourth, the eco-spiritual attitude toward nonhuman life rejects the notion that the world is composed of fundamentally antithetical forces that must struggle for supremacy. It also rejects the market liberals' ideal of an invisible hand that accommodates rival aspirations through the maximization of rational self-interest. Thus, while the Dalai Lama affirms that political conflicts are reconcilable without resort to violence, the agent of such reconciliation is not egoistic competition but enlightened self-interest. Ultimately one's own happiness is best served by acts of loving-kindness toward others. In this, his eco-spiritual praxis fulfills the ultimate purpose of America's Sacred Ground, the pursuit of the good.

What follows is a delineation of more specific ways in which eco-spirituality enriches, informs, and expands the functioning of the two-tiered public fora of America's Sacred Ground in dealing with environmental issues.

The Civic Public Forum

The inclusion of "dependent origination" in environmental political discourse sheds light on a central feature of McGraw's fundamental law of consistency. The norm of reciprocity that lies at the heart of this law cannot be misconstrued as naïve altruism when it is conjoined with dependent origination, because the latter stipulates that one's personal well-being is inextricably implicated in the well-being of others. So understood, the law of consistency does not require people to act contrary to their own interests. Because intersubjectivity is a fundamental reality of existence, humans are simultaneously both individual and communal. Each person is one element in a series of systems, from family to nation to biosphere, the functioning of which both reflects and shapes the functioning of the person. One can be fully free only when the individual and collective elements of the self are integrated in such a way that they sustain all creation.

While recognizing the equal and infinite moral worth of every soul, the Dalai Lama also recognizes that every right implies a responsibility to respect and honor the other's corresponding right:

> To develop a sense of universal responsibility—of the universal dimension of our every act and of the equal right of all others to happiness and not to suffer—is to develop an attitude of mind whereby, when we see an opportunity to benefit others, we will take it in preference to merely looking after our own narrow interests.[15]

Eco-spirituality also contributes to the Civic Public Forum by rejecting anthropocentric attitudes without falsely underplaying the power of humans. The characteristic American belief in the autonomy of the individual is not an adequate basis for responding to environmental decline. But humans are not inconsequential inhabitants in the overall functioning of the planet. Eco-spiritual praxis must involve the human voice and experience in a profound way without making them the central focus or seeing them as radically distinct from nonhuman nature.[16] Metaphors such as the "trustee," "caretaker," and "steward" suggest that humans are in charge of managing the earth. While an improvement over more domineering metaphors, they still imply that humans are separate from and superior to the rest of creation.

By contrast, the ecological thought of the Dalai Lama treats the "person-in-community" as the primary unit, transcending the false dichotomy between anthropocentrism and ecocentrism. Persons are conceptualized as active constituents of larger social and natural systems, which to some extent guide and constrain their activities and to which they contribute. The Dalai Lama says,

> If all phenomena are dependent on other phenomena, and if no phenomena can exist independently, even our most cherished selves must

be considered not to exist in the way we normally assume. . . . We come
to see that the habitual sharp distinction we make between "self" and
"others" is an exaggeration.[17]

So while he devotes most of his attention to *human* happiness, his way of
thinking overcomes the strict separation between one person and another,
one religion and another, or one sentient being and another. Eco-spirituality
reinserts humanity back into nature as a whole, regarding one's fellow creatures not merely as means but as ends in themselves.[18]

Furthermore, deliberations about environmental issues in America's Civic
Public Forum tend to assume that the natural world is a collection of objects
and "resources" that can be manipulated through technology for economic
interests, valuable only to the extent that they can be bought, sold, developed, or inhabited. In deliberations over environmental policy, management
issues are often the primary focus. Discussions about mechanisms of control
often take priority over discussions about the ecological purposes or functions of environmental phenomena.

In ecological thinking, however, while the mechanism of a system is
found at lower levels (in its parts), its purpose is found at levels above (in the
wholes). For example, take an organ, such as the human heart. Its mechanism (how it works) is found through its tissues and cells and what they
do—contracting, expanding, and so forth. Its purpose or function, however,
is found by understanding the role the heart plays in the body of which it is
a part. Similarly, holistic thinking about the environment is less interested in
"how" questions than in "why" questions. It focuses on purposes rather than
mechanisms. So when addressing environmental problems in the Civic Public Forum, eco-spirituality urges each person to ask: What is the function
(the role, niche, or purpose) of this person, group, species, or natural feature
within the larger ecosystem?

But the major contribution of eco-spiritual activists to the Civic Public
Forum stems from their sense of community with nonhuman nature. Human
spirituality connotes kinship with all life and reverence for nature's beauty
and abundance. For eco-spiritual activists, this sense of connectedness
acquires a profound intensity that is not simply an emotional response, but
also a firm commitment founded on reason.[19] By overcoming the split
between spirit and matter, the affinity for the natural world reclaims the
sense of the natural world as enchanting, sublime, and wondrous. This perception of nature as holy squares with McGraw's conclusion that "for the
founders . . . the temporal world, that is the 'secular' world, is sacred too."[20]
In other words, America's "ground" is sacred in both the literal and figurative
sense.

Thus eco-spirituality provides a persuasive argument for prioritizing the
multiple claims on our universal responsibility, by ranking them according to
the relative urgency of the need involved. Since the very prospect of achiev-

ing human happiness presupposes a livable planet, the ecosphere has claims that are prior to those of individuals. Individuals share the universal responsibility for maintaining the conditions necessary for human existence by harmonizing their lives with the natural world in which they are embedded. This implies, among other things, a duty not to exploit, squander, or hoard components of the world's ecological infrastructure. At the next level of priority, the human need for health and safety implies a responsibility to assist those whose life or health is threatened and to refrain from actions that cause harm to others. Third, the need for acceptance, esteem, and a sense of belonging implies the duty to honor diversity and to make the well-being of others our own concern. Finally the need for freedom—in both the inner and outer sense—carries with it the responsibility for honesty, integrity, and accountability in our dealings with other sentient beings.

According to this perspective, the laws of Civic Public Forum imply a commitment to sustainability, that is, to avoid hoarding, squandering, or exploiting nonhuman nature. It expands the scope of the law of no harm and the law of consistency. Biophilia approaches the loss of habitat, the extinction of species, and the polluting of nature as sources of grief. Indeed, the Dalai Lama's premise is that not just all *humans* but all *sentient beings* are equal in their desire for happiness and their right to attain it. This calls everyone to extend compassion not just to those near and dear to them, but to sentient beings everywhere.

Thus, one of the ethical implications of eco-spiritual holism is the broadening of reverence for life to include a positive regard for the ecosphere. Eco-spirituality's recognition of the fundamental interdependence of human and nonhuman nature leads to the understanding that the biotic community of which humans are a part is a living system that now has claims on personal moral consideration as well. By doing so, eco-spirituality furthers the historical trend toward enlargement of the American political community that has been marked by the inclusion of non–property owners, nonwhites, and women. As McGraw points out, this tendency toward greater inclusivity is "inherent in the system, itself, and has remained there as a latent force continually moving toward its full realization."[21]

The Conscientious Public Forum

How are deliberations about environmental issues in the Conscientious Public Forum altered when the person, the community, the culture, and the ecosphere are recognized as interconnected levels? First, eco-spiritual thinking repudiates both the illusion of self-sufficiency, on the one hand, and the romanticized immersion of the self in nature on the other. From this perspective individuals are made by, and make their relations in reciprocity with, other individuals (human and nonhuman) and their environments. The unique, separable, individual agent is deemphasized. Social and natural interdependence are givens. Decisions, creative acts, and learning each become viewed as transactions or patterns of relationship connecting us with the larger context of life.

Second, the eco-spiritual framework emphasizes the primacy of the inner life as a first step in addressing environmental problems. The Dalai Lama has demonstrated through his own actions that public engagement is a spiritual path, which is consistent with the duty to discern what conscience directs:

> So long as we carry out our work with good motivation, thinking, "My work is for others," it will be of benefit to the wider community. But when concern for others' feelings and welfare is missing, our activities tend to become spoiled.[22]

Further on he observes, "If we change internally—disarm ourselves by dealing constructively with our negative thoughts and emotions—we can literally change the whole world."[23]

This underscores the feedback between political engagement and spiritual growth. The hub of his ethical program is the symbiotic relationship between concern for self and concern for the world, both human and nonhuman. His concern is not with the private enlightenment of separate individuals, but the lives and consciousness of all sentient beings. His emphasis is on universal responsibility (chi sem), transcending the false dichotomy between rights and duties by linking compassionate action to personal enlightenment. This is congruent with Lockean political theology in which the inner life is primary, but in which there is correlative duty to bring conscience to life through civic engagement. The goal of America's Sacred Ground can be seen as harmonizing the vox Dei, the "still, small voice" and the vox populi.

But to affirm the political primacy of inner transformation in this way is to alter how society approaches environmental problems. Although the most devastating consequences of environmental degradation are visited on indigenous peoples and people in developing countries, the eco-spiritual view is that the root cause of the environmental crisis is what Americans (and the developed world generally) believe. It is in the very fabric of individuals' lives, not "out there" somewhere. It arises, as Susan Griffin says, ". . . from a consciousness that fragments existence . . . [w]ithin this particular culture . . . which has grown into an oddly ephemeral kind of giant, an electronic behemoth, busily feeding on the world, the prevailing habit of mind is to consider human existence and above all human consciousness and spirit as independent from and above nature."[24]

This inside-out approach to the environmental crisis challenges us to confront taken-for-granted patterns of thinking as an indispensable step toward sustainability. One example is the notion of an ever-accelerating rate of production and consumption rushing into an open-ended cornucopian future. Another central assumption of American political discourse—sometimes in the foreground, sometimes in the background—is anthropocentrism, the belief that humans have a privileged status among the forms of life making up the biotic community. As a result of these thought patterns, Americans generally see the nonhuman world as the supplier of natural resources, aspects of earth that satisfy human wants.[25] Notice how often policymakers refer to "wildlife management" and "resource management," as though the nonhuman world could not possibly get along on its own. The Dalai Lama reminds us that it is more accurate to say that humans are the ones who need management.

These harmful attitudes, in turn, hinge on one's idea of where life resides. For if only organisms are imbued with life, then beings like us are important and all else is relatively unimportant. For most Americans the earth is thought to consist of important entities called organisms and their relatively inconsequential nonliving environments. However, organisms are "brought to life" only within the matrix of air, land, and water. In natural cycles, matter and energy circulate over and over through organic and inorganic phases, including the air in our lungs, the water in our tissues, and the minerals in our bones. It is false consciousness to believe that human populations exist apart from the natural systems that support and sustain them. Groups, cultures, and nations are not free-standing; they are Earth-dependent. "Life" is a property of ecological systems, not of organisms per se.

By recognizing the crucial political role that one's state of mind plays in the political process, eco-spirituality illuminates an important aspect of America's Sacred Ground. Western political thought has tended to equate liberty with the freedom to choose from among alternatives according to one's preferences—that is, to exercise choice *in the absence of external restraints.* The Revolutionary War, constitutional limits on governmental power, the ongoing struggles for the rights of labor and for racial and sexual equality, all reflect this country's concern with independence from outside forces: governmental tyranny, economic dependency, and legalized exploitation.

Without denying the importance of these threats to freedom, the Dalai Lama's view is that when our spiritual life is neglected there is no hope of securing the common good. His "form follows consciousness" approach emphasizes the inner sources of outward environmental harm:

> The overriding question concerns the individual's spiritual state, their overall state of heart and mind in the moment of action. . . . When our intentions are polluted by selfishness, by hatred, by desire to deceive, however much our acts may have the appearance of being constructive, inevitably their impact will be negative, both for self and others.[26]

He thereby reminds everyone that political, economic, and legal coercion are not the only enemies of human happiness. Suffering—especially the suffering of the natural world—also results from noncoercive, psychospiritual factors such as the individual's attachment to sensory gratification, status, and wealth. In order to overcome these barriers to political emancipation, one must confront adversaries of a different sort. These include the insidious influence of psychological manipulation, subtle persuasion, and conformism in both the marketplace and the political arena. The use of sophisticated mass marketing techniques and public relations tactics has become increasingly commonplace in education, religion, and civic life generally.

Consequently, to achieve environmental sustainability, it is necessary to resist control by others in the Civic Public Forum, as well as to develop inner discipline, which the Dalai Lama calls "the ethic of restraint," in the Conscientious Public Forum. At least the founding fathers and mothers, the southern slaves, and the northern union organizers knew who their enemies were. For the eco-spiritual activist, on the other hand, while eternal vigilance remains the price of liberty, the first person to watch out for is oneself.

Moreover, biophilia connotes a call to civic engagement, in accord with the duty to participate in the Public Forum. Traditionally the movement back to nature has marked a form of withdrawal or spiritual retreat from civic life.[27] For spiritually motivated environmental activists, however, one's affinity for nature does not turn one away from the world, even if the experience of intimacy with nature is utterly private and contemplative. Instead it opens channels of loving-kindness aimed at the liberation of all sentient beings. The Dalai Lama says:

> I have suggested that we all desire happiness, that genuine happiness is characterized by peace, that peace is most surely attained when our actions are motivated by concern for others, and that this in turn entails ethical discipline.[28]

He therefore understands that the purpose of political life is to promote happiness by fostering compassion—a politics that responds to the legitimate needs of human and nonhuman life while teaching civic virtue in order to counteract selfishness.

CONCLUSION

Social upheaval is often the midwife of political transformation. Historically, new political ideas, institutions, and practices have been sparked by breakdowns in the existing order. The growing evidence of environmental decline suggests that we now face such a turning point. When politics exalts narrowly defined self-interests, dehumanizes people, and devalues nature, upheaval is sure to follow. The scope of suffering today in both the natural and human realms requires a new way of thinking about politics, one that is rooted in America's Sacred Ground, while expanding previous conceptions regarding its scope and function. Eco-spirituality succeeds in doing this by articulating a holistic understanding of the self and a restructured relationship with the environment.

The world's suffering tells everyone that this new relationship with the totality of life must be fundamentally moral, not simply biological. Like many spiritually based environmentalists, the author welcomes new assumptions into the civil discourse, new aspirations, and new assertions about political life that are better suited to twenty-first-century political realities, where the present environmental predicament is both a political crisis and a spiritual one. As Edmond O'Sullivan writes, "We need a spirituality whose scope and magnitude will open us up to the wonder and the joy of the universe. We are in need of a spirituality which has embedded within it a vision that keeps us vitally connected to the natural world and to the unfolding of the universe."[29]

In keeping with America's Sacred Ground, eco-spiritual thought is not an overarching, hegemonic worldview. It is innately eclectic, heterogeneous, and idiosyncratic. Its objective is not to combine religious doctrine with sovereign political power. Rather it seeks to persuade people to improve their conscious contact with the sacred depths of nature, not only as a means of personal transformation but also to empower them to achieve a more sustainable world.

Tenzin Gyatso, the present Dalai Lama, unifies his spiritual work with an ecological understanding of responsible citizenship. Brought up as a Tibetan monk, he was thrust onto the stage of international affairs by the Chinese invasion of Tibet in 1959, when he fled to India. His subsequent life and public service embody many features of the spiritual/political dialectic that lies at the heart of America's Sacred Ground. His political life continues to be a crucible of both inner and outer transformation, each informing the other. Here he summarizes, in terms that echo the Lockean roots of America's Sacred Ground, the distinctive way that spiritually motivated citizens contribute to public life:

> Spiritual practice . . . involves, on the one hand, acting out of concern for others' well-being. On the other, it entails transforming ourselves so that we become more readily disposed to do so. To speak of spiritual practice in any terms other than that is meaningless.
>
> My call for a spiritual revolution is thus not a call for a religious revolution. Nor is it a reference to a way of life that is somehow otherworldly, still less to something magical or mysterious. Rather it is a call for a radical reorientation away from our habitual preoccupation with self. It is a call to turn toward the wider community of beings with whom we are connected, and for conduct which recognizes others' interests alongside our own.[30]

This eco-spiritual vision presupposes a fundamentally new relationship not only among humans but also between humans and the ecosphere. It is a political vision that counterbalances the spiritual vacuum of contemporary American society and the pervasive alienation from self, others, and nature that American politics has come to promote. This in turn fosters a return to a spiritual understanding of ourselves, our place, and our purpose—one that fulfills America's Sacred Ground's call to make a better world through an ecological understanding that involves the heart and the soul as well as the mind.

Chapter 6

The Mormon Religion, Cultural Challenges, and the Good Society

John R. Pottenger

INTRODUCTION: A UNIQUELY AMERICAN RELIGION AND AMERICA'S SACRED GROUND

The Second Great Awakening (1790s–1830s) spawned dozens of new religions during the early decades of the American republic. With society awash in religious pluralism and in an attempt to satisfy their spiritual needs, an increasing number of Americans sought unorthodox approaches to those offered by conventional Christian denominations. Since the early nineteenth century, many of the alternative religious movements have survived and even prospered well into the twenty-first century. Certainly no exception to this phenomenon is the Church of Jesus Christ of Latter-day Saints (the LDS Church or Mormons). Founded by Joseph Smith and five others in western New York in 1830, the LDS Church initially met the needs of thousands of Americans who felt spiritually and socially adrift. Today, the church has grown exponentially and has become the fifth-largest denomination in the United States. The LDS Church has approximately sixty thousand full-time, proselytizing missionaries throughout the world and more than 12 million members worldwide.[1] Recognizing the phenomenal growth and universal appeal of the LDS Church, non-Mormon historian Jan Shipps asserts that

Mormonism is on the verge of becoming a major world religion.[2] In the same way that Christianity grew into a distinct religious tradition despite its origins in Judaism, Shipps argues that Mormonism is emerging as a new religious tradition even as it claims to be Christian.

From the moment of its contentious appearance, the LDS Church has captured the attention of observers who have grappled with the implications of this new and controversial religion.[3] Contemporary social critic Harold Bloom asserts that the imagination of Joseph Smith, independent and unfettered by European religious beliefs and institutions, led to the creation of a uniquely American religious tradition.[4] Referring to the Mormon prophet as a religious genius, Bloom maintains that Smith offered new religious teachings, while recognizing that his followers would have to "become a people" for the new faith to survive. In addition to teaching novel doctrines and sacred rituals, Smith organized his followers into communities with distinct political, economic, and familial arrangements. To expedite the growth of the new faith, he also sent missionaries to seek new converts in foreign countries.

Yet since its inception, conflict has existed between Mormons and others in American society. Those with more orthodox Christian beliefs, as well as the U.S. government, have periodically attempted to thwart the appeal and growth of the new religion. Today, the LDS Church perceives a growing threat from secularism to its community of believers, as the gap widens between the moral teachings of the church and the cultural relativism of American society. In addition to the mounting intensity of the culture war, the church is also wary of the expansion of government's reach into private social relations, as American liberal democracy increasingly favors removal of religion from the public square.

Liberal democracies have long recognized and encouraged a distinction between two competing theories of politics. Liberal theory argues for the supremacy of the rights of the individual and one's self-interest over the demands of a likely tyrannical majority. Democratic theory argues for the preeminence of the mandate of the majority to achieve the common good rather than the usually self-serving and socially disruptive interests of the individual. Through a historically evolutionary process, liberal democracy's civil society has forged a practical tension between the forceful imperatives of the two theories, such that the interface between private endeavors and political arrangements do not collapse into either anarchy or totalitarianism.[5] The tension arises from the legitimacy of both theories' values that arise from opportunities for voluntary participation in a plethora of activities of a nonpolitical and noneconomic character, from family life to self-help associations to religious organizations.[6] In turn, a vibrant market economy and a responsible pluralist democracy provide the conditions necessary for a well-developed civil society.[7] Thus a self-contained whole is obtained that gives the liberal democratic model its stability as diverse individuals and groups compete with each other for political influence. Nevertheless, Barbara A. McGraw argues that American liberal democracy has an innate normative intent in the way it is constructed that provides a foundation for the United States, which she refers to as "America's Sacred Ground" and which has too often been ignored.[8] Having rediscovered America's Sacred Ground, McGraw makes a case for the need to transcend the politics of self-interest and to return to the original pursuit of the common good.

McGraw argues that America's Sacred Ground recognizes the necessity of, and encourages the search for, the common good. Given its liberal origins, this normative ground gives preeminence to the individual in that search. Adapting the views of John Locke on the purpose and limits of government regarding individual conscience, McGraw maintains that the pursuit of the common good arises from the individual's need to act morally to achieve happiness.[9] Locke believes that an individual can discover God's will through reasoning about how to live a just life and even the characteristics of a just society. Consequently, it is of supreme importance that the individual be free to think and discuss with others his or her views regarding divine will. McGraw argues that a two-tiered structure of public forums supports the intent of America's Sacred Ground: the Conscientious Public Forum and the Civic Public Forum.

The Conscientious Public Forum defends voluntary associations, religious diversity and tolerance, and religion in the public square, and promotes religious pluralism in the search for understanding the nature of the good society.[10] In this forum, religious individuals and organizations attempt to convince each other of the theological correctness and moral righteousness of their positions regarding matters of spiritual salvation, individual morality, social ethics, and the common good. Furthermore, since religious associations claim special insights into understanding divine intent, McGraw believes that they ought to be heard in the public square and involved in the public policy debates of the Civic Public Forum. In the Civic Public Forum, religious denominations may express concerns that emanate from the Conscientious Public Forum. Various constitutional arrangements and legal mechanisms of representative government, such as periodic elections, separation of powers, checks and balances, federalism, and majority-rule decision making, provide the means for translating citizen preferences into public policies. However, unlike proponents of individualistic liberalism who argue that any democratic majority may hold sway in the political realm, McGraw argues that majority-rule decision making is limited by America's Sacred Ground. The majority may only translate citizen preferences into public policies as long as those policies do not violate the delimiting principles of the Civic Public Forum.

In the Civic Public Forum laws are only legitimate if they are consistent with the limits set by two normative principles: no one may harm another in his or her life, liberty, or property, and no one may deny to others what one is not willing to deny oneself.[11] The Civic Public Forum, then, is restrained by inalienable rights of the freedoms of conscience and association, which permit divine intent for the common good to be revealed through personal reflection and public debate. Since voluntary associations are based on moral autonomy, individuals are not coerced to be involved. In this way, defense of individual rights results in a greater likelihood of identifying the common good. Lockean individualism makes authentic communities (what McGraw refers to as "communities of conscience") possible in the Conscientious Public Forum and attaining the common good achievable in the Civic Public Forum. Consequently, the rights of freedom of conscience and freedom of association are core civil rights. According to McGraw, John Locke and the nation's founders perceived these conditions and stipulations as necessary for attaining a good society. Since Lockean rights necessary for public debate and policy determination have divine intent, both forums are founded on a "sacred ground" of rights necessary for individual choice and democratic institutions to function independently as well as cooperatively. Given America's Sacred Ground, then, how can the Civic Public Forum embrace pluralism, yet not impede the building of religious communities in the Conscientious Public Forum?

Using McGraw's framework, terminology, and thesis regarding the need to recover and recognize America's Sacred Ground, the LDS Church's role in public debate can be addressed. Specifically to be addressed are the ways in which the church and individual Mormons have been active in the Civic Public Forum and the Conscientious Public Forum. In these forums, Mormons endeavor to protect their unique identity as well as defend and promote their sense of community. Along with defense of religious liberty, the LDS Church focuses primarily on public policy issues related to the family as the primary social unit of society. Through its proselytizing efforts in the Conscientious Public Forum, the church's exclusive message regarding salvation and free will motivates its missionary efforts in increasing the number of adherents to its faith and admonishing others toward virtuous social behavior. As an increasingly key political actor in the Civic Public Forum, the church also participates politically as a special-interest group in legislatures and courtrooms and mobilizes church members as voters to support or defeat particular state propositions. The LDS Church, then, participates in both public forums with a distinctive attitude toward society and spirituality, culture and morality, democratic politics, and the separation of church and state. Although the church believes its social and political activities contribute to building the good society, Mormonism's unique history and peculiar theology have prevented it from forming deep alliances with either the religious right or the secular left.

Mormonism's attitudes and politics formed during failures regarding America's Sacred Ground and the treatment of the LDS Church. The emergence of Mormonism offended non-Mormons in the Conscientious Public Forum and led to violations of basic rights in the Civic Public Forum. In its struggle to survive, the LDS Church forged an approach to its participation in both forums that has ensured the survival of its own "community of conscience" as well as enhanced its ability to influence the direction of public policy debates.

Fundamental traits provide the key to understanding Mormonism's support for America's Sacred Ground and its participation in both forums. These include Mormon religious exclusivism, theocracy and disestablishment, modern scriptures and separation of church and state, and challenging social issues in the quest for the good society. How Mormonism addresses these issues reveals the direction and restrictions of the LDS Church's participation in the two-tiered Public Forum.

MORMON EXCLUSIVISM

The Conscientious Public Forum comprises certain conditions with an end in mind.[12] The end of this forum is to encourage the use of individual freedom of conscience in discovering the common good, and then to discuss particular findings with others. In this forum, only moral suasion may be used to convince others of the virtue of one's position; as long as consistency is upheld and harm is avoided, government force is not permitted. Consequently, voluntary compliance is to be sought in convincing others to change their beliefs and behavior. Through free and open dialogue, members of the Conscientious Public Forum will be able to apprehend divine will and its implications for their daily lives, including its relevance in identifying the common good. Also in this forum, an examination of the marketplace of religious ideas reveals that exclusivism is frequently unavoidable on moral and epistemic grounds. Religious exclusivism assumes that certain tenets of belief are true, and if those tenets are incompatible with others, then the others must be false.[13] As a result of exclusivist claims of the Mormon faith, profound theological differences serve as obstacles to the LDS Church's ability to form lasting ecumenical alliances and political coalitions with religious and other organizations.

Unlike other religious adherents, such as Catholics and Baptists, who attempt to demonstrate a historical lineage of authority to New Testament figures, Mormons believe that careful research will reveal that no such divinely sanctioned lineage exists. According to Mormon interpretation of history, a study of historical Christianity reveals an unfortunate straying or "Great Apostasy" from the true teachings and intentions of the gospel of Jesus Christ, as well as a loss of divine authority among men to conduct necessary rituals or ordinances of salvation.[14] The LDS Church maintains that Jesus not only taught his gospel of redemption and salvation for all humankind but established a church guided by his twelve apostles to further the Great Commission or proselytizing efforts. Furthermore, the apostles were given priesthood authority by Jesus to preach the gospel and conduct sacred ordinances, including baptism, necessary for individual salvation. Traveling throughout the Mediterranean world, generally going two by two, they preached the gospel and organized local congregations of Christ's true church.

Yet in the years following Jesus' crucifixion, resurrection, and ascension, according to the LDS Church, the apostles were unable to maintain regular communication with and religious cohesion among the rapidly growing and diverse congregations. With their own untimely deaths and the inability of the fragmented and disparate church leadership to replace them, the established and necessary lineage of priesthood authority of the apostles ceased.[15] Furthermore, the following centuries witnessed a gradual corrosion of the essence of the gospel teachings, through errors in the translating and copying of divinely inspired manuscripts, the incorporation of noninspired texts, and misunderstandings and faulty interpretations. According to Mormon belief, the gospel that had been taught from Adam to Moses and Abraham, and finally culminating in its fulfillment with Jesus, was lost in its purest form. For nearly seventeen hundred years, only a corrupted expression could be detected in an imperfect collection of scriptures, the Bible, with religious ecclesiastical institutions bearing only faint resemblance to that originally established by Jesus and his apostles. In its dark and misguided state, human civilization had been in need of the restoration of the gospel of Jesus Christ, according to Mormonism.

Nevertheless, given man's free will and disposition toward morally destructive, self-interested behavior, certain social conditions had to obtain before a divine restoration could take place. The conditions necessary would have to include the formation of a society that valued individual initiative and responsibility, particularly in matters of personal morality. Furthermore, such a society would have to permit freedom of conscience and association, especially with regard to religious beliefs and practices.

Consequently, according to Mormonism's interpretation of history, faint stirrings of religious liberty began to appear toward the end of the medieval era, particularly in the influential writings of Martin Luther, Philipp Melanchthon, John Calvin, and John Wesley.[16] The desire for religious freedom in the face of powerful church-state arrangements forced dissenters, pilgrims, puritans, and others to leave the "old world" in search of a "new world" free of intolerance and oppression. The most prominent location ultimately became the North American continent, where tolerance of diversity was a necessary condition for survival. The influential writings of the Protestant dissenters as well as British and Scottish thinkers, such as John Locke and Adam Smith, laid the foundation for an alternative public philosophy that would emphasize individual rights over government authoritarianism.[17] With the development of America's Sacred Ground, a new political culture arose, culminating in the writing of the Declaration of Independence and the U.S. Constitution. Under these conditions, the LDS Church maintains that a unique opportunity existed for the restoration of the gospel. With the Conscientious Public Forum in place, the restoration would begin with a divine epiphany before a poorly educated but receptive farm boy—Joseph Smith—in western New York in 1820.

In this First Vision, both God the Father and His Son Jesus Christ appeared, thus confirming the existence of two separate, divine beings.[18] The two divine beings called Joseph Smith to be the new prophet of the final era or dispensation of human history. The LDS Church believes that, since Adam, several dispensations of time have witnessed teachings and ordinances of the gospel revealed to man through duly called and ordained prophets. Each dispensation ended with the loss of pertinent teachings and authority due to general unrighteousness and apostasy from divine instructions.[19] As the new prophet, Smith ushered in the final dispensation with the restoration of the gospel. In subsequent years, numerous biblical prophets and apostles, including Moses, Elijah, John the Baptist, Peter, James, John, and other angels, would appear to and communicate with this latter-day prophet. These divine visitors revealed to Smith the gospel in its purest form, and bestowed upon him the priesthood authority to conduct divinely sanctioned and thus legitimate baptisms and other ordinances of salvation. As the new leader of the true priesthood, Smith then organized a church with an ecclesiastical structure along the lines of that which existed during and briefly after Jesus' ministry. As the new prophet in communication with Jesus for spiritual and moral guidance of church members, Smith sent an army of proselytizing missionaries with divine authority to various parts of the world to seek converts by preaching the restored gospel. He also ordained twelve apostles— the Quorum of the Twelve— to coordinate and guide the rapidly growing network of congregations, as well as control and exercise priesthood authority for matters of individual salvation and church operations.[20]

The claim by the LDS Church that the heavens were once again opened to divine communication between God and man suggested that new revelations for the welfare and salvation of humankind would be forthcoming. In fact, Joseph Smith brought forth a new volume of scripture to complement the initially inspired yet historically transmitted and flawed Bible. With the assistance of an angel, Smith maintained that he had located ancient writings with divinely inspired stories of past civilizations of North America; these writings included an account of a visit by the resurrected Jesus before his ascension. The LDS Church teaches that Smith translated the writings through divine inspiration and published them in 1830 as the Book of Mormon.[21]

The LDS Church maintains, then, that it is not only a Christian church, but "the only true and living church upon the face of the whole earth."[22] That is, the LDS Church exclusively contains the complete teachings of the gospel of Jesus Christ. Furthermore, the LDS Church believes itself to be uniquely endowed with divine authority to conduct sacred rituals or ordinances necessary for individual salvation. It does recognize the generally well-intended efforts and teachings of other Christian denominations and sects, as well as those of non-Christian religions. However, Mormon exclusivism does not recognize the sacraments and rituals of other denominations, either as holy or sanctioned by God; nor does it accept many of their teachings as theologically legitimate and sound. Consequently, in its proselytizing efforts, the LDS Church requires that a prospective adherent foreswear his or her current religious allegiance and affiliation, regardless of the individual's previous participation in another denomination's sacraments, such as baptism; membership in a priesthood of the clergy; or devotion to any other non-Mormon religious ritual or practice.

Mormon exclusivism conflicts with essential teachings and beliefs of historical Christianity.[23] Both claim that certain theological propositions are necessarily true, or required to be accepted as true, yet many propositions of one are contradictory to those of the other. Since the LDS Church accepts the Bible as generally inspired, but flawed, it has expanded and enhanced the quality of the Christian canon by adding the Book of Mormon and other contemporary scriptures. This expansion is antithetical to historical Christianity, which accepts only the Bible as authoritatively inspired and complete and thus believes the canon to be closed. In addition, the LDS Church rejects the Nicene and Apostles' creeds, since they were formulated after the apostasy that took true Christianity from the earth. Mormons generally find the creeds, essential to Christianity, to be theologically in error. Specifically, Mormonism rejects the Christian concept of the trinity, teaching instead the existence of the Father, Son, and Holy Ghost as separate, anthropomorphic deities, whereas historical Christianity teaches that the three are coequal entities in one substance.[24] The incompatibility of doctrines and beliefs has blocked ecumenism between Mormon Christianity and historical Christianity. Consequently, the refusal by most Christian denominations to accept the LDS Church as one of their own has hampered efforts to form political alliances on certain social issues, such as increasing legal restrictions on abortion providers.[25]

FROM REVELATION TO THEOCRACY TO DISESTABLISHMENT

In addition to Mormon exclusivism, the LDS Church's own historical experience with the nineteenth-century American culture of radical individualism, pluralist politics, and market economics contributes to the contemporary Mormon framework for developing a spirituality that participates in politics. Arising out of a social milieu that included sexual and economic experimentation, from advocacy of celibacy (Shakers) to communal property and "complex marriage" (the Oneida community), Joseph Smith developed a theology that linked this world and the next through the eternal nature of the extended family.[26] He questioned why the Old Testament practice of select prophets of God taking more than one wife had been abandoned by historical Christianity. Believing his calling was to restore ancient yet timeless teachings of God, Smith received a revelation regarding the practice of "plural marriage" or polygamy.[27] He taught that human relationships are imperfect yet perfectible images of relationships in the hereafter. The place where these proper relationships are to be found, he maintained, is in the extended family.

In an attempt to develop a Mormon community of conscience with intent to extol the virtues of the extended family, Smith also implemented the Old Testament emphasis on the priestly as well as prophetic character of everyday life. That is, religious considerations were to include temporal concerns, as well as how to meet spiritual needs. The church organized by Smith played a comprehensive political role, as religious leaders also served as political leaders. The community's worldly laws were based on biblical teachings as interpreted by the church's prophet and its other ecclesiastical officials. Under theocratic rule, the church's leaders included communal economic arrangements to fulfill better the demands of production and distribution in order to be self-sufficient from American society.

Smith's social practices of polygamy as well as economic communalism and the superiority of theocracy gave a sense of identity and community to the fledgling religion in frontier America, as the Mormons sought to build their Zion.[28] However, as new Mormon communities were established with thousands of converts, friction arose between the Mormons and their more independent, individualist, and monogamous non-Mormon neighbors. In the Conscientious Public Forum, the controversial Mormon congregations were perceived as a threat to the decency of the prevailing social values. In addition, the principles of the Civic Public Forum were increasingly violated. As the storm gathered and as a minority religion, Mormon communities were the recipients of violent persecution, including deadly attacks, from intolerant neighbors.[29] Many of the attacks were frequently instigated with the full knowledge and support of local and state government authorities.[30]

By 1846 open conflict and even warfare, including the murder of Smith and other LDS Church leaders, ultimately forced the greater part of the Mormon communities to emigrate from Ohio, Illinois, Missouri, and other states of the Midwest to the relative obscurity and safety of present-day Utah, then under Mexican sovereignty.[31] At the conclusion of the Mexican-American War, Mexico ceded the Rocky Mountain West to the United States, which included myriad Mormon settlements. Once again, conflict intensified between Mormons and non-Mormons with the arrival of American settlers from the east. In 1856, the Republican Party had campaigned on ending the "twin relics of barbarism": slavery and polygamy. Although the Democratic candidate, James Buchanan, won the presidency, he was also under increasing pressure to end polygamy in the territories. In 1857, Buchanan sent a military expedition to subdue the Mormon theocracy in the Utah territory. Brigham Young, the new Mormon prophet, instigated a scorched-earth policy to resist the U.S. army. With the army unable to reach Salt Lake City, open warfare was averted and resolution of the "Mormon problem" was delayed until after the Civil War.[32]

After scrutinizing the Utah territorial theocracy, the U.S. Congress passed legislation banning polygamy, dissolved the corporation of the LDS Church, restricted further Mormon emigration to the Utah territory, placed territorial schools under federal government jurisdiction, and abolished woman suffrage in Utah. Challenging the statutes in the federal courts, the LDS Church argued that its freedom of religion was violated. Ignoring the Civic Public Forum's principle of no harm, the Supreme Court in *Reynolds v. United States* (1878) and subsequent cases relied solely on a narrow interpretation of the forum's principle of consistency to uphold the restrictions of Congress.[33] The court permitted the federal government's use of force to curtail the religious rights of Mormon citizens engaged in private and voluntary behavior, but the restrictions applied equally to all citizens, regardless of denominational affiliation.

By the end of the nineteenth century, with significant immigration of non-Mormon Americans and increased military presence of the U.S. government throughout the Utah territory, the Mormons' religious liberty had been severely restricted and their polygamous family practices curtailed. With no practical alternative to withdraw once again from U.S. territory, limited accommodation to secular demands imposed by the federal government now appeared to the LDS Church as preferable to the real possibility of extermination, which would end its temporal and spiritual mission.[34] Accommodation had to be made primarily with regard to Mormon economic arrangements, such as the United Order (one type of several versions of economic communalism practiced in Utah); polygamy, despite its implementation by only approximately six percent of the male population; and political centralization under Brigham Young's theocracy.

With relative peace established between the U.S. government and the LDS Church, the Mormon leaders of the Utah territory sought statehood as a means to regain a measure of political autonomy. Among several prerequisites to statehood, the U.S. Congress insisted on changes in Mormon family practices and an end to the Mormon theocracy. In 1890, to comply with Congress's mandates, the LDS Church issued the Manifesto, which formally abolished the practice of polygamy.[35] In 1891, the Mormons' People's Party was also disbanded, with church leaders asking members to affiliate with either the Democrat or Republican parties to create a two-party system. In 1896, Congress granted statehood to Utah, and later that same year, the LDS Church issued the Political Manifesto, which required its ecclesiastical leaders to commit to separation of church and state. With its temporal property and voting rights restored, the church could now direct the preponderance of its attention toward spiritual concerns and proselytizing efforts. Even so, the LDS Church has possessed the most political influence in Utah from statehood to the present time. The pronouncements and teachings of church leaders and scriptures guide the church's activism in the Civic Public Forum.

MODERN SCRIPTURES AND SEPARATION
OF CHURCH AND STATE

Religious texts may be valued as more than a source of personal ethics; they may also serve as a font of political ideas for a particular religious culture.[36] Sacred texts play a major role in shaping that religion's cultural tradition and political outlooks.[37] As the scriptural cornerstone of the Mormon religion, the Book of Mormon appeared during some of the most socially and politically trying times for the LDS Church. The book contains numerous stories that have shaped Mormon attitudes toward politics.

One of the more popular stories in the Book of Mormon centers on the theme of defending religious freedom in the face of persecution by corrupt government authorities.[38] The protagonist in the story is Moroni, the field commander of an army protecting his country from an enemy on its borders. Word reaches him that religious dissension among the Christian population has broken out in the capital. Wishing to take advantage of the dissension to solidify their positions, evil rulers in government foment further social upheaval by promoting diversity of religious opinions and acrimonious debate, appealing to crass materialism, and persecuting true-believing Christians. Angry with the corrupt government as well as the weak-willed Christians, Moroni raises a "title of liberty," a banner inscribed with the slogan "In memory of our God, our religion, and freedom, and our peace, our wives, and our children."[39] After donning his armor, Moroni prays to God for "the blessings of liberty to rest upon his brethren, so long as there should a band of Christians remain to possess the land." He then lifts his banner and exhorts his troops to covenant with him to remain steadfast in their faith and to join him in returning to the capital to defend Christianity, their families, and liberty. Upon arrival, his army has grown and out of fear, the corrupt rulers flee the capital. Moroni has succeeded in restoring his country to the followers of Jesus Christ.

Like Joseph Smith's condemnation of religious confusion and diversity during the Second Great Awakening in the American frontier, the Book of Mormon story implicitly criticizes religious pluralism and disinterested government. While the story concludes with Christianity's political dominance restored, contemporary Mormons tend to interpret the story in terms of the millennial expectations stated in their other modern scriptures. Believing that the proselytizing efforts will grow in efficacy, Mormons have faith that "every ear shall hear it, and every knee shall bow, and every tongue shall confess" the truth of the restored gospel of Jesus Christ.[40] Thus the new scriptures contain stories that affirm the Mormons' unique calling and inspired confidence in a future free of bigotry and oppression where they will be free to preach the gospel.

Furthermore, other passages in the Book of Mormon often depict what Mormons believe to be the North American continent as a land of liberty, a promised land, which will only remain free so long as its inhabitants lead righteous lives.[41] Many prophetic references to the discovery of America, the founding of the republic, and the necessity of religious liberty as a prelude to the restoration of the gospel of Jesus Christ abound in the book. Other modern scriptures of the LDS Church and statements of its leaders have also contributed to the Mormon political outlook and its affirmation of America's Sacred Ground.

Public statements of early LDS Church leaders and revelations contained in the new scriptures also inculcate reverence for the Declaration of Independence and the U.S. Constitution as inspired documents. Claiming that he was the world's greatest advocate of the Constitution,[42] Joseph Smith asserted, "Hence we say, that the Constitution of the United States is a glorious standard; it is founded in the wisdom of God."[43] Utah Mormon leader Brigham Young often preached that "the signers of the Declaration of Independence and the framers of the Constitution were inspired from on high to that work."[44] Other nineteenth-century Mormon leaders, such as George Q. Cannon of the Quorum of the Twelve, stated that "the men who established that [U.S.] Government were inspired of God—George Washington, Thomas Jefferson, John Adams, Benjamin Franklin, and all the fathers of the Republic were inspired to do the work which they did."[45] Hence Mormons have been instilled with a strong belief and pride in the historic and universal role that the rise of America's Sacred Ground played in the restoration of the gospel.[46] Even so, Mormons do not officially claim that the framers of the Constitution were equivalent to saintly prophets of old or that the Constitution should be regarded as holy scripture. Instead, they argue that these important documents proclaim and protect the God-given gift of individual free will, particularly with regard to religious freedom of the Conscientious Public Forum, and the necessity of rule of law in the Civic Public Forum to protect the individual's right to make choices regarding religion and other personal matters.[47]

In their modern scriptures, particularly the Doctrine and Covenants, Mormons are taught to uphold the principles of the Civic Public Forum by respecting civil authority "according to the laws and constitution of the people, which I [the Lord] have suffered to be established, and should be maintained for the rights and protection of all flesh, according to just and holy principles."[48] Indeed, they are exhorted to "let no man break the laws of the land, for he that keepeth the laws of God hath no need to break the laws of the land."[49] They are urged to pray that "those principles, which were so honorably and nobly defended, namely, the Constitution of our land, by our fathers, be established forever."[50] Furthermore, they are encouraged to become active in politics and "support honest and wise men" for office.[51]

With the Mormon commitment to the U.S. Constitution as an inspired document juxtaposed with tragic encounters of religious bigotry, the LDS Church solidified its commitment to the separation of church and state. In its scriptures, the church finds the following: "We do not believe it just to mingle religious influence with civil government, whereby one religious society is fostered and another proscribed in its spiritual privileges, and the individual rights of its members, as citizens, denied."[52] Mormon scriptures assert that "rulers, states, and governments have a right, and are bound to enact laws for the protection of all citizens in the free exercise of their religious belief."[53] In one of its Sunday school manuals, the LDS Church states that civil government cannot guarantee religious freedom completely without keeping church and state separate: "If church and state are one, political influence may easily be exercised over religion and one church may be favored over others. Therefore, separation of church and state is essential for the independence of religion from both state domination and the power of the dominant church over minority groups."[54] The LDS Church is wary of any attempt by a religious denomination to use the state for its own ends.

SOCIAL ISSUES CHALLENGING THE DIVIDE BETWEEN THE CIVIC AND CONSCIENTIOUS PUBLIC FORUMS

Despite a century of having abandoned polygamy, Mormon teachings have continually emphasized the importance of the extended family. Mormon doctrine teaches that a seamless whole exists between family life in this world and the kingdom of God in the next. Indeed, this belief in the eternal nature of the family goes to the heart of Mormon moral theology and practical ethics. In developing its peculiar community of conscience in the Conscientious Public Forum, the church gears its primary teaching and conducts various programs to strengthen the home. In the Civic Public Forum, the LDS Church strenuously resists the politicization of its beliefs and practices, carefully evaluating the moral merits of social issues affecting the family before it becomes politically involved. For example, fearing too many unacceptable conditions that would undermine its teachings, the church has refused to support the faith-based initiative proposed by the administration of President George W. Bush. Gordon B. Hinckley, LDS Church president and prophet, stated, "I am in favor of complete separation of church and state, and while we appreciate the offer of federal funding, we like to do ours on our own. Once the government is involved, regulations follow."[55] Having suffered government restrictions that threatened the integrity of Mormon beliefs and practices throughout its history, the LDS Church has considerable experience in developing independent programs to meet the spiritual and temporal needs of its members.

In its community of conscience, the LDS Church teaches that an individual cannot achieve "exaltation" (the highest state of salvation) without family unity, without the husband and wife being "sealed" to each other in one of the LDS Church's holy temples. In order to be married and participate in other sacred rites in the temple, Mormons are required to profess and exhibit genuine allegiance to their faith, conduct their lives in a morally exemplary way, and pay tithes to the church on their annual income.

The church uses tithing money to enhance its proselytizing efforts; to support other religious activities, including building more temples; and to help its needy members. Members are asked to fast from food and drink one day per month and to donate to the church the equivalent of the money that would have been spent on meals. In turn, it uses these contributions as well as profits from its extensive agricultural, communications, insurance, and other business enterprises to support needy members through the Church Welfare Program. During times of economic distress, the welfare program provides Mormons with financial support, food and housing, and employment opportunities. Indeed, church members are strongly discouraged from relying on government welfare programs and instead encouraged to seek assistance first from their immediate family and then from the church.

Myriad other church programs support the ideal concept and unity of the family, including the Home Teaching Program and LDS Social Services. In the former, each family in a ward (similar to a parish) is visited on a monthly basis by designated representatives of the local ward to assist in meeting any spiritual and temporal needs. In the latter, the church provides counseling services and other assistance with regard to family problems such as drug abuse and unplanned pregnancies.

To avoid further entanglement with potential government restrictions, the LDS Church does not endorse candidates for public office, nor will it permit its buildings to be used by candidates for political purposes. For example, the church refuses to permit the Christian Coalition to distribute voter guides at Mormon chapels on the Sunday before an election. These prohibitions are an attempt to preserve the church's perception of a distinction between "moral issues" and "political issues," a distinction it perceives as necessary to preserve religious liberty while resisting secular threats to the family. According to Dallin H. Oaks, a member of the Quorum of the Twelve, as a practical matter, "our Church has to have a general characterization that rules out Church positions on most legislative issues. The moral vs. political distinction is that general characterization. What I understand it to mean is that our Church will rarely take a position on any political issue."[56]

McGraw argues, however, that in the Public Forum, moral inquiry occurs in both the Conscientious Public Forum and the Civic Public Forum. Reflection on the character of individual moral behavior necessarily includes how others as well as the community are affected, leading to the development of a social ethic. Thus, consideration of public policy issues necessarily consists of a moral dimension, inasmuch as others are affected.[57] While Mormon consideration of public policy issues recognizes that a moral aspect exists, the LDS Church generally adheres to the Lockean argument for permitting the widest personal latitude of freedom of conscience among church members with regard to politics. Given its teachings regarding the preeminence of individual free will and religious freedom, fear of being tainted by the corruption of a degraded and materialist society, and frank admission of not being an expert in all matters of temporal importance, the LDS Church resists the allure of seeking political power to change the world. According to President Hinckley, "Our strength lies in our freedom to choose."[58]

> Well, the church itself as an institution does not involve itself in politics nor does it permit the use of its buildings or facilities for political purposes. Now, we do become involved if there is a moral issue or something that comes on the legislative calendar which directly affects the church. We tell our people who are citizens of this land and other lands that they as individuals have a civic responsibility to exercise the franchise that is theirs so they become very active. But as a church, as I have said, we do not become involved in tax matters or any other kinds of legislation unless there be a moral issue which we think is of great importance or something that may be directed to the church, harmfully as we view it, and then we would become involved. We do very little politicking. We look at Washington [D.C.] and smile.[59]

By rarely taking a position on political issues, the LDS Church attempts to act consistently with its scriptural teachings that endorse separation of church and state, thus supporting the conditions necessary for all citizens to search for and come to accept voluntarily an understanding of the common good discovered in the Conscientious Public Forum. On those moral issues identified as necessary for upholding the search for and achieving the common good, the church will be active in the Civic Public Forum. Given this distinction, the LDS Church behaves in consonance with the normative imperative of America's Sacred Ground.

In the perspective of the LDS Church, the family is necessary to teach children moral values that transcend self-serving and socially destructive attitudes. In addition to teaching religious doctrines regarding personal salvation, Mormon children are taught the value of mutual assistance and loving relationships based on Christ-like service to others, both in the family and community. Furthermore, to search for and discover the common good, family members are taught how to exercise their basic civil rights of America's Sacred Ground. The family's promotion of freedom of conscience prepares children to identify and accept those values that sustain the good society. Formal church instruction and structured programs also assist family members as they meet daily challenges, from tribulations associated with personal ethics and religious conviction to clarifying their civic duties.

Upon adulthood and with a firm commitment to the faith, the LDS Church encourages individual Mormons to become active in the Conscientious Public Forum where religious doctrines, including those advocating the eternal nature of the family, may and ought to be promulgated and discussed with their fellow citizens. Inculcating a strong sense of civic virtue, the church also encourages Mormons to participate freely in public policy debates on political issues in the Civic Public Forum.

However, the Civic Public Forum also may involve debate about moral issues with policy solutions that the LDS Church holds will have a deleterious effect on the family. The LDS Church maintains that those public policies that impair the family's ability to serve as a social support structure in the search for the common good and teach values that support a sense of community violate the Civic Public Forum's principle of "no harm." For example, in the view of the LDS Church, social policies that permit elective abortion and same-sex marriage are contrary and harmful to the structure and intent of family life. In these cases, the LDS Church itself will become active in the Civic Public Forum to protect the family from harm in the church's effort to achieve the common good.

The LDS Church maintains that many policies that endorse intemperate behavior in the name of personal freedom, such as elective abortion and same-sex marriage, undermine and thus weaken the sanctity and socially crucial role of the family. Elective abortion and same-sex marriage often eschew personal responsibility toward others in favor of irreal rights of egoism that harm individual life and disrupt family harmony through confusion of gender roles. The church's own exceptions to its prohibition on abortion, including preference for the life of the mother over that of the fetus, reveal that harm to the family is of greater concern to the church than harm to the individual. Nevertheless, the church's own preference for the mother and the family does not obviate the fact that the preponderance of elective abortions fail to meet the church's standard for legitimate exceptions to its prohibition. On the contrary, they tend to reflect a devaluation of human life by placing concern for personal convenience, material objectives, or other self-centered desires over the welfare of the unborn child.

The LDS Church's position regarding same-sex marriage is generally in line with the argument that the Lockean concept of rights makes no distinction between homosexual and heterosexual individuals. That is, the usual catchphrase of "homosexual rights" unwittingly deflects attention from the ontological claim that there exist inalienable rights of the individual, regardless of sexual preference. Consequently, the individual rights of homosexuals must not be construed as a moral right of homosexuality.

With regard to public policy and legal matters, then, it is certainly the case that the equal protection of the laws, a staple of the Civic Public Forum's principle of consistency, requires that all individuals be protected equally in their civil rights. As a political matter, defining the institution of marriage as only between a man and a woman opens the institution to all individuals as a civil right. Consequently, it is not a violation of an individual's civil rights to preclude the possibility of same-sex marriage, since the legal sanctions regarding this definition apply to both homosexuals and heterosexuals; if both wish to participate in the institution, both must marry a member of the opposite sex. That some homosexuals and heterosexuals may not wish to participate in the institution likewise incurs no penalty from the state, inasmuch as participation for both is nonobligatory. Consequently, the use of the equal protection clause and the claim of a violation of civil rights in a court of law to demand that the legal definition of marriage be changed to accommodate same-sex couples is philosophically untenable, reflecting conceptual confusion over the meaning of legal categories. One political approach supported by the LDS Church to delimit the impact of erring judges who agree with such flawed arguments is to remove through state or national constitutional amendment processes the definition of marriage from their interpretive jurisdiction.

More problematic for the LDS Church, however, are the potential outcomes of political processes of the Civic Public Forum that reflect changes in the broader culture. Preaching personal moral responsibility in the Conscientious Public Forum, the church argues that sexual immorality, including homosexuality, weakens the individual's ability to lead a life of virtue and integrity. Recognizing that issues of appropriate sexual behavior are a matter of personal conscience and that homosexuals may otherwise engage in self-less activities of value to society, the social consequences of exposing children to immoral arrangements may nonetheless demand attention in the Civic Public Forum. However, as tolerance of homosexuality increases in the Conscientious Public Forum, public debate in the Civic Public Forum may be expected to revisit the legal limits of acceptable sexual practices. Under mounting pressure from a culture of immoral indulgence, according to church leaders, it is possible that the definition of marriage will be changed to include same-sex unions or other nontraditional arrangements.

Those opposed to changing the present legal definition of marriage frequently argue that the historical understanding of the concept of marriage has at its core a committed relationship between a man and a woman. However, arguments based on appeals to history are often fraught with difficulties, particularly the unwitting use of the genetic fallacy. The fallacy frequently occurs in arguments that rely solely on references to the accepted beliefs and social practices of the past as justification for their continuance in the present. Historical descriptions are insufficient premises to construct a moral syllogism wherein the conclusion must include a prescriptive or normative claim. For this reason, such arguments are neither logically nor morally defensible, regardless of historical precedent.

Cultural and legal legitimacy extended to many earlier institutions, such as slavery, have been countenanced today as morally illegitimate according to the Lockean values of America's Sacred Ground, regardless of the historical longevity of the institution. Should the trend of public debate in the Civic Public Forum lean toward political and legal recognition of same-sex marriage, the LDS Church would have to rely less on appeals to history and more on theological arguments in the form of moral exhortations, which raises questions of appropriate language and effective means of public discourse in an increasingly multicultural and religiously diverse society. For this reason, the church expends considerable resources in the Conscientious Public Forum to influence cultural norms in opposition to sexual immorality. The LDS Church anticipates that its positions on such moral issues will be understood by the public as legitimate for law and public policy because, in effect, if not explicitly, those positions serve well the principles of the Civic Public Forum.

Given the centrality of family unity in Mormon teachings, then, the LDS Church will avoid taking a principled stand on political issues, such as gun control, while weighing in on moral issues affecting the family, such as same-sex marriage and abortion. Indeed, Oaks maintains that "Latter-day Saints cannot afford to ignore a worldwide climate that threatens the family."[60] In fact, in tandem with its worldwide proselytizing efforts, the LDS Church has increased its presence in international forums regarding family matters. In 1997, the church established the World Family Policy Center (WFPC) at Brigham Young University (BYU) in Provo, Utah. It is a cooperative effort of BYU's J. Reuben Clark Law School, the David M. Kennedy Center for International Studies, and the School of Family Life. The WFPC "facilitates international policy debate by serving as an exchange point for the discussion and evaluation of emerging international legal norms and as an active participant in the examination of UN documents."[61] The WFPC represents a family perspective before the United Nations and other forums, which unfortunately "have been much more preoccupied with the individual and the individual's rights than with the basic social unit within which individuals survive and thrive."[62]

While the LDS Church wishes to protect its independence from state domination, it has been equally concerned about attempts by the national government to distance itself completely from religious influence on public policy matters as well as what appear to be attempts to ban religion from the public square. Although they support the separation of church and state, current church leaders have expressed reservations regarding the nature and height of "the wall" between the two. Oaks harbors serious questions concerning the legitimacy of the wall; in his assessment, "The modern popularity of the wall metaphor should not conceal its inappropriateness as an expression of current church-state relationships."[63] In other words, there is and ought to be a constructive role for the church to play regarding moral issues in the two-tiered Public Forum. The state should encourage contributions from all sectors of society, including from the religious communities of conscience.

Venturing into the Civic Public Forum, the LDS Church emphasizes the importance of understanding the nature of the family and defending the family's role "as the fundamental unit of society."[64] To this end, the LDS Church teaches that it is the purpose of the family to teach children proper values necessary for the family unit to survive temporally and remain intact eternally. The church believes that threats to the contemporary family originate primarily with the promotion of ethical relativism as a result of radical individualism of secular society in the Conscientious Public Forum. Given the political pressure of radical individualism, the church perceives various legislative initiatives and other public policies in the Civic Public Forum as endangering the family. The church concludes that it must be actively involved in politics to counter this trend.

To defend their faith, the LDS Church and individual Mormons have been politically active in resisting perceived threats to religion and family unity, by participating in electoral politics, legislative lobbying, and judicial challenges of the Civic Public Forum. For example, in the late 1970s, the church provided financial aid and mobilized local members in certain states to oppose ratification of the proposed Equal Rights Amendment to the U.S. Constitution.[65] The church perceived the amendment as a threat to its religious liberty, particularly with regard to its patriarchal organizational structure and fundamental teachings and beliefs about the distinct and divine nature of gender roles.[66] Particularly with regard to gender roles, the danger posed by the amendment for Mormons developed into a moral issue, unlike women's suffrage a century earlier, which was deemed a political issue of equality and no threat to moral values. Similarly, in 1996, the LDS Church joined with the Catholic Church in Hawaii to form the political organization "Hawaii's Future Today" in successfully opposing legislation recognizing same-sex marriages.[67] The LDS Church also filed an *amicus curiae* brief in the case of *Baehr v. Miike* (1999), in which the Hawaii Supreme Court ultimately found that Hawaiian law did not discriminate by defining marriage as only between a man and a woman.[68]

According to Oaks, proponents of homosexuality threaten the divine nature of the family in their attempt "to undermine the principle of individual accountability, to persuade us to misuse our sacred powers of procreation, to discourage marriage and childbearing by worthy men and women, and to confuse what it means to be male or female."[69] In the case of *Boy Scouts of America v. Dale* (2000), the LDS Church entered the federal courts of the Civic Public Forum to file an *amicus curiae* brief in support of the scouting organization's rule that prohibits homosexuals from serving in leadership positions, which was upheld by the Supreme Court.[70]

In 2003, the issue of same-sex marriage came to the fore in presidential and local politics when certain state court decisions affirmed a civil right of homosexual couples to marry. Perhaps the opinion that precipitated the latest conflict in the culture war was that of the Supreme Juridical Court of Massachusetts of November 2003. Later on February 4, 2004, the court stated that when "barred access to the protections, benefits and obligations of civil marriage, a person who enters into an intimate, exclusive union with another of the same sex is arbitrarily deprived of membership in one of our community's most rewarding and cherished institutions."[71] Massachusetts Governor Mitt Romney, the son of the late George Romney (four-term governor of Michigan and 1968 candidate for the Republican presidential nomination and active member of the LDS Church), responded with an argument that contains the standard Mormon position of defending the traditional understanding of the family, while also defending the right of the individual to choose alternative lifestyles. With regard to defense of the family, Romney stated the following:

> Marriage is a fundamental and universal social institution. It encompasses many obligations and benefits affecting husband and wife, father and mother, son and daughter. It is the foundation of a harmonious family life. It is the basic building block of society: the development, productivity and happiness of new generations are bound inextricably to the family unit. As a result, marriage bears a real relation to the well-being, health and enduring strength of society.[72]

While he believes that government has a role to play through legislation and constitutional amendments of the Civic Public Forum in defending this concept of the family, Romney also argued that government should not be used to restrict individual choices regarding lifestyle in the Conscientious Public Forum:

> It is important that the defense of marriage not become an attack on gays, on singles or on nontraditional couples. We must recognize the right of every citizen to live in the manner of his or her own choosing. In fact, it makes sense to ensure that essential civil rights, protection from violence and appropriate societal benefits are afforded to all citizens, be they single or combined in nontraditional relationships.[73]

In addition, throughout 2004 local magistrates in other states had begun to issue licenses for same-sex marriages. Political pressure mounted on the national and state governments to enact laws and constitutional amendments to permit states the right of refusal in permitting and recognizing same-sex marriages. In Utah, the editorial board of the *Deseret Morning News*, an LDS Church–owned newspaper, endorsed President Bush's call for an amendment to the U.S. Constitution to protect traditional marriage.[74] The LDS Church itself publicly released on July 7, 2004, the following official statement: "The

Church of Jesus Christ of Latter-day Saints favors a constitutional amendment preserving marriage as the lawful union of a man and a woman."[75]
However, the church did not endorse any specific amendment under consideration.

Another crucial aspect of the extended family has to do with procreation.
One threat to the sanctity of procreation troubling to Mormons is that of elective abortion. According to the LDS Church, the possible exceptions for
abortion "are when the pregnancy resulted from rape or incest, or a competent physician has determined that the life or health of the mother is in serious jeopardy, or the fetus has severe defects that will not allow the baby to
survive beyond birth."[76] Given the LDS Church's opposition to elective abortion but with its recognition of morally legitimate exceptions, particularly
with regard to rape or incest, the consistency of its position can only be
defended by accepting the proposition that the life of the fetus is less important than the continuation of a particular view of family unity. Similar in
argument, the positions of many Mormon members of the U.S. Congress can
also be understood in terms of the LDS Church's position in support of individual free will, wary of government control, and defending an ideal concept
of the family.[77]

With regard to abortion, Sen. Orrin G. Hatch (R-Utah) maintains that "the
real issue, however, is not whether we have the freedom to choose but what
we choose with that freedom. To me, the question is not whether we are free
to terminate a life for our personal convenience but what moral consequences the choice will have for us, our families, including the unborn child,
and society as a whole."[78] Typically, Mormons are taught that free will, which
is a gift from God, is necessary for the individual to exercise moral autonomy
and responsibility. While individuals are free to make immoral choices, the
desire is that they will choose to act morally. In terms of personal salvation,
the exercise of free will has eternal consequences, for which the individual is
morally responsible. In addition, the social impact of particular choices is the
moral responsibility of the individual, for which he or she will also be held
eternally responsible. With this focus on the end to be served and not just
the means to the end, Hatch is then able to support federal funding in the
Civic Public Forum to explore the promise of certain techniques of regener-
ative medicine, such as stem-cell research.

Hatch's position on the issue of federal funding of stem-cell research is in
opposition to that of many pro-life advocates of the religious right. Pro-life
advocates claim that research using stem cells destroys potentially viable
human embryos in the process; in their judgment, the destruction of the
embryos amounts to abortion and hence is morally unacceptable. However,
Hatch argues that the same moral obligation that exists to defend pre-natal
life also exists to defend life "outside the womb." That is, "an advocate for life
has to consider not only our obligations to a group of cells with the potential for life but also our obligation to our fellow citizens—men, women, and

children—who will face untold suffering and lose many years of life unless there is a medical breakthrough."[79] Hatch draws a distinction between the origins of the researcher's destroyed or unused embryos and those produced through natural procreative processes. For example, he finds human cloning of babies as morally repugnant and as "a completely unjustified intrusion into the creation of life that should be the sacred responsibility of a husband and wife."[80]

Key to Hatch's defense of using stem cells for scientific research is the role of the mother's womb: "For me, human life begins in a mother's nurturing womb and is impossible without it. The blastocysts used for stem cell research are not conceived in the traditional sense of a sperm and an egg uniting, nor are they transplanted into a mother's womb. Consequently, they are not really the same as either a person or a fetus."[81] Hatch supports federal funding of research in this area as both "pro-life and pro-family." Similarly, on June 10, 2004, the *Deseret Morning News* published an editorial in support of lifting President Bush's executive order restricting stem-cell research: "[I]t is significant to note that some members of Congress who are staunch opponents of legal abortion-on-demand have concluded they are not compromising their beliefs by supporting this. Generally this comes after the realization that the embryos used for this research would otherwise be destroyed. . . . The president ought to revise the rules."[82]

The LDS Church and Senator Hatch oppose elective abortion as a threat to the essence of the family and support stem-cell research as a means to improve the health of the family.[83] Their positions coincide with that of John A. Widtsoe, an early-twentieth-century member of the Quorum of Twelve, who concisely stated the LDS Church's attitude regarding the extended family: "The conception of an actual relationship among all humanity places upon every human being a family responsibility."[84]

WEATHERING THE STORM

In contrast with the liberal state that focuses on the preeminence of the individual, the tendency of religion, including the Mormon religion, is to focus on the preeminence of the moral community as a prerequisite for the good society. To this end, along with the long-standing defense of its religious beliefs and practices, Mormonism emphasizes the need for the maintenance of moral behavior throughout civil society, particularly in defense of the family, in the face of cultural challenges to the contrary.

The LDS Church has accumulated considerable resources to proselytize and exercise significant political influence in the two-tiered Public Forum of America's Sacred Ground.[85] For example, in the Conscientious Public Forum, recent conflicts with evangelical Christians have already led to a rapprochement between responsible parties on both sides. Two organizations, the Standing Together Ministries, an evangelical ministry in Salt Lake City, and the BYU Richard L. Evans Chair for Religious Understanding, recently arranged for an internationally renowned evangelical Christian preacher to speak at the LDS Church's famed Tabernacle in November 2004.[86] Ravi Zacharias, known for editing an authoritative guide to religious cults, which includes Mormonism, spoke on the divinity of Christ before a Mormon audience in the Tabernacle. Not since 1871, when Brigham Young invited Dwight L. Moody, founder of the Moody Bible Institute in Chicago, has an evangelical Christian spoken in the Tabernacle.

Nevertheless, while it occupies a place in civil society's religious pluralism, Mormonism's unique history and unusual theology have prevented it from forming deep alliances with either the religious right or the secular left. The LDS Church and individual Mormons frequently find themselves joining forces with those on the religious right on certain social, moral, and political issues and distancing themselves on others. For example, the LDS Church has been influential in public policy debates on abortion in the Utah state legislature, often with the support of pro-life Christians. However, various pro-life movements, such as the Center for Reclaiming America, a political advocacy organization of the Coral Ridge Ministries, have been attempting to block changes in legislation regulating abortion procedures for Utah state hospitals receiving federal funding.[87] The changes, which would more closely reflect the position on abortion preferred by the LDS Church, are seen as too liberal by the pro-life advocates.

Mormonism's theological embrace of the U.S. Constitution, particularly as it advocates defense of religious liberty in the public square and its promulgation of patriotism and loyalty to the federal government, has also made the LDS Church suspect in the eyes of the secular left. Conservative Mormons in politics and business, such as Ezra Taft Benson (U.S. secretary of agriculture in the Eisenhower administration and later president of the LDS Church), Brent Scowcroft (national security advisor in the Ford and G. H. W. Bush administrations), Terrel H. Bell (U.S. secretary of education in the Reagan administration), Rex E. Lee (solicitor general in the Reagan administration), and J. Willard Marriott (Marriott Hotel chain), have generally contributed to the image of the LDS Church as a member of the religious right. Yet liberal Mormons have also been prominent in the public square, such as Marriner Eccles (chairman of the Federal Reserve Board during the F. D. Roosevelt administration), Sterling M. McMurrin (U.S. commissioner of education in the Kennedy administration), Esther Peterson (U.S. assistant secretary of labor in the Kennedy administration), David M. Kennedy (U.S. secretary of the treasury in the Johnson administration), and Stewart Udall (U.S. secretary of the interior in the Kennedy administration).

According to some observers, the continued suspicion of secular government policies and programs encourages individual Mormons to be active in politics, while at the same time the LDS Church refuses formally to align itself with a particular administration by refusing to endorse political parties and candidates for office.[88] The church participates in the Civic Public Forum by encouraging debate on the moral aspects of select public policy issues, while it continues to be wary of government intrusion into religious life in the Conscientious Public Forum.

Curiously, this distinction between moral issues and political issues serves as a restriction on the LDS Church with regard to its participation in the Civic Public Forum. Many other denominations attempt to use the political machinery of this forum as a means to influence public policy with regard to diverse issues, from controlling local school boards to insert religious teachings in the curricula to encouraging members of the U.S. Congress to adopt a pro-Christian foreign policy. The LDS Church, however, limits its participation primarily to issues directly affecting familial matters. In this way, the church's activities appear to accord more closely with the intent of America's Sacred Ground. The church avoids many of the temptations to violate the principles of no harm and consistency of the Civic Public Forum and participates more actively in the Conscientious Public Forum to build its community of conscience, while engaging in public debate regarding the nature of the public good.

Despite theological and organizational limits on their ability to form and join political coalitions, Mormons will weather the storm as they defend select social institutions that they believe are under assault from diverse cultural challenges.

Chapter 7

American Muslims and the Rediscovery of America's Sacred Ground

M. A. Muqtedar Khan

INTRODUCTION

The American Muslim community is at a crucial crossroads. It is experiencing an existential crisis. Students of Islam in the West are beginning to ask questions about the future of Islam, and Muslims in an increasingly Islamophobic West are growing wary of the unrest and growing tide of extremism in the Muslim world.[1] At the same time, American Muslims have reached a critical mass. This gives them a presence that promises influence in the mainstream society, and a visibility that also attracts a backlash, as people fear its growth and influence. Some scholars, such as Fawaz Gerges, maintain that the contemporary Arab and Muslim experience is similar to that of communities such as American Jews and Irish Americans, who too were assimilated only after being discriminated against, marginalized, and oppressed.[2] The difference is that the catastrophic events of September 11, 2001, and the open-ended "war on terror" has exaggerated and traumatized further the potential for Muslims to become fully participating members in the greater American society.

The determination of the American Muslim community to make an impact on the political, theological, and cultural scene on North America, and the growing fear and prejudice against Islam and Muslims in the United States, has created a unique situation for Muslims. Unlike Protestants, Catholics, Jews, Mormons, and others, American Muslims do not yet have a place in American society.

To understand the relative standing of various religious communities in the United States, consider this: since 2004, the State Department has been mandated by Congress to produce an annual report on global anti-Semitism. The purpose is to protect Jews worldwide from prejudice, hatred, and violence.[3] The United States now also funds many Christian projects through its faith-based-initiative programs.[4] But the same government also supports the PATRIOT Act and other initiatives that systematically target Muslims and violate their civil rights on the basis of their religion. This less-than-equal status of the American Muslim community has resulted in American Muslims being the victims of illegitimate laws passed in the Civic Public Forum.[5]

One only has to visit the Web sites of several evangelical Christian churches and communities to witness the horrific levels of Islamophobia that exist today. The case of General Boykin, while in charge of intelligence at the Department of Defense, is such an example. He visited Churches and indulged in anti-Islam and anti-Muslim rhetoric. Numerous Islamophobic comments made by prominent Christian leaders such as Rev. Franklin Graham, Rev. Jerry Falwell, Rev. Jerry Vine, and Rev. Pat Robertson also clearly suggest that there is an atmosphere in the United States that encourages anti-Muslim prejudice to thrive in the Conscientious Public Forum.[6] Having said that, it is also important to recognize that many Christian groups have come forward in solidarity with Muslims to protect their civil rights, that gradually an interfaith space has emerged sympathetic to Muslim conditions, and that many are working together to redress the situation.

American Muslim's internal struggles and outreach have generated a moral dialogue in the Conscientious Public Forum, which is developing a strong civil society movement to raise public awareness to impact the Civic Public Forum institutions that victimize Muslims. Because of these developments, American Muslims are uniquely poised to help all Americans rediscover America's Sacred Ground.

ASPIRATIONS OF THE AMERICAN MUSLIM COMMUNITY

Muslim immigrants who started coming to the United States in the early 1960s had already tasted the elixir of Islamic revivalist fervor and experienced the brutality and autocracy of their governments of origin, which were interested in either crushing or co-opting emerging Islamic movements. Several members of the various Islamic movements such as the Muslim brother-

hood and the Jamaat-e-Islami came to America, and many of them soon discovered the epochal opportunity that America provided.

In a society where there is political and religious freedom, Muslims could
quickly organize and freely establish Islamic movements that were constantly
repressed in the heartlands of the Muslim world. While there was deep hostility and prejudice towards Islam and Muslims, it was nothing compared to
the stifling character of despotic regimes in Egypt, Iraq, Iran, Saudi Arabia,
Libya, Sudan, and Palestine (under Israeli colonialism).

The easiest and often the only way for these Muslims to come to America
was through the route of higher education. They came; they earned their
Ph.D.s in natural and social sciences, and they stayed to create a crucial mass
of intellectual Muslim elite in the United States. The nature of this immigration became a filtering process, allowing only better-educated and intellectually sophisticated individuals to enter from the Arab world. Add to this the
flow of Muslim professionals and scholars escaping poverty and poor
economies from India, Pakistan, and Bangladesh, and the result was a Muslim leadership capable of articulating enlightened self-interest and formulating a far-reaching vision for the revival of Islam and Islamic values.[7]

Whereas the freedom to rethink the Islamic civilization project and to
indulge in serious rejuvenation of the stagnant Islamic sciences was not available in the Muslim world, American Muslims found that their new home in
the United States opened new possibilities. Islamists who found themselves
in leadership positions in the emerging American Muslim community essentially had one overriding goal: to revive Islamic civilization throughout the
world, including in the United States.[8] They strongly believed that the key to
reviving Islamic civilization was the intellectual revival of the Ummah
(Islamic community or nation), which is in effect a top-down, overarching
worldview approach to government. Intellectuals such as Ismail Farooqi and
his Islamization of Knowledge Project, and Seyyed Hossein Nasr and his
Islamic Philosophy and Islamic Sciences Project are indicative of this thinking. The founding of the Association of Muslim Social Scientists[9] was the first
step towards establishing this revivalist thinking within some kind of institutional setting.

The freedom available in the West led to further institutional development
of this revivalist agenda and led to the establishment of the International
Institute of Islamic Thought (IIIT) in Virginia and the Islamic Foundation in
Leicester, United Kingdom. These are think tanks dedicated to the intellectual revival of Muslims. The idea was simple. Freedom of religion and
thought in the West, and in America in particular, would produce Islamic
ideas and ideology and then be exported back to the Muslim world where
they would be introduced and tested in the hope that they would stimulate
and galvanize social and religious reform. Both centers have produced pro-
lific literature in the forms of books and journals on various aspects of

Islamic sciences and social sciences. The most spectacular of such endeavors was the establishment of the International Islamic University of Malaysia.

IIU Malaysia is a product of American Muslim expertise and Malaysian resources. The president of IIIT, Abdul Hameed Abu Sulayman, who was also a founding member and president of the Association of Muslim Social Scientists (AMSS), left the United States to take over as the rector of IIU Malaysia. He took with him not only the ideas of *Ismail al-Faruqi*, the Islamization project, but also many Muslim social scientists and intellectuals who had emerged in the free and challenging environment of American academia. There he sought to unite the so-called secular and sacred sciences in an attempt to create a generation of Muslim students well versed in modern as well as traditional studies, the essential ingredients for the reconstruction of a thriving Islamic civilization.[10]

Muslim leaders of this generation also created Islamic political organizations that are trying to increase their political and economic influence in the United States in the hope that it can be leveraged to improve the condition of the Muslim world. Such organizations include the Council on American Islamic Relations (CAIR), American Muslim Council (AMC), Muslim Political Action Committee (MPAC), Kashmiri American Council (KAC), American Muslim Alliance (AMA), and American Muslims for Jerusalem (AMJ).[11] They use the resources of the American Muslim community to fight for freedom, democracy, and self-determination in the Muslim world.[12]

In the United States, the emerging leadership realized that the single most important goal was not to assimilate and disappear into the great melting pot, like many who had come before them. The need to defend and consolidate Islamic identity became the primary goal in the United States. Muslims were not in the United States to assimilate. They were in the United States to take their place in American society and be accepted. Thus, the development of the American Muslim community in the last three decades, at least among the immigrants, can be divided into two phases. The first phase entailed consolidation of the Islamic identity and the second phase entailed making an impact on the American society.

To realize these goals, nearly two thousand Islamic centers and over twelve hundred Islamic schools have mushroomed within the last three decades. Several Islamic movements, such as the Islamic Society of North America (ISNA), Islamic Circle of North America (ICNA), and the Islamic Assembly of North America (IANA), emerged to galvanize momentum and fervor in adherence of Islamic practices so that the Islamic identity of the immigrant community did not dissipate. Traditionalist movements like the *Tablighi Jamaat*, a movement that focuses on ritual purity and revival, have taken root along with the *Naqshbandi Sufi* movement.[13] Further, the Islamic community has enjoyed the great advantage that comes from conversions. Even as assimilation took away many, reversion and conversion to Islam brought many new believers within the fold and kept the critical mass of the community sufficiently large to preclude complete assimilation.[14]

The leadership of the intellectual elite, the resonant echo of the Islamic revivalist fervor of the Muslim world, the gradual transformation of America from melting pot to a multicultural society, and the rapid rate of conversion of Americans, both white and black, to Islam all provided energy and momentum for the sustenance of Islamic practices in America. Thus, the aspirations of American Muslim leadership became as follows:

1. Defending the Islamic identity of Muslims in America against assimilation.
2. Developing intellectual and political resources capable of making significant social and political changes in the Muslim World.
3. Making an impact on American society.

In the pursuit of these goals, the American Muslim identity gradually emerged as its community coped and adjusted to challenges within and without the community.[15]

INTERNAL AND EXTERNAL CHALLENGES

Yet the American Muslim leadership realized that the challenges to becoming fully accepted and respected participants in American democracy were two-dimensional. First, there were *barriers to acceptance* posed by ignorance of Islam and prejudice toward Arabs and Muslims, which was widespread in American society and fostered meticulously by America's political leadership and media.[16] Second, Muslims realized that there was *resistance to adjustment* within their community itself that would pose a major barrier to engagement with the American mainstream. Both of the challenges, internal and external, had an equal impact on the aspirations that the American Muslim community had set for itself.

Prejudice, Resistance, and the Progression of Islam in America

Prejudice against Islam in the American mainstream presented several barriers to the practice of Islam. Every time there was a major political development in the Middle East, the American media would unleash attacks on Islam and its values. Islam was and is still presented as an irrational, undemocratic faith that is opposed to equality, freedom, and peace. The Western imagery of Islam as antithetical to Western values made it extremely difficult in the past for Muslims to publicly declare their commitment to Islam. The demonization of Islam in the media, and the prejudice, hatred, and intolerance it bred, made practicing Islam in the public arena a dangerous prospect.[17]

Muslim women could not wear the headscarf in schools, at shopping malls, or in workplaces. For example, Muslim women wearing headscarves were usually screened out at the interview stage of applying for a job. If they started wearing scarves after they obtained a position, they were often terminated without cause. Teachers would object and send Muslim girls home for wearing the headscarf. Girls were punished when they refused to wear revealing clothes in gym classes or swimming pools. Social interactions in the workplace, which often take familiarity between people of different genders as given, were alien to many Muslim women.

Men faced discrimination for wearing beards or caps, and for wanting a longer break on Fridays to offer the congregational Friday prayers. Both men and women faced resistance to their requests for time off for Islamic festivals. Many Muslim scholars and intellectuals faced discrimination when seeking jobs in higher education and when writing on politics, particularly on Middle Eastern issues, from an Islamic perspective. The pressure to consume alcohol at parties, to eat non-*halal* food, and to participate freely in mixed environments remains very high. Moreover, Muslim men in high level managerial positions found that their careers could be jeopardized because Islamic etiquette and dietary laws socially marginalized them. Such ignorance of Islamic gender practices led to deliberate or unintended discrimination of Muslims. Work and school environments that lacked sensitivity to Muslim needs tended to become hostile.[18]

Ignorance about Islam and hostility toward it presented several challenges. The pressure to assimilate, to "normalize," was very high. As a result, many Muslims began to use Americanized versions of their names to hide their Islamic identity and even their foreignness. Muhammad became Mo, Jeffery became Jeff, Ali became Al. Others resisted and sometimes made a breakthrough and at other times paid the price.

Muslim families found that American public schools offered reasonable education for their children at no cost, but the public schools did not inculcate values consistent with the values of Islam. The food was not *halal*, the stories and the lessons were either based on Christian folklore or secular ethos. Muslim children found it difficult to resist the desire to be like their non-Muslim peers. Most parents struggled to establish themselves in their careers and found that they had little time to provide their children with the religious and cultural education that they needed.

Many Muslims, though, were neither disturbed nor concerned. They were pleased with their material success and tried to gain acceptance in the mainstream culture by distancing themselves from Islam and Islamic practices. For those who were not keen on defending their Islamic identity, life in America was full of promise. Many realized the American dream, and enjoyed the prosperity and freedom available in America. A large segment of this group returned to Islam in significant ways once their children grew up and began to manifest some of the social ills of American society, such as sexual promiscuity, drugs, moral indifference, and other negative behaviors. Some still remain assimilated, finding themselves on the fringe of both the Islamic society in America and the general American society.

But many Muslims who came to America for political and economic reasons were determined to resist assimilation. They answered the call from the Islamists and Muslim intellectuals and *Dawah* (invitation to Islam) workers to join the various Islamic movements that mushroomed in the 1970s and 1980s. The first thing that Islamists did was to take over the National Arab Students Association, a secular ethnocentric organization, and dissolved it. They replaced it with the Muslim Students Association National. The national MSA and its branches at various campuses started working with local communities to establish small Islamic *Halaqas* (study circles) and *Musallahs* (prayer centers) in classrooms or rented apartments.

After graduation, with the help of the Muslim leadership that came out of the MSAs around the country, these small communities started establishing Islamic centers. In the late 1970s, the Gulf States had become cash rich with the rise in oil prices. Many of them gave generously to Muslim communities all over the world, seeking to establish mosques and Islamic schools. Some of the most important Islamic centers, like the Islamic Centers in Washington, D.C. and New York, were built with generous donations from them.[19]

With some foothold in communities and universities, Islamic movements began to fight against the pressure to assimilate. In the 1970s and 1980s, the response was purely defensive as the primary focus was to build large numbers of Islamic centers and Islamic schools. Islamic centers and their activities kept adults in touch with their beliefs and their heritage, and Islamic schools taught Islamic values and inculcated Islamic practices among the young. As mentioned previously, there are at the moment over two thousand Islamic centers and over twelve hundred Islamic schools in North America.[20]

These centers also became the hubs for activities by Muslims who in their countries of origin belonged to various Islamic movements. For example, the *Tablighi Jamaat*, an Islamic movement that is a loose network of activists who focus on Islamic rituals and encourage each other to pray regularly, quickly took root in many mosques, especially in Florida, Chicago, Upstate New York, and New York City. This apolitical and mildly spiritual movement is one of the largest Islamic movements in North America, with over one hundred thousand participants.

Similarly, ISNA and then ICNA expanded, focusing their activities on Islamic centers. Gradually all of the Islamic movements began holding annual national and regional conventions, which bring scholars from North America and the Muslim world to large convention centers. There, thousands of Muslims converge every year to listen to lectures on Islam and participate in various community and faith-related workshops. Currently, the annual convention of ISNA attracts over thirty-five thousand participants and over one thousand scholars. The regional *Tablighi Ijtimas* (gatherings) attract anywhere between ten thousand and fifteen thousand attendees. ICNA averages between ten thousand and twelve thousand participants at its annual conventions.[21] At all these conventions, Muslim scholars and intellectuals from North America and the rest of the Muslim World interact with American Muslims and each other, providing a preview of the Islamic civilization that Muslims dream about.

A New Generation: Working in the Civic and Conscientious Public Forums for Civil Rights and Acceptance of Muslims

By the beginning of the 1990s, the community as well as the leadership became more confident.[22] A new generation of American Muslims had grown up and emerged. Some were lost, but many of the young American Muslims made their senior generation proud. They were confident, successful, and deeply committed to Islam and the well-being of the Muslim *Ummah*. By then, the American landscape was dotted with Islamic landmarks. It was thought that it was time to have the same impact on American culture.[23]

While members of the senior generation were content to defend, the new generation was eager to be more proactive. They were not satisfied with the mere preservation of Islamic identity. They wanted Islam to be accepted and recognized as a constituent element of America itself.

This increase in confidence resulted in three major changes. The first was the emergence of the Council for American and Islamic Relations (CAIR) and its culture of "action alert activism." CAIR is a watchdog organization seeking to battle prejudice against Islam in both the Civic Public Forum and the Conscientious Public Forum. CAIR has a very large electronic mailing list, with over five hundred thousand names, according to Ibrahim Hooper, its communications director. Whenever an incident of Islamophobia is reported, CAIR sends an email to its members asking them to call, email, or write letters to the offending party.

In the Conscientious Public Forum, CAIR specializes in fighting negative stereotypes of Muslims and the demonization of Islam in the media, although it has not been as successful in this arena as it has been in the Civic Public Forum. There, among other things, CAIR fights discrimination in the workplace. Now, when employers fire Muslim women for wearing headscarves, they are likely to face the ire of CAIR. In addition, in the Civic Public Forum, CAIR is ready to take every available legal action to fight discrimination— from public exposure of discrimination to lawsuits. It also helps organizations by providing sensitivity training.

CAIR's biggest contribution, however, is the education it provides to the community about how to fight discrimination and prejudice. In the last few years, CAIR has enjoyed considerable success in restoring jobs and obtaining compensation for Muslims suffering from discrimination. Following CAIR's success, several other organizations now also use the action alert activism made popular by CAIR to mobilize the community whenever and wherever prejudice and discrimination surfaces.

The second significant change has been the operating style of the college and university Muslim Students Associations, which have had a major impact in the Conscientious Public Forum. When the senior generation was in charge, the MSAs were focused on Muslims and sustaining their faith and Islamic practices. But with the MSAs' new generation at the helm, many more Muslims are outwardly focused. They are at ease with their Muslim identity and more interested in presenting a positive image of Islam.

Unlike the *halaqas* of the past, the biggest activity of the MSAs is the Islam Awareness week they organize, usually in October–November each year on hundreds of campuses in North America. Lectures on Islam, art exhibitions, and cultural events are organized to introduce America to the true dimensions of Islam. This is the new form of *Dawah* (invitation to Islam) developed by the new generation of American Muslims. The Islam Awareness weeks are so well-established that they have become nearly as ubiquitous on American campuses as hamburgers and Coca-Cola.

The third major development in the Conscientious Public Forum in the 1990s was the explosion of Islamic media on the Internet. The Internet provided American Muslims with an excellent opportunity to share information with other Muslims and to provide news and opinions from Muslims' perspectives on various topics. For decades, Muslims complained about bias in Western media. Now at least the Internet allows Muslims to disseminate the news that concerns them and to advance opinions and views on current events from an Islamic perspective. Websites like Iviews.com compete with CNN and other major global news providers for Muslim viewers and readers. The Internet has also facilitated fundraising, networking, and discussions and dialogue among Muslims from various perspectives, and has helped build consensus among Muslim activists in the United States.[24]

This newfound confidence resulted in the trend in the institutional development of the Muslim community of America to increase exponentially. Muslims have stopped spending all their resources, human and material, on institutions for identity preservation in mosques and schools and have begun to turn those resources to the Civic and Conscientious Public Forums. The 1990s experienced the emergence of organizations like the American Muslim Council (AMC), Muslim Political Action Committee (MPAC), American Muslim Alliance (AMA), American Muslims for Jerusalem (AMJ), and Center for the Study of Islam and Democracy (CSID). The explicit purpose of these organizations is the political mobilization of American Muslims to accumulate power that can be used to effect change in the Muslim world.

These organizations educate American Muslims in the nuances of democracy, pluralism, and interest-group politics. They mobilize Muslims to participate in American politics at every level, from voting in elections to running for office. They actively lobby Congress and the executive branch to change American foreign policy toward Palestine, Iraq, Pakistan, and Kashmir in particular and the rest of the Muslim world in general. Hundreds of seminars and workshops have been conducted in Islamic centers all over the country and at regional and annual conventions of Islamic movements like ISNA and ICNA to encourage Muslims to participate in the American political process.[25]

By the end of the 1990s, all of the major developments discussed here indicated that American Muslims had begun to influence American politics and culture in the Civic Public Forum and the Conscientious Public Forum. Muslims have never lacked in commitment or zeal. Now they not only had gained a base to work from but also had developed the know-how to resist assimilation effectively and defend their identity from the social pressure to conform.

By the turn of the century, there was an upbeat mood in the community as it began to flex its political muscle. In reality, however, it was still in the infancy stage and needed considerable resources before Muslims would be able to match the powerful lobbies of such groups as Jewish and Cuban Americans. Small successes, such as the appointment of the first Muslim as a U.S. ambassador (to Fiji), the first Muslim federal judge, the first Muslim activist to the Congressional Commission on International Religious Freedom, and the first Muslim as deputy secretary of agriculture, all helped to fuel Muslim enthusiasm. These successes also gave credence to the claims of Muslim leaders that participation would bear fruit. In the presidential election of 2000, Muslims endorsed and voted as a bloc for the eventual winner, George W. Bush. For the first time, Muslims gained recognition as a political force of consequence.[26]

The Impact of the Tragedy of September 11, 2001

It is difficult to articulate fully the impact of the attacks of September 11, 2001, on the American Muslim community. Suffice it to say that American Muslims were devastated. In fact, American Muslims were double victims of these attacks. On the one hand, hundreds of American Muslims died in the attack itself and during the rescue operation. On the other hand, American Muslims had to face drastic consequences as a result of America's response—the "war on terror."

Before September 11, American Islam was on the rise. The charisma of Islam was alluring to many. Islam was winning converts from all groups—whites, blacks, Hispanics, Jews, Hindus, Catholics—among both men and women who were drawn to Islam. Mosques were on the rise in every major city in North America, as well as Islamic schools and Islamic political action committees. American Muslim leaders, who had for a long time been a frustrated and marginal group, suddenly found themselves in the company of presidents. Islam was the fastest-growing religion in America, in Europe, and in Australia, with 1.4 billion adherents worldwide, 6 million in the United States alone.

In the minds of American Muslims, their votes had made the difference in Florida, and Muslims were primarily responsible for placing George W. Bush, their choice, in the White House. Many American Muslims believed it was just a matter of time before the American Muslim population would outpace other groups in American society. Thus, they believed they would soon become a very powerful political force, enabling Islam to manifest itself in its truest form in America, and further empower America to become a great society. In November 2000, after the arrival of American Muslims as a political force, it was difficult to separate reality from fantasy.

However, September 11 abruptly changed all of this. Now, defending and preserving the existing achievements and assets, such as the nearly two thousand mosques, the various Islamic schools, charities, and access to media and government itself, became uphill battles. The two sources of Islam's growth, immigration and conversion, were now both arrested. Former Attorney General John Ashcroft's crusade, the domestic dimension of the "war on terror," targeted American Muslims and their institutions, and therefore put an effective stop to the flow of Muslims into the United States. Furthermore, the negative publicity regarding Muslims and Islam fomented very high levels of Islamophobia.

The media's strong association of Islam with extremist political violence sustained by Al Qaeda and the insurgency in Iraq did unimaginable harm to Islam's image in America. Not only has the community lost developmental momentum, but also most of its hard-earned goodwill has dissipated. Now Islam and America Muslims face hostility and prejudice as never before.

The most important aspect of the institutional development of American Muslims in the past thirty years was an implicit faith in American freedoms. Muslims never worried about their civil rights in America. So they invested in institutions that would either preserve the Islamic identity of the next generation such as mosques and Islamic schools, or advance the interests of Muslims overseas through the various charities and organizations dedicated to the Palestinian, Pakistani, Kashmiri, and other "back home" causes.

The attack on civil rights that has come in the form of various programs and legislation has caught the community off guard. The PATRIOT Act is a prime example. It has effectively nullified the Fourth, Fifth, Sixth, and Eighth Amendments to the U.S. Constitution directly, and the First and Ninth Amendments indirectly. American Muslims never expected, and were not prepared, to fight a major civil rights battle, and they have not yet begun to respond in earnest.

This shattering of the American Muslim dream and the crisis of civil rights has the community in total disarray. It is afraid, confused, and extremely insecure about its future. Most American Muslims have very little use for the radicalism of militants that belong to Al Qaeda or the Taliban, which is primarily why they are in the United States and not in their countries of origin. They do not support terrorism or the extremism that is now threatening America. But they also cannot support the assault on their civil rights launched by the administration that they helped put into power. Increasingly, they are wary of the anti-Islam rhetoric coming from the Christian Right and its growing influence on the White House.

In a sense, American Muslims are caught between the war on terror and what they see as a war on Islam. They are not with bin Laden; they were never with him, but they are finding it increasingly hard to be with President Bush and his campaigns at home and abroad. Intuitively, American Muslims are seeking a third way, one that will save Islam from extremism and America from the decline in its civil rights standards. Unfortunately, however, American Muslim leaders are not yet able to articulate the third way.

THE STRUGGLE WITHIN AMERICAN ISLAM
AND REDISCOVERING AMERICA'S SACRED GROUND

As this chapter has shown, the transition of American Muslims from a fragile group focused on defending Muslim identity to an intrepid community determined to make an impact has been difficult. To understand the political dynamics and the various contentions, it is important to return to the two images of the West that Muslims currently entertain—America as a democracy and America as a colonial power. For the purpose of this discussion, the term "Muslim Isolationists" will be used to characterize those American Muslims who give greater significance to the imperialistic tendencies of the United States overseas in conceptualizing American identity. "Muslim Democrats" will be used to describe American Muslims who support American democracy. "Muslim Assimilators," a third group discussed earlier, will refer to those American Muslims from the senior generation who chose assimilation, i.e., "normalization," into mainstream American culture, rather than challenging what assimilation entailed.

The relationship between Muslim Democrats and Muslim Isolationists can best be described as a love-hate relationship. On Conscientious Public Forum issues concerning the defense of Islamic identity, such as establishing and maintaining Islamic centers and schools, these two groups cooperate fully, and the community appears to be seamless. But on political issues in the Civic Public Forum, these two groups break apart and do not see eye to eye on any issue. It is safe to say that, when preserving belief and rituals, these two groups have common ground, while they clearly entertain different conceptions of the role that Muslims, as Muslims, should play in American civic life. At the same time, Muslim Assimilators have succumbed to a secularized approach to American politics and culture, eschewing Islamic identity as not particularly relevant to either the Civic or Conscientious Public Forums. It is in the clash of all of these differences in the wake of September 11 that American Muslims may help America rediscover America's Sacred Ground.

Muslim Isolationists: Identifying and Focusing on U.S. Excesses

Muslim Isolationists hold that the United States is an evil empire dedicated to global domination. As a result, Muslim Isolationists focus their attention on events that support this view of America's imperialistic tendencies. In this decade alone, they maintain that the United States benefited from the Iran-Iraq War, then destroyed Iraq—the most advanced Arab nation— in the Gulf War, and made billions of dollars in profit by billing Muslims for that war. They have stressed how U.S.-led sanctions gradually squeezed the life out of Iraq, resulting in the deaths of hundreds of thousands of Muslim children. They have watched in horror as the Israeli military has killed over three thousand Palestinians since September 2000 alone (nearly as many as the victims of September 11)[27] using a war machine that has benefited from U.S. aid—about $4–6 billion every year, in excess of $80 billion in total.[28] And now the Iraq War has raised even more alarm.

Muslim Isolationists have expressed alarm as they hear report after report in the media blaming the Palestinians for dying, and as they have witnessed the United States refusing to blame or admonish its ally Israel, while claiming to be the defender of human rights. Muslim Isolationists are incensed with the United States for what Muslim Isolationists view as its utter disregard for Muslim lives and Muslim society. This impression occurs in a context where, as this chapter has previously discussed, the American media demonizes Muslims, as well as Islam itself, at home and abroad.[29]

Most importantly, Muslim Isolationists report that they are not impressed with America's record on democracy or its values of freedom and equality. First, they point to the use of secret evidence on the basis of the Anti-Terrorism and Effective Death Penalty Act of 1996, as well as the PATRIOT Act, used only against Muslims, which violates these values by not allowing defendants full and equal access to due process of law.[30] Second, they view American society as immoral, sexually decadent, greedy, and exploitative of the weak at home and abroad. Third, philosophically, Muslim Isolationists do not appreciate the values of freedom and tolerance because they fear that they will give people the opportunity to stray from what Muslim Isolationists think is true Islam. Fourth, theologically they disagree with democracy as a means of political governance because, for these Muslims, democracy is an institution that legitimizes the basest instincts of humanity and is an affront to divine laws. Muslim Isolationists describe the American political and legal system as *kufr*, that is, a system against the laws of Allah and the Islamic *Shariah*, and therefore reject it totally.

The frustration and animosity that Muslim Isolationists feel as a consequence of American foreign policy excesses is translated into a rejection of all that is American and Western, including democracy and religious tolerance. The hostility toward America is also extended towards people of other faiths and makes Muslim Isolationists suspicious and paranoid even when they see the United States doing something that supports Muslims, like intervening in Bosnia and Kosovo to protect Muslims against a Christian state.

Muslim Isolationists argue that American Muslims must participate in an effort to revive the institution of *Khilafah* [Islamic Caliphate] that will magically take care of all Muslim problems. Some of the isolationists have organized themselves under the banner of *Hizb-ul-Tahreer*, a fringe political movement that advocates a narrow and harsh interpretation of Islam. In the last few years, the Muslim Isolationists have focused their attention on preventing the Muslim Democrats from engaging Muslims in the Civic Public Forum. However, their attempts to create intellectual and political ghettos have failed, as more and more Muslims are participating in the American political process.[31]

Muslim Democrats: Contributing to the Promise of America's Sacred Ground

On the other hand, Muslim Democrats have transformed American Muslims from a marginal, inward-looking immigrant community to a reasonably well-organized and coordinated interest group. It is able to fight for Muslims' own rights and to assert their views at the national, as well as international, level. The key to the success of Muslim Democrats has been their understanding of the West and their liberal vision of Islam.

Muslim Democrats were quick to grasp the significance of the constitutional guarantee of religious freedom in the United States. In the beginning, religious freedom led them to organize institutions and movements solely focused on preserving the Islamic identity of American Muslims. This was a reaction to the perceived loss of Muslim identity that had taken place when Muslim Assimilators, who had come before them, had been culturally mainstreamed and therefore had lost all connection to Islam. But as more and more Muslims came to America, they answered the rallying call of Muslim Democrats. In so doing, they began to see a dream—a dream of a model Muslim community, practicing Islam as well as playing a role of moral leadership, guiding not only other Muslim communities, but also America herself toward a life of goodness and God consciousness. In this, they also answered the call of America's Sacred Ground to raise consciousness to God in order to discern what conscience directs and participate fully in American public life from that perspective. That is, they saw themselves, in effect, as working to build the good society in America from the ground up.

Today, Muslim Democrats see in America not merely its imperialist impulse, but also the ideal of the respect for law and fellow human beings, which is embodied in the nonharming and legal consistency principles of the Civic Public Forum, as reflected in the Bill of Rights. Of course, Muslim Democrats are aware of the hypocrisy of the United States with regard to its own principles, when treating "mainstream" American citizens differently than Muslims. But this is not new to Muslim Democrats; they have witnessed Muslim nations employing disparate standards when dealing with others. Still, Muslim Democrats are frustrated with the United States when it does not fulfill its commitments to democracy and human rights in the Muslim world and violates its own fundamental principles.

Yet Muslim Democrats are also quick to acknowledge that Muslims are better treated in the United States than they are in Muslim countries. They have seen democracy, pluralism, and cultural and religious tolerance in action, and are fascinated by the ability to resolve political differences peacefully in the United States. They wish that Muslim societies, too, would be able to escape the political underdevelopment from which they currently suffer and rise to manifest Islamic virtues like those virtues that America's Sacred Ground presents to the world. Most of all, they admire America for its commitment to consultation and desire to rule wisely through deliberation in the Civic and Conscientious Public Forums—an ideal to which Muslim Democrats aspire.

Muslim Democrats have had several successes in their struggle against Muslim Isolationists. First, they have been able to assume leadership positions quickly in nearly every avenue of American Muslim activism. Whether it is in the political arena of the Civic Public Forum or in religious affairs in the Conscientious Public Forum, Muslim Democrats hold sway. Second, they have been able to advance a vision for the American Muslim community, which makes American Muslims proud of themselves and galvanizes them to contribute their money and time in the pursuit of their vision of an ideal Muslim community that serves as a vanguard for other Americans. Their greatest achievement has been their liberal interpretation of Islam.

Through thousands of seminars; persuasive articles in monthly magazines and Islamic center newsletters; lectures at regional and annual conventions of ICNA, ISNA, AMC, CAIR, MSA, MYNA (Muslim Youth of North America), workshops, and leadership retreats in the last thirty years; and the Friday *Jumma* prayers across the nation, Muslim Democrats have campaigned to alter the way Muslims think about America and about Islam itself. They have fought for the legitimacy of their ideas against traditional scholars and battled against the siege mentality that has prevented Muslims from opening up and taking a fresh look at the world, as well as themselves, from the new perspective that their experience in America has given them.[32]

In the last three decades, Muslim Democrats have shifted the Muslim community's focus from battling Western values to building bridges with them. Muslim Democrats have rejuvenated the tradition of *ijtihad*, independent thinking amongst Muslims, and now openly talk about *fiqh al-akhliat*, that is, Islamic law, or the interpretation of the *Shariah* for places where Muslims are in the minority.[33] They have emphasized Islamic principles of justice, religious tolerance, and cultural pluralism.[34] They have Islamized Western values of freedom, human rights, and respect for tolerance by finding Islamic sources and precedence that justify them. Consider the following examples:

Islam's first amendment
There is no compulsion in religion. (Quran 2:256)

The Quranic sources for religious tolerance
Those who believe (in the Qur'an), those who follow the Jewish (scriptures), and the Sabians and the Christians,—any who believe in Allah and the Last Day, and work righteousness,—on them shall be no fear, nor shall they grieve. (Quran 5:69, 2:62)

The Quranic sources on pluralism
O mankind! We created you from a single (pair) of a male and a female, and made you into nations and tribes, that ye may know each other, not that ye may despise (each other). Verily the most honored of you in the sight of Allah is (he who is) the most righteous of you. And Allah has full knowledge and is well acquainted (with all things). (Quran 49:13)

And among His signs is the creation of the heavens and the earth, and the differences in your languages and colors; indeed in this are signs for people who know. (Quran 30:22)

To each among you have we prescribed a law and an open way. If God had so willed, He would have made you a single people, but (His plan is) to test you in what He hath given you: so strive as in a race in all virtues. The goal of you all is to God; it is He that will show you the truth of the matters in which ye dispute. (Quran 5:48)

The Quranic injunctions on moderation
We have made you a nation of moderation (Quran 2:143) . . . *so establish justice and moderation.* (Quran 55:9)

Quranic injunctions on democracy
Conduct your affairs through mutual consultation. (Quran 42:38)

The liberal understanding of Islam is also taking institutional form. A very good example of this development is the establishment of the Center for the Study of Islam and Democracy (CSID) that explores common ground between Islamic governance and democratic governance that emphasizes rights and consent.

Thus, in the battle for American Islam, Muslim Democrats have enjoyed a resounding success. They have gradually marginalized Muslim Isolationists and rendered their arguments and positions illegitimate. However, there are still pockets of resistance that are confined largely to Internet-based discussion groups or Web sites. In the run-up to the election of 2000, the struggle between the two types of Muslim elite in America had intensified, but by that election the Muslim Democrats had prevailed. Muslim Democrats succeeded in mobilizing Muslims to register to vote, and they have voted since in such large numbers that the media and political parties now acknowledge them as a significant voting bloc. American Muslims have become not only eager to participate and make an impact in both the Civic and Conscientious Public Forums, they have made an impact already.[35]

On the other hand, Muslim Isolationists do not have a program or vision that attracts Muslims. Their call to establish *Khilafah* is without substance and lacks credibility because the vast majority of American Muslims have embraced the fundamental framework and values reflected in the American ideal—America's Sacred Ground—even if those ideals are not fulfilled completely in the United States today. For example, some of the Muslim Isolationists are disingenuous in their explanation about religious freedom in America and argue that all the positive things that are happening to Muslims in America are from Allah and that the American values of tolerance, freedom, and democracy do not contribute to such positive developments because they are just empty slogans. However, Muslim Isolationists do not apply the same determinist approach in explaining the misfortunes of Iraqis or the Palestinians. Muslim Isolationists contend that the bad things that are happening to them are not from Allah, but as a consequence of American and Israeli colonialism.[36]

There is an element of hypocrisy too in the manner in which Muslim Isolationists conceptualize their own role in America—a clear violation of the consistency principle of the Civic Public Forum. Muslim Isolationists maintain that, since the American system is not divinely ordained and is not geared towards realizing the Islamic *Shariah*, participation in that system constitutes (in their minds) violation of Allah's decree in the Quran (5:45) that Muslims shall not rule by anything other than what Allah has decreed. That is, Muslim Isolationists do not support a system that provides equal participation by all. Participation, they argue, means endorsement of the system; therefore they are opposed to Muslim participation in American politics—in violation of the American Sacred Ground duty to participate. However, they ignore the fact that in theory both the American Constitution and the Islamic state seek justice and the protection, as well as the moral and material well-being, of their citizens.

Other evidence of their hypocrisy is that, though Muslim Isolationists reject the entire American system, they have no qualms about participating in the American economy. They take jobs and pay taxes (to support the system); some of them even start businesses in the system where, like the polity, the economy is also un-Islamic. When quizzed on this inconsistency and pressed further by suggestions that since they disapprove of the system they should migrate (which is an Islamic thing to do), Muslim Isolationists resort to accusing Muslim Democrats of being agents of the State Department and of being in league with the enemies of Islam.

Tahreer, the strict Muslim sect referenced earlier that is preferred by some Muslim Isolationists, has been shut down in most Muslim countries, most recently in Pakistan. The only places where Muslims are free to pursue *Tahreer* in the open and without any fear of state reprisal is in the West—the United Kingdom, Canada, and the United States. Yet ironically, *Tahreer* condemns the United States and other countries of the West for their belief in democracy and freedom, while at the same time it is clearly evident that the very belief in religious liberty has helped those who adhere to *Tahreer* to escape political extinction.

With such a record, it is no surprise that Muslim Isolationists' activism is now limited to harassing activist Muslim Democrats and trying to place hurdles in their paths, such as spending Muslim Isolationists' resources attacking Muslim Democrats for "inventing" an American Islam in conjunction with American scholars like John Esposito and Yvonne Haddad that emphasizes the softer side of Islam.

LESSONS FROM THE MUSLIM DEBATE

The debate between Muslim Democrats and the Muslim Isolationists has been engaged on the theme of the American Muslim identity and on the issue of whether and to what extent Muslims should engage with the American mainstream. As Muslim Democrats continue to prevail in that debate, there has been a newly emerging trend among Muslims in America. The community's decision to vote as a bloc in 2000 underscored the extent to which Muslim Democrats had succeeded in marketing the idea of democratic politics and pluralism to Muslims in America.

In political and social terms, Muslims had intuitively grasped the essence of America's formative Sacred Ground and had begun to cultivate their future in its fertile soil. By engaging American politics on its terms, Muslim Democrats underscored two important elements of the American polity. First, they began to view America as being a nation of nations, a community of communities, a polity of subpolities. Therefore, they came to understand that political debates and the formation of identity and interests would always take place through what Robert Putnam calls "two-level games."[37] Initially, each community experiences an internal debate about its self-identity, norms, and values, and also negotiates the specific interests it wants to pursue in the larger political arena—the Civic Public Forum. Once the community is able to resolve who it is (identity) and what it wants (interests) in the context of its internal sphere—as, in McGraw's terms, a "community of conscience"—then it is ready, indeed empowered, to engage in the Civic Public Forum. Thus the prerequisite to engage American politics requires self-empowerment.

The second element is the transmission of the identity and interests to the Civic Public Forum. Thus, after Muslims debated what kind of Muslims they were and what they wanted in America, using both parameters of discourse and values deeply entrenched in Islamic ethos, they then had to assert in the Civic Public Forum that they were Americans like everyone else. They also had to assert that they had the same goal that everyone else should have: a better, more prosperous, more multicultural, and more open America that listens to all of its citizens.

Thus, American Muslims transitioned from an insular community focused on forming and preserving their identity in their new home to a community engaged in the Civic Public Forum. There they had to articulate their identity and values not in ethnocentric language but in legal and rational terms so that those who belonged to other identity spheres, such as American Jews, American Catholics, and African Americans, could understand them and accept them, so that they could participate in the continual pursuit of the realization of America's promise in America's Sacred Ground.

But the response of the Bush administration to the events of September 11 has resulted in new challenges as once again the discussion about the place of Muslims in America has been reopened. The Muslim Isolationists had receded into the background after the triumph of the Muslim Democrats in the debate over participation during the presidential elections in 2000. But now, with the systematic profiling of Muslims by the Department of Homeland Security, increased negative media attention, and Muslims feeling estranged and marginalized, Muslim Isolationists have returned with great vigor.

Muslim Isolationists have three powerful arguments, which have forced Muslim Democrats to reimagine Muslim identity in America and rearticulate Muslim goals. First, they claim that the war on terror is actually a war on Islam. Second, they contend that the United States is determined to use "moderate Muslims," a derogatory term in their lexicon, to distort Islam and undermine Muslim societies worldwide. Third, they maintain that the U.S. commitment to democracy and freedom is questionable. Indeed Muslim Isolationists question the very premises of the idea of democracy and pluralistic society as a cover for separating Muslims from Islam.[38]

Although the return of the Muslim Isolationists has once again reopened the old issues in the community, the shock of September 11 and its consequences also have galvanized the community in favor of the Muslim Democrat perspective, resulting in an extraordinary reaction. To taste liberty and see progress toward equal justice, and then see it severely curtailed, has made the Muslim community even more aware of the importance of the "no harm" and "consistency" principles of the Civic Public Forum. It sees the need to participate from its unique perspective to help build American society as a good society in accordance with these principles. This realization has, in turn, resulted in the expansion of the number of individuals and organizations involved in Civic and Conscientious Public Forum debates to steer the United States toward its Sacred Ground.

Muslim participation in the Civic Public Forum has increased exponentially. Muslims are spending more money and time to influence the outcome of Civic Public Forum issues. Young Muslims have dropped out of medical schools and other science-related programs to join law schools to become civil rights lawyers. Furthermore, many individuals who had remained indifferent to the community's internal dynamics and its engagement with America have now joined the debate in earnest. The Muslim participation in the Public Forum has never been as animated, as diverse, and as rich as it is now.[39]

With the emergence of a more highly active progressive and liberal Muslim component, the internal Muslim dialogue also has taken new forms, touching upon issues ranging from the role of women in society to the role of Muslims as citizens in non-Muslim societies. The debates are theological, political, ideological, and also tactical.

These current debates are giving depth and substance to Muslim self-understanding and providing many dimensions on which they are engaging mainstream society. New think tanks have emerged that are geared towards domestic policy and fighting poverty,[40] and new groups have emerged that seek to reform Muslim understanding of Islam.[41] There are more intense discussions about U.S. policies at home and abroad; most importantly, American Muslims have transformed the focus of their identity—which hitherto was centered around their Muslimness—to their Americanness. Their fear that they may have become pariahs in their own nation is reshaping their self-conception and their notions of their host society.

Today, through their own experience of adversity, Muslims have come to understand that America is not a place to plant a new religious vision of a top-down state. Instead, the ideal of liberty and equal justice for which America stands, even when its government does not follow that ideal, is worth defending. For that reason, Muslims are now deeply concerned that America remains true to its foundations in America's Sacred Ground. Consequently, Muslims hope to dissuade the United States from its recent turn toward top-down governance under the influence of the emerging Christian political bloc.

CONCLUSION

As a new generation of Muslims joins the community, the influence of Muslim Democrats is being consolidated. While the new generation is familiar with the problems of the Muslim world and its bill of complaints against the United States, life, as they know it, is in America, with all its pluralities and diversity—and with all of its own failures to realize its full promise. Muslims are strongly in the corner of the Muslim Democrats and have come to manifest and articulate the third way that they were seeking—the one that would save Islam from extremism and America from the decline in its civil rights standards. That third way is not to be Americans who are Muslims or Muslims who are born in America, but to be *American Muslims*.

American Muslims believe in Islam, they are democratic, and they respect human rights. They are economic and political liberals and social conservatives. They believe in freedom of religion and the right of all peoples, ethnic as well as religious, to be treated equally. They are aware of their economic and political privileges and grateful to Allah for it. They dream of making changes in Muslim attitudes, as well as Muslim conditions in other countries, so that their fellow Muslims can also learn the bliss of practicing Islam by choice and without any fear of the state or a dominant group.[42]

As Muslim Democrats seek to find a place for Islam and Muslims in America, they are reviving America's sacred traditions. Muslims have entered the Conscientious and Civic Public Forums as Muslims, where Muslims debate and articulate and even rethink their values, identity, and interests through internal democracy using the logos and ethos of Islam. Then they translate the will of the community into the logos and ethos of pluralist America and seek to realize that will on America's Sacred Ground.

Chapter 8

The Black Church: Sacred Cosmos Meets Sacred Ground

James Lance Taylor

INTRODUCTION: SLAVERY, DELIVERANCE, AND THE
REDISCOVERY OF AMERICA'S SACRED GROUND

In *Rediscovering America's Sacred Ground*, Barbara McGraw perceptively critiques the presumption that freedom of religion in American society vis-à-vis the Establishment Clause necessarily means freedom from religion in the public life of the nation. Her appeal to the original intentions of the founders concerning the place and role of religion in public life is a rediscovery of the pervasive influence of Lockean liberal thought on matters of religious tolerance. It is, indeed, one that supersedes the popular and intellectual debates that continue to rage in contemporary public discourse and constitutional challenges. McGraw accomplishes this by highlighting viewpoints that act to "strain at the gnat and swallow the camel" concerning the proper balance between religion and public life.

America's Sacred Ground simultaneously discredits left "accommodationist," and right "separationist" oriented positions and absorbs them in its framework. They are welcome to participate in the two-tiered Public Forum that partly constitutes the nation's founding principles, which are America's Sacred Ground. The very fact of the right to express individual conscience, whether in matters of religion or of "secular" concerns, is provided by America's Sacred Ground. McGraw insists, for instance, that the sometimes bloody history of theocratic expressions of Christianity in pre-Enlightenment pogroms informed both Locke's and the founders' reticence toward an establishment of any specific tradition, while at the same time inviting Christian social and political discourse in the Conscientious Public Forum where persuasion is a driving force. Christians, Muslims, Hindus, Jews, and others violate the tenets of America's Sacred Ground when the apparatus of the state, with its tools of law, policy, and violent coercion, is sought in the Civic Public Forum to the detriment of religious or other minority populations.

The particular experiences of African Americans in the American political system are consonant with the premises of America's Sacred Ground. This is precisely because while African Americans sought to persuade the nation's ruling elites to use federal power to end their oppressive condition, especially in the South, their efforts were informed by a theological worldview of deliverance. But that worldview avoided any theocratic assumptions. African American elites, from radical abolitionists David Walker and Frederick Douglass to the generation of Martin Luther King Jr., attempted to combine a ground-up vision of an active God in human history with an activist national government, and the explicitly *religious means* they utilized had *political ends*.

In *Black Religion and Black Radicalism*, Gayraud S. Wilmore defines Black religion "as a complex concatenation of archaic, modern, and continually shifting belief systems, mythologies, and symbols, none of which can be claimed as the exclusive property of any one religious tradition—yet sharing a common core related to Africa and racial oppression."[1] This suggests that the religiosity among entire generations of Africans—although not accepted unanimously or uncritically—reflects a Black American *weltbild* (view of the world) and *weltanschauung* (worldview). This special approach resulted from Western European and Euro-American slavery and its importance in the Black protest narrative at least through the immediate post–civil rights era. From the vantage of the Conscientious Public Forum, African Americans sought to speak truth to power in the Civic Public Forum, and in doing so, advocated for freedom from racial oppression by way of religious protest. In some ways the Black struggle was one great and protracted moral reform struggle against both the state and society—all the while using each to prompt the other toward corrective and remedial action that could relieve them of their oppressive condition.

The thesis of America's Sacred Ground reflects the logic of African American politics through its delineation of the Public Forum of social and political discourse. More so than any collective of individuals in American society, African Americans have simply never embraced the Manichean-styled separation of church and state parceling of their faith commitments from their democratic social justice commitments theorized and codified in its founding documents. Their predicament warranted national action, thus invoking moralistic appeals to engage the Civic Public Forum. Although the Civic Public Forum was closed to them—where, as McGraw acknowledges, the laws, judges, and courts were complicit in their oppression—African American leaders nonetheless caucused among themselves in effective national conventions, insisting that the power of the state be put to use in their interests. This was due in large part to David Walker's and later Frederick Douglass's early example of insisting that the federal government act to end slavery in the South. And while much of the advocacy of early abolitionist efforts among African Americans was presented in religious terms of "exodus" and liberation, African Americans never sought the state's power for religious ends. Still, religion has had utility in the expression of Black politics.

America's Sacred Ground is as concerned with other forms of domination that are not necessarily religious in nature, as it is with matters of religious tolerance, mutual respect, and plurality. This explains McGraw's acknowledgment that "the oppressed hold a special place for America's Sacred Ground, as they did for Locke, because they guide America to an ever-unfolding understanding of the depth of the sacred civil rights—as has occurred throughout American history." And yet the porous character of America's Sacred Ground invites liberationist religious strategies in the interest of the oppressed, that is, in the Conscientious Public Forum, to undermine dominant and oppressive structures there and in the Civic Public Forum. McGraw readily acknowledges this dynamic in the context of Martin Luther King's approach to civil rights protest. She notes, "clearly, King's efforts on behalf of African Americans involved the Civic Public Forum because his efforts had to do with the Civic Public Forum goals of liberty and equality, which he sought to obtain for African Americans by changing the law. Whereas prior to his efforts, African Americans were extremely limited in their ability to express conscience in the Public Forum, after King's work (and the work of others who continued in his quest), their participation was greatly enhanced and the law continues to evolve in this vain."[2]

There is little agreement among scholars on the political role of the Black church and African American religion prior to the emergence of Martin Luther King Jr. Yet, there is some consensus, as W. E. B. DuBois recognized, concerning religion's importance both as "the central organ of the organized life of the American Negro,"[3] and its latent power to mobilize people's courage and sense of political efficacy. Black theologian Gayraud S. Wilmore explains further that

> the transmutation of spiritual energy into a political movement for freedom has been an inherent characteristic of black religion from the slave period. It played an important part in slave insurrections in the United States and in the militancy of a significant sector of the black church down to the present.[4]

In each of the major movements in which African Americans participated in their interests *as* African Americans, religion provided important psychological and mobilization resources. Scholars of African American religion and politics have exposed the traditionally "otherworldly" orientation of African American churches and religionists between the Reconstruction (1865–1877) period and the modern Civil Rights Movement (1905–1965).[5] It is the one major religious orientation of African Americans that undermined African American participation in the tow-tiered Public Forum of America's Sacred Ground. According to Lewis Gordon, Black scholars such as Mays and Frazier emphasized the "strong strain of conservatism in black churches that encouraged 'withdrawal from social and political involvement in their communities.'"[6] Prior to its institutionalization in churches and formal organizations, the early expression of African American religion reflected John Locke's view concerning a "right to revolt" that could be invoked when the sacred rights of the people are violated by hierarchical structures of power—whether monarchical or racial. The insurrectionary commitments of Black antislavery preachers such as "Black Gabriel" Prosser in Richmond, Virginia (1800); Denmark Vesey in Charleston, South Carolina (1822); David Walker in Boston (1829–1830); and most famously, Nat Turner in Hampton, Virginia (1831) were consistent with this aspect of Locke's political theology. In this sense, America's Sacred Ground speaks to and reciprocates the African American experience in politics. At the same time, the manner in which Locke and many of the Revolutionary generation participated in the regime of African and African American slavery required that African American religious elites combine their religious ideals with the tenets of modern liberalism that Locke and Jefferson epitomized.[7]

As a result, few recognize the Civil Rights Movement as a religious achievement. R. Drew Smith notes, for instance, how "despite the instrumental value of black churches to black electoral politics, the religious content that black churches contributed to civil rights movement politics has been less welcomed within post–civil rights movement politics."[8] Practitioners of African American religion have also participated in important episodes of social justice commitment that suggest that periods of protest and periods of acquiescence alternate in a pendular manner in terms of high or low protest saliency, and always within the space provided by the two-tiered Public Forum of America's Sacred Ground. Critical figures to America's Sacred Ground, such as John Locke and Thomas Jefferson, provided the theoretical and intellectual arsenal that would contribute significantly to liberal doctrines of property (in persons and in the purpose of government) and to the right of revolution. These seemingly irreconcilable political orientations provide the narrative of much of the political mobilization characteristic of African American religion and politics beginning with the American Revolution, intensifying in three decades of Black abolitionism prior to the Civil

War, and culminating in the debates and contentions concerning African American religion in the Civil Rights Movement.

What then, to the African American religious tradition, is America's Sacred Ground? Has it served as a tool of Black American oppression or an instrument of Black liberation? How does America's Sacred Ground relate to the social, political, and religious experiences of African American individuals and collectives? Have African Americans renounced or appealed to the very structures of liberty provided in seventeenth-century Lockean liberalism and eighteenth-century Revolutionary ideals such as those in Jefferson's Declaration of Independence? Or, did Jefferson's *Notes on the State of Virginia* undermine the natural law sentiments of the Declaration of Independence? To what have African Americans appealed when the architects of the foundational and first principles of America's Sacred Ground participated in the soil of race oppression and indifference?

In this chapter it is first important to contextualize the relationship between the broad religious worldview of African Americans and its encounter with the pertinent tenets of America's Sacred Ground. It is important to note that Black religion throughout the colonial era functioned mostly autonomously and within the guise of some vestigial African influences. The implication is that the Sacred Cosmos which African Americans developed in both accommodation and protest to their predicament in America had antecedent influences. These were later coupled with the moral ideals of Christianity and liberalism of the founding generation, which otherwise operated against the natural rights of African Americans.

Second, it is important to address the pre–Civil War colonization projects and abolitionism which places David Walker's many criticisms of Thomas Jefferson in the *Appeal to the Colored Citizens of the World* at the center of analysis.[9] David Walker epitomizes how Black religionists, especially those who were committed to the social justice orientation of African American religion, spoke truth to power. Walker focused his arguments in the *Appeal* specifically on Jefferson. They took the form of political sermons and were presented as representative of the pre–Civil War agitation against the racial status quo. Walker's *Appeal* concretized African Americans' participation in America's Sacred Ground by way of a reciprocal participation in its Conscientious and Civic Public Forums. This is an integral narrative of African Americans' involvement in social and political movements at each stage of the Black liberation struggle.[10]

Thus, prior to and within church institutions Black religion has engaged Black politics in the modern civil rights reform movement as an oppositional force. At various times Black religion has called for violent rebellion, but more commonly, it has called for moral reform, mainly through what some scholars have called the Black or African American "jeremiad,"[11] that is, the political sermon tradition used earlier by Walker and others. The relevance of the Black jeremiad to America's Sacred Ground is that it has been a major instrument of persuasion used by African American religious elites, committed to the prophetic "social justice" orientation in Black religion. This rhetorical method has been used in the Conscientious Public Forum to bring about a shift in the consciences of many, which has led to reforms in the Civic Public Forum with regard to laws and public policy that directly impacted the social and political status of African Americans. Throughout the nineteenth and twentieth centuries Black religion functioned as the primary instrument of social protest among African Americans in Black protest discourse. Prior to the passage of the 1965 Voting Rights Act—which was an achievement of mostly Black religious functionaries such as King, Ella Baker, Ralph Abernathy, and Bayard Rustin—without Black religion, Black politics would be *impossible*.

THE POLITICS OF RACE OPPRESSION AND BLACK RELIGION'S APPEAL TO THE PRINCIPLES OF AMERICAN DEMOCRACY, OR THE SACRED SOULS OF AMERICA'S BLACK FOLK

Harvard political scientist Michael Dawson understands ideology in a manner consonant with the operational functions of the worldview provided in Black religion to the extent that he sees it as

> a worldview readily found in the population, including sets of ideas and values that cohere, that are used publicly to justify political stances, and that shape and are shaped by society. Further, political ideology helps to define who are one's friends and enemies, with whom one would form political coalitions, and, furthermore, contains a causal narrative of society and the state. Cognitively ideology serves as a filter of what one "sees" and responds to in the social world. . . . Individuals develop a politicized sense of racial identification which influences both their ideological view of the social world as well as their political behavior.[12]

Historian Eugene Genovese maintains "that a significant thrust in black culture emanated from the African tradition. If that thrust had European counterparts, so be it. If those counterparts reinforced or encouraged certain features of black religion, well and good. Black America's tie with an African tradition nonetheless remained and helped shape a culture entirely its own. . . ."[13] The question of divine rescue powerfully shaped the ideological and political orientations utilized by African Americans in their social and political struggles to define their relationship to the American political system. Genovese suggests, "The philosophical problem of religion, its truth and falsehood, represents a domain only partially separate from that of politics. Since religion expresses the antagonisms between the life of the individual and that of society . . . it cannot escape being profoundly political."[14] Hence Black Americans have relied on the principles of American democracy as the primary source of social, economic, psychological, and political liberation from conditions that seemingly implicated the work of hostile cosmic and supernal powers. The trauma and ontological dizziness of slavery (even in its most paternal or "benevolent" forms) and the "triangular trade" in Black labor forced Africans on all ends of its time and spatial trajectory to give supernal explanation for their hellish circumstances. It would thus be unthinkable for Africans, even before contact with the West, to conceive of natural disasters, sickness, disease, premature or tragic death, or any abnormality, separate from an understanding of their proximate favor with God, native deities, or the ancestors. They contemplated whether a great sin committed before the gods or insult to the ancestors had warranted such a fate as several centuries of racial slavery in a nation of liberty. Monarchical tyrannies made no promise of individual liberty; democracy did. Hence the democratic impulses extant in African American religious tradition were born first in the condition of slavery and extended through several centuries of protest. To suggest, in the absence of chattel slavery, that Black Americans would ordinarily yield comparable levels of religiosity or religious expression to what they have historically would be to attribute to Black individuals a more powerful source of solidarity than is apparent among other groups that had experience in oppression—with the exception of Jews, groups that have historically yielded lower scores on religiosity scales. The point is that slavery provided a uniform point of reference for Africans and American Blacks. R. Drew Smith notes that "slavery was the one issue that drew black churches into the public arena."[15]

Scholars largely agree that African American politics grew out of a structure that gave religious leaders early primacy among African Americans in their social organization. In *The Souls of Black Folk*, DuBois contends that two of the most important *antecedent* entities to emerge among antebellum Black people were an at-large Black church, which preceded the Black family structure under chattel slavery, and the office of the Black preacher, which DuBois regarded as "the most unique personality developed by the Negro on American soil."[16] For sociologist E. Franklin Frazier, plantation religion among slaves was identified as an "invisible institution."[17] The importance of religion in the historical narratives of Black Americans collectively and in individual biographies points to a structure that subsumed all facets of life—economic, social, political, and cultural—and resonated throughout the diaspora of African and hyphenated African peoples for much of four centuries. It encompassed the myriad ideological, organizational, associational, institutional, and individual-level groupings and subsequent subhistories, even though it may have developed differently in, say, Brazil or Haiti than in the United States.[18] Thus, when African Americans would encounter

Christianity and the ideals of America's Sacred Ground, they were already predisposed to interpret their reality in religious terms.

Political scientist Cedric Robinson contends that "the transport of African labour to . . . the Americas meant also the transfer of African ontological and cosmological systems; African codes embodying historical consciousness and social experience; and African ideological and behavioural constructions for the resolution of the inevitable conflict between the actual and normative."[19] The development of the cosmological system is consistent with Emile Durkheim's classic sociological explanation of religion in *The Elementary Forms of Religious Life*.[20] In it, he viewed religion as a social product that emerges out of the shared experiences of groups and individuals, as well as experiences such as slavery and its social, legal, and political consequences.

The context in which these experiences occur relates to the various material circumstances of people of African descent and powerfully shapes the character of individual, group, or national consciousnesses. Nevertheless, the modernist constructions of race and racism provided a basis for African American concerns such as deliverance, freedom, democratic idealism, racial realism, and moral agency in the form of a Black religious ethos.

The Hegemony and Inversion of Race Domination

There are clear comparisons between the totaling power of monarchy against which the Revolutionary generation (e.g., Jefferson, Paine, and Franklin) dissented and the totaling power of white supremacy which many in turn meshed with Victorian moral codes, republicanism, and liberalism. As a result, African Americans and other diasporan Black people employed religion in various ways in their social movements oriented toward the goals of freedom and liberation. Michael Dawson contends, for instance, that the religious and political ideology of "black nationalism had a sufficient social base throughout the 19th century, except during Reconstruction, to insure that substantial sectors of the black community were always at odds with all of America's versions of 'the' liberal tradition."[21]

The ubiquitous, omnipresent, and seemingly omnipotent power of the Crown that loomed large in the consciousness of eighteenth-century Western European and North American societies was to Anglos and other whites what racial domination would represent to African Americans under liberalism; that is to say, that what monarchy violated in the individual in eighteenth-century Europe and North America, global racial domination violated in Native and African American individuals. Much of the African American encounter with religion in the New World was thus forged with markedly different understandings than those forged among whites in Europe and North America. Emerging from its "dark age" after several centuries of Islamic "Blackamoor" domination between the eighth and twelfth centuries,

European cosmological thought shifted "from a terrestrial social order to that of a spiritual kingdom: Christendom."[22] Christianity eventually constituted the cultural religion of Europe and its "Great Commission," comported well with the merchant ambitions of the emergent European bourgeoisie which sought, above all, exploitable labor. In time the absolutist monarchical and clerical hierarchies would be replaced or supplemented by ideological ones (i.e., liberalism) among Europeans largely because of the writings of individuals such as John Locke and later Thomas Jefferson and Thomas Paine.

African Americans were confused by the liberal tenets of America's Sacred Ground precisely because, as they were seen dialectically (religion in absolutism versus bourgeois liberalism) by whites who understood the latter as a ground up antiabsolutist oppositional ideology, in practice they operated undemocratically with regard to Africans and American Blacks. Among most European and Euro-American groups—Catholic and Protestant—religion acted as top-down phenomena before the various liberal states and societies relegated it to the private sector of civil life. African Americans sought to employ religious faith, spiritually and socially, as a ground-up means to undo the effects of the liberal racial hierarchies which Du Bois's *The World and Africa* (1946) and Robinson's *Black Marxism* (1983) maintain were in part the product of Western European aristocratic, intraracialist and hierarchical thought.[23] The differences, or what Jefferson identified in *Notes* as "the real distinction that nature has made," between Native, African, and Anglo Americans made the narrow promotion of Lockean liberalism, Paine-styled commonsense democratic values, and aristocratic republicanism more plausible in the young nation. This was a fact that might otherwise have betrayed many of the same class-based leveling tendencies that plagued France in its contemporary revolution. Over a period of several centuries, Europe's white slaves and indentured laborers would be uniquely incorporated into the "master class" in the New World. Cedric Robinson contends that racism

> ran deep in the bowels of Western culture, negating its varying social relations of production and distorting their inherent contradictions. The comprehension of the particular configuration of racist ideology and Western culture has to be pursued historically through successive eras of violent domination and social extraction which directly involved European peoples during the better part of two millennia. Racialism insinuated not only medieval, feudal, and capitalist social structures, forms of property, and modes of production, but as well the very values and traditions of consciousness through which the peoples of these ages came to understand their worlds and their experiences.[24]

White race solidarity was forged at the expense of alternative interracial "proletarian" coalitions between poor African American and white workers and individuals. The majority of Blacks' status as slave noncitizens was facilitated by the reinforcing powers of race, which consolidated white majority domination. Historian Edmund Morgan relates the contradiction of freedom-loving slaveholding in noting:

> Aristocrats could more safely preach equality in a slave society than in a free one. Slaves did not become leveling mobs, because their owners would see to it that they had no chance to. The apostrophes to equality were not addressed to them. And because Virginia's labor force was composed mainly of slaves, who had been isolated by race and removed from the political equation, the remaining free laborers and tenant farmers were too few in number to constitute a serious threat to the superiority of the men who assured them of their equality.[25]

Morgan insists further that it was not that "a belief in republican equality had to rest on slavery, but only that in Virginia, and probably in other southern colonies, it did. The most ardent American republicans were Virginians, and their ardor was not unrelated to their power over the men and women they held in bondage."[26] Humanitarian ideals such as equality, fraternity, and liberty could only be realized at the expense and exclusion of Blacks as individuals and as a collective in the larger American society. Jefferson scholar Paul Finkleman notes, for instance, that "during Jefferson's presidency, Sir Augustus John Foster, an English diplomat, observed that Virginia planters could 'profess an unbounded love of liberty and of democracy in consequence of the masses of people, who in other countries might become mobs, being there nearly altogether composed of their own Negro slaves.'"[27]

Slavery and racial oppression in unprecedented ways homogenized Africans and consequently created a procrustean Black American racial identity. They subsumed lost African ethnicities beginning with the slave ship journeys known as the "Middle Passage" and shed them almost entirely by the American Civil War period. Charles Joyner notes that among Colonial plantation slaves "a new culture, predominantly African in origin, but different from any particular American culture, began to take shape."[28] No subsequent movement, political ideology, or cadre of individuals has had so powerful a socializing effect as the Black American slavery epoch and racial oppression in accordance with hegemonic use of liberally derived white law, religion, economics, and violence. This experience provided a way of ordering the world for African Americans historically and spatially and it ran adjacent (but not subordinate) to the "big idea" of white supremacism that developed out of modern liberal market and Christian missionary ambition. Africans and American Blacks developed an essential way of reading the world and interpreted the contours of social and political relations.

The religious worldview of African Americans derived from a definite shared experience in racial oppression. The lived experience of their subalternation actually renders the fact that race is a socially constructed "least common denominator" which forges African American solidarity, totally irrelevant in a heretofore racist society. For centuries it was omnipresent among Blacks, slave and free, educated and illiterate, New Englander and southerner, male and female alike—as was the ideology of white supremacism. Thus the Black Sacred Cosmos arose out of the condition of slavery and oppression, and the democratic principles that liberalism promoted had great appeal in it.

Origins of a Black Sacred Cosmos

In terms of the origins of the Black Sacred Cosmos, scholars have vigorously debated whether religion or religiosity among African Americans (past/present) is a cultural vestige or remnant of the African past. Anthropologist John Langston Gwaltney argues, for instance, that it is important to recognize how "core black culture, . . . its values, systems of logic and world view are rooted in a lengthy peasant tradition and clandestine theology" in the United States.[29] The source of the Sacred Cosmos was an important element in the unsettled debate between Jewish anthropologist Melville Herskowitz and African American sociologist E. Franklin Frazier concerning the larger question of African survivals among subsequent generations of Black people in diaspora.[30] Herskowitz's *Myth of the Negro Past* (1934) points to a "tenaciousness of African religious beliefs," which endured even after the earliest generations of Africans passed. He forcefully insists, "there is no more theoretical support for an hypothesis that they [African Americans] have retained nothing of the culture of their forebears, than in supposing that they have remained completely African in their behavior."[31] Frazier's *The Negro in the United States* argues against any substantive cultural nexuses between Africans and African Americans.[32] He contends that the slavery experience obliterated all African cultural remnants; the Negro is an American product and his cultural productions are wholly American, and partly imitative of white cultural outputs. In his later work, *The Negro Church in America*, Frazier contends that Christianity became a substitute for the social bonds and the social cohesion that were lost in the traumatic encounters with capture, the "Middle Passage," and the slavery regime of the plantations.[33] In order to clarify its authenticity, DuBois suggests that Black religion be studied "as a development, through its gradual changes from the heathenism of the Gold Coast to the institutional Negro Church of Chicago."[34] Moreover, DuBois describes the "successive steps of the social history" of the Black religious life:

> [N]o such institution as the Negro church could rear itself without definite historical foundations. These foundations we can find if we remember that *the social history of the Negro did not begin in America.* He was from a definite societal environment. . . . *The first church was not at first by any means Christian nor definitely organized*; rather it was an adaptation and mingling of heathen rites among the members of each plantation, and roughly designated Voodooism. *Association with the masters, missionary effort and motives of expediency gave these rites an early veneer*

> *of Christianity, and after the lapse of many generations the Negro church became Christian.*[35]

Lawrence Levine suggests that

> the preliterate, premodern Africans, with their sacred worldview, were so imperfectly acculturated into the secular American society into which they were thrust, were so completely denied access to the ideology and dreams which formed the core of the consciousness of other Americans, that they were forced to fall back upon the only cultural frame of reference that made any sense to them and gave them any feeling of security. [In fact their predicament contributed to the sharing of a] fundamental outlook toward the past, present, and future and common means of cultural expression which could well have constituted the basis of a sense of common identity and worldview capable of withstanding the impact of slavery.[36]

The African American cosmos derived from a ground-up uplift ethos and was responsive to what had, by the era of the revolution in science and reason, developed into an overarching system of racial domination. This is a system that McGraw refutes as a violation of America's Sacred Ground. Lincoln and Mamiya identify these theological perceptions interchangeably as either "the black sacred cosmos or the religious worldview of African-Americans,"[37] which made sense of the world by giving explanation for, and meaning to, the structures of domestic and global white supremacy. The formulation of the sacred worldview was widespread among African Americans, but it did not constitute an overarching worldview such as McGraw rejects in *Rediscovering America's Sacred Ground*, primarily because African Americans entered social relations from the standpoint of being a dominated people, dominated by the overarching worldview of white supremacy that colored political and social relations for several subsequent centuries.

The elements of the Sacred Cosmos are not fixed in a systematic theology or a formal system of beliefs; indeed this worldview transcended the doctrinal idiosyncrasies of specific religious groups or organizations. According to Lewis Baldwin, the early churches among African Americans shared a

> fundamental agreement concerning the need to challenge the status quo. They had a common understanding of the Christian faith and its implications for addressing human need and inequality. In other words, there was a consensus of beliefs, attitudes, values, and expectations that bound them together despite the incidentals that distinguished them from one another. Thus, they were able to establish a broad, interdenominational tradition of shared involvement in the struggle for a just and inclusive society, one that contributed enormously to the vitality of black churches as social institutions.[38]

Thus the emergence of an African American worldview had more to do with theodicy in relation to experience than with a set of measurable affirmations or theological properties. It has not acted as a hegemonic and uncontested force as did the Medieval cosmos of Western Europe, which is clearly rejected by John Locke and the democratic premise of America's Sacred Ground. Throughout the modern Civil Rights Movement (1895–1965), African American politics and history reflected the strong sense of group destiny presented in the biblical narratives. This sense of destiny was regardless of the political accommodationism that characterized the period since Reconstruction. The Hebrew exodus story and the statement that "Ethiopia shall stretch forth her hands to God" (Ps 68:31) led generations of African and African American elites such as AME Bishop Henry McNeal Turner to anticipate the eschatological "Coming of the Lord" and to have faith in God's interest in the social and political plight of Black people in Africa and in diaspora. Lincoln and Mamiya contend that the "direct relationship between the holocaust of slavery and the notion of divine rescue colored the theological perceptions of black laity and the themes of black preaching particularly in those churches closest to the experience."[39] Cornel West argues:

> Black strivings are the creative and complex products of the terrifying African encounter with the absurd *in* America—and the absurd *as* America. . . . They constructed structures of meaning and structures of feeling in the face of the fundamental facts of human existence—death, dread, despair, and disappointment. Yet the specificity of black culture—namely, those features that distinguish black culture from other cultures—lies in both the *African* and *American* character of black people's attempts to sustain their mental sanity and spiritual health, social life and political struggle in the midst of a slaveholding, white supremacist civilization that viewed itself as the most enlightened, free, tolerant, and democratic experiment in human history.[40]

The ability of the slaves to make the Judeo-Christian texts instrumentally useful in the absurdity enabled them to create an alternative perspective that combined the best of their folk culture with lingering African components and the religion of the New World.

WHAT THE FOUNDERS INHERITED, WHAT THE FOUNDERS WROUGHT: SACRED COSMOS MEETS SACRED GROUND

Between Locke (1632–1704) and, say, Jefferson (1745–1826), America's Sacred Ground was formed in an epistemological, ideological, and cultural milieu. In it, Africans and their American "Negro" progeny were relegated to the status of invisible, quasi-human noncitizens, and thought bereft of Western European and North American Enlightenment and "civilization." McGraw reiterates the philosophical influence of John Locke on Thomas Jefferson and his contemporaries, especially in the *Two Treatises of Civil Government*. At the time, Locke found himself in the middle of the religious and

political controversies between the antiabsolutist Whigs and the more pro-
absolutist Tories. With the theoretical rationale provided by what would
become identified as Lockean liberalism, the Whigs sought and gained
statutory controls over the king, while the Tories viewed monarchical authority as inviolable. Locke contended that absolute monarchy was irreconcilable
with civil government and society "and so can be no form of civil government at all." In chapter 7, "Of Political or Civil Society," Locke states:

> In absolute monarchies, indeed, as well as other governments of the
> world, the subjects have an appeal to the law, and judges to decide any
> controversies and restrain any violence that may happen betwixt the
> subjects themselves, amongst another . . . what security, what fence is
> there, in such a state, against the violence and oppression of this
> absolute ruler. . . . To ask how you may be guarded from harm or injury
> on that side where the strongest hand is to do it, is presently the voice
> of faction and rebellion. As if when men quitting the state of nature
> entered into society, they agreed that all of them but *one* should be
> under the restraint of laws, but that he should retain all the liberty of the
> state of nature, increased with power and made licentious by
> impunity.[41]

Civil society must protect against arbitrary power encroachments, kingly
or otherwise, on minority or unorthodox belief through the legal provisions
of established law, a dispassionate judiciary, and courts with sufficient power
to enforce decisions. Intellectually Locke recoils at domination in the interest of one man or one group of people over another in society.

Among the American founders, Virginia's Thomas Jefferson is to many
singly the most important. *Rediscovering America's Sacred Ground* acknowledges Jefferson's preeminence in American political history and John Locke's
influence on him. Locke's impact on the Revolutionary generation, nearly
one century later, is paramount in the development of classical liberal
notions of liberty and property (including one's labor, body, and person) that
would come to permeate American political consciousness. According to
McGraw, the American surrogates to Locke's "political theology"[42] borrowed
liberally from his iteration of the sacredness of life, liberty, and property, and
they were "accepted, adopted, and referenced universally by the American
colonists in the formative documents of the states."[43] In *The Declaration of
Independence* by Carl Becker, the noted author wrote that "so far as the
'Fathers' were, before 1776, directly influenced by particular writers, the
writers were English [as opposed to French or Rousseauan], and notably
Locke. . . . The lineage is direct: Jefferson copied Locke."[44] He and Franklin
were most representative of the American provincial version of the Enlightenment philosophes.

John Locke believed that each individual has "a *property* in his own *person*: this nobody has a right to but himself. The labour of his body, and the

work of his hands, we may say, are properly his."[45] Among the founders of
the American Republic who studied him, Locke's teaching on slavery and
property did not apply to Africans; the ideal of property in one's person
would be inverted to property in *other* persons.[46] Where, as McGraw notes,
Thomas Jefferson "amended" Locke's conditional tolerance that discrimi-
nately extended sacred rights only to professed believers, Jefferson was true
to Locke's exceptionalism in forging a homegrown, American version of it
with regard to individuals and groups in society such as women and Native
and African Americans. For instance, Locke takes note of the "property of
labour" in "several nations of the *Americans*,"[47] but says nothing of their
African and Negro populations that could lead his students to advocate an
antislavery position. McGraw just the same reminds us that Jefferson felt
". . . no wonder the oppressed should rebel, and they will continue to rebel
and raise disturbance until their civil rights are full[y] restored to them and
all partial distinctions, exclusions and incapacitations removed."[48] Of course,
the right to rebel did not pertain to Negroes whom Jefferson believed in the
Notes, if emancipated, would be motivated by the "ten thousand recollec-
tions" of the "injuries they have sustained."[49] Nor could it apply to the insurrectionary Black slaves led by Toussaint L'Ouverture who were in revolt
against the French in Hispaniola (Haiti) at the start of his presidency.[50]

John Locke, in fact, believed that the enslavement of individuals created
"a state of war" between master and slave.[51] Locke's support for an individual right to private property in one's person provided a structure of religious
and political dissent that could be creatively used by literate, insurrectionary-
minded African Americans. One example was David Walker, who was on the
adverse side of social relations and political power even after the earth-shat-
tering American Revolution. Locke's support for revolutionary opposition to
oppression corresponds neatly with the religiously inspired social justice
protest orientation that later developed among African Americans in which
Walker would focus on Jefferson.

David Walker's *Appeal* to Thomas Jefferson

Slavery opponent John Adams, along with Jefferson, drafted the final document of the Declaration of Independence after it went through eighty-six
revisions in the Continental Congress, which deleted one-fourth of the original text.[52] The most noteworthy deletion was an antislavery clause charging
King George III with "waging cruel war against human nature itself, violating
its most sacred rights of life and liberty." Virginia delegate George Mason,
who owned the lion's share of slaves among the delegates at the Philadelphia
Convention, understood the moral and religious implications of slavery on
Africans and whites as he noted, "every master of slaves is born a petty
tyrant. They bring the judgment of heaven on a Country . . . [and] by an
inevitable chain of causes and effects providence punishes national sins, by

national calamities."[53] More famously, however, was Jefferson's jeremiad stating the following:

> And can the liberties of a nation be thought secure when we have removed their only firm basis, a conviction in the minds of the people that these liberties are a gift of God? That they are not to be violated but with his wrath? Indeed I tremble for my country when I reflect that God is just; that his justice cannot sleep forever; that considering numbers, nature and natural means only, a revolution of the wheel of fortune, an exchange of situation is among possible events; that it may become probable by supernatural interference! The Almighty has not attribute which can take side with us in such a contest.[54]

If Locke was the towering figure among the American Revolutionists, Thomas Jefferson was the chief inspiration for African American political indignation. Historian Wilson Jeremiah Moses writes for instance, "David Walker's *Appeal in Four Articles* . . . contained many bitter references to Jefferson's assertion in *Notes on the State of Virginia* that emancipation could never be effected unless accompanied by deportation 'beyond the reach of mixture.'"[55] Moses also notes that Black writers and critics such as Walker "in the early republic were to repeat the themes of the Jeffersonian jeremiad with enthusiasm for the next several decades" after he wrote *Notes on the State of Virginia* (1781–1782).[56] According to Moses, Jefferson's noted statement concerning God's opposition to oppression was a major inspiration for David Walker's jeremiadic response, which exemplified the intense feeling of agitation among free, northern African American elites mainly in New York, Philadelphia, and Boston just one generation after the American Revolution.

It is important to recognize the detail that the founders of the American political system did not *create* American slavery; they *extended* it. As it would become known, the "peculiar institution" existed in the nation for more than 150 years *before* Jefferson wrote the Declaration of Independence and the delegates of the 1787 Philadelphia Convention established the United States of America as a political federation. Moreover, the Articles of Confederation made provisions for slavery in the colonies. Nevertheless, the institution of American slavery was on retreat throughout the northern states around the time of the Revolution, before it expanded primarily due to the technological advances evident in Eli Whitney's "Cotton ('gin) Engine" in 1793.[57]

David Walker was born free in Wilmington, North Carolina, in 1785.[58] His clarion call to revolution—which was often followed with an invitation to whites to repent for race oppression and slavery—was the major influence among African Americans in Boston, and it is he, not William Lloyd Garrison, who was the principal leader among Black abolitionists.[59] Walker migrated to Boston in 1825 and wrote the *Appeal* mainly as an answer to the recently deceased Thomas Jefferson's racist speculations about African and Negro inferiority in *Notes on the State of Virginia*. Written out of disappointment rather than hatred, the *Appeal* contained a ferocity that conveys the intensity of Walker's feelings about the man whom he perceived as the most enlightened of white men. He produced a treatise calling for the slaves to rebel in a general uprising.[60]

In the four articles entitled "Our Wretchedness in Consequence of Slavery," "Our Wretchedness in Consequence of Ignorance," "Our Wretchedness in Consequence of the Preachers of the Religion of Jesus Christ," and "Our Wretchedness in Consequence of the Colonizing Plan," Walker unequivocally participated in the Conscientious Public Forum of America's Sacred Ground. Marxist historian Herbert Aptheker insists, "Never before or since was there a more passionate denunciation of the hypocrisy of the nation as a whole—democratic and fraternal and equalitarian and all the other words."[61] He adds further, "Walker is among the pioneer antagonists to racism. . . . He selects [Thomas Jefferson] exactly because he is of the finest and because, as the author of the Declaration of Independence, as a slave owner and as one who, in his Notes on Virginia, embraces—though with hesitation—the idea of the innate mental inferiority of Negro people, Jefferson symbolizes, as it were, the contradictions consuming the Republic."[62] Moses insists, "Black sermons and pamphlets continued to play upon the Jeffersonian theme, that slavery was a violation of natural and divine law. Their authors may be interpreted as loyal informers, in a sense, issuing a warning to whites, revealing the hostility and resentment that pervaded black communities North and South, slave and free."[63] According to Moses, Walker's *Appeal* was "an extreme example of the jeremiadic tradition," but still just one of the many put forth by religiously motivated African Americans. Walker especially highlighted the fact that African and Negro slaves in the Americas suffered more severely at the hands of Christians than other peoples had suffered historically under "heathen" nations and that a chief influence on their thinking was Thomas Jefferson. Being motivated by both conscience and a sense of social justice, Walker writes:

> I ask every man who has a heart, and is blessed with the privilege of believing—Is not God a God of justice to all his creatures? Do you say he is? Then if he gives peace and tranquility to tyrants, and permits them to keep our fathers, our mothers, ourselves and our children in eternal ignorance and wretchedness, to support them and their families, would he be to us a God of justice? I ask, O ye Christians!!! Who hold us and our children in the most abject ignorance and degradation, that ever a people were afflicted with since the world began.[64]

In Article II of the *Appeal*, Walker takes up the discussion of Jefferson's influence on the racial attitudes and political ideals of many whites. Jefferson's *Notes on the State of Virginia*, which informs most of Walker's criticism, was Jefferson's only full-length scholarly intellectual work. Aside from the Declaration of Independence, Jefferson did not dominate American political thought as widely as Walker gives credence, but lending his prestige to thoughts such as those expressed in *Notes* is of particular concern to Walker as he notes:

> I call upon the professing Christians . . . to show me a page in history, either sacred or profane, on which a verse can be found, which maintains, that the Egyptians heaped the *insupportable insult* upon the children of Israel, by telling them that they were not of the *human family*. . . . Can the whites deny this charge? Have they not, after having reduced us to the deplorable condition of slaves under their feet, held us up as descending originally from the tribes of Monkeys or Orang-Outangs? O! my God! I appeal to every man of feeling—is not this insupportable? Is it not heaping the most gross insult upon our miseries, because they have got us under their feet and we cannot help ourselves? Oh! Pity us we pray thee, Lord Jesus, Master.—Has Mr. Jefferson declared to the world, that we are inferior to the whites, both in the endowments of our bodies and of minds? It is indeed surprising, that a man of such great learning, combined with such excellent natural parts, should speak so of a set of men in chains.[65]

Clearly the most disturbing feature of Walker's *Appeal* among white southerners was his call to insurrectionary revolt. Just a raft journey away from the southern United States, the specter of the Haitian Revolution loomed large in the consciousness of whites and African Americans. The *Appeal* was a call not to revolution for the purpose of establishing some new political order except to the extent that the young republic would be rid of its sin in slavery. In Article II, Walker refers to whites as "our natural enemies" and urges his readers, in the event of a general insurrection, "if you commence, make sure work— do not trifle, for they will not trifle with you—they want us for their slaves, and think nothing of murdering us in order to subject us to that wretched condition—therefore, if there is an *attempt* made by us, kill or be killed."[66] Despite his willingness to raise the sword, Walker culminates the *Appeal* with an olive branch to whites:

> I speak Americans for your good. We must and shall be free I say, in spite of you. You may do your best to keep us in wretchedness and misery . . . but God will deliver us from under you. And woe will be to you if we have to obtain our freedom by fighting. Throw away your fears and prejudices then, and enlighten us and treat us like men, and we will like you more than we do now hate you, and tell us no more about colonization, for America is as much our country, as it is yours. Treat us like [people] and there is no danger but we will all live in peace and happiness together. . . . What a happy country this will be, if the whites will listen.[67]

In the end, the *Appeal* effectively spoke from the Conscientious Public Forum and spawned an air of tense fear over its potential to incite rebellion among the slaves. It also spawned southern political elites in the Civic Public Forum to ban the pamphlet. Their fears were not unfounded. Nat Turner's famous insurrection followed just one year after Walker's *Appeal* was published in its last edition. Walker's *Appeal* demonstrates that despite the founders' best intentions in forging America's Sacred Ground, they were, with regard to Africans in America, themselves in violation of it.[68] In particular, elites and the popular majorities violated the cardinal tenets of America's Sacred Ground—that is, that no one may harm another in his life, liberty, and property, and that the law of consistency and no harm must be applied to all.

Important to understanding the impact and inherent contradiction of the founders' role in forging both America's Sacred Ground and extending African Americans' peculiar predicament of being a dominated people is McGraw's insistence that America's Sacred Ground includes certain principles that transcend the actions or inactions of the founders. These principles were more important than any single founder's failure to live according to its precepts; ironically, this is not much different than how a given religionist's failure to live up to the moral codes of belief leaves the system of belief intact despite individual hypocrisy. Indeed, even where they failed to live up to their own ideals, the raw "stuff" of America's Sacred Ground provided the structure of dissent—even to the point of violence—for traditionally oppressed populations, such as Native Americans, descendants of Africa, and women. Just the same, America's Sacred Ground reserves a preferential option to the oppressed who, in McGraw's words, "hold a special place for America's Sacred Ground."[69] Whenever any sacred right was violated, there apparently stood a "right to revolution" which the American founders recognized for themselves, but not for the likes of their onetime compatriot Daniel Shays and his agrarian uprising, nor for the Native and African populations in the burgeoning country.

This perspective on the African American encounter with America's Sacred Ground encapsulates the extent to which the founders' complicity in fortifying slavery and the slave trade in the United States spoke to a larger validation of the inferior status of African Americans. How, for instance, was it possible that the founders of the young nation, including Washington and Jefferson, also set up the rules that would require three centuries of protracted struggle and movements beginning with the early-nineteenth-century abolitionist movement, which was inspired by David Walker's Christian militancy, to overcome? On this score, however, McGraw argues that "we should not conclude that because the founders violated their own principles, those principles were not still fundamental to the American system."[70] She insists further, "on the contrary, what those who understood the full reach of America's Sacred Ground did not accomplish at the time of the founding was nevertheless inherent in the system, and has remained there as a latent force continually moving toward its full realization."[71]

This violation of the central principles of the multitiered public discourse abrogated African American civil and political rights in a manner that would shape their politics in profound ways. It should be apparent at this point that America's Sacred Ground is more than religious discourse. It addresses the dangers of *any* dominant worldview that obviates the good society. McGraw contends, for instance, that "the good society is not something conceived by those in power at the top of a grand societal hierarchy with 'an overarching worldview' to impose on the people. Rather the good society is achieved through debate and action of the people pursuing the good according to conscience from the ground up by virtue of the shared expression of the plurality of their perspectives. In this way, America's Sacred Ground preserves maximum liberty while making possible pursuit of the good."[72]

Despite their hypocritical participation in the very regime that undermined their construction of America's Sacred Ground, Locke's and the founders' writings and rhetoric created the space for the dissent and liberationist ideals in which individuals such as Walker and his contemporaries participated. The perennial influence of liberal thinking would be evident in important African American texts stretching from David Walker's *Appeal* in response to Jefferson and beyond King's 1963 appeal in "I Have A Dream," which invoked Lincoln's intellectual debt to Jefferson. Between Walker and King, Africans and African Americans spent much of their spiritual and religious capital, in Martin Luther King's words, attempting "to make real the promises of democracy," and the promises of America's Sacred Ground. The clear fact of African Americans' inferior status in the context of burgeoning liberal and European and North American democratic societies led Muslim minister and King nemesis Malcolm X to conclude in his own jeremiad that "this is American justice, this is American democracy, and those of you who are familiar with it know that in America democracy is hypocrisy. . . . Democracy is hypocrisy. If democracy means freedom, why aren't our people free? If democracy means justice, why don't we have justice? If democracy means equality, why don't we have equality?"[73] McGraw in turn concedes that the efforts of King and the disposition of Malcolm X (whom she does not reference in the book) ". . . was caused by the failure to open the Public Forum to them. Moreover, they have shown how the omission of their admittance to the Public Forum is a violation of the rule of constituency/no hypocrisy because it is a denial to them of what those in power—the majority—have not denied to themselves."[74]

CONCLUSION: WHITHER AFRICAN AMERICAN RELIGION? WHITHER THE OTHERWORLDLY BLACK CHURCH?

Three major strategies in African American protest history have been identified by social scientists. The first is known as the "social justice" orientation; the second is referred to as a "spiritual otherworldliness" or "opiate" orientation; a third is known as a "compensatory" perspective, which is barely distinguishable from the otherworldly orientation.[75]

America's Sacred Ground speaks to the major organized religious orientations that African Americans have adhered to in terms of their approach to politics. Prior to the abolition of the centuries-long slavery epoch, Black religion—here understood as the at-large African American religious experience mainly in Protestant ecclesiastical traditions in the United States but with some antecedent African and subsequent Islamic influences—operated in social and political movements within the venue of the Conscientious Public Forum of America's Sacred Ground as the primary means by which African American religious and political elites sought to effectuate changes in its Civic Public Forum venue that had limited, frustrated, and denied their participation in the social and political life of the nation.[76]

The social justice orientation is reflected variously in insurrectionary efforts to use violence as a *means* to liberation; it never has advocated violence for the sake of violence. This is true of the jeremiads of Walker as well as Malcolm X. Despite being derided as a co-opted "Uncle Tom" by many student activists in the 1950s and 1960s, Martin Luther King Jr.'s direct action, civil disobedience strategies were a politics of "this world." His efforts were derived from the "prophetic" dispositions of early African American religionists, and he categorically rejected the more conservative and politically disengaging "priestly" perspective inherent in the otherworldly orientation.[77]

McGraw's insistence that there is a "duty to participate in the Public Forum" through "speech, action, and by listening to others' views in accordance with conscience and mutual respect" exposes the "otherworldly" orientation of African American political theology as an obstacle to the good society. According to McGraw, "the founders established America's Sacred Ground for a purpose—to make possible the pursuit of the good society through the debate and action of individuals of conscience from a plurality of perspectives. Consequently, regardless of the fact that we, the people, cannot be forced by law to comply, we, nevertheless, have conscientious moral obligations in the Conscientious Public Forum."[78] Failure to engage in public discourse as motivated by one's conscience, especially on the behalf of the oppressed, profanes the moral foundation of society. In her view, one cannot opt out of participation, because disinterest in fulfilling one's civic duties is considered a form of participation.[79]

In the chapter "Of Mr. Booker T. Washington and Others" in *The Souls of Black Folk*, W. E. B. DuBois lists militant Christian individuals as representing one of two major religious orientations that were consistent with, and subverted by, Booker T. Washington's accommodationist political orientation.[80] The accommodationist orientation of Washington rejected overt political agitation in the interest of civil rights. The institutionalization of Black religion from its early status as the "invisible institution" to its organizational formations in the "African" church (pre–Revolutionary Era), the "Negro" church (antebellum era to post–WWII era), and still later, "Black" church (1960s–1990s), have influenced the predominant scholarly views on Black religion. Gary T. Marx's *Protest and Prejudice* is well known for its elaboration of the "quietist" propensities of African American religion that inhibit "attitudes of protest," and "an important factor working against the widespread radicalization of the Negro public."[81] This scholarly opinion emerged, however, mainly from the research of E. Franklin Frazier, who emphasized the opiate-like "compensatory," character of African American religion *before* the achievements of Martin Luther King Jr. It is not an overstatement to suggest that the *political* disposition of the African American church can be divided into BK and AK; that is, before King and after King.[82]

Where some scholars might be reluctant to give credence to a rhetorical and literary device such as the jeremiad, it has nevertheless functioned as much as a historical and political instrument in American politics as a theological one, particularly as it could be variously used to perpetuate, for instance, the Anglo-Saxon Protestant cultural status quo or to oppositionally speak truth to power as many African American political elites attempted across several centuries. Michael Eric Dyson adds,

> The centrality of Christianity in African-American culture means that the moral character of black protest against racism has oscillated between reformist and revolutionary models of racial transformation. . . . Black Christian reformist approaches to racial transformation have embraced liberal notions of the importance of social stability and the legitimacy of the state. Black Christian reformist leaders have sought to shape religious resistance to oppression, inequality, and injustice around styles of rational dissent that reinforce a stable political order.[83]

Yet African American participation in the Conscientious Public Forum of persuasion and voluntary acceptance of the antiracist moralist views that they have conveyed therein have not been altogether Christian—as the post–World War I fashion of urban and cosmopolitan agnosticism and the emergence of "Black Islam" reveal—and, while they have sought its moral reform, African American religionists have readily understood that there were major moral limitations in the state. Indeed, African American elites have used the jeremiadic tradition of social criticism in the Conscientious Public Forum as a means to the end of persuading the American public, the electorate, and citizenry to engage and persuade elected and appointed political elites to take action in the Civic Public Forum of laws and public policy.

According to Moses, "Uncle Tom" became synonymous with race betrayal during the height of the Garvey era after World War I.[84] At that juncture, which Gayraud Wilmore identifies as parcel to the "deradicalization of the Black church" (more accurately, the "Negro church"), the church failed to engage in political movements *as Black Christians*. In its place emerged the northern urban cults out of which the Nation of Islam was founded in 1930.

The "pie-in-the-sky" orientation of the "otherworldly" political theology served as the distinctive criticism of Malcolm X and his attacks on King and other Christian leaders—African American and white. But King was on the front line of the Civic Public Forum, while Malcolm X—in the Nation of Islam—engaged in persuasion in the rhetoric of the Conscientious Public Forum. Barbara McGraw holds that any orientation in religion and politics must adhere to the "first moral principle" of the Conscientious Public Forum, in which "each individual has a duty to move beyond one's own wants and desires, and to broaden one's sights to the 'universal' or, if one prefers, the whole collective . . . and try to reflect on and discern through conscience (however conceived) what it is that promotes the good for society within the context of the Public Forum of America's Sacred Ground." More pertinently, the "second moral precept" which she emphasizes is that "each individual has a conscientious moral obligation to do one's best to contribute, within the context of America's Sacred Ground, to the development of a good society. This is done not only through one's own speech and action, but by listening sufficiently to 'take in' and understand the views of others, so that conscience is informed and the good can be revealed and confirmed."[85]

If the otherworldly orientation of African American religion minimizes the moral force that McGraw demands in America's Sacred Ground, the social justice orientation is consonant with its recognition, vis-à-vis Locke, of a right to revolution. The social justice or liberationist theology in African American religion also meets the participatory tests in the Conscientious Public Forum because it is has been consistent with the duty to engage the public and political elites in reform efforts to protect civil rights. Where the otherworldly orientation is criticized for its apolitical essence, the social justice orientation was rejected by the majority of African Americans because of its advocacy of violence as a means to liberty. However, McGraw allows for this because the violation of an individual's sacred rights "rather than effecting peace, such attempts result in civil unrest as the people rise up to oppose their oppressors, and the authorities rush to quell the dissidents to restore the imposed unity, leading again to more civil uprisings until there is either revolution—or complete totalitarian suppression."[86] Although violence is not preferred as a first option in America's Sacred Ground, McGraw after all, sees King as the most noteworthy African American practitioner of America's Sacred Ground. Nevertheless, she concedes not only a "political motivation for rebellion, but a religious impetus to revolution—a 'Revolutionary revival,' and that impulse had Locke woven into the very fabric of the revolutionary spirit."[87] The right to rebel, according to McGraw, derives "from this initial theological premise: There is God who created human beings free and equal."[88] When individuals sense injustice imposed by arbitrary "overarching worldviews," they have an inalienable right, through conscience—which is the voice of God—to revolution.

The persistence of the Nation of Islam in African American religious and political history, through Malcolm X, deeply influenced the Black Power feelings of young activists in the 1960s in such a way that even "Black Power" implicated a larger frustration with the failure of the African American churches to develop of "culture of doing politics," independent of King's brief interregnum.

Religion is integral to understanding Black politics even though Black politics has undergone a fundamental process of secularization commencing at the turn of the twentieth century and culminating in the 1960s Black Power phase of the African American liberation struggle. Yet this statement is not intended to overstate the "secular" quality of "Black Power," precisely because its main target was Martin Luther King Jr. and the Southern Christian Leadership Conference (SCLC), which had dominated the Civil Rights Movement, and its primary inspiration was Malcolm X. The failure to appreciate the fundamental religious stimulus, even to Black Power, is to ignore the primary instrument of social protest among African Americans in Black protest discourse. Malcolm X tapped the prophetic ethos that David Walker made attractive to Black Bostonians in the nineteenth-century protest discourses.

Despite valiant efforts among Black intellectuals and theologians such as James Cone in the "Black Theology" movement of the 1960s and 1970s, the African American church—while still the critical institution in African American life—has largely abandoned the prophetic role of speaking truth to power, and has once again reverted to its priestly duties of "preaching to the choir." Here Jesse Jackson has little remaining moral credibility, and T. D. Jakes's charisma has become substitute for critical prophetic discourse in the Conscientious Public Forum, while in too many areas of life, African Americans—especially the youth in the cities—languish in a despair that perhaps only their slave ancestors could appreciate.

Today the largest segment of Orthodox Muslims in the United States is made up of African Americans, and the advent of the 1995 Million Man March—with its controversial but important leader, Louis Farrakhan, having expanded his influence in Black politics—further highlights the fundamental weakness of post–Civil Rights and Black Power African American Christianity, which is either a lack of will or ability to speak in the Public Forum to the African American existential predicament from the vantage point of radical Black Christianity epitomized by David Walker and Martin Luther King Jr. Should the pendulum swing back to some massive, "ground-up" effort as it has only episodically, then the participatory vision that Barbara McGraw poses bodes well for African American religion and political life. If, as McGraw insists, it makes claims to rediscovering America's Sacred Ground, the vision will also be important for the practitioners of African American religion to rediscover the roots of Black radical Christianity. Those roots patently ignored the facile notion that religion, in the Conscientious Public Forum, should be separate from political discourse in the Civic Public Forum.

Chapter 9

The Hindu Tree on America's Sacred Ground

Anantanand Rambachan

INTRODUCTION: THE HINDU WORLDVIEW

Hinduism is an astoundingly diverse tradition, as indicated by the name "Hindu" itself. Hindu is not the personal name of a founder nor is it descriptive of a central belief or practice. "Hindu" is the Iranian variation for a name of a river that Indo-Europeans referred to as the Sindhu, Greeks as the Indos, and British as the Indus. Those who lived on the territory drained by the Indus were derivatively called Hindus. They did not necessarily share a uniform religious culture, and today the Hindu tradition reflects the astonishing variation in geography, language, and culture across the Indian subcontinent. It helps to think of Hinduism as a large, ancient, and extended family, recognizable through common features, but also reflecting the uniqueness of its individual members. Necessary generalizations will not be misleading if there is attentiveness to this fact of diversity.

The Significance of the Vedas

Many of the common features of the Hindu tradition are derived from the scriptures known as the Vedas. The four Vedas (Rig, Sama, Yajur, and Atharva) are considered by orthodox Hindus as revelation and have a privileged authoritative status. Particular Hindu groups regard many other texts as revelation, but the Vedas enjoy an almost unanimous recognition as revealed knowledge. Each Veda may be broadly divided into two sections. The first section of each text provides information and rules for the performance of religious rituals. The last section of each text contains a series of dialogues known as the Upanishads, which are the most important sources of religious and philosophical thinking in Hinduism. Any Hindu tradition that seeks the stamp of orthodoxy tries to establish, through commentaries, that its interpretations are faithful to the Upanishads.

The Four Goals of Human Existence

Contrary to popular stereotypes, the Hindu tradition is neither life-denying nor otherworldly. It does not uphold the attainment and enjoyment of material things as life's highest end, but has acknowledged their significance in the scheme of human existence. Wealth (*artha*) and pleasure (*kama*) are among the four legitimate goals of life. While affirming these, Hinduism also reminds us of their transience and inability to fully satisfy us.

Wealth and pleasure must be sought by being responsive to the demands of the third goal, referred to as *dharma*. *Dharma* derives its meaning from the fact that every human being is inseparably connected with and dependent on other human beings as well as nonhuman realities. The goal of *dharma* requires attentiveness to the well-being of the whole, even as human beings are nourished and sustained by it. *Dharma* is violated when human beings obsessively and narrowly pursue private desires that destroy the harmony of the community on which human lives depend. Noninjury (*ahimsa*) is regarded as the highest expression of *dharma*.

While the Hindu tradition ascribes great value to the practice of *dharma*, it does not see this as the ultimate goal of human existence. Hinduism's highest and most valued goal is *moksha*. The Sanskrit term *moksha* means freedom, and keeping in mind the diversity of Hinduism, it is not inaccurate to say that this freedom is primarily from ignorance (*avidya*). It is a common view in the Hindu tradition that ignorance of the true nature of the human self (*atman*) and God (*brahman*) is the fundamental human problem and the underlying cause of suffering. Freedom or liberation cannot be obtained without right knowledge of reality.

For three of the great theologians and traditions of Hinduism, Shankara (Non-dualism—Advaita), Ramanuja (Qualified Non-dualism—Vishishtadvaita), and Madhva (Dualism—Dvaita), the self (*atman*) cannot be equated fully with the time-bound physical body or the ever-changing mind. In its essential nature, the self is eternal. Consciousness and bliss constitute its essence. For Shankara, the self is ultimately identical with *brahman* (the Ultimate "One"); for Ramanuja, it is inseparably related to *brahman* as part to whole, while for Madhva, it is entirely different from but completely dependent on *brahman*.

The Doctrines of *Karma* and *Samsara*

Ignorant of the true nature of the self, one wrongly identifies it with the body and mind, imposes the limitations of these on the self and becomes subject to greed and want. To obtain the objects of desire, one puts forth actions (*karma*) of various kinds. Desire-prompted actions generate results for which the performer of actions is responsible and which lead to subsequent rebirths in order to experience the consequences of these actions. All traditions of Hinduism adhere firmly to a belief in the doctrine of *karma* as a law of cause and effect that includes the moral dimensions of human life.

The belief in a cycle of multiple births and deaths, referred to as *samsara*, is intrinsically related to the doctrine of *karma*. The latter affirms that every volitional action produces a result that is determined by the nature of the action and the motive that underlies it. Because of the cycle of multiple births, it is readily conceivable that a storehouse of the effects of previous actions exists that cannot be exhausted in a single lifetime. Future births are thus necessitated for the purpose of experiencing the desirable and undesirable consequences of past and present lives and for the attainment of unfulfilled desires. In these future lives, the effects of new actions are added to the storehouse of *karma*, and the cycle of *samsara* is perpetuated.

Moksha is consequent upon the right understanding of the nature of the self. While, as noted above, the self is understood differently within the tradition, *moksha*, in all cases, implies the recognition of the self to be more than the psychophysical apparatus and to be immortal. Such an understanding of the self's essential nature brings an end to the cycle of birth, death, and rebirth. For Shankara, liberation is possible while the individual is alive in the body. When one knows the self, one ceases to equate the self with the body and is free. For Ramanuja, on the other hand, the self can never recover its innate purity as long as it remains associated with the body. Freedom must await the death of the body. For all traditions of Hinduism, *moksha* implies freedom from suffering, greed, and mortality.

HINDUISM IN THE UNITED STATES

The year 1965 marked a turning point in the history of Hinduism in the United States. The Immigration Act of 1965, initiated by President John F. Kennedy and signed into law by President Lyndon B. Johnson at a ceremony at the foot of the Statue of Liberty, eliminated national origins quotas and made it possible for significant numbers of Asians and other non-Europeans to take the first steps to becoming U.S. citizens.

The Restriction of Asian Immigration

Prior to 1965, it is estimated that Indian immigrants to the United States numbered less than fifteen thousand. Many of these were farmers from the Punjab who first settled in British Columbia, Canada, in the late nineteenth and early twentieth centuries. Some of these then migrated south into the states of Washington, Oregon, and California. In 1923, the U.S. Supreme Court ruled that Hindus could not be citizens of the U.S. "Hindu," as Diana Eck, points out, was interpreted as a racial and not a religious category.[1] The case that resulted in this ruling involved an application for U.S. citizenship by Bhagat Singh Thind, a Sikh settled in Canada. The court argued that Hindus were not "free white persons" under the law and, therefore, not entitled to citizenship. A federal law of 1790 permitted only white immigrants to become naturalized citizens. The Immigration Act of 1924 established a national origins quota system and excluded Indians, along with immigrants from China, Korea, and Japan, from entering the United States.

The Influx of Hindu Immigrants

While the Immigration Act of 1965 was restrictive in the sense that it gave priority to immigrants with professional skills, the influx of Indian immigrants to the United States was significant. The 1980 census listed 387,223 "Asian Indians" as permanent residents. In the 1990 census, this number had climbed to around 1.7 million. The estimated Hindu population in the United States is now 930,000.[2] As a consequence of the restrictive immigration policy, they constitute a distinct group, "with a higher proportion of educated and skilled individuals than Indian populations elsewhere in the world."[3] Hindus are concentrated largely in the metropolitan areas of New York, New Jersey, Illinois, Texas, and California, although there are few urban areas without a Hindu presence. It is estimated that approximately 40 percent of Indian immigrants in the United States come from Gujarat and about 20 percent from the Punjab. Following these are immigrants from the Hindi-speaking states of north and central India: Tamils, Telugus, Keralites, and Bengalis.[4]

The Transcendentalists and Swami Vivekananda

While the arrival of Indian immigrants to the United States after the passage of the Immigration Act of 1965 significantly hastened the growth of Hinduism, these were not the first to cultivate the seeds of Hinduism on American soil. The credit for this must go to the New England Transcendentalists, and, in particular to Ralph Waldo Emerson and Henry David Thoreau. They encountered Hinduism through sacred texts like the *Bhagavadgita* and the Upanishads and were attracted to its nonexclusive character and its vision of a single reality underlying all phenomena. The writings of Emerson and Thoreau created a climate of interest and familiarity with strands of Hindu thought for Swami Vivekananda, who arrived in the United States in 1893 to speak at the World's Parliament of Religions, held in conjunction with the Chicago World's Fair. Vivekananda's impact at the Parliament was memorable, and it was followed by two years of intense lecturing along the eastern and western coasts of the United States, but also in cities like Minneapolis, Des Moines, Detroit, and Memphis. He established branches of the America's first Hindu organization, the Vedanta Society, in New York (1894) and San Francisco (1899).

Today, with over seven hundred temples and centers, Hinduism has become a visible part of America's sacred geography. The tradition continues to reflect the rich diversity of doctrine and practice that are associated with its history and development in India. Prominent among its faces are those who follow the path of Advaita (nonduality), the disciplines of Yoga and meditation, or one of the dualistic, devotional strands of Hinduism emphasizing love (*bhakti*) of God and a life of surrender and service.[5] As the tree of Hinduism secures its roots on America's sacred soil, it will be nourished, challenged, and transformed by the elements of this soil, while enriching this soil with its unique gifts and insights.

THE RELATIONSHIP BETWEEN CIVIC AND THEOLOGICAL PLURALISM

Civic Pluralism and Theological Exclusivism: The Paradox of American History

At the heart of what Barbara A. McGraw refers to as America's Sacred Ground, the core values and ideas sustaining the American political system, is the embrace of pluralism. Pluralism implies encouraging and valuing a diversity of expressions in the Public Forum, an approach, as McGraw notes, endorsed by the founders. This includes the diversity of religious expressions.

The necessity for pluralism as a shared and unifying value is even more important today in the light of America's unmatched diversity of cultures, religions, and traditions. One of the interesting paradoxes of American history, as Eck rightly notes, is the fact that the "positive civic view of pluralism clashes directly with the negative religious views of pluralism held by some conservative Christians."[6] While the protection of freedom of conscience by the U.S. Constitution has secured pluralism in the religious sphere, it is quite likely that pluralism, political and religious, is better guaranteed when a philosophy of political pluralism is complemented by a theology of religious pluralism. A theology of religious pluralism checks the tendency and temptation on the part of religious exclusivists to see the state as instrument for enforcing a particular religious doctrine and limits the desire of a state to use a particular religion to sanction its edicts. It may act as an antidote to what McGraw characterizes as a top-down system in which a religious institution attempts to use the power and agencies of the state to enforce its doctrine. In a top-down system, the state seeks its legitimacy from religion through the enforcement of religious dogma.

Pluralism as an Expression of the Human Condition

Unlike the Christian tradition, which in many cases is theologically exclusivist in orientation, Hinduism has developed approaches and insights that are essentially pluralistic in character and which complement and are congenial to America's value for pluralism in the political sphere.[7] This is the consequence of the antiquity and interaction among India's diverse religious and cultural traditions. Hindu justifications for pluralism are articulated largely with reference to religious and philosophical diversity. As will be seen, however, the arguments that are employed by the tradition are also applicable to the political sphere. Pluralism, as a key value in America's Sacred Ground, will find considerable justification and support from Hinduism.

The different Hindu philosophical systems are referred to as *darshanas* (literally, ways of seeing). These different ways of seeing express temporal, spatial, and cultural locations as well as identities, individually, and as members of groups. Plurality, in other words, is a natural expression of the human condition and needs to be accepted as such. The classic metaphor of the five blind men who touched various parts of an elephant and described it differently describes well this human reality. One touched the tail and described the elephant as giant broom, while another touched the leg and described the elephant as a pillar, and so on. Each advanced a reasonable description of the elephant, but each was limited by the partiality and specificity of his window of experience.

Pluralism and the Limits of Language

Along with arguments for pluralism rooted in the diversity of human nature and locations, Hindu traditions have also called attention to the limits of human language. Admittedly, the concern with the limits of language has been articulated with particular reference to the naming and defining of God. God is always more than can be defined, described, or understood with humans' finite minds: descriptions will, of necessity, be plural. This is the point of the often-quoted Rig Veda (1.64.46) sentence, "The Real (sat) is one, but sages name it variously." The text is a comment on the finitude of all human language in relation to the absolute. In trying to describe it, language will be plural, since the absolute exceeds all descriptions. Each word formula is inadequate and reflects the historical and cultural conditions under which it occurs. The consequence is an epistemological and philosophical humility expressing itself in a theology of pluralism that can accommodate different views about God. This approach is consistent with freedom of conscience, which was so important to both John Locke and the founders and therefore central to America's Sacred Ground.

The acknowledgment of the limits of language and the relativity of the human condition preclude any Hindu claim to the ownership of truth in its fullness and finality. While firmly rooted in the view that the universe has its source and being in the One, which the Upanishads refer to as *brahman*, the tradition has consistently admitted that this One transcends all limited human efforts at definition and description.[8] The Taittiriya Upanishad (2.9.1) speaks of *brahman* as "that from which all words, along with the mind, turn back, having failed to grasp." The Kena Upanishad (2:3) expresses the impossibility of comprehending the infinite as one does a limited object by delighting in the language of paradox: "It is known to him to whom It is unknown; he does not know It to whom It is Known. It is unknown to those who know well, and known to those who do not know."

The point of such texts is not to demean human language or to negate its value, but to remind people of its limits and of their limits in relation to God. A God whose nature and essence could be fully revealed in human words, or who could be contained within the boundaries of people's minds, would not be the One proclaimed in our traditions. This recognition of the intrinsic human limitation in attaining or formulating a complete knowledge of God means that no intellectual, theological, or iconic representation is ever full and final. Each struggles to grasp and express that which is ultimately inexpressible, and each attempt reflects and is influenced by the cultural and historical conditions under which it occurs. The various traditions are *darshanas*, ways of seeing and understanding, but in relation to the limitlessness of the One, the fullness of knowledge cannot be claimed.

Pluralism and Openness to the Value of Diverse Expressions

If it is impossible to confine the One within the boundaries of religion or to represent it entirely through the language of its theologies, human beings must be open to the possibility of meaningful insights from others that may open their hearts and minds to the inexhaustible and multifaceted nature of the divine. The confession of the limits of human understanding and language provide a powerful justification for a pluralistic outlook and for relationships of humility and reverence with people of other traditions. Religious exclusivism and arrogance are the consequence of thinking that one has a privileged relationship with God. It is the outcome of limiting God to one's community, sacred text, and place of worship.

Hindu theories are often accused, with some justification, of failing to distinguish between one revelation and another and of overlooking the significance of religious differences. While there is some truth to this charge, it is not a necessary outcome of the Hindu approach. Take, for example, the previously quoted text from the Rig Veda (1.64.46), "The Real (*sat*) is one, but sages name it variously." This text is sometimes employed to explain away doctrinal differences as merely semantic ones. The text does offer the suggestion that religions speak differently even as they speak of the One, but does not conclude that the different ways in which people speak about the One are insignificant. It does not also mean that all ways of speaking about the One are equally true and valid or that the ways that people speak make no difference. Surely, the ways in which people speak about the absolute are important since these not only reveal their understanding of its nature but also form the basis for their lives in the world.

The point of the Rig Veda text is not to gloss over doctrinal differences. Rather, it offers a far richer insight for pluralism. The text may be read as a comment on the limitations and finitude of all human language in relation to the One. Human discourse about God will inevitably be multiple since God exceeds anything that can be said about God. While doctrine and discourse are not redundant, any discourse about the divine should not be absolutized, and language or other symbols should not be confused with the reality to which these point.

Pluralism and One God "However Understood"

The one Hindu doctrine that perhaps best expresses its approach to pluralism and relates to Locke's idea of the one God understood differently is the Hindu teaching on the *ishtadeva*. *Ishtadeva* is Sanskrit for "chosen God," and implies a context in which God-choices are available. From among these, a person chooses one that becomes her or his *ishtadeva*. The most popular *ishtadevas*, today, include Shiva, Vishnu—especially one of Vishnu's human incarnations like Rama and Krishna—and the Goddess in one of her many forms such as Durga or Kali. There is no doubt that at times in the history of Hinduism, the various *ishtadevas* were perceived as different and competing gods and their worshipers as rival communities. Many of the myths connected with Vishnu or Shiva, for example, aim to verify the superiority of one over the other and there are still traditions within Hinduism in which such rivalry persists and one *ishtadeva* is subordinated to another. Although it may be impossible to trace the history of the *ishtadeva* doctrine in Hinduism, it seems to this author that the doctrine is precisely a response to such exclusive and sectarian claims and rivalries about the true God. Although it is possible to subscribe to the doctrine of the *ishtadeva* while admitting some measure of reality to other gods and subordinating these to one's own, this violates the intent and spirit that underlies the teaching.

The historical context of the doctrine, as already noted, is the existence of diverse cultural and religious communities with their own distinctive images, liturgies, and theologies. As these communities interacted, understood better each other's claims, and were enriched by the influence of the other, there was a movement from exclusive viewpoints which rejected the God of the other as false or which hierarchically subordinated the other's God to one's own. The *ishtadeva* doctrine, in fact, implies a rejection of the real existence of many gods and affirms the reality of the One.[9] At the same time, the doctrine presupposes that this One is imagined, named, and worshiped in different ways and that human beings are choosing from among the many names and images of the One.

From the *ishtadeva* perspective, there are not literally many Gods in the universe. The world does not have room for Christian, Hindu, and Muslim gods, but it certainly has room for multiple understandings of the nature of God as envisaged in these traditions. *Ishtadeva* points to a diversity of human conceptions of God while denying multiple divinities. It helps to think of the person in another religious tradition, not as a stranger with an alien deity, but as a fellow human being whose God is our God. While such an attitude may be found today among some descendants of the Abrahamic traditions, it is yet to be extended, in any significant way, to people of other faiths. The God worshiped in Hindu temples and homes is rarely thought of as identical with the God honored in churches, synagogues, and mosques.

Pluralism and Humility in the Religious and Civic Spheres

Hindu arguments for religious pluralism are, in the main, epistemological, and these can easily be incorporated into a more comprehensive doctrine, justifying the necessity and value of a variety of expressions in the Public Forum. Hindu arguments about the spatial, temporal, and cultural limits of the human condition and about the limitations of language have relevance for debates and discussions in the civic sphere in America. McGraw calls attention to the problematic contemporary polarization of political discourse in the United States and the division of the nation into two competing camps. Winning votes and attaining power are more important than "the pursuit of the good society." Hinduism espouses an epistemological and philosophical humility that is antithetical to the privileging of a single viewpoint, religious or political, and recognizes the enrichment that diversity affords. The desire for religious or political hegemony and homogeneity is not in accord with America's Sacred Ground or the foundations of the Hindu worldview.

SACRED PERSON AND SACRED GROUND

The Principle of Equal Dignity and the Equal Presence of the Divine

Pluralism, as a cornerstone of America's Sacred Ground, and as embodying a belief in the value of multiple voices and perspectives, finds its justification in freedom of conscience and expression and in equal dignity and equal justice. These are among the core principles of America's Sacred Ground identified by McGraw. In the case of the Hindu tradition, the inherent worth of the individual human person proceeds from the belief that each one embodies the infinite divine spirit (*brahman*). The various traditions of Hinduism have characterized the relationship between the divine spirit and the human self (*atman*) in various ways, dependent on their philosophical standpoints. The nondualists (*Advaitins*) speak of the ultimate identity of the two, the qualified nondualists (*Vishishtadvaitins*) describe the relationship as one of inseparability and not identity, and the dualists (*Dvaitins*) understand the soul to be different from but under the control of God. All of them agree, however, on the fact that the divine exists equally and identically in all beings. As the *Bhagavadgita* (13:27) puts it:

> One who sees the supreme Lord,
> Existing alike in all beings,
> Not perishing when they perish,
> Truly sees.[10]

The profound significance that the Hindu accords to this truth may be appreciated from the fact that its discernment is equated with liberation (*moksha*), the highest goal of human existence. The divine, in Hinduism, does not have to be mediated by religious institutions or elites. The religious challenge in Hinduism is not one of bridging a spatial or temporal distance between oneself and God. Whether people know it or not, they exist in and are inseparable from God. Human beings are not spatially, but epistemologically distant from God, and this distance is bridged by an awakening in the human mind and heart to the reality of God here and now.

Hinduism's Accord with the "Ground–Up" System of America's Sacred Ground

This Hindu approach is much closer to the "ground-up" system of America's Sacred Ground and quite different from the top-down system opposed by the founders, where access to God is made possible through authoritative individuals and structures. God, in Hinduism, is discovered directly in the heart of each human being, and the enlightened conscience (*atmasantosha*) is an important source of ethical values.[11]

The human problem, in relation to the divine, is described as one of ignorance (*avidya*), similar to a form of blindness that prevents people from seeing what is right before their eyes. *Moksha* is awakening to the identical presence of the divine in oneself and in all beings and the transformation of life that follows from this awakening. The *Bhagavadgita* (18:20) commends the wisdom that enables a person to see, "one imperishable Being in all beings, undivided in separate beings." This vision does not call upon people to ignore or deny the uniqueness of individuals and communities, but to perceive the unity that underlies all and to realize the value of each one that flows from it. One cannot profess value for the divine and despise the multiplicity of beings into which the divine has willingly entered.

The Principle of Equal Justice and the Equal Presence of the Divine

While the social and political implications of this truth are not detailed in the classical texts, the requirements are unmistakable. When the implications for human relationships are enunciated, these are done in terms of equality. As the *Bhagavadgita* (5:19) states it:

> Even here on earth, those whose minds are impartial overcome rebirth. God is perfect and the same in all. Therefore, they always abide in God.[12]

Justice, understood as equality of treatment and a principle of the Public Forum, is a consequence of the equal presence of the divine and is a condition for liberation and oneness with God.

The Law of No Harm and Ahimsa

The Hindu doctrine of the unity of existence through the divine, and in the sacredness of all life that expresses the divine, is the foundation of its cardinal ethical principle, *ahimsa* (noninjury), which may be equated with the law of no harm in the Civic Public Forum. Belief in divine immanence requires the demonstration of reverence and consideration for life in all its forms and the avoidance of injury. In his understanding and interpretation of the meaning of *ahimsa*, Gandhi explained that in its negative form it means abstention from injury to living beings. In its positive form, *ahimsa* means love and compassion for all. For Gandhi, *ahimsa* also implies justice toward everyone and abstention from exploitation in any form. "No man," claimed Gandhi, "could be actively non-violent and not rise against social injustice no matter where it occurred."[13] *Ahimsa*, if construed positively, would be read as a respect for the life, liberty and property of others. Equality will flow from the social and political application of the doctrine of divine equality.

The Law of Consistency and the Identity of Self

The divine is identified, especially in the nondual tradition of Hinduism (*Advaita*) as the ground of human selfhood, and the divine (*brahman*) is spoken of as nondifferent from the human self (*atman*) in its most fundamental nature. With this ultimate identity in mind, scriptural texts speak interchangeably of seeing the self (*atman*) in all beings and/or seeing the divine (*brahman*) in all beings.[14] Isa Upanishad (6), for example, reminds us that the wise person who sees all beings in the self and sees the self in all beings is liberated from hate. The *Bhagavadgita* (12:13) puts this same point positively and describes such a person, not only as free from hate, but as friendly and compassionate to all. The Hindu ideal of seeing all beings in one's own self and one's self in all beings ought not to be interpreted passively. It is, at heart, a call to learn to enter compassionately into the lives of others, seeing through their eyes, sharing their emotions, understanding their thoughts and responding to their needs. It is identifying with others in joy and in sorrow and learning to own their pleasures and pains as one's own. The ethical implication is faithfulness to the law of consistency in the Civic Public Forum expressed in the Mahabharata teaching, "Do nothing to others which, if done to you would cause you pain; this is the sum of duty."

Liberation and the Conscientious Public Forum Duties to Raise Consciousness and Participate in the Public Forum

The knowledge of oneness, the indivisibility of the self, properly understood, leads to a deeper identity and affinity with all, which is faithful to the Conscientious Public Forum's duty to raise consciousness to the divine, the universal. Liberation in Hinduism does not alienate, isolate, or separate one from the community of other beings, but it awakens one to the truth of life's unity and interrelatedness. The value which one discovers for oneself when one understands one's true nature as nondifferent from *brahman* is a value that extends to and includes all beings.

In the *Bhagavadgita*, the discussion on the identity of the self is followed by a verse (6:32) which praises the highest *yogi* as the one who, because of knowing the truth of the self, owns the pain and suffering of others as his own. If the knowledge of the identity of the self in all leads to seeing the suffering of another as one's own, undertaking actions for the alleviation of suffering, whenever possible, becomes a necessary outcome. Seeing the suffering of the other as one's own suffering becomes rather meaningless if this important truth does not instigate action to help the other.

The vision of the one self in all beings makes it possible to identify with others beyond the boundaries of nationality, ethnicity, tribe, religion, and culture, to share suffering and rejoice in prosperity. It challenges attitudes of uncaring indifference toward the suffering of others with whom people do not normally identify because of traditional boundaries of the kinds mentioned above. It enables people to see living beings as constituting a single community and provides a philosophical basis for a compassionate and inclusive community where the worth and dignity of every human being is affirmed and where justice, at all levels, is sought.

This leads to fulfillment of the Conscientious Public Forum duty to participate. The *Bhagavadgita* (3:20) holds before us the ideal of *lokasangraha,* or action, that is motivated by compassion to build a good society. This is the highest human motivation and one which, in the words of the text, can summon as much energy, commitment, and dedication as action intended for personal benefit.

> Even as the unwise act with personal attachment, so should the wise act, without personal attachment, desiring the good of the world.[15]

The *Bhagavadgita* puts such great emphasis on voluntary action for the good of society that it provides a new and brilliant definition of the meaning of renunciation and the renunciant. In traditional understanding, the renunciant was one who relinquished social and family obligations in favor of pursuing personal liberation. The *Bhagavadgita* (6.1), however, redefines the renunciant as the person who unselfishly fulfills obligations to society and family and not the one who abandons these. The heart of being religious, in other words, is not inactivity, but engagement in action for the good of others. It is cooperative action to build what McGraw refers to as "communities of conscience."

TRANSFORMING AND BEING TRANSFORMED

While the core values underlying America's Sacred Ground will be enriched by the unique insights and arguments of the Hindu tradition about pluralism and human dignity, it is also clear that the tradition will be challenged and transformed by the ingredients of American soil. A distinctively American expression of Hinduism, consistent with the central ideas of America's Sacred Ground, will emerge.

The Top-Down Reality of Hindu Society: Caste and Gender Injustice

The Hindu tradition, as noted above, offers a profound theological justification for equal dignity and justice rooted in the teaching about the equality and inclusivity of God's presence. The perception of the divine as the self (*atman*) of all helps people to understand that harm to another is harm to one's own self.[16] Although Hinduism, as noted before, offers a theology that is close to the ground-up approach of the founders, its potential for an all-encompassing idea of equality and justice was constrained in India by a hierarchical ordering of society into the *varna* or caste system, that unequally distributed rights and privileges. In this system, rights are not universally specified, but are determined on the basis of caste, station in life (*ashrama*), and gender. The integration of caste and life stages is referred to as *varnashramadharma*.[17]

Whatever might have been its historical origin or intent, the caste system developed into a hierarchical and unequal ordering of society into four groups, differentiated on the basis of ritual purity and occupation. At the top of the social order are the *brahmins*, who are the teachers, priests, and custodians of the sacred knowledge. Following the *brahmins* are the *ksatriyas*, who are the warriors and political leaders, defenders of the community and guarantors of political order and stability. Next comes the *vaishyas*, who are the merchants and farmers, the generators and distributors of wealth, and the *shudras*, who are the laborers and servants of all others. The first three castes are referred to as the *dvijas* (twice-born), since they alone are entitled to the rite of initiation (*upanayana*) that is a prerequisite to traditional study of the Vedas. The system also led to the creation of a large group of outcastes or untouchables who were considered ritually impure and denied all privileges and rights belonging to members of the caste order.

Caste was justified on the basis of the doctrine of *karma*. The argument was that better karma in past lives leads to rebirth in a higher caste. Since caste limited occupational choices, marriage, and social relationships on the basis of birth, it was the antithesis of the notion of freedom and equality. Manu (ca. 200 B.C.E.–100 C.E.), ancient India's influential lawgiver, in his *Manava Dharma Shastra* (Treatise on Human Duties), specifies the occupations appropriate to each caste as divinely ordained.

> But in order to protect this universe He, the most resplendent one, assigned separate (duties and) occupations to those who sprang from his mouth, arms, thighs and feet. To brahmans, he assigned teaching and studying (the Veda), sacrificing for their own benefit and for others, giving and accepting (of alms). The ksatriya he commanded to protect the people, to bestow gifts, to offer sacrifices, to study (the Veda), and to abstain from attaching himself to sensual pleasures. The vaisya to tend cattle, to bestow gifts, to offer sacrifices, to study (the Veda), to trade, to lend money, and to cultivate land. One occupation only the lord prescribed to the sudra, to serve meekly even these (other) three (varnas).[18]

Duties and rights were also prescribed on the basis of gender differences. Manu treats women as constituting a group of their own, and they are not to be accorded the same privileges as males. In lawsuits, for example, they are entitled to give evidence only on behalf of other women.

> Women should give evidence for women, and for twice-born men (of the) same kind, virtuous sudras for sudras and men of the lowest (varna) for the lowest.[19]

Men do not owe women the same moral obligations as they do other men. Manu minimizes the outcome of a false oath made to a woman.

> Let no man swear an oath falsely, even in a trifling matter; for he who swears an oath falsely is thus lost in this (world) and after death. No crime, causing loss of caste is committed by swearing (falsely) to women, the objects of one's desire, at marriages, for the sake of fodder for a cow, or of fuel and in (order to show) favour to a Brahmana.[20]

Examples can be multiplied, but it is clear that Manu, Hinduism's most famous lawgiver, articulated a doctrine of human inequality contrary to notions of liberty, equal justice, and equal dignity in America's Sacred Ground and in Hinduism's own core teaching. The structure of traditional Hindu society, with its caste and gender biases, privileged males of the upper caste and did not promote or encourage equal participation in public discourse.

The Struggle to Return Hinduism to its Egalitarian Roots

The rise of the Indian nationalist movement in the late nineteenth and early twentieth centuries witnessed a vigorous attempt, especially by Gandhi, to recover and put into practice Hindu teachings about human equality, dignity, and equal justice. Gandhi was concerned, not merely with freedom from British colonial rule, but with overcoming the injustice and inequality perpetrated by Hindus. He refused to accept that the Hindu tradition, at its core, was synonymous with human inequality.

> Birth and the observance of forms cannot determine one's superiority and inferiority. Character is the only determining factor. God did not create men with the badge of superiority or inferiority; no scripture which labels a human being as inferior or untouchable because of his or her birth can command our allegiance, it is a denial of God and Truth, which is God.[21]

Like the American founders, Gandhi identified with the poor and down-trodden. Eck describes him as, "the advance guard of what would later be liberation theology with its 'preferential option for the poor.' "[22] He made the removal of untouchability one of the principal goals of his life and fought against it not only through public speeches, but by undertaking the work of untouchables, sharing meals with them and inviting them to become residents in his community. He brought women out of the seclusion of homes into the forefront of the political struggle, paving the way for their freedom and emancipation.[23]

The concerns of Gandhi and other Indian leaders were reflected in the contents of the Indian constitution, adopted when India became an independent nation in 1947. The Indian constitution actually guarantees more fundamental human rights than the provisions of the American Bill of Rights.[24] Among these are the "Right to Equality," "Right to Freedom," Right Against Exploitation," "Right of Freedom of Religion," "Cultural and Educational Rights," "Right to Property," and "Right to Constitutional Remedies." Special laws, such as the Protection of Civil Rights Act, 1976, have been enacted to give meaning to the constitutional provisions.

The Persisting Legacy of Caste

In spite of such measures, however, the phenomenon of untouchability persists in contemporary India, and Hindus continue to define the meaning of Hindu identity over and against those who are deemed polluting and, for this reason, marginalized. The sharp distinctions between self and other, the boundaries of the pure and impure, are still drawn sharply in Indian villages, where the character of human and economic relationships are still governed by the hierarchies of caste and where reports of violence against persons of lower castes are common. Although the conditions of life in Indian cities are quite different from those in rural areas, cities are not free from the travails of caste and untouchability. In urban areas, discrimination expresses itself in more subtle forms and in limited job choices that push untouchables into menial tasks. In a city like Hardwar, on the banks of the Ganges, physical segregation is evident in the fact that the upper-caste dwellings are closer to the pure water of the river, while the lower castes are relegated, depending on relative degree of purity, to locations farther away from the river.[25] Kancha Ilaiah has commented that the movement from rural to urban locations does not change the socioeconomic relations because of the pervasive character of caste. "We had hoped," writes Ilaiah, "that the decolonized Indian capital would make caste dysfunctional by giving us equal rights in politics, in economic institutions, cultural institutions, educational institutions and administrative institutions. But that has not happened. The migration from rural to urban centers has not changed our socioeconomic relations as caste discrimination has been built into every structure."[26]

In addition, as John Carman rightly notes, the Indian constitution does not ground its rights "in anything, whether in individual human nature, the requirements of human community, or the creative intention of God." He poses the challenge for Hinduism in this crucial question. "Are there features in traditional Indian society that could help prepare for a shift in social values from the duties of those with different social roles to universal rights for all citizens . . .?"[27] Mitra also contends that the struggle for human rights among Hindus "demands not only social reform movements, but also exploration, investigation, and reinterpretation of the theoretical foundations underlying the social hierarchy of Hinduism."[28]

CONCLUSION

The answer to John Carman's critical question is in the affirmative, and this chapter has already identified the theological grounds that will justify the shift to "universal rights for all citizens." The theological vision that guarantees human freedom, equality, and justice will enable the Hindu tradition to continue enriching America's Sacred Ground, a process that started centuries ago with its influence on Ralph Waldo Emerson and Henry David Thoreau. Through the encounter with Hinduism, they both came to a deeper appreciation of religious plurality and the unity of the divine in all things. At the same time, America's Sacred Ground may have the catalytic effect of moving Hinduism more swiftly to affirming those indispensable elements of its worldview that are consistent with the principles of freedom, equal justice, and dignity. It may also enable the tradition to see clearly the inconsistencies between its teaching about the sameness of the divine in all beings and structures of inequality. The doctrine of divine equality, so deeply established at the heart of Hinduism, will become, on America's Sacred Ground, a powerful searchlight illumining and healing exploitative and oppressive structures of Hindu society.

The social and political implications of this Hindu teaching will be vigorously pursued, but the effects of this inquiry will not be limited to the transformation of the tradition in the United States. The American Hindu community has very close ties with the Indian subcontinent. The ease and frequency of travel and communications enhances the possibility that the effects of the transformation of Hinduism in the United States, through engagement with America's Sacred Ground, will have worldwide implications. Even as the theological vision of Hinduism helps to secure America's Sacred Ground, that ground will enable Hinduism to realize with consistent clarity the social and political implications of its vision. The relationship between Hinduism and America's Sacred Ground will be uniquely symbiotic, with enriching fruits for the good of all (*lokasangraha*).

Chapter 10

Staking Out America's Sacred Ground: The Baptist Tradition of Religious Liberty

Derek H. Davis

INTRODUCTION

In her provocative book, *Rediscovering America's Sacred Ground: Public Religion and Pursuit of the Good in a Pluralistic America*, Barbara McGraw explores the founders' intentions regarding the relationship between religion and state, arguing convincingly that the underlying basis of the founders' project is what she calls "America's Sacred Ground." This Sacred Ground, she claims, is the much-needed compass that provides the foundation for analyzing popular and political discourse about public religion and its role in shaping American values. Further, she argues that America's Sacred Ground is the fundamental moral and practical framework that makes open debate possible.

McGraw locates the roots of America's Sacred Ground in the ideas of John Locke, whose views were in turn accepted and expanded by the American founding fathers. In explaining how so few persons today understand the theological dimensions of Locke's project, she wants Americans to rediscover the sacred foundations of the collective political life they all share. McGraw thus argues that all Americans have the right to engage in political discourse and present their views in making contributions to the sociopolitical order, but that none have the right to elevate their ideas and beliefs above others at the level of public policy or lawmaking. She argues that the founders wanted no winners, so to speak, only an open forum for rational argument to take place.

McGraw devises some helpful terminology to advance this idea: the two-tiered Public Forum. The Conscientious Public Forum entertains all ideas and beliefs in public discourse, religious and nonreligious, toward improving the entire democratic order. The Civic Public Forum operates at the level of law, is built on the goal of advancing the common good, and constitutionally prevents favoring the views of any one faction or group. Together these two fora allow for maximum participation in political discourse and prevent stagnation that would ensue if America's Sacred Ground were violated by endorsing some worldviews over others.

This chapter argues that the historic Baptist tradition of religious liberty in America fits squarely within the framework of America's Sacred Ground. The vigorous promotion of religious liberty has been a central tenet of Baptist faith and practice for centuries, and Baptists historically have sought religious freedom not only for themselves but for persons of every faith. Baptists have been on the front lines of combating religious oppression everywhere it occurs, in America and elsewhere. According to traditional Baptist belief, a government that gives preferential treatment to certain religious beliefs breaches the eternal and inalienable rights of each individual, and disobeys the will of God. Governments that establish certain religions, advance mere toleration as opposed to complete religious freedom, advocate the religious life in preference to the nonreligious life, or proscribe the reasonable religious practices of any faith group—in short, inordinately mix church and state— have been consistently opposed by Baptists.

But fidelity to ideas is never easy. Today the commitment of many Baptists to protecting church-state separation, and thus religious liberty, has diminished dramatically. In the belief that secularism is overtaking American culture, some Baptists have increasingly begun to call for moral reform through increased government advancement of religion. This includes more prayer in the public schools, more government dollars spent for religious education, increased government postings of the Ten Commandments and other religious symbols, and more government monies spent to support churches and other religious groups in administering "faith-based" social programs. The sentiment seems to be that America is in trouble morally and that only a loosening of the constitutional prohibitions on government involvement and oversight of religion can stem the tide of moral decline. Thus, today, many Baptists have abandoned the tradition of religious liberty of their forbears and in so doing have lost their footing on America's Sacred Ground, an essential piece of the democratic framework which owes so much to Baptists. Arguably now more than at any other time in America's history, the nation needs the strong voice of the traditional Baptist witness on religious liberty. It is the voice that affirms America's Sacred Ground as that which makes possible the participation of all religious voices in the public square, and it is the voice that embraces the vision of the founding fathers to create a public order with sacred dimensions in which no religious worldview triumphs over others.

Many Baptists mistakenly think that separation of church and state equates to no religion in the public square, and to the enshrinement of secularism as a national policy. But church-state separation and secularism are not one and the same. Secularism contemplates the marginalization of religion, even its elimination. The founding fathers never intended to promote secularism, unlike the leaders of the French Revolution. To the contrary, they sought to structure the nation in such a way that harnesses religion and religious people as the very bond that would ensure the long-term success of the nation. They knew the nation must be made up of a virtuous citizenry to ensure its success, and they looked to religious people and institutions to provide this virtue.[1] The founders never envisioned a society that could succeed without a strong religious makeup. They knew from history, however, the problems and disasters that resulted from government being an advocate of religion, of the potent dangers of inordinately mixing government power with religious zeal. The separation of church and state, in the mind of the founders, was therefore an integral part of preserving America's Sacred Ground.

Many Baptists have opted for a government that is more "hands on" in terms of advancing "family values" and "basic morality" because they are unaware of their heritage. The Baptist tradition affirms separation of church and state as vital to religious integrity, as essential to authentic free exercise without government monitoring or control, as essential to the church's prophetic role in society, and as necessary to protect the religious consciences of persons of all faith traditions. Despite good intentions, these Baptists violate America's Sacred Ground. They see in government the ability to "fix" what they perceive to be wrong with America—a drift toward a culture that embraces godlessness, abortion, homosexuality, sexual immorality, and a host of other concerns. But they go too far. They abuse the Civic Public Forum by using it to achieve their own Christian ends, ignoring other voices that are equally entitled to contribute to the common good. This is one of the ends of church-state separation: to prevent any religious group from achieving dominance in the formulation of law and public policy.

This mistake has not been characteristic of most Baptists throughout American history. It is important, therefore, to review the rich Baptist heritage, beginning in the seventeenth century, to better appreciate and consider the Baptist principle of religious liberty and how it has helped shape America's Sacred Ground, but which is, regrettably, presently under attack. Having presented the tradition of religious liberty as observed by Baptists in America, this chapter then moves to a consideration of those present-day Baptists who lay siege to the principles of the two-tiered public forum of America's Sacred Ground, with emphasis on the error of their ways.

THE BAPTIST HERITAGE OF LIBERTY: AMERICA'S SACRED GROUND ESTABLISHED

> For we do freely profess that our lord the king has no more power over their consciences [Roman Catholics] than over ours, and that is none at all. For our Lord the king is but an earthly king, and he has no authority as a king but in earthly causes. And if the king's people be obedient and true subjects, obeying all human laws made by the king, our lord the king can require no more. For men's religion to God is between God and themselves. The king shall not answer for it. Neither may the king be judge between God and man. Let them be heretics, Turks, Jews, or whatsoever it appertains not to the earthly power to punish them in the least measure. This is made evident to our lord the king by the scriptures.[2]

One of the earliest Baptists, Thomas Helwys, wrote these powerful words in *The Mystery of Iniquity* in 1612. He would be imprisoned that same year by King James I, who refused to tolerate heretical notions such as those expressed by Helwys—that men are answerable only to God for their religious opinions, not to kings. Helwys later died in prison because of his bold pleas for religious liberty for all.[3] Helwys, along with other leading Baptists of the seventeenth century, including John Smyth and Leonard Busher, would become some of the most prominent figures in Baptist history. Within years of Helwys's death, English Baptists would risk the two-month voyage across the tumultuous waters of the Atlantic Ocean in search of a land where true religious liberty might become the standard. These Baptists would perform a leading role in shaping America's experiment in religious liberty. Significantly, though, they sought an equal religious liberty for all, not just for themselves as Baptists. They understood Locke's project before Locke was even born.

Roger Williams

The paramount importance placed on religious liberty in America today is undoubtedly due in part to the bold and enduring religious pilgrimage of Roger Williams. Williams came as a Puritan pastor to Massachusetts in 1631, but was banished in 1635 because of his criticism of the colony's theocratic political order and overt suppression of religious dissenters. Using the Bible, he contested New England's theological justifications for church and state cooperation within the colony. For Williams, Massachusetts had violated the biblical doctrine of soul freedom through its intolerance of religious diversity and convergence of church and state. Williams adamantly objected to mandatory church attendance for all citizens within the colony. In addition, he objected to religious tests for holding public office and to the colony's "Freeman's Oath," which required an oath to God before one could obtain citizenship. He argued that, for non-Christians, such an oath was tantamount to the state's coercion of prayer, and for Christians, it could not be taken since only the kingdom of heaven, not the temporal state, is to be established by oaths to God.[4]

Roger Williams was convinced that the separation of church and state is necessary to ensure that the state performs its essentially secular tasks and the church is free to perform its spiritual tasks. He was America's first separationist, and was clearly far ahead of most political thinkers of his day. His views would closely coincide with one of America's pivotal founders, Thomas Jefferson. Baptist leader J. M. Dawson offered this comparison: "Granted that Williams was concerned to 'free the church from the state while Jefferson thought to free the state from the church,' the views of the two add up to the same thing—separation."[5]

As was common in his day, Williams separated the Ten Commandments into the first table (duties to God) and the second table (duties to fellow man). He did not advocate anarchy and conceded that civil authorities should be empowered to regulate violations of the second table of the Decalogue; however, no civil authority could legalize the first table and regulate or punish offenses against it.[6] To enable civil authorities to regulate matters that were strictly between man and God was an invasion of sacred space. Banished from Massachusetts in 1635, Williams fled to Providence, where he founded the first Baptist church in America. While he remained a Baptist for only a few months, opting instead for a path as a "Seeker," Baptists have never hesitated to adopt him as one of their own since his views on religious liberty and other basic biblical doctrines are so closely aligned.

Williams returned to England almost a decade later to obtain the provisional charter for the Rhode Island colony he had founded in Providence. While in England, Williams penned his grand treatise on religious liberty, *The Bloudy Tenet of Persecution*. The "Bloudy Tenet" represented the failure of human governments to delimit their authority in matters of religious conscience. He passionately argued for the notion of complete religious liberty, demonstrating a "careful history of strife over conformity in Old and New England."[7] This champion of religious liberty threatened the prevailing political structure in both England and Massachusetts, since it was commonly believed that the separation of church and state would lead to the moral degeneration of society and the decline of religion as the glue of society. Many Americans today, some Baptists among them, are suggesting that this concern has come to fruition, thus necessitating a closer union between church and state. Williams, however, more than a half century before Locke's ideas prominently appeared on the scene, was an advocate of a political order that respected equally all religious traditions.

Roger Williams's Rhode Island became a haven for the religiously persecuted. It was not a Christian colony, but a free colony. For Williams, a Christian state, or "Christendom," could not exist; history had demonstrated too many times failed attempts to "wrap the mantle of Christ around everything they said, everything they did."[8] Christianity dealt with each individual's heart and soul, while "Christendom" obviated Christianity and fostered only temporal politics, religious persecution, and coercion.[9] But while Williams would never have erected a Christian state, as a strong advocate of natural law,[10] he would have been a strong proponent of the Sacred Ground concept.

John Clarke

John Clarke accompanied Williams on one of the latter's three trips to England on behalf of the charter for Rhode Island. Having studied law at Cambridge, Clarke was a student of politics and was capable of leading dissenting Baptists in New England in the fight for religious liberty. As Williams's contemporary, Clarke's work coincided and paralleled that of the more famous Williams; both sojourned the separationist road of Baptist life to press for complete religious liberty. Equally disappointed by the level of religious intolerance in Massachusetts, Clarke joined Roger Williams, who assisted Clarke in acquiring a pleasant coastal island to be named Newport. In 1640 he organized and pastored the First Baptist Church of Newport—the second Baptist church in America. He would serve in this capacity for nearly forty years, until his death in 1676.

Clarke's contribution to religious liberty is best depicted in his efforts to secure a permanent charter for all the communities in Rhode Island. Clarke embarked upon the arduous journey to London to petition to deaf ears for his charter. Nevertheless, the fortitude, persistence, and patience of this Baptist minister, doctor of medicine, and political theorist finally paid off in 1663 when Charles II, under the restored monarchy, sanctioned the royal charter.

On the strength of the indefatigable efforts of Clarke, King Charles II granted to Rhode Island a permanent charter, the first such document to ensure religious liberty for English citizens. While religious liberty remained an embryonic idea throughout the other American colonies where Baptists and other dissenters remained persecuted and oppressed, the Rhode Island Baptists, consistent with their religious heritage, continued to plant seeds of religious liberty. They would soon take root in the charters of New Jersey, Carolina, and Pennsylvania and eventually blossom throughout the budding nation. Like Williams, Clarke believed in a political principle of equal religious freedom for all humankind, and a secular state to guarantee it.

Isaac Backus

Over the next century, Baptists, in the wake of the Great Awakening, began to grow and flourish amidst the abundant religious harassment and maltreatment that was still readily apparent in most colonies, Massachusetts in particular. Religious favoritism and preferential treatment were a persistent problem. Consistent with the currents of revolutionary zeal for political and religious liberty, Isaac Backus led Baptists and other nonconformists in a movement to end discriminatory government practices against those who rejected the Puritan creed.

Through tracts, speeches, protests, and petitions, Isaac Backus (1724– 1806) led the charge in pursuit of religious liberty during the tumultuous period of the American Revolution. Backus recognized the importance of church-state separation and freedom of the soul and was anxious to see these ideas advanced in the new nation. Dartmouth historian John Mecklin acknowledged Backus's importance: "Patient, tolerant, wise and brave in the face of institutionalized intolerance and petty persecution, he illustrated, in simple and unpretentious fashion, principles which were later to become embodied in organic law and made the guarantee of our democratic liber- ties."[11] In addition, noted Mecklin, "John Cotton, Cotton Matther, John Wise, and even Jonathan Edwards, belonged to their day and age, but Isaac Backus belongs to every age and to all men who love liberty."[12]

Backus's fight for religious liberty was carried out chiefly with his pen. He has been recognized by many as *the* historian of the early New England Bap- tists. He was convinced that producing a written history would be beneficial to his primary purpose in life, advocating liberty of conscience for Baptists and others. "Through careful, diligent research in Massachusetts, Rhode Island, and Connecticut," wrote Baptist ethicist T. B. Maston, "Backus was able to write a history of New England Baptists that was widely recognized in his day and has been accepted as standard since that time."[13]

Backus was instrumental and successful in facilitating the use of a specific organization to provide a united stance and cooperative approach toward the fight for religious liberty. The Warren Association called Backus to lead its "Grievance Committee" after 1772, in representing its efforts to redress the wrongs done toward Baptists in the New England region. In an effort to seek relief, the task of this committee was to assemble and present to courts and legislators "well-attested" cases of religious persecution. This association made important contributions that correlated with Baptist efforts in the fight for religious liberty. Backus served as their spokesman before the Continen- tal Congress in Philadelphia in 1774.[14]

Lockean ideas of individual liberty were commonly accepted among the people of the day.[15] Backus quoted from Locke often in his tracts written dur- ing the pre-Revolutionary period. This is in all likelihood because Backus found in Locke ideas to help substantiate and advocate his own Baptist beliefs concerning liberty of conscience and separation of church and state.[16] Backus argued that the church is an undeniably important and vital part of civil life. In a letter to George Washington, Backus asserted, "No men are more necessary and useful to human society than faithful religious teachers or ministers."[17] However, in his proposed Bill of Rights for the new Consti- tution of Massachusetts in 1779, Backus wrote:

> Nothing can be true religion but voluntary obedience unto his revealed
> will, of which each rational soul has an equal right to judge for itself;
> every person has an inalienable right to act in all religious affairs accord-
> ing to the full persuasion of his own mind, where others are not injured
> thereby. And civil rulers are so far from having any right to empower any
> persons to judge for others in such affairs . . . under any pretense what-
> soever.[18]

Backus abhorred Massachusetts' use of its power to support one particular
church, clearly a form of "taxation without representation." It was a violation
of religious liberty for Massachusetts to demand either a renunciation of one's
faith or payment of a tax that supported one established church. He deemed
it a "heresy for any men to develop laws to bind others in religious matters,
or to loose any from the laws of Christ in the government of his church."[19]

His proposed language to end the Congregational establishment was not
included in Article III of the 1780 Massachusetts Constitution. Although the
article on establishment was retained and remained in effect until 1833, the
words, writings, and character of Isaac Backus forever symbolized and influenced the Baptist struggle for religious liberty for generations to come and
helped to shape the American tradition of church-state relations.

If Backus is to be criticized, it is perhaps in his belief that the American
order should be infused with a specifically Christian character. True, he was
a vigorous advocate of church-state separation, but as a necessary tool to prevent the elevation of any one *Christian* denomination over others. He thus
envisioned a kind of "national" faith, but clearly one that was Christian in
makeup as opposed to anything else. He lived, of course, in a day in which
Protestantism was the overwhelming faith represented throughout the land.
Like the founding fathers that he influenced, he might have envisioned a
"sacred" order, but one built on the strength of the Bible, not the natural law.
He even went so far as to require a religious test for holding public office in
his native Massachusetts: "No man can take a seat in our legislature until he
solemnly declares, 'I believe the Christian religion and have a firm persuasion
of its truth.'"[20] Roger Williams would have unalterably opposed Backus on
this point. Isaac Backus did not understand completely America's Sacred
Ground. Indeed, he abused what McGraw has called the Civic Public Forum
by using it to impose a particular religious worldview on his fellow citizens.

John Leland

A generation later John Leland (1754–1841) carried on the struggle of
Backus and his predecessors. Living until 1841 allowed Leland to witness
not only the ratification of the U.S. Constitution and Bill of Rights but also
the end of the Congregational establishment in Massachusetts in 1833. For
Leland, the latter was cause for celebration, as Massachusetts was the last
holdout among states that once embraced formal religious establishments.

Religious liberty dominated Leland's writings and constituted much of his life's work. Known by his peers as shrewd, witty, and eccentric, Leland was a widely read and well-informed evangelist and agitator throughout most of his life. Although a native of Massachusetts, Leland labored tirelessly in Virginia from 1776 to 1791. As a vibrant and bold preacher, Leland promoted the Baptist message during these crucial years of Virginia's struggle for religious liberty.

His passionate defense of liberty coincided with the efforts of Thomas Jefferson and especially James Madison, who were at the forefront with Leland in Virginia's fight for religious liberty. Leland championed the Baptist notion of rights of conscience as inalienable to every man. As such, he worked vigorously to sever any remaining ties between Virginia and the Episcopal Church, concluding:

> Government has no more to do with the religious opinions of men, than it has with the principles of mathematics. Let every man speak freely without fear, maintain the principles that he believes, worship according to his own faith, either one God, three Gods, no God, or twenty Gods; and let government protect him in doing so.[21]

Defending religious liberty with Jefferson and Madison, Leland was also instrumental in helping to gather signatures for Madison's legendary *Memorial and Remonstrance*, "even as he lobbied for enough votes to help pass Jefferson's Bill for Establishing Religious Freedom."[22]

At the federal level, Leland was appointed in 1779 to represent the Virginia General Committee in correspondence with President George Washington concerning major Baptist issues. Baptists were primarily concerned that, even though it was arguably implied, the Constitution itself did not spell out the religious liberty in which they so passionately believed. Leland wrote to Washington with a diplomatic and persuasive prowess:

> When the constitution made its first appearance in Virginia, we, as a society, had unusual strugglings of mind, fearing that the liberty of conscience, dearer to us than property or life, was not sufficiently secured. Perhaps our jealousies were heightened by the usage we received in Virginia under real government, when mobs, fines, bonds and prisons were frequent repast. . . . Amidst all these iniquities of mind, our consolation arose from this consideration—viz., the plan must be good, for it has the signature of a tried, trusted friend, and if religious liberty is rather insecure in the Constitution, "the Administration will certainly prevent all oppression, for a *Washington* will preside."[23]

Washington attempted to placate the committee's fears by asserting that if he ever conceived that the Constitution might possibly endanger religious liberty, he would never have affixed his signature to it. Further, Washington stated, "I beg you will be persuaded that no one would be more zealous than myself to establish effectual barriers against the horrors of spiritual tyranny, and every species of religious persecution."[24] Not fully satisfied that the Constitution was adequately clear on these points, the Virginia Baptists, led by Leland, mounted a campaign to prevent ratification. Leland sent Madison a copy of ten Baptist objections to the Constitution, all grounded in the lack of a bill of rights or written guarantees of religious liberty in the Constitution. These objections clearly make the point that Leland sought no favors for Baptists or even for Christians under the new Constitution. Leland was entirely Madisonian-Jeffersonian in his approach to religious freedom: if it was not equal freedom for all, it was not true freedom. America's Sacred Ground had a friend in John Leland.

A great deal has been written about a meeting between Madison and Leland in 1788, which was instrumental in striking a "deal" between them, thereby gaining Baptist support for the Constitution. Madison agreed to introduce amendments to the Constitution, "spelling out the freedoms which the Baptists desired."[25] While Madison's suggested wording was considerably modified once presented to Congress, its fundamental ideas survived, including the principles of no establishment and free exercise that are the heart of the American tradition of religious liberty. While most Americans would hail James Madison as the man most responsible for American religious liberty, J. M. Dawson put forth the notion that if James Madison were asked who was responsible, he would quickly reply, "John Leland and the Baptists."[26] It is definitely the case that Madison received much insight and inspiration from the Baptists, and perhaps, asserted Dawson, "[w]ithout the Baptists Madison might never have been."[27]

The list of valiant Baptist advocates for religious liberty does not end with the close of the eighteenth century. Baptist leaders in the nineteenth and twentieth centuries recognized that the American experiment of religious liberty is revolutionary and requires constant nurturing. In the delicate experiment that is American democracy, it is expected that complications concerning the achievement of religious liberty will arise; undoubtedly the nuances of modernism have presented many complex issues and circumstances for Baptists. Nevertheless, Baptists have remained vigilant in seeking to protect the fundamental principles of religious liberty that many of their predecessors suffered and struggled to secure. The leading Baptist in the fight for religious liberty in the nineteenth and twentieth centuries was George W. Truett.

George W. Truett

George Washington Truett is ranked among America's most outstanding Baptist orators and statesmen, and he was particularly well known for his vigorous defense of religious liberty. He tirelessly articulated the major Baptist principles, all centered in the inalienable relationship between the individual soul and God. As fundamentalist leaders in Texas were working to disman-tle the Southern Baptist tradition, says Baptist historian Bill Brackney, "it was George Truett's force and content which kept the witness united."[28] Truett served as pastor of the First Baptist Church in Dallas, Texas, for forty-seven years, presided over the Southern Baptist Convention from 1927 to 1930, and headed the Baptist World Alliance from 1934 to 1939. George Truett passionately felt that the progress made toward greater religious liberty and separation of church and state was a Baptist idea, regarding it as the "supreme contribution of the new world to the old."[29]

George Truett took up the concept of a free church in a free state, arguing that the church "needs no prop of any kind from any worldly source, and to the degree that it is thus supported is a millstone hanged about its neck."[30] He encouraged Baptists, Americans, and the world never to forget the prin-ciple of religious liberty, as forgetfulness and complicity in this realm explain many of the religious woes that have and do afflict the world. Truett, as much as anybody, understood the grand importance of "absolute right" over "mere toleration" when speaking of religious liberty:

> Our (Baptist) contention is not for mere toleration, but for absolute lib-erty. . . . Toleration is a concession, while liberty is a matter of principle. Toleration is a gift from human beings, while liberty is a gift from God. . . . Religion must be forever voluntary and uncoerced, and that it is not the prerogative of any power, whether civil or ecclesiastical, to compel men to conform to any religious creed or form of worship, or to pay taxes for the support of a religious organization to which they do not belong and in whose creed they do not believe. God wants free wor-shipers and no other kind.[31]

Truett powerfully pierced the heart of tyranny and religious oppression throughout his Baptist journey. He forcefully preached that the individual's right to private judgment is the "crown jewel of humanity, and for any per-son or institution to dare to come between the soul and God is a blasphe-mous impertinence and a defamation of the crown rights of the Son of God."[32] George Truett was a true advocate of equality under the law for all religious traditions; indeed he too understood, however presciently, Amer-ica's Sacred Ground.

Having surveyed some of the major Baptist defenders of religious liberty, and seeing that the beliefs of most of the true Baptist leaders fit squarely within McGraw's notion of America's Sacred Ground, it is important also to review some of the major Baptist organizations formed in the twentieth century that deal with political issues. Here it is possible to begin to see a divide, a break by some Baptists with older Baptist beliefs on religious liberty in favor of a stance that would, a la Isaac Backus, more vigorously identify the American public order with the Christian faith.

BAPTIST ORGANIZATIONS AND THE DEFENSE OF RELIGIOUS LIBERTY: AMERICA'S SACRED GROUND CHALLENGED

As was so with other Protestant denominations in America, Baptists were not prone to create formal organizations to advance religious liberty until the twentieth century. In the twentieth century, however, several Baptist organizations began to distinguish themselves, nationally and internationally, in becoming strong advocates for religious liberty. In particular the Baptist World Alliance (BWA) and the Baptist Joint Committee on Public Affairs (BJC) won well-deserved reputations for championing religious liberty. In the late 1980s, however, the Southern Baptist Convention (SBC), the largest Baptist organization in the world with a membership of approximately seventeen million, began a series of steps to distance itself from traditional Baptist views on religious liberty. The SBC had always looked to its own Christian Life Commission (CLC) but also the more independent BJC to handle its work on religious liberty. But in 1988 it eliminated the CLC and created the Christian Ethics and Religious Liberty Commission (ERLC) to represent its increasingly conservative stances on religious liberty. Then in the early 1990s, the SBC formally broke ties with the BJC because of the latter's "liberal" stances on church-state issues. Then in the early 2000s it broke ties with the Baptist World Alliance (BWA) for the same reason.

With the creation of the ERLC, the SBC made a dramatic turn away from traditional Baptist views on religious liberty. It will be suggested here that these latter-day Baptists departed from the founders' project and that they failed to understand the underlying founders' commitment to what McGraw has called America's Sacred Ground. Further, it will also be suggested that they contributed to the misguided movement among American conservatives to restructure church and state in America in a way that trumpets Christianity and politically treats it as superior to other faiths.

The Baptist World Alliance

The BWA was formed on July 17, 1905, nearly three hundred years after the formation of the earliest Baptist church in England in 1612. The BWA does not function as a judicial or legislative body, but rather serves as a Baptist fellowship, working tirelessly to keep its constituents informed on many issues, including religious liberty. The BWA has consistently challenged Baptists across the globe to remain committed to their vital denominational principles and heritage, including religious liberty. Birthed from nineteenth-century ecumenism, the BWA was founded primarily through the efforts of the three largest Baptist groups: the American Southern Baptists, the American Northern Baptists, and the British Baptists.[33]

In his presidential address in 1955, F. Townley Lord summarized the achievements of the first fifty years of the BWA, emphasizing in particular its preservation of the basic Baptist ideals of religious liberty. At this same fifty-year celebration, the president of Andover-Newton Theological Seminary, Herbert Gezork, addressed some of the pressing issues of this era, reemphasizing the Baptist distinctive of religious liberty. He eloquently stated:

> The Baptist position on the matter of religious liberty is crystal clear. We have no sympathy for the agnostic or the atheist, but we shall stand for his freedom to hold his religious or anti-religious beliefs, as we stand for our own freedom.[34]

Gezork iterated further that, given their passion for religious liberty, Baptists must continue to strive for true religious freedom for all and reject the practice and idea of mere religious toleration. Placing the power of the state behind one form of religion, merely tolerating others, he said, "is not religious liberty," but instead, is a concession or "subtle form of coercion."[35] Passionately pleading for Baptists to guard jealously their precious heritage of religious liberty, Gezork said it was absolutely imperative to hold on to this belief in a world that was facing a terrifying and impending threat to civilization—the totalitarian state:

> For the tendency towards increasing power of the State is observable everywhere, and therefore the Christian must be twice vigilant every where. He must guard existing civil rights. He must oppose efforts to make people think and believe alike. . . . He will be willing to render to Caesar what is Caesar's, but he will not allow Caesar to determine what is his and what is God's; he will reserve that right for his own free conscience under God. . . . If ever there was a time for Baptists to proclaim in word and life their great principle of soul-liberty, that time is now.[36]

Gezork's remarks are typical of the BWA's attempts to sound a steady note to Baptists everywhere to stand fast in protecting religious liberty.

The BWA has strived for religious liberty for all peoples through a variety of means, including praying, speaking, and writing to government and church leaders in many countries, including Hungary, Spain, Russia, Czechoslovakia, China, Cuba, Bangladesh, Liberia, South Africa, and countries throughout Eastern Europe. The BWA's valiant efforts to remain true to the Baptist principle of religious liberty as a fundamental human right is to be commended.

While the BWA remained a lighthouse for religious liberty around the world, in the United States Baptists commensurately recognized and championed religious liberty. In the midst of the tumultuous 1930s, many Baptist leaders grew increasingly wary of Franklin Roosevelt's New Deal administration and the emerging federal government programs like Social Security and their effects on philanthropic activities of the churches.[37] Under the auspices of this period of national transition, Baptist groups across the nation, including the Northern, Southern, and National Baptists, began to hearken more fervently back to their roots of religious liberty, speaking with a united voice on a variety of fronts. Whether it was urging the U.S. State Department to investigate charges of Christian persecution in Romania in 1937, President Roosevelt's 1939 appointment of Myron C. Taylor as a diplomat to the Vatican, or the public funding of parochial institutions, "[t]o many Baptists, the 'wall of separation' had been breached in unhealthy ways and an effective form of redress had to be made."[38]

The Baptist Joint Committee on Public Affairs

In 1942 the Northern, Southern, and National Baptist conventions, in a welcome spirit of cooperation, united as the Joint Conference Committee on Public Relations. This organization became known four years later as the Baptist Joint Committee on Public Affairs (BJC). William Brackney explains:

> Issue by issue the associated committees and what became permanently the Baptist Joint Committee on Public Affairs in 1946 provided a "watchdog" surveillance on matters of church-state relations. . . . U.S. Baptists pressed through diplomatic channels and won freedom from persecution for Romanian Baptists. . . . While President Roosevelt did not recall his ambassador to the Vatican and aid to church-related schools did continue, Baptists had proven that joint resolve was indeed an effective tool.[39]

For nearly sixty years the BJC has served as the principal Baptist voice to the U.S. government and the world on a wide range of religious liberty issues. BJC activities have included, among others, informing Baptist church members of presidential and legislative proposals and policies affecting religious freedom, developing Baptist positions on those issues, filing *amicus curiae* briefs with courts on First Amendment cases, and direct interaction with the White House. The BJC has maintained a strong record of opposing all forms of constitutional amendments that would support prayer in public schools, as well as vigorously opposing all types of public assistance to parochial schools, including tuition tax credits.

Under its first executive director, Joseph Martin Dawson, the BJC wasted no time in vigorously addressing religious liberty concerns, for example, opposing state support of parochial schools, opposing state-supported religion in the public schools, and opposing appointment of a U.S. ambassador to the Vatican. Also, the BJC maintained a firm stance against the federal tax aid to parents and parochial school children in *Everson v. Board of Education of Ewing Township* (1947). Baptist Joint Committee Chairman E. Hilton Jackson argued the *Everson* case on behalf of the appellant before the Supreme

Court.[40] In response to the High Court's unfavorable ruling, the BJC in February 1947 adopted a forceful resolution assessing the ruling:

> We deplore this opinion and are convinced that it will divide the people of the nation at a time when unity is greatly needed. In view of the religious heritage of America, which Associate Justice Black so eloquently reviewed, the decision is all the more to be deplored. As Baptists of the United States we are resolved that the struggle for religious liberty, in terms of the separation of church and state, must be continued. We have lost a battle, but we have not lost the war.[41]

The BJC opposed President Harry Truman's announced appointment of Mark W. Clark as a full-fledged ambassador to the Vatican. This issue undoubtedly strained relations between Truman and Dawson,[42] as a heated exchange between them was surely one of the most direct confrontational encounters the BJC has had with the White House over religious liberty concerns in its entire history. Dawson "waged a stiff battle against confirmation," speaking "from one end of the country to the other."[43] Following these protests by the BJC, in January 1952 Clark withdrew his name for the ambassadorship. Truman never announced a new appointment prior to leaving office in 1953.

Under the leadership of Emanuel Carlson (1954–1971), the BJC faced many of the same battles it had fought in past years. On the practice of religion in public elementary and secondary schools, the BJC was heavily involved in landmark cases such as *Engel v. Vitale* (1962) and *Abington Township School District v. Schempp* (1963). In *Engel*, for instance, the Supreme Court ruled that vocal prayers delivered in the public schools, written by state officials, are unconstitutional. Justice Hugo Black, a Baptist, concluded that such a policy contradicted the "first and most immediate" principle of the Establishment Clause: "a union of government and religion tends to destroy government and to degrade religion."[44] Representing the Court majority, Black wrote that when "the power, prestige, and financial support of government is placed behind a particular religious belief, the indirect coercive pressure upon religious minorities to conform to the prevailing officially approved religion is plain."[45]

While government sponsorship of religion remained of paramount concern to the BJC, it also fought for religious liberty in a variety of other areas. For example, it opposed making Good Friday a legal holiday in America, supported West Point cadets in their struggle to do away with compulsory chapel, and supported tax exemptions for churches in *Walz v. The Tax Commission* (1970). Further, the BJC defended the right of John F. Kennedy to campaign for the U.S. presidency, basing its defense on the constitutional forbiddance of religious tests for public office.

The BJC faced many of the same religious liberty issues while under the direction of James E. Wood Jr. (1972–1980). These included the appointment of ambassadors to the Vatican and federal funding of sectarian institutions, IRS regulation of churches, use of missionaries for government intelligence, government prohibition of abortions, and the rise of the religious right. Wood's spirit of ecumenism led to productive relations with other advocacy groups with similar religious liberty concerns.

In 1979 the BJC again faced a familiar foe in the form of legislative attempts to promote the practice of prayer in the public schools. The BJC vigorously opposed a strong campaign by Senator Jesse Helms to legislate school prayer and remove the Supreme Court's jurisdiction concerning the issue. The BJC's effort was joined by President Jimmy Carter, who urged Congress to defeat the campaign, cautioning that "Congress not get involved in the question of mandating prayer in public schools."[46] In a shift of loyalties that was formalized in the 1990s, the SBC, under the leadership of President Adrian Rodgers, changed its support to Senator Helms's efforts.[47]

PRESERVING AMERICA'S SACRED GROUND: THE NEW BAPTIST DIVIDE

During Wood's tenure as director tension peaked between the BJC and the SBC and its Christian Life Commission (CLC). The CLC voiced concern over what it felt was an overstepping of boundaries on the part of the BJC. Even before its formal inception, objections had been raised about the BJC going beyond its specific duties of providing a national Baptist presence in the nation's capital and speaking out on issues without first receiving specific requests or a consensus from the various conventions involved. While it was generally expected that groups such as the CLC would focus primarily on the moral issues of the day, while the BJC primarily addressed the nation's government entities, some overlap was inevitable and had been generally accepted.

Foy D. Valentine, executive secretary of the CLC since 1960, continued to bring attention to what he and others within the SBC considered unnecessary program duplication between the two Baptist agencies.[48] Thus, the role of the BJC was being questioned and its existence threatened. The rise of the fundamentalist arm of the SBC created a massive rift in leadership that began to cripple the BJC and its goal of furthering religious liberty. Many from the fundamentalist wing of the SBC yearned for a "return" to the country's "religious roots," which many felt would cure the malaise of the world's social diseases. These new voices in the Baptist fold increasingly wanted the BJC to reflect its views.

James Dunn assumed the helm of the BJC in 1981 and sought to limit the BJC's agenda to those specific controversies that directly affected church-state relations and religious liberty in the United States. Dunn's tenure involved many of the same battles fought over previous decades. School choice again surfaced as a national issue, and once again, the BJC maintained a firm stance against the use of public funds for private schools. The "school choice" plan pushed by President George Bush was opposed by Dunn and the BJC as "the same old repeatedly rejected schemes to divert tax dollars to private and parochial schools."[49] Consistent with the growing schism between the CLC and the BJC, ERLC director Richard Land remained open to the proposal, suggesting that the issue deserved further consideration.[50]

In 1982, the BJC released a statement condemning President Reagan's proposed amendment to the Constitution to permit public school prayer, saying, "[i]t is despicable demagoguery for the President to play petty politics with prayer. He knows that the Supreme Court has never banned prayer in schools."[51] Another sharp rift occurred that same year when the SBC leadership passed a resolution defending the proposal put forth by President Reagan, asserting that the amendment did not provide for direct government regulation.[52] The BJC retorted that someone would have to review and approve said prayer to assure its inoffensiveness to some religious groups, ultimately leaving a generic and heavily diluted prayer that would constitute a wasted effort for a controversial practice.

It was in 1991 that the schism between the BJC and the SBC reached its climax as the SBC discontinued its funding contributions to the BJC. However, many other organizations, such as the American Baptist Convention, quickly filled this major gap in funding, and consequently, the BJC is currently funded by a much broader base of support from organizations, individual contributors, and independent churches. As the SBC extended its relations with the political right and wavered on traditional Baptist commitments to religious liberty, it became inevitable that these two organizations would eventually part ways.

It is the author's view that in the latter part of the twentieth century the conservative element among Baptists fell into a fatal error that has ravaged human societies for millennia: grounding political identity in religion. It is true that the SBC did not advocate the creation of a national church, or intentionally relegate non-Christian minorities to secondary status, but increasingly it sought to structure America as a religious state. Such a state would be driven by its people's historic attachment to Christianity which, in the end, would favor Christian ideas, programs, political candidates, and activities, and thus create a kind of Christian establishment achieved by entry "through the back door." In so doing, the SBC departed from traditional Baptist views that deny that America is a religious state. The founders sought not to erect a wholly secular state, but neither did they seek to achieve superior status for Christianity in American public life. The foundation of America's Sacred Ground is built upon natural law, which enables all groups, religious as well as nonreligious, to have access to public policy debates while denying to any the right to control or dictate policy. The SBC gradually moved away from being satisfied with the ability to speak at the level of McGraw's Conscientious Public Forum to believing that, as a representative of God to help preserve America's values, it should promote Christian values in the Civic Public Forum.

But the Civic Public Forum is a meeting ground for all American citizens. It formulates laws based on what is best for all the people, not just some. There exists in America a large religious community, as well as a considerable nonreligious community, that does not want to make abortion illegal, mandate prayers in public schools, or fund private religious schools. They oppose funding social service programs administered by churches and other houses of worship, posting religious symbols on public property, preventing gay marriages, or otherwise imposing what is a conservative "Christian" vision on the entire nation.

The SBC would surely counter by arguing that it is attempting to structure law in a way that benefits all Americans, and that in so doing it must push for such legislation because other citizens, blinded by their own lack of an ability to ascertain God's will, do not know what is truly best for the nation as a whole. But this approach is blind to its own intolerance of others' conscientiously held views, and fails to acknowledge that its own views are not adequately supported to become law. This is why so many conservative Baptists accuse moderate Baptists (for example, those who align with the BJC's approach) of aligning with the interests of secularism. They see moderate Baptists as uncommitted and willing to give America over to less religiously inspired voices, but this is a false charge. Moderate Baptists are as concerned as anyone about building a moral America, but they wish to respect the common good. Therefore they decline to elevate their own views over others' and are satisfied with law and public policy that more deeply respects the diversity of America. In other words, they respect the Civic Public Forum as a forum that acts as a restraint on factional takeovers.

Theoretically, it is possible that the SBC and other like-minded citizens, by continuing to make arguments for a change in perspective at the level of the Conscientious Public Forum, might one day be successful in bringing about a new consensus that widely supports their views. But until that day arrives, the SBC should recognize that it violates America's Sacred Ground by attempting to legalize its own views.

It is possible to see clearly, then, how the principle of the separation of church and state, by which no religious worldview is to be elevated above others at the governmental level, is entirely consistent with America's Sacred Ground. Both work in tandem to encourage and preserve a moral framework in the private and public realms, but together they prevent any one faction in America from violating others' conscientiously held views. Such factions do this by seizing control of the Civic Public Forum and enshrining their own views when no broad consensus exists as to how such views are in accord with the principles of the Civic Public Forum as given effect in the Bill of Rights.

Meanwhile, the BJC refused to support particular parties or candidates and, instead, tried to remain focused on specific issues and their effects on Baptists and the world. In 1992, James Dunn, in concert with a host of diverse leaders, issued a statement opposing religion as a method for judging political candidates:

> Faith in God should unite us, not divide us. We begin with the proposition that God is neither Democrat nor Republican nor, for that matter, American. God transcends all national and political affiliations. God's precinct is the universe. Identifying the Kingdom of God with any political party is presumptuous.[53]

In 1995, the BJC once again opposed efforts by some in Congress to further entangle religion and government through a school prayer amendment to the Constitution. In response to this latest wave of attacks against religious liberty, the BJC, along with fourteen other religious groups, expressed their opposition to this proposal to President Clinton. Later that year, the BJC continued to deflect the barrage of proposals issued from Republican congressmen to establish a constitutional amendment that would bar government from discrimination against or denial of benefits to groups or individuals "on account of religious expression, belief or identity."[54] In its consistent opposition, the BJC concluded that such an attempt to amend the Constitution would be far more detrimental than beneficial to the cause of religious liberty. In line with the growing divergence between the ERLC and the BJC, the ERLC supported the congressional proposals. They noted that such an amendment would permit "prayer and religious expression, out loud, so long as it was not materially disruptive of the school program," and the "wall [of separation] which equates separation from church and state [does not mean] separation of religious speech from public life."[55] The ERLC argued that their support of the amendments was an attempt to "protect student religious liberty without sacrificing Baptist principles of church-state separation and freedom of conscience."[56] But the reality is that a public policy that permits prayer in public schools will inevitably favor Christian prayers since the American public overwhelmingly identifies with the Christian faith. Advocates of school prayer know this, of course, and are satisfied that while the policy might enable some kinds of non-Christian prayer, the overwhelming number of prayers that ensue will be Christian. If this is not the creation of a Christian establishment "through the back door," what is? This goes beyond the ERLC using the Conscientious Public Forum to *promote* its ideas to using the Civic Public Forum to *legalize* its views.

While the divide between the BJC and the ERLC has always been apparent, it is in no way suggested here that these groups are positioned at completely different ends of the religious liberty spectrum on all issues. On the contrary, the ERLC has joined the BJC in supporting or opposing many issues in recent years. In the wake of the landmark Supreme Court case of *Oregon v. Smith* (1990),[57] which most religious lobbies thought was a threat to religious liberty, both groups supported the Religious Freedom Restoration Act (RFRA). They viewed it as an attempt to legislatively revive the pre-*Smith* requirement that the government must demonstrate a "compelling state interest" before it can deny the enjoyment of a citizen's religious activity. Although it has since been invalidated in its application to the states, the RFRA was signed into law on November, 17, 1993, due in some measure to the two Baptist groups' common support of the measure.[58]

In 1999, J. Brent Walker, who had served as general counsel for the BJC from 1993 to 1999, became the organization's fifth executive director. Upon assuming duties, Walker summarized the important role the BJC has played since its formation in 1942:

> No voice at the intersection of church and state has been more consistent, reliable and sensible during the past six decades than that of the Baptist Joint Committee. That's why no voice today is more trusted. As we face the challenges of the year 2000 and beyond, we recommit ourselves to the proven principle that separation of church and state is the best way to ensure religious liberty for all.[59]

In 2002, the BJC joined other prominent religious organizations in opposing "The House of Worship Political Speech Act," sponsored by Representative Walter Jones, saying that such a proposal "would harm, not help religion in America."[60] The Act sought to allow churches to engage in partisan politics without forfeiting their tax-exempt status. In large part due to the aggressive lobbying of the BJC and other major religious lobbies, the bill failed to gain a majority in the House of Representatives and lost in October 2002. K. Hollyn Hollman, BJC general counsel, remarked that Congress "properly rejected Rep. Jones' invitation to politicize churches," arguing that it was unfortunate "that some members purport to protect churches by promoting legislation that politicizes them."[61]

The BJC has recognized that the efficacy of its ministry also depends upon its ability to work with other groups and diverse religious traditions where, despite their theological differences, they have been able to "find common ground in the quest for religious liberty and the separation of church and state."[62] For example, joining with the American Jewish Committee and the Religious Action Center of Reform Judaism, the National Council of the Churches of Christ, and the Interfaith Alliance Foundation, the BJC released a statement titled *A Shared Vision: Religious Liberty in the 21st Century*. It articulates dedication to religious liberty and outlines how the religion clauses of the First Amendment operate to ensure it.

During Walker's tenure, the ERLC continued to represent a more conservative stance on public policy issues than the BJC. Headed by Richard Land from its beginning, the ERLC increasingly sided with Republican administrations on most issues. It supported school prayer amendments, school vouchers, and other programs to fund private religious schools with government funds, and while it expressed concerns about the George W. Bush administration's drive to provide government funding to faith-based institutions to administer social programs, it nevertheless was reluctant to criticize the initiative.

The advocacy of the SBC and the ERLC can be criticized along the line of concerns that Barbara McGraw highlights in her book. She wants Americans to rediscover the sacred foundations of the collective political life in which they all share. In her view, the secular left, the religious right, and a group she calls accommodationists all misconstrue the nature of America's Sacred Ground. The ERLC and its parent Southern Baptist Convention could never be mistaken for representing the views of the secular left, of course. But its members are to be found in great numbers within the other two groups.

The religious right, including a large number of Southern Baptists, looks to the overwhelming presence of Christian persons and institutions that informed the founding and concludes that Christianity is the foundation of the American polity. McGraw argues that the religious right, however, just like the secular left, seeks to impose constitutionally a "top-down, overarching worldview/unifying moral order"[63] upon other Americans, which is inconsistent with America's Sacred Ground and the advancement of the good society that the founders envisioned.

While the SBC is now well populated with members of the religious right who want to legalize Christian perspectives, it also counts among its constituents many accommodationists who seem satisfied to compete in a free-for-all for dominance in the public square. Their misguided solution, as McGraw contends, is to permit all citizens to assert their own worldviews, and rely on the hope that ultimately this process will have a counterbalancing effect such that no one group is able to seize too much political power. However, this in no way prevents any of them from *trying* to elevate legally their worldview over others by persuading others to overlook the principles underlying the Constitution. Thus, they too fail to see that the sacred nature of the American order protects the religious consciences of all persons and denies them the right to position their perspectives above others in political or legal terms—at least until a clear consensus emerges. Such a consensus would have to be one that would sanction the legalization of views, but only when they are in accordance with the underlying practical, political, and moral framework of the nation: America's Sacred Ground.

CONCLUDING OBSERVATIONS: PROTECTING AMERICA'S SACRED GROUND

Religious liberty for each individual is a treasure of the Baptist faith that has been passionately and sacrificially guarded. Unfortunately, many Baptists today remain unaware of their rich heritage of religious liberty and are more concerned with creating a "Christian" nation, or at least a nation that more genuinely reflects Christian values, through legislative and judicial means. Waves of fundamentalism have crashed upon the shores of Baptist organizations, through leaders such as Jerry Falwell, Pat Robertson, Paige Patterson, and Charles Stanley. The fundamentalist faction of Baptists in the United States has sought to shift major Baptist principles in an effort to "recapture God for America."[64] Fortunately, Baptist moderates such as James Wood have rightly said that "it is unnecessary and wrong for any religious group or individual to seek to Christianize the government. . . . It is arrogant to assert that one's position on a political issue is 'Christian' and that all others are 'un-Christian.' "[65]

It is arguable that no Christian denomination has made greater contributions toward preserving religious liberty in America and in the world than Baptists. Birthed in persecution, Baptists have fought for religious freedom and have tirelessly resisted all efforts, whether from civil or ecclesiastical powers, to compel religious conformity. Valiant and emboldened Baptists such as Roger Williams and John Clarke inaugurated a tradition of religious liberty, guaranteed by the separation of church and state, which has become the backbone of the vigorous religious life that is seen in the United States. Baptist leaders such as John Leland and Isaac Backus were strong influences on the founding fathers' decision to construct a framework of religious liberty in the Constitution. Collectively the Baptist commitment to religious liberty has been carried on by organizations such as the Baptist World Alliance and the Baptist Joint Committee. Together, they represent a host of Baptists across the globe who know their historical roots and believe unequivocally in religious liberty for all persons of all faiths.

Undoubtedly, the historic Baptist position on religious liberty, enshrined in the American system since the founding era, is now threatened. The genius of the American system has always been that in religious matters the government is neutral—by law. This commitment allows all citizens to practice their religious faiths freely without having religion imposed upon them by government. Regrettably, many Baptists today lead the modern assault on the separation of church and state. Many would have government be the mentor, the overseer, the advocate of religion. In the name of halting "moral drift," many critics of church-state separation would have Americans return to prayer in the public schools and allow the posting of the Ten Commandments in public places. They would support government subsidies of churches to administer social programs; government monetary support of religious educational institutions; more religious symbols, such as the national motto, "In God We Trust," on public property; and on and on.

Many Christians wrongly believe that Christianity will flourish in a more Christian political environment. History shows the opposite to be true. Christianity grew more rapidly than at any time in history in the first three centuries after Christ's death when Christians were persecuted for not bowing the knee to Caesar. Christians understandably sought more favorable political conditions for themselves. By the fourth century, Christianity was so widespread that it became impossible to control it by means of outright persecution; the emperor Constantine placed it on a neutral basis with other religions in A.D. 313 and in A.D. 380. Theodosius made it the official religion of the empire. The faith thereafter lost much of its vitality, distinctiveness, and vigor, owing to its preferred political status. Merged with government, Christianity became consumed with temporal affairs—armies, police, crime, taxation, commerce, economics, etc.—and less focused on the mission outlined for it by Christ and the apostles. In its witness, the church gradually began to rely less on the power of its spiritual message than on the power of the sword to enforce its political will. The persecuted had turned persecutor. More recently, much the same phenomenon occurred in China following the Communist Revolution in 1949. An immediate crackdown on religion that lasted some twenty-five years resulted in the greatest spread of Christianity to have occurred in China before or since.

The author would hope not to be misunderstood here. He is not advocating indifference to politics. As John Courtney Murray once said, politics is part of the moral universe, and Christians are rightly concerned with morality. The Sacred Ground concept captures this well; America was always intended to be a fit and moral place in which to live, and Christians have much to contribute to a moral America. But in their daily lives, Christians are to be Christian *citizens*, not merely Christians. Because the Bible does not require that political and governmental affairs be Christian, those who are Christians are free to join with non-Christians in America's democratic form of government. They may make laws that, from the perspective of its people as a whole and *not* from the perspective of Christians' own interpretation of the Bible, best ensure the common good. In this process, negotiation and compromise are not dirty words, and Christians should be satisfied with laws that fall short of biblical standards as they understand them. Biblical standards may dictate the contributions that Christians make toward formation of laws, but Christians do not fail God if the negotiated product, even laws on such controversial areas as abortion, school prayer, and homosexuality, do not meet their standards. The goal, even duty, of Christians should be to assist the government in the promotion of the welfare of *all* American citizens based upon a shared morality, not to set up a kingdom of God on earth.

Proposals to "Christianize" the nation through political means misconstrue America's Sacred Ground. These proposals do not respect America's

Sacred Ground because they inject a religiosity into American public life that violates the right of other Americans to be citizens of a republic that does not favor one set of religious views over others. This is a clear violation of the Consistency Principle of the Civic Public Forum. American Sacred Ground is one of freedom, and as McGraw so appropriately notes, "the ultimate purpose of freedom" is the "pursuit of the good,"[66] which is itself grounded in God who in the name of conscience protects *all* pursuits of the good.

In the United States, the First Amendment's proscription against religious establishments and its allowance for the free exercise of religion virtually guaranteed a religiously pluralistic society—with the understanding that no one form of faith would achieve dominance. Increasingly Americans seem to be on the verge of adopting a whole new framework of fusion of religion and government. In essence, they are abandoning the principles of America's Sacred Ground and a return to the classical and medieval top down, overarching worldview polity in which government actively promotes religion as the glue of the social order. Americans are on the verge of destroying America's Sacred Ground.

The divisiveness that has emerged over the past few decades has wounded but not defeated the Baptist voice for religious liberty. This is because "even in the face of new voices in their own family who would ironically seek to establish a Christian Commonwealth not unlike attempts of the seventeenth century, Baptists have continued to be 'stubborn for liberty.'"[67] Americans would do well to remember the words of James Madison: "The religion then of every man must be left to the conviction and conscience of every man. . . . In matters of Religion, no man's right is abridged by the institution of Civil Society and . . . Religion is wholly exempt from its cognizance."[68] These words, issued by a prominent non-Baptist but who nevertheless stood firmly with Baptists fighting for religious liberty in his own day, indeed capture the true essence of the Baptist tradition of religious liberty, a tradition fully committed to preserving America's Sacred Ground.

Chapter 11

Buddhist Contributions to the Civic and Conscientious Public Forums

Rita M. Gross

INTRODUCTION

> We put thirty spokes together and call it a wheel;
> But it is on the space where there is nothing that the use-
> fulness of the wheel depends.
> We turn clay to make a vessel;
> But it is on the space where there is nothing that the use-
> fulness of the vessel depends.
> We pierce doors and windows to make a house;
> And it is on these spaces where there is nothing that the
> usefulness of the house depends.
> Therefore, just as we take advantage of what is,
> We should recognize the usefulness of what is not.
> *Tao te Ching*, Chapter Eleven[1]

In April 2003, I experienced something new. I was in Bhutan, and the symbols of my religion, Vajrayana Buddhism, were everywhere—on the money,
in the streets, on people's houses, everywhere. I found this experience

exciting and affirming. As a result, I found myself thinking for the first time that maybe I understood why Christians in the United States are so eager to put up Christmas displays including manger scenes in public parks, something to which I have always been adamantly opposed. That set me to thinking again about issues of church and state, religion and the public square. I had to ask myself if my two reactions constituted a double standard, something I always try to avoid. I asked myself again why I am so opposed to displays of Christianity in the public square.

Almost immediately I also realized that it is not the displays themselves to which I am opposed. I am opposed to and frightened by the theological and political packaging surrounding that desire to put Christmas displays in public parks and the Ten Commandments in county courthouses. Not only do proponents of such displays claim exclusive truth for Christianity; a significant percentage of them also claim that the United States is a Christian nation and that the separation of church and state is not actually part of our constitutional framework. That combination, exclusive truth claims and opposition to the separation of church and state, is what makes religious displays in public space extremely dangerous. However, there is also a natural longing to express one's religious understandings and symbols publicly, as my experience in Bhutan taught me. My new question became, "What would it take for public displays of religion to be safe?"

The Larger Framework: American Religion and Politics in the Context of Religious Studies

Solving that riddle is the purpose of this chapter. Using a Buddhist response and a discussion of Barbara McGraw's provocative book *Rediscovering America's Sacred Ground: Public Religion and the Pursuit of the Good in a Pluralistic America*, this chapter places the riddle in the broader context of the author's work as a scholar of comparative studies in religion. It will use critical-constructive thought, be grounded in "the comparative mirror"[2] and be centered in knowledge beyond European thought. These comments are grounded more in that critical-comparative perspective than in European enlightenment thought or American political theory.

In the author's view, the most fundamental shift of attitude required for religious discourse to be both safe and possible in what McGraw refers to as the Civic and the Conscientious Public Forums is a new and more realistic acceptance by all parties of the inevitability of religious diversity. From a theological and philosophical perspective, people of all faiths must renounce exclusive truth claims regarding their verbal and symbolic accounts of religion and accept that there never will be (and never has been) one universally accepted faith. This is simply a fact, and theology that cannot cope with facts is faulty theology. If deep acceptance of the inevitability of religious diversity were present, Christmas displays in public parks, preferably without Santa and the reindeer, would not be so threatening. It is the exclusive claims of many religious people that make the entry of religious discourse into any public arena so scary. Paradoxically, if people were to give up their claims to the exclusive relevance of their verbal or symbolic forms, their viewpoints would be much more likely to be welcomed by others in both the Civic and the Conscientious Public Forums.

This change of heart can be fostered in part by a clearer understanding of how much the United States has changed religiously since it was founded. When the much admired constitutional framework of the United States was devised, the country was no where nearly as religiously diverse as it is today. In the eighteenth century, most inhabitants of the United States were Protestants. Then and through the nineteenth century, the public arena and American culture were dominated by a Protestant worldview. Everyone knows that this is no longer true. Members of every religion on earth now live in the United States in growing numbers. This vast change in the religious demography of the United States is under-appreciated by Christians (both Catholic and Protestant); it may not even register in the consciousness of some of them, which may be one reason that it is so easy for them to think of the United States as a "Christian" nation. But this simple and vast change in religious demography is, in the author's view, one of the key realities driving the need for a new assessment of how to safely integrate religious discourse into both the Civic and Conscientious Public Forums.

Furthermore, even though McGraw has argued in her introductory chapter and in *Rediscovering America's Sacred Ground*, that the founders contemplated religious pluralism in America that went well beyond Christianity, the founders knew little about religions other than Christianity. Consequently, their model of religion necessarily was highly colored by a Christian lens. But today, thinking about religion that way, though still very common, is simply outdated, given the knowledge that now exists about religions throughout time and space—knowledge that is readily available. (As an aside, the author claims that this is why academic courses in the study of world religions are such an important piece in thinking through how individuals can safely admit religious discourse into the Civic and Conscientious Public Forums.)

The change of heart from making exclusive truth claims to accepting religious diversity as inevitable is also fostered by a new understanding. It is that the dichotomy between the secular left and religious right, so often invoked within the context of American politics, makes no sense, given what the academic study of religions reveals about how religions work. Indeed, McGraw herself has argued in *Rediscovering* that the category "secular," as it is most often used in American political debates, makes little sense. Moreover, it does not accurately describe how religions and societies work. The category "secular" is usually understood as being, in McGraw's terms "non-religious," or as this scholar-practitioner would say, "outside the sanctuary." But the questions raised especially by the knowledge of world religions are whether or

not it is possible to stand outside all sanctuaries, and more important, outside of which sanctuary. One may step outside a specific sanctuary, but, nevertheless, one usually steps into another sanctuary—another overarching
worldview and set of assumptions. One can call that new orientation "secular" only in reference to the abandoned sanctuary. There is no clear definition
of religion upon which all agree. Therefore, there are no criteria by which
everyone can define secularity apart from whatever is understood locally by
"religion." In a pluralistic religious context, labeling anyone or any orientation "secular" is very difficult. For ideological reasons, various partisans may
wish to claim that some other orientation is "secular," but what does that
mean? Does it make any sense?

Study of most religious and cultural situations around the world partially
validates one claim of conservative Christians. Religion is hardly ever merely
a set of ideas entertained in private, and it is never devoid of implications for
how to live the good life. Furthermore, societies are almost never devoid of
religion if religion is defined as overarching worldviews that guide life and
provide values. Thus, claims usually attributed to or made by the so-called
secular left—that can live without religion—are severely undercut by the evidence of how societies generally work.

The whole notion of a public realm radically opposed to or separate from
religion falls apart in the evidence of comparative studies in religion, which
demonstrates that religion is usually a whole way of life, not merely a private
set of ideas that do not spill over into everyday life. The European enlightenment notion that religion is a matter of individual, private belief that need
not be expressed except privately and with one's co-religionists is not usually
found in traditional religious contexts. The goal of operating the public realm
with purely "nonreligious" secular values is probably a lost cause. To this
extent, claims made by conservative Christians have a certain validity, but
something is missing in attempts to completely segregate religious concerns
from public life.

What contemporary knowledge of world religions grants conservative
Christians with one hand, it takes away with the other. If it is difficult to be
"secular," that is "outside the sanctuary," the question still remains, "which
sanctuary?" The evidence that it is difficult to be "outside the sanctuary" by
no means validates the claims of conservative Christians that there is only
one sanctuary in which to be—theirs. The study of religions also demonstrates that more than one sanctuary and competing claims for religious allegiance exist, even in relatively more traditional contexts. The internal
divisions and conflicts in many nonmodern religions and cultures are more
than ample evidence of this fact.

If evidence of how religions usually work demonstrates the difficulty of
being truly secular or outside all sanctuaries, it also invalidates the use of the
label "secularist" as a relevant way to call people bad names. For example,
"secular Jews" are usually understood as people who do not observe tradi-

tional Jewish practices, such as the dietary laws, but does that by definition mean they are secular people? There are other sanctuaries than the Jewish one, including social service, such as serving in Doctors without Borders or the Peace Corps. Likewise, conservative Christians often assume that the only alternative to their point of view is secular nonreligion, which simply is not true. Thus, to call someone a "secularist" usually means nothing more than that they are outside *my* sanctuary. Given the reality and validity of religious diversity, that conclusion is almost meaningless and simply will not do. There is not, never has been, and never will be only one sanctuary within or outside of which one stands. Rather, there has always been a dizzying array of sanctuaries, though in cultural isolation it is more difficult to see them. This author suggests, as does McGraw, that "secularism" is a hegemonic category that has not been well thought through and is best abandoned.

As an aside, it should be noted that the situation is made even more complicated by post-Enlightenment knowledge that makes it painfully obvious that many ideas previously labeled as "secular" and "neutral" are actually rooted in a weak version of Christianity and Western thought in general. But this knowledge does not strengthen the claims of conservative Christians; it weakens them. For example, their argument that no one should mind the "under God" clause because it is a generic, almost nonreligious notion becomes ridiculous. With this claim, religious conservatives trivialize the uniqueness and profundity of their own religion. In a religiously plural nation, how is it possible to justify forcing the phrase "under God" onto all citizens in the oath they use to swear allegiance to that nation, whether or not they believe in God?

Belief or nonbelief in God, by the way, has nothing to do with supposed "secularity," or dislike of religion. People whose religion does not include belief in a deity, such as Buddhists, simply do not want a foreign religious ideology forced upon them if they wish to pledge allegiance to their country out loud, formally, and publicly. They would prefer not to have to choose between pledging allegiance, but lying during the pledge, or being denied the opportunity to pledge allegiance publicly, formally, and out loud. They would rather discuss the pros and cons of believing in God in the Conscientious Public Forum, rather than appeal to God in public national rituals, even though participation in those rituals may not be mandatory. Public national rituals are too important to be arenas in which members of any one religion are singled out as "more American" than members of other religions whose consciences are troubled by the content of these rituals. Appeal to God in national public rituals fosters the false impression that America is a "Christian nation," one of the most dangerous of recent political heresies.

The "under God" clause is only one example among many of how a weak version of Christianity is imposed on people of all faiths in the United States. This author would also argue that conservative Christian positions on many other questions, such as gay rights or abortion, are also local and provincial, rather than universal. Their lack of universality, however, does not mean that their positions are untenable or invalid. It only means that they cannot be issues decided in the Civic Public Forum, that is, legally enforced universally and expected of everyone.

So what is the solution? A more explicitly proactive theology of religious pluralism than is usually attributed to the American founders. The answer lies in a public theology of religious pluralism that recognizes the inevitability of religious diversity. A theology of religious pluralism that does not regard other religions as unfortunate mistakes is needed by every religion in a religiously plural society because the "we are right and you are wrong" stance makes for bad discourse in the Conscientious Public Forum, as well as oppressive legislation in the Civic Public Forum. If such a theology of religious pluralism were in place, it would not be so dangerous to admit religion into discourse in the public square; it might even be beneficial, and it would certainly be more realistic. What has been said previously bears repeating. Ironically, the benefit from giving up exclusive truth claims in religion would be greater freedom to express one's religious views on public issues without so much resistance from others. Everyone would feel much less threatened if those who make exclusive truth claims no longer argued that everyone else should do things their way, that they should be allowed to legislate their morality onto everyone in the society.

BUDDHISM AND REDISCOVERING AMERICA'S SACRED GROUND

Probably there were no Buddhists in the United States when the Constitution was written, and certainly none were involved in the drafting process. Probably the founders knew almost nothing about Buddhism. Yet Buddhism accords well with the constitutional framework that guarantees freedom of religion and separation of church and state, even though it has not explicitly generated such ideas in its own history. However, this author is more interested in exploring how certain Buddhist understandings might help everyone to think through some of the impasses in current discussions of church and state. This is not to suggest that Buddhism should be adopted; it will remain a small religion in the United States in the foreseeable future. But its attitude about its insights is more "take and apply" than "you need to become one of us," at least in the admittedly idiosyncratic Buddhism of North America.

It must be understood that in this section of the chapter, the author is speaking from an academic perspective of Buddhism as well as from the experience of thirty years of personal Buddhist practice and contemplation, complemented, of course, by considerable academic knowledge of Buddhism. Therefore, the author claims the label "scholar-practitioner" and works from within that perspective to suggest ways out of some of the impasses discussed above.

SOME CENTRAL BUDDHIST TEACHINGS RELEVANT TO THE DISCUSSION

Before linking Buddhism with the concerns of *Rediscovering America's Sacred Ground*, some Buddhist approaches to life should be explained. First, Classic Mahayana Buddhist statements about form and emptiness can be utilized to show how the universal experiences named by these Buddhist terms literally open up the space for a Civic Public Forum. They are devoid of specific religious content (though not "secular" in the usual sense of that term) at the same time as the inevitability, necessity, and desirability of a pluralistic Conscientious Public Forum become obvious.

One translation of the full version of this statement says: "Form is emptiness. Emptiness is also form. Form is none other than emptiness. Emptiness is none other than form." For the sake of brevity, Buddhists often speak of "form" or of "emptiness," depending on which is being emphasized more. The key word that must always be remembered is *inseparability*. Form and emptiness are inseparable; one is never found without the other, though limited vision usually pushes the individual to see one rather than the other. If inseparability is forgotten, many mistakes are easily made, and these mistakes are often devastating. The inseparability of form and emptiness is also talked about as the two truths—absolute and relative truths—and their inseparability. The absolute truth pertains roughly to the realm of emptiness, while the relative truth pertains more to the realm of form, of phenomena, of things conventionally perceived. The hard part is to remember that these truths are inseparable; it is not that the absolute truth is somehow "truer," as many English speakers would assume. It is a matter of knowing which applies when, how, and to what.

These statements are usually entirely enigmatic when first encountered, especially if one has always thought exclusively in "either-or" methods and rejected "both-and" methods as nonsense. Inseparability is about the "both-and" of form and emptiness. Though the statement sounds enigmatic, it is utterly central and basic to Mahayana Buddhism (and certainly no more enigmatic than the notion of the Trinity). It has also become important in certain segments of Christian theology in recent years,[3] though often with a one-sided emphasis on emptiness.

To go further into this exploration, it is important to attempt some explanation of these terms. Counterintuitively, emptiness is the starting point, though it will be possible to see quickly that to explain emptiness, it is also important to talk about form or phenomena. "Emptiness" is the literal translation of the original Sanskrit term *shunyata*, but it is not necessary to go further into linguistic explorations. It is said that all things, all forms, all phe-nomena are "empty," and often also that they are, therefore, "nonexistent." No wonder Buddhism seems exotic, esoteric, incomprehensible, and maybe profound! Some forms of Buddhism, especially Zen, tend to leave things there and wait for the student to "get" what that means. But there is also a tradition of explaining this view as best as can be done in words so that one can contemplate and meditate upon the meaning of these words. This approach is more suitable for non-Buddhists trying to understand and per-haps apply Buddhist wisdom to their own contexts. Therefore, this approach is usually the one used by Buddhists in multifaith explorations.

The key points: When Buddhists say that forms, phenomena, are empty, the question is "empty of what?" If Buddhists say that they are nonexistent, in what sense are they nonexistent? They do not exist *as permanent, separate, and independent entities.* However, this statement does not mean that phe-nomena *have no relative existence as impermanent, mutually dependent phenom-ena.* The problem is that people usually think and act as if phenomena truly existed in an absolute sense, rather than having existence relative to one another.

To say that phenomena are empty or nonexistent is to say that they are empty of self-existence and are not self-caused. Without exception, all forms, all phenomena are impermanent, always changing, never the same for two seconds in a row, completely dependent on causes and conditions outside themselves, not existing in any way apart from their matrix. Put another way, but very important for most Buddhists, is that nothing in them or their expe-rience is changeless and eternal. This nonexistence interlaces every moment of experience and every fiber of one's being. There is a sudden blank, a sud-den stop. That sudden blank is always happening, but just missed, and imposed with an individual's version of reality on top of it. There is nothing else, though it would be even more accurate to say that emptiness is *beyond* and encompasses the "is–is not" dichotomy. Certainly that insight, when actually taken in (which usually does not happen even when people think they understand it), has profound, thoroughgoing implications for every iota of conventional understanding of reality and people's lives—a key point in any discussion of political and social issues.

The great danger of slightly missing this point has always been nihilism. The Buddhists who first began to talk of emptiness recognized this danger themselves and warned about it. How does emptiness become nihilistic? The answer is, when it is *believed in,* when it becomes an ideology, a new fix on reality, and when it is used to say that because everything is empty, nothing matters. It is a problem to believe that things, especially oneself, actually do exist, but it is a bigger problem to believe that they do not exist. These mat-ters are always said to be beyond concept, nonconceptual, so that words are like writing on the water. Yet words are one of our most effective means of communication. Because of this tendency toward nihilism, the author has some misgivings about a contemporary Christian theological attempt to fix the problems of a God who has become too concrete, too specific, too relativized, by talking of God as empty.[4] Any talk about emptiness must be balanced by awareness of the inseparability of emptiness with form.

The question of whether "emptiness" is the best way to render what is pointed to here has become quite important in contemporary Buddhist discussions. It was the standard translation of early Buddhalogists, but contemporary Asian Buddhist teachers who have become expertly fluent in English are wary of the nihilistic connotations of the word for English speakers. The Dalai Lama now prefers "interdependence," which is said to be the same as emptiness in the important Sanskrit text that is the foundation for these discussions. Thich Nhat Hahn has made the term "inter-being" almost a common English word. In English, these two terms probably convey better the inseparability of form and emptiness than "emptiness" by itself. What people must understand is that not only are they not; they are not in the midst of all things, which also are not. People cannot just spin off into emptiness; they must relate with all other empty phenomena because they really have no other choice.

Recently, when trying to help non-Buddhists gain a bit of nonconceptual understanding of these matters, the author has found it useful to draw abrupt attention to the space and silence that undergird all expressions. "Space" and "silence" are equally cogent and less abstract ways of pointing to the sudden stop occurring in the midst of all experience all the time. They are especially effective with academics and theologians, who fill up every possible moment and are always talking, who actually believe that their words convey truth, rather than point to truth. Silence is central to all genuine religious or spiritual traditions; it is also the matrix within which sounds arise. But most people usually miss the silence, both in words and in music. Likewise, space is the matrix within which phenomena arise and into which they subside. But, like the paper on which words are written, the background space is usually missed while the space that is filled up with letters or pictures is the focus of attention. Deliberately cultivating awareness of space and silence, which is quite possible, enhances the understanding of phenomena, of things, and completes the picture so that it is possible to go beyond a one-sided emphasis on forms. Truly, without space and silence, words and forms could not arise and subside. What people think exists depends completely on what they usually do not notice, but exists more truly than all the things upon which they focus.

Discussing forms or phenomena is easier. For one thing, because phenomena and space are inseparable, much has already been said about phenomena, including the phenomena of concepts, beliefs, theologies, and ideologies. For another, people live in the world of form and phenomena almost all the time, so they are very familiar with them. As a result, most people are much more familiar with concepts, theories, ideologies, and theologies than with reality. However, that does not mean that phenomena are constantly misunderstood. The most important thing not already emphasized about phenomena is that they are necessarily multiple, diverse, limited, and relative, as well as ever-changing and impermanent. But humans really do not want phenomena to be diverse, limited, and relative, or ever-changing and impermanent. The true implications of their multiplicity also escape people. Humans want a singular truth; they dislike diversity; they do not want change (most of the time); they certainly do not want impermanence (again, most of the time). It is very hard for them to concede that everything that is focused upon is only relative and limited, both in its reality and in their understanding of it. People are terrified of space and silence, which are much more reliable than any phenomenon or concept, and so they seek something solid, permanent, and true in what, by definition, cannot be permanent and true—the phenomena, forms, and concepts with which they are so familiar.

As the great failing of too much reliance of emptiness is a tendency toward nihilism, the great failing of too much reliance on forms is absolutizing the relative. Since people live so much in the realm of form, of conventionality, it is very easy to absolutize the relative; it is done almost continuously. This is what can make both political and religious discourse so painful, and when the two realms of politics and religion are intertwined, the pain can be intensified exponentially. Absolutizing the relative is usually accompanied by a great deal of self-assurance and self-righteousness. Clear and simple, even simplistic declarations of what is good and evil, and considerable ideological aggression in expressing those views are common. Focusing in the realm of form or phenomena does not require such difficult and disruptive styles of communication, but if there is no attunement to space and silence, they become much more likely. This demonstrates again why it is so important to remember the inseparability of form and emptiness.

Religions, including Buddhism, often take themselves too seriously and easily absolutize their relative verbalizations or symbols of reality. In fact, religions and religious people constantly mistake their symbols for reality rather than the reality to which they point. Or, if they recognize the constant temptation to absolutize the relative, they always exempt their own formulations from being relative.[5] If asked, what about Buddhism and about this author's passionate discussion of form and emptiness—that too, of course, cannot be more than a, perhaps quite good, relative attempt to point to something. There are better and worse relative pointers, but no pointer is more than that. As to what it points to—space and silence currently seem to be the best words for that. But since those pointers are relative, changing, limited phenomena, tomorrow another pointer might seem more adequate.

For those who say that religion has to provide them with more certainty, this author would reply that they are asking for the impossible—for phenomena and space/silence to be the same thing, rather than to be inseparable. They are inseparable, but it makes no sense to think of them as the same thing. In fact, such attempts to merge relative phenomena, including religious concepts, and space/silence are dangerous and are the source of much of the human-caused misery, suffering, and anguish in the world.

If religion is not about doctrinal certainty, then what is it for? The Buddhist answer has always been consistent. Religion is a tool for transformation of both oneself and society. The words "tool" and "transformation" are equally important. To say religion is a tool is to say it is a method, not an end in itself. It also means that religions point to Reality, but they cannot grasp it or really show it to others. The most famous analogies are that the teachings are a raft, meant to take us to the other shore, not something to carry around, or that the teachings are like a finger pointing to the moon. The first analogy is expressed in a famous and often quoted text: "O bhikkhus, even this view which is so pure, so clear, if you cling to it, if you fondle it, if you treasure it, if you are attached to it, then you do not understand that the teaching is similar to a raft, which is for crossing over, and not for getting hold of."[6] Regarding the second analogy, it is said that the person who focuses on the finger instead of using it as a pointer is extremely unfortunate, even stupid. All this means that all religious doctrines, symbols, and so on, are in the realm of form or phenomena; they point to the space and silence, but they are not the same thing.

Another way to express this same point is to appeal to another famous Mahayana inseparable pair—Wisdom and Compassion, or skillful means. Wisdom is realizing the inseparability of form and emptiness, and out of this wisdom spontaneously arises compassionate skillful means. "Skillful means" concerns knowing what is the right tool for the situation. One tool cannot do all tasks; any craftsperson will need a variety of tools. It is more compassionate to have and to provide the right tools for the situation than to always try the same tool and always give the same answer to people who ask for help. A skillful instructor assesses the situation and provides appropriate tools, that is, spiritual practices. Therefore, it is assumed that there will be multiple religious teachings and practices. Thus, from another angle we see that religions necessarily will be multiple. Doctrines and practices are part of the relative world of form, not the absolute realm of silence and space, and anything in the world of phenomena is necessarily plural. Counterintuitive as it seems at first, according to Buddhism, religious teachings and practices are not about truth; they are about compassionate skillful means. Being in the realm of form or phenomena, religious teachings and practices cannot be the truth. That has to be found in the realm of space and silence.

However, to regard religious doctrines and practices as tools rather than truth does not mean, as so many initially suppose, that any doctrine is as good as any other doctrine. A leaky raft will probably not get one to the other shore, and there is a great deal of Buddhist debate about which practices or doctrines are leaky rafts. The tool of religion is for the purpose of transforming oneself and society. If transformation from more aggressive to less aggressive behavior and from less kind and compassionate to more kind and compassionate acts do not occur, then the tool is not working or the wrong tool is being used.

Buddhist teachers often say that, given that people do have beliefs while on earlier stages of their spiritual journeys, it is always better to hold beliefs that lead to kindness and compassion rather than to harming and aggression. Constant checking of this process is recommended. An important implication of this teaching is that Buddhists usually recommend moral rather than metaphysical or doctrinal criteria for evaluating doctrines and practices. Thus, the process of doctrinal debate is more to eliminate problematic views, views that lead in the wrong direction, rather than to find some final truth. However, many provisional teachings are said to lead in the right direction, even if one later moves on to another view, on the basis of further or deeper experience.

BUDDHISM AND AMERICA'S SACRED GROUND

Echoes of the relevance of these teachings to America's Sacred Ground reverberated almost continuously through the preceding comments. It is time to make more explicit what was written earlier: The universal experiences named by these Buddhist terms literally opens up the space for a Civic Public Forum devoid of specific religious content (though not "secular" in the usual sense of that term), while at the same time the inevitability, necessity, and desirability of a religiously plural Conscientious Public Forum become obvious. By this point, it should be easy to see that the Civic Public Forum roughly corresponds to the realm of emptiness, space, and silence, while the Conscientious Public Forum roughly corresponds to the realm of form, phenomena, concepts, and practices.

First, it should be noted that "space" and "ground" are very similar religious metaphors. Buddhists tend to talk of "space" and "sky" rather than "ground" when pointing to the matrix in which things happen and the basis that people usually miss, but they mean much the same thing. The space discussed in this chapter, like the ground of Barbara McGraw's title, provide both the room for and the basis upon which things can unfold properly. In the long run, space, like the ground, cannot be discovered or made up; it can only be "rediscovered," an important verbal nuance.

For rediscovering America's Sacred Ground, nothing seems more essential than recovering some sense of the spacious, vast, open quality that has been evoked as basic Buddhist sensibilities. The contemporary American political situation is intensely claustrophobic because of too much ideology, which is to say, too many relative ideas being taken as absolutes by whatever group promotes them. The "right" and the "left" are equally guilty on this score.

Somehow, it is necessary to get past this stifling situation. Figuring out how is the responsibility of the various traditions that occupy the Conscientious Public Forum, for it is clear that most people are not going to suddenly start to talk about space and silence as their guideposts. But there are ways in which Christian concepts of God could promote appreciation of the basic "ground" or "space." For example, the apophatic theological tradition focuses on the way in which one cannot truly know what God is, but only what God is not; and monotheists warn that we can make anything, including concepts of God, into idols. It is not the author's place to make those suggestions, especially in this context. However, any life changes that promote quietness and contemplation rather than more speed and busyness would be very helpful. With such quietness and spaciousness in place, people would find it easier to let issues that should remain matters of the Conscientious Public Forum rest there, rather than trying to propel them into the Civic Public Forum, which is the main reason for the difficulties surrounding several current issues.

In an America that is much more religiously plural than when its Constitution was framed, the Civic Public Forum must be as minimal as possible and do everything it can to avoid framing any laws or practices that would establish or favor one religion over another. For one religion to try to establish laws or practices that would make its principles binding on adherents of all other religions, or on those who profess to have no religion, is oppressive and therefore harmful, and does not advantage that religion in any way.

Although it is easier to determine what is to be avoided whenever possible rather than precisely what should be done in each and every circumstance, it is mpt useful to enumerate the positive functions of the Civic Public Forum. To list when legal authority and coercion are appropriate would require a list in constant need of adjustment and refinement as situations change. Only one positive general principle applies to the Civic Public Forum. The laws of the Civic Public Forum must ensure that no citizens are harmed by economic, legal, or social situations that leave them vulnerable to and unprotected against more powerful interests that seek to take advantage of them. For the most part, negative guidelines for the Civic Public Forum are far safer, and far more in accord with the wisdom of both the founders and the great religious traditions, including Buddhism. McGraw discusses the guiding principles of the Civic Public Forum: "the law of no harm," which states that no one may harm another in his/her life, liberty, or property, as well as the "law of consistency/no hypocrisy," which means that one should not deny others what one is unwilling to deny oneself. Relying on the evidence of forty years of the comparative study of religions—that the only universal teaching, whether theological or ethical, is an ethic of causing as little harm as possible—the author concurs with McGraw and others who make a similar case. The principle of nonharming is even more basic than the injunction to do good. People often may not really know what would be good for someone else, but usually it is easy to discern what is harmful to them.

Only one small refinement is still required. It is unrealistic to demand absolute nonharming in all cases. Life feeds on life; even agriculture usually destroys some life forms. Therefore, the most careful translations of the Buddhist ethic of nonharming use the word "avoid." One should always avoid harming, doing the least harm possible given the circumstances. It is not helpful to argue that some actions are impermissible because they cause harm to someone somewhere if they are the least harmful alternatives.

Taking these minimal ethical guidelines into account, several contentious issues can be examined to show how Buddhist appreciation of space and silence could help individuals separate the Civic and the Conscientious Public Forums, which is the main issue. Those who seek to impose their own specific religious or moral values on all others confuse the Civic and the Conscientious Public Forums, making religious discourse in the Conscientious Public Forum difficult for everyone.

This can be illustrated with the insertion of the "under God" clause into the Pledge of Allegiance. It is difficult to understand what Christians and other monotheists would be giving up or how they would be harmed if the clause were absent, whereas the presence of that clause obligates those whose religions do not include such beliefs to public lying whenever they recite the oath of allegiance. On any grounds, such obligatory lying is harmful. *Absence* of the clause does not amount to *denial* of the existence of God; it only returns a question about which there is legitimate disagreement to the Conscientious Public Forum, where believers are free to urge others to believe in God, but without using aggressive scare tactics in that process.

Regarding another contentious current issue, gay rights, it is truly difficult to see how others are harmed when gay people have the same civil rights as everyone else, including the right to marry. Furthermore, one could argue that the lack of equal civil rights is harmful to gay and lesbian people, in the same way as lack of civil rights was harmful to blacks and other people of color. If marriage did not involve enormous legal and economic benefits, such as access to health insurance, the issue would not be so serious. No religion could be obligated to perform its marriage rituals for those whom it does not consider fit to marry each other, a condition that can also apply to heterosexual couples. But depriving people of legal and economic rights enjoyed by all other people is harmful to them. It seems easier to grant gay and lesbian people the right to civil marriage than to try to undo all the economic and legal benefits and obligations that go with marriage.

In no case is the confusion between what belongs in the Conscientious Public Forum and what belongs in the Civic Public Forum greater than in the current furor over abortion. The muddled language surrounding the abortion debate intensifies the confusion. No one is "pro-abortion." No one suggests that having an abortion is a life experience that should not be missed. The moral ambiguity and pain of a situation that ends in abortion is quite clear to many so-called pro-choice people. Frances Kissling, long-term president of Catholics for a Free Choice, has published an article in which she urges pro-choice advocates to be more forthcoming about the grief and pain associated with having to make the choice.[7]

The difficulty and uniqueness of this situation is that it is impossible to avoid harm, no matter what course of action is taken. When there is an unwelcome pregnancy, harm necessarily will occur. The very word "unwelcome" makes this clear; the time and circumstances are not appropriate for childbearing. Either the fetus will harm its mother, family, community, and environment in ways too numerous to enumerate, or this particular life stream of the fetus will be ended and it will be asked to move on to another existence. Women have dreams and visions for their vocation, including a spiritual vocation, and those dreams and visions of the purpose of her life are greatly harmed when a woman who does not want to bear a child is forced to remain pregnant. Biographies of Buddhist women saints often contain stories of how harmful forced marriage and maternity can be to women. The fetus will suffer whether or not abortion is the option chosen; being an unwanted child is not a good fate. In addition, societies and the environment are greatly harmed when asked to support populations far beyond their carrying capacity. The question is, then, in each situation: What choice results in the least harm? As a traditionally trained Tibetan lama writes, "Abortion may not be a good thing, but in certain circumstances it may be more beneficial to have an abortion than not to have one."[8] The stereotype that "religious" people are anti-choice, while pro-choice is a "secular" position, could not be more misleading. Many religious people are both pro-choice and antiabortion, a position that honors life and is in no way self-contradictory.

Japan is a nation with a large Buddhist population. In terms of the realm of phenomena and form, the realm of verbal doctrines, Buddhism is as "antiabortion" as Roman Catholicism. Yet the rate of abortion in Japan is quite high, much higher than in the United States, partly because birth control is relatively unavailable. What is the practical response of Japanese Buddhists to such difficulty? All forms of Japanese Buddhism provide a ritual of grieving and forgiveness for those who have suffered an abortion—both parents and fetuses. This ritual is commonly and publicly performed; mementos of the ritual are quite obvious in many Japanese Buddhist temples. One scholar who has studied this ritual in depth remarks that this way of dealing with the ambiguity of abortion means that Japanese society is not torn apart by the issue.[9]

Thus it is possible to see once again how attention to space and silence, to the formless realm, and to the relativity of all forms can point to a way between, or a way out of the extremes that plague discussions of abortion in North America. If any issue should be a matter of the Conscientious Public Forum rather than the Civic Public Forum, this is it. There is nothing wrong with people trying to convince others not to have abortions, without using aggressive tactics in their persuasion. But to make this one religious position binding on people whose conscience takes them to another decision is as oppressive, and therefore as harming, as legally mandated abortions would be.

At a more abstract level, the most important insight that could come from a discussion of emptiness/space/silence and the Civic Public Forum is the recognition that space is not negative. As pointed out in earlier discussions of emptiness, a focus on blank space is not a nihilistic denial of forms and phenomena; it is what allows them to arise and subside. Literally, things arise and appear because there is space for them to do so. Space, rather than denying or negating anything, provides room for multiple arising and thriving. (People's immediate question about the arising of "evil," always a relative rather than an absolute phenomenon, is taken care of by appeal to principles of non-harming, kindness, and compassion.) Thus, if no specific religious forms are imposed, all can arise and thrive in their own appropriate contexts. The absence of the Ten Commandments in the courthouse does not negate them. It simply puts them in their proper context as the moral code of two or three religions that thrive in a religiously plural America. The same applies to the "under God" clause, as mentioned previously. This point—that the absence of specific, often familiar forms is not a negation or denial of them—could be very important for those who are so troubled when their forms are found inappropriate for the Civic Public Forum. The lack of specific forms in the Civic Public Forum actually makes space—makes possible the arising of these forms in the appropriate context, including the Conscientious Public Forum.

Sometimes in a pluralistic society, it is suggested that instead of minimizing forms that are publicly mandated, more representative forms should be added from other traditions. The classic example is adding a Hanukkah Menorah to solve the problem of the manger scene in the public park. One could imagine that instead of removing the Ten Commandments from the courthouse, one could add representations of basic legal codes from other traditions, though it is doubtful whether or not those who want the Ten Commandments in the courthouse would be satisfied by that solution!

In some ways, especially in schools and other educational institutions, there is much to be said for this solution to problems that inevitably arise with pluralism. The problem, however, is that such positive inclusiveness always excludes someone, setting up another round of complaints. A good example is interfaith meetings that seek to include all religions, but often leave out the pagan traditions and sometimes leave out indigenous traditions. This author once witnessed the frustrations of a pagan, wearing her pentagram and wondering where she was supposed to fit into a supposedly inclusive gathering. As a Buddhist, this practitioner felt almost as excluded because of all the God-talk. In the long run, open space is much more inclusive than any list intending to include everyone. No one is rejected by or excluded from space and silence, and no one can eject them.

School prayer can serve as a final example of how attentiveness to the underlying, basic space and silence can help solve divisive issues. The answer seems stunningly simple—silence. Any verbal solution will fail; introducing Christian prayers, even allowing non-Christian children an alternative, is simply inappropriate in a religiously plural society. The inclusive solution of adding prayers from many traditions is awkward and will not be satisfactory to those who do not want to be subjected to prayers from other traditions. Silence undergirds the spiritual practices of all traditions and is actively practiced in most, and one can safely assume that silent prayers are frequently said in schools; there would be no way to prevent them. Disciplined silence during the school day could be quite helpful for everyone, especially the staff.

As the last point regarding the Civic Public Forum, the author suggests that today there is a need for further disestablishment of generic Protestantism. It is no longer the religion almost all share. Much of the contention over religion currently is due to the fact that, especially as America becomes more religiously diverse, Americans are making adjustments to the Civic Public Forum to accommodate to that fact. Such alterations are constantly necessary because people's understandings of what constitutes genuine non-harming in the Civic Public Forum changes, especially as new groups find their voices.

In many ways, the original Constitution and the way it was interpreted were admirable, but in other ways they were not. Slavery continued to be allowed, and women were virtual noncitizens. Some of these unsavory elements were allowable by Christian tradition; slavery was defended as allowed by the Bible and Christianity has a stubborn stream of male dominance and misogyny. Many other aspects of Christianity were actually established as state-sponsored religion, for example, Sunday blue laws and allowing prayer in public schools. As mentioned earlier, in the light of greater cross-cultural knowledge, many portions of the original constitutional framework that seemed neutral and universal have been shown to be a version of generic Protestantism as well as Eurocentric.

Thus, the portions of the national vision and constitutional framework that promote nonharming and equal protection, the two principles of the Civic Public Forum, have been eroding some aspects of what was previously included in the Civic Public Forum. That actually contradicts the vision of some of the founders, as well as attention to the formless realm of space and silence. Slavery is gone, and women's rights, including the right to vote, have significantly increased. Nearly all blue laws and school prayer are gone, though some wish to bring them back. Other issues are currently under contention—for example, gay rights and how to integrate all the new religious communities in our presence into the fabric of our national life. In that process, what was once a weakly established religion of generic Protestantism has become less and less able to impose its forms on the whole society (with some exceptions, such as the "under God" clause in the Pledge of Allegiance).

It is understandable that some pain would be involved in that process and that complaints and attempts to retain dominance over the Civic Public Forum might result.

But "recognizing the usefulness of what is not," recognizing that space accommodates all things, should give assurance that the absence of certain forms in the Civic Public Forum does not involve their disappearance but the recognition of their relativity, which does not change anything about them. *It only recognizes what was always the case.* These forms did not become relative whereas once they were absolute; they always were absolutized relatives. As shown in this chapter, absolutizing the relative is the great temptation of all religions. Furthermore, these forms do not disappear in some "secular" void, nor are they relegated to private life. They are still there in the profound space and silence which accommodates them, as well as other religious forms. And they are still welcome and relevant in the Conscientious Public Forum. No one is asking religious conservatives to take on some other theology. All that is expected of them is that they not ask for more share of the Civic Public Forum than any other group, and that they be nonaggressive and nonimperialistic in how they put forth their own voices in the Conscientious Public Forum.

Sometimes it is said that the national motto is *e pluribus unum* (from the many, one). That motto serves Americans well, but it also needs to be understood that from the matrix of emptiness, space, and silence emerge many forms, many phenomena, many points of view. It never has been different and never can be different. The realm of form is necessarily plural, which is becoming ever more evident in America. Those many forms are not necessarily all compatible, or essentially the same, as some would insist. There are genuine differences in points of view, and it is necessary to learn how to live with those differences.

In both the Civic and the Conscientious Public Forums, one thing above all makes it difficult, if not impossible, to live with differences—exclusive truth claims, at least if intended for public consumption, and they usually are. At this point, it is important to return to an initial claim about the inappropriateness of exclusive truth claims in a world that is necessarily and inevitably religiously plural. In other contexts, this author has strongly argued that they are theologically inappropriate and unnecessary, even counterproductive to the well-being of a religion. Now, it is important to point out how devastating they are to both the Civic and the Conscientious Public Forums.

The one positive universal value found to guide both forums, but especially the Civic Public Forum, is nonharming, often phrased as not doing to others what one does not want them to do to us. No one wants to be on the receiving end of exclusive truth claims, especially in a public forum of any kind. Therefore, they are harmful behavior. Everyone in a pluralistic society has the responsibility to curb their harmful behaviors as much as possible. There are many good reasons to give up exclusive truth claims, as pointed out elsewhere and earlier in this chapter. In the end, however, it is also an obligation to give them up, at least in public discussions.

Such a spiritual discipline is the one thing that could most improve the quality of the Conscientious Public Forum. It is so pervaded by ideology and aggression that it is unpleasant and unattractive to participate in it at present. With less opinion that everyone else must necessarily be wrong, there could be and should be much more civility, gentleness, and nonaggression in our Conscientious Public Forum. These practices would also bring the basic principle and ethic of nonharming into our Conscientious Public Forum.

Part of realizing how to practice these spiritual disciplines of avoiding exclusive truth claims and practicing civility, gentleness, and nonaggression, especially in public speech, is recognizing that being on the right side of an issue or cause is not enough. It simply is not enough to be right, a point that often comes as a shock when this author insists upon it to feminists, peace activists, environmentalists, and others who are on the "right" side of various causes. When these causes use the tactics of anger, confrontation, shouting, and aggressive demonstrations, they come close to invalidating their position by making obvious their inability to present their values to those on the other side. It is difficult to distinguish right from wrong in the case of two angry groups of people shoving at each other. If there is one thing necessary to current public debates, it is nonaggression and civility in speech and interaction, born of long and deep acquaintance with and appreciation for space and silence.

CONCLUSION

I did enjoy seeing my religious symbols on public display in Bhutan. Surely there can be a way that we can make it safe for religious symbols and values to be more visible in our Public Forums. So, in the end, let us pray, that "speedily and in our time,"[10] it might be safe to allow Christmas displays, including manger scenes, in our public parks. Because I enjoyed seeing my own religious symbols in public in Bhutan, I can understand how Christians might feel. But there are conditions for that freedom to display religion publicly. The condition of dropping exclusive truth claims in return for that freedom is nonnegotiable. As for what might be contained in a public display of Buddhist symbols in the United States, solving that problem will have to wait for another time and place!

Chapter 12

Unsecular Humanism: The Supreme Court and American Public Culture

David W. Machacek

Phillip E. Hammond

INTRODUCTION

In his book *Constitutional Faith*, Sanford Levinson wrote, "It is obvious to anyone observing American political culture that much of our disputation is in some sense organized around constitutional categories."[1] Although this "constitutionalization" of American public culture began at the very founding of the nation, it became more apparent over the course of the twentieth century, as a public culture largely defined by Protestant religion gave way to one defined in constitutional terms of respect for individual rights.

During the nineteenth century, the Supreme Court had focused its efforts on the questions of the proper extent and limit of federal power over the states and, later, federal power to regulate the economy. Indeed, James Hutson notes, from the time of its ratification in 1791 until well into the twentieth century, the Bill of Rights, concerned as it was with individual rather than state rights, "fell into a kind of national oblivion, . . . not to be 'discovered' until the beginning of the World War II."[2]

During World War II, explains H. Jefferson Powell, "Governmental propaganda and public opinion alike identified freedom of speech, press, and religion as among the chief moral and political values the Western Allies were defending against fascism."[3] Although his primary intention was to overcome judicial resistance to the New Deal economic agenda, Franklin Delano Roosevelt's appointment of progressive justices to the Supreme Court during his second term in office led to a "revolution" in Supreme Court jurisprudence. It was what Hammond, Machacek, and Mazur note not only upheld progressive economic legislation, but also signaled "the beginning of a period of concentration on civil rights and liberties that would become the hallmark of the remainder of their twentieth-century work."[4] The result, Hutson continues, has been that the "Bill of Rights has enjoyed a remarkable resurgence in our national consciousness."[5] Indeed, the authors of this chapter would argue, a constitutional language of rights has become the *lingua franca* of public moral discourse; the courts, as custodians of America's constitutional culture and arbiters of its constitutional values, have assumed the sovereignty lost by the mainline churches in American public life.

In reaction to this development, some on the so-called religious right have charged the courts, particularly the U.S. Supreme Court, with a "judicial activism" that deprives religion of a public moral voice and establishes antireligious, amoral secularism as the official religion of the nation. The authors argue here that the public culture that the Supreme Court has advanced is decidedly *unsecular* because it assumes the existence of a universal order of moral law that precedes and transcends secular law—a universal order of moral law based on the values of humanism. Hence, the moral tradition of American constitutionalism can be described as "unsecular humanism."

As anyone familiar with contemporary debates over abortion, gay rights, and school prayer knows, America's constitutional tradition is embattled. Specifically, some Americans now charge that rather than objectively interpreting the foundational document, the justices use their power to impose private moral judgments in opposition to the democratically enacted will of the people. Contemporary battles over the role of federal courts in resolving disputes over these contentious issues, in other words, reveal a crisis of moral legitimacy—specifically, the legitimacy of the Supreme Court's claim to speak as the final authority on American constitutional values. As this chapter shows, by insisting on a distinction between what may be decided by law and what must be left to individual conscience, the Court's decisions in these controversial areas appear to be reaffirming, if not "rediscovering" America's Sacred Ground.

THE LOSS OF PROTESTANT SOVEREIGNTY

Protestant Christianity was formally disestablished early in the nineteenth century, Massachusetts being the last state to disestablish its state church in 1833. But it was so prevalent in the American culture up to that time, that it could be said that the state was secular, but the nation was Christian.

Deprived of access to the coercive powers of law, Protestant religion remained sovereign in public life, defining the language and values by which public issues were discussed and debated. The mainline churches, in particular, could be seen—and were seen by both social scientists and most Americans—as custodians of the public culture.

That the mainline churches began to lose custodianship of the public culture following the Civil War is now indisputable, with the result being that the public culture itself underwent dramatic changes, becoming less and less identifiably Protestant or even Christian. However, the roots of this shift in public culture predates the Civil War era. With the First Great Awakening (ca. 1730–1760) and especially the Second Great Awakening (ca. 1800–1830), churches had relinquished a good deal of their public authority. Orthodoxy of any sort was made vulnerable by these two waves of religious fervor, which, by emphasizing emotion in religion, deemphasized doctrine, instruction, and prescribed ritual. Certainly, too, clerical authority in the wider community was compromised, however strategic some clergy may have been in the religious experiences of their flocks.

It is not that religion was without effect; the revivals' impact on social institutions such as education, health care, journalism, reform movements, and so on is well known. It is rather that religion became undeniably *voluntary*, and in becoming voluntary further lost sovereignty. The freer people were to be religious in their own way, the less important it became *how* they were religious or even *if* they were so.

Further, there is no doubt that nineteenth-century America experienced a vast multiplication of religions. Not only did Protestant groups proliferate, but Jews also increased in number and Roman Catholics came in massive waves. Meanwhile Transcendentalists, Spiritualists, Millerites, Mormons, and many more religious groups added to the obvious religious heterogeneity. All would, in due time, establish their right to exist and propagate. Pluralism took a quantum leap during this period.

Before the Civil War, America had a "Protestant" culture, its images and symbols drawn largely from Protestant sources, however varied. Non-Protestant alternatives, if acknowledged at all, were "tolerated" by a cultural elite still dominated by Protestants. By the turn of the century, however, the cultural elite was no longer Protestant-dominated, and neither were the challenges to Protestantism simply other religions. They included noncreedal programs such as socialism, as well as compelling alternatives to historic creeds like evolutionary implications for biblical interpretation. Moreover, these challenges penetrated every major denomination in Protestantism and performed analogous subversions in Judaism and Catholicism. A direct effect of these challenges was the emergence of "liberal" Protestantism, well symbolized by the creation in 1908 of the Federal Council of Churches. An indirect effect was acknowledgment by these churches that, when it came to influencing society, they would now have to compete with other persons and groups on equal footing.

Although the upshot in Protestantism of the Social Gospel movement was clearly a move in a this-worldly direction—as the churches tried new ways to make their presence felt in redeeming the world—it meant a further reduction in the hegemony of Protestant Christianity. The Social Gospel movement revealed deference by the mainline Protestant churches to the growing influence of the social sciences in American public culture. Martin Marty writes:

> From the 1880s to World War I the mainline Protestants saw much of their intellectual leadership adopt various versions of the new theology and much of their reformist passion shaped into a new social gospel. Biblical criticism, evolutionary thought, and modern secular philosophy were absorbed into the liberal Protestant patterns.[6]

In other words, Protestantism was acknowledging the legitimacy of sources of public authority outside of itself and of standards other than its own by which social issues and the public response to social issues would be judged.

The social impact of the recognition of external standards was monumental because it allowed cooperative efforts with non-Protestant groups to reform society. Social programs, in other words, could now be legitimated by appeal to the findings of secular social science, making it possible for reasonable persons of whatever religious stripe to recognize the public health and productivity benefits of, for example, limiting the number of hours in the workweek.

However, if the social sciences provided a language and a logic by which a religiously diverse public might evaluate the *effectiveness* of social policies, they failed to provide a language and logic by which a religiously diverse public might debate the desirability of those policies. The social sciences were—or at least claimed to be—value neutral. Yet a religiously plural public also required a language for public moral discourse that did not presume the truth of any one particular faith. A constitutional moral-legal language of individual rights influenced by decisions of the U.S. Supreme Court came to play that role.

THE SOVEREIGNTY OF CONSTITUTIONALISM IN AMERICAN PUBLIC LIFE

The rediscovery of individual rights in the twentieth century has much to do with America's experience in World War II, and that historical context says much about the culture of rights that has emerged. The limit to the ability of a constitutional system to protect rights was gruesomely demonstrated by the Holocaust. After the war, the Nuremberg and Tokyo trials, and conflict with communist regimes, renewed America's commitment to the idea that rights derive from a source that transcends government—that indeed those who govern can be held accountable for what came to be codified in the Universal Declaration of Human Rights in 1948 as "crimes against humanity." Those experiences could not have been a more potent reminder to Americans of their own struggle against King George III, a struggle justified in the name of rights that derive not from written constitutions but from a source that precedes and transcends human laws.

The impact of the World War II experience on the Civil Rights Movement in the United States is well known. Having just fought a brutal war that revealed horrendous abuses of human rights by fascist regimes abroad—regimes characterized by the violent suppression of minorities and political dissidents—Americans could hardly fail to notice the abuses inflicted against Black Americans at home, abuses tolerated and sometimes sanctioned by the legal system. The legitimacy of the law came to be seen as resting on the morality of law, but the morality of the law was henceforth to be evaluated in terms of fundamental, or "sacred," human rights rather than terms derived from Protestant Christianity. That is, the morality of the law was to be evaluated on the basis of unsecular humanism.

To be sure, civil rights leaders invoked the language of Protestant Christianity, but their appeal was effective precisely because people did not have to share the religious viewpoint of Black Baptists—or Methodists or Muslims—in order to perceive the justice of their cause. One could disagree with Martin Luther King Jr.'s exegesis of Exodus and still recognize the legitimacy of the moral claim he was making. Black Americans could lay claim to rights not because they were Christian but because they were human.

Put another way, discrimination against African Americans was not seen as sinful because the Bible or some religious leaders said it was sinful—indeed, some religious leaders advanced biblical arguments to legitimate discrimination. Discrimination was sinful because it violated the values of human dignity and equality embedded in the Constitution. In this sense, it might be said that the Civil Rights Movement does not represent the impact of Protestantism on American constitutional culture so much as *it represents Protestantism absorbing constitutional values into itself.*

As the twentieth century unfolded, Americans who felt unjustly burdened by the laws increasingly turned to the courts for relief, and the Supreme Court, using a language of constitutional or civil rights, played an increasingly prominent role in defining the terms of public debate about civic moral issues.

Machacek and Fulco's analysis of the public debate over gay marriage in Massachusetts offers evidence of this assertion. They analyzed responses posted on the *Boston Globe* Web site to the 2003 Massachusetts Supreme Judicial Court decision declaring the state's ban on same-sex marriage to be unconstitutional. These responses revealed three distinct conversations: a religious conversation about the morality of homosexuality, a conversation about constitutional rights, and a conversation about prejudice against homosexuals. By far, the greatest number of people who posted opinions, 203 or 32 percent, framed their opinion of the decision in terms of constitutional rights. Another 112, or 18 percent, framed their opinion in terms of religious belief, while 88 or 15 percent, framed their opinion in terms of attitudes about prejudice.[7] These results suggest the degree to which the debate was framed in terms of constitutional values of respect for individual rights and equality. Machacek and Fulco discovered that even religious leaders who opposed the decision tended to do so, "publicly, on secular-legal, rather than religious, grounds. . . . Thus, even religious objections to same-sex marriage are often translated into a constitutional-legal language for the purpose of public debate."[8]

It is clear, therefore, that a language of rights drawn from the Declaration of Independence and the Constitution and defined by the courts increasingly serves as the *lingua franca* of public moral discourse—and with profound consequences. Of those in Machacek and Fulco's study who framed their opinion on gay marriage in constitutional-legal terms, 93 percent favored it. Although more divided, the majority (66 percent) of those who framed their opinion in religious terms opposed legalizing gay marriage.[9]

AN UNSECULAR HUMANISM

Given the implications of the shift of sovereignty from religion to a constitutional culture of individual rights for the public culture, it is not surprising that it has met with the objections of religious conservatives, even as liberals celebrate it. But the charge among some religious conservatives that the Court has established an antireligious, amoral "secular humanism" as the official religion of the nation is simply false.

The American culture of rights presumes the existence of a sacred order of law that precedes and transcends human law. That is to say, rights are not "created" by human legislation; their origins are *not* "secular." However, they come to be known through conscientious reflection on the human experience—the constitutional culture is humanist. Thus, it is more appropriate to characterize the American culture of rights as "unsecular humanism." But the contemporary debates over the direction that the culture of rights has taken do not really revolve around such semantic issues. They revolve, instead, around the question of institutional authority to interpret rights.

Regardless of one's ideological perspective, the belief that the morality of the secular law is to be judged with reference to a sacred, universal order of human rights necessarily raises an epistemological question: How is this transcendent law to be known? The perspective of America's Sacred Ground provides the answer.

As McGraw notes, the American founders rejected the notion that the divine will for ordering society was given from the "top down" through divinely anointed rulers informed by church establishments. Thus, as has often been noted, the founders rejected the authority of tradition—religious and political—as evidenced by the legal disestablishment of religion and by provisions for the revision of the laws, including as Article V of the Constitution provides, the supreme law of the land. Knowledge of the transcendent law would emerge from the "ground up" by persons of conscience engaged in free debate about the good, through an ongoing deliberative process in which all are free to participate on equal terms. Thus, while the Constitution was believed to reflect ultimate principles of justice, its opening line announced that the Constitution was the creation of "We the people."

Although the doctrine of constitutional adjudication was established early on, resting institutional authority to interpret the Constitution in the Supreme Court, the Court, as we have seen, did not immediately assume responsibility for protecting individual rights. While it was generally understood that the Bill of Rights protected certain individual rights against actions of the federal government, it did not empower the national government to intervene against actions of the states. For the first hundred years of its existence, therefore, the Court exercised its power to restrain the national Congress from overreaching its power as against the states.

However, the Fourteenth Amendment, passed to aid the national government's reconstruction efforts after the Civil War, provided that no state shall "deprive any person of life, liberty, or property, without due process of law." The Due Process Clause cast the Court in a new role, as protector of constitutionally guaranteed individual rights, which became increasingly apparent as the Court began to consider the substance of the clause.

THE COURT ESTABLISHES ITS MORAL AUTHORITY ON AMERICA'S SACRED GROUND

At first, the doctrine of substantive due process developed primarily in the Court's economic liberty jurisprudence—the cases involving contract and property rights that had held back the New Deal economic reforms. Starting in *Lochner v. New York*[10] in 1905, in which a statute limiting work for bakers to ten hours a day and sixty hours a week was challenged, the Court had invalidated much state and federal economic regulation by citing the Due Process Clause. Labor contracts, which involved the transfer of property (work in exchange for money), the Court said, were immune to regulation by the state.

The sum and substance of the "constitutional revolution" that followed the reelection of FDR in 1936 was that the Court, although it never actually overturned its earlier economic liberty decisions, stopped consistently applying substantive due process to economic liberty cases. However, it continued, and with increasing frequency, to apply substantive due process in cases involving other areas where the laws restricted individual autonomy. That is, while it stopped applying substantive due process to "property rights" cases, it increasingly applied it in cases involving "liberty rights." Developments in the areas of religious freedom and privacy are of particular significance from the perspective of America's Sacred Ground.

If liberty, along with life and property, form the substantive concerns of the Due Process Clause, the Court, in order to adjudicate disputes arising under the Fourteenth Amendment, had to be able to say what "liberty" meant. At the very least, the Court said, liberty included the rights and freedoms enumerated in the Bill of Rights, and the Court expressed particular concern with the First Amendment. Thus, in a 1925 case involving a criminal anarchy statute (*Gitlow v. New York*), the Court noted that "we may and do assume that freedom of speech and of the press . . . are among the fundamental personal rights and 'liberties' protected by the due process clause of the Fourteenth Amendment from impairment by the States."[11] In *Palko v. Connecticut*, a 1937 "double jeopardy" case, the Court extended that interpretation to the entirety of the First Amendment as well as other parts of the Bill of Rights. Justice Cardozo wrote for the majority:

> [T]he due process clause of the Fourteenth Amendment may make it unlawful for a state to abridge by its statutes the freedom of speech . . . or the like freedom of the press . . . or the free exercise of religion . . . or the right of peaceable assembly . . . or the right of one accused of a crime to the benefit of counsel. In these and other situations immunities that are valid as against the federal government by the force of specific pledges of particular amendments have been found to be implicit in the concept of ordered liberty, and thus, through the Fourteenth Amendment, become valid as against the states.[12]

As Hammond notes in *With Liberty for All*, the "incorporation" of the First Amendment into the definition of liberty in the Fourteenth Amendment forced the question, "What is religion?" Wanting to avoid getting mired in questions of orthodoxy, which would have placed the Court in a position of distinguishing "true" from "false" religions—particularly problematic in a religiously plural society that guarantees religious freedom—the Court eventually recognized that it is individual *conscience* that the Free Exercise Clause of the First Amendment protects.[13]

This shift in jurisprudence is vividly illustrated in cases involving conscientious objection to military service. "Conscientious objection," Hammond notes, "had long been recognized in American law," but until 1948 "membership in a so-called peace church (often Mennonite or Quaker) determined one's eligibility."[14] That is, the Court was concerned with group, as opposed to individual, conceptions of religious truth and morality. Over the years, however, the eligibility rules were relaxed to allow conscientious objector status based on, according to the 1948 Selective Service Act, "an individual's belief in a relation to a Supreme Being involving duties superior to those arising from any human relation."[15]

In 1965, the Court granted conscientious objector status to a self-proclaimed atheist in *United States v. Seeger*. The decision was based on the grounds that his "purely ethical creed" was a "sincere and meaningful belief which occupies in the life of its possessor a place parallel to that fulfilled by the God of those admittedly qualifying for the exemption."[16] Religion, the Court was saying, was to be equated with individual conviction, not membership in some one or another organized religion or even belief in the existence of a god or gods. Moreover, what mattered was not that one used religious language to express one's conscience, but rather that it was conscience that was being expressed. Thus, the Court's free-exercise jurisprudence was moving in the direction of America's Sacred Ground, which held that divine truth is revealed not through institutional authorities but through the individual exercise of conscience and participation of individuals of conscience in the Public Forum.

Even as the Court's understanding of religion was changing, it was also handing down decisions intended to protect the free public expression of conscience. Thus, in 1940 the Court reversed the conviction of a Jehovah's Witness for violating a breach of peace ordinance in *Cantwell v. Connecticut*.[17] The Court said that Cantwell's right to try to persuade others of the truth of his religious convictions immunized him from a statute requiring a license to engage in solicitation. Licensing and breach of the peace laws could not be used to silence the expression of religious conviction in public, so long as his actions did no harm to others and posed no threat to public safety.

Likewise, in 1944, the Court upheld the acquittal of Guy Ballard on charges of mail fraud in *United States v. Ballard*.[18] Ballard, the leader of the I AM movement, had been charged after he sent pamphlets in the mail promising healing in exchange for financial donations. So long as Ballard was sincere in his convictions, the Court said, the coercive powers of the federal law could not be used to silence him, even if his convictions looked like "rubbish" to members of the Court.

Indeed, as Hammond, Machacek, and Mazur illustrate in *Religion on Trial*, beginning with the *Cantwell* decision and continuing until recently, the Court was actually expanding the possibilities of free conscientious expression by insisting that government policies that restricted the free exercise of religion be justified as serving a legitimate state interest in the least burdensome way, the so-called *Sherbert* test.[19] From the perspective of America's Sacred Ground, it can be seen that in this line of cases, the Court was protecting and expanding the Conscientious Public Forum. Here, individuals were free to express and try to persuade others of their own religious views (and to live their lives accordingly), while the use of legal sanctions to punish or privilege particular views was forbidden.

The Court was also, in its voting rights and antidiscrimination cases, protecting access to the Civic Public Forum. A footnote to the Court's 1938 *Carolene Products* decision provided the rationale for the Court's "activism"—that is, nondeference to legislative enactments—in terms entirely consistent with America's Sacred Ground. Justice Harlan Stone identified three circumstances when the Court, an unelected body whose decisions were not generally susceptible to normal democratic means of revision, could act to overturn democratically enacted legislation: (1) "when legislation appears on its face to be within a specific prohibition of the Constitution, such as those of the first ten amendments"; (2) when legislation interferes with the democratic process itself (i.e., laws restricting access to the vote or interfering with the freedom of speech); (3) when "prejudice against discrete and insular minorities . . . tends seriously to curtail the operation of those political processes ordinarily to be relied upon to protect minorities" (i.e., when the prejudice is so widespread that the political alliances that minority groups need to influence legislation are unlikely or impossible).[20]

As others have noted, this footnote provided the rationale for the "switch in time that saved nine."[21] The Court's deference to the legislature in economic matters could be justified because economic regulations were susceptible to revision through normal democratic means; if Americans did not like the regulations, they could elect representatives who would work to change them. But it left open the possibility of judicial action in cases where fundamental rights protected by the Constitution were at stake, including especially the right to participate in both the Conscientious Public Forum (explicitly protected by the First Amendment) and the Civic Public Forum (necessary to protect the democratic process itself). *Brown v. Board of Education*,[22] the 1954 case that ruled school segregation unconstitutional, was a direct result.

The paradox involved in this shift in priorities has not been lost on the Court's critics. In essence, the Court abandoned an activist jurisprudence and adopted a jurisprudence of deference to the legislature in property rights cases, but abandoned a jurisprudence of deference to majority opinion and adopted an activist jurisprudence in liberty rights cases. That paradox is not of concern here. What is of concern is what the activist jurisprudence in liberty rights cases meant for America's Sacred Ground.

In these two lines of cases, the Court can be seen to be protecting the moral foundation of the two-tiered public forum. That is, in the first instance, the Court preserved a public forum where conscience could be expressed and where one is free to try and persuade others of one's own views without fearing the violence of the state. In the second instance, the Court preserved a public forum in which all persons could, on equal terms, participate in deliberations about matters of public policy and law, including especially those whose fundamental rights might be harmed if they were left out of the deliberations.

The Court was clearly positioning itself as the custodian of the moral commitments embedded in the Constitution and Bill of Rights. However, those moral commitments could be seen as having come about from the ground up, through a deliberative process in which all were free to participate in equal terms because the moral commitments embedded in the Constitution and Bill of Rights had been accepted by "We the people." As Powell notes, judicial activism in these cases could be reconciled with the theory that the authority of the laws derived from their democratic origins because one could "explain constitutional adjudication as the enforcement of generally shared traditions . . . , the interpretation of rules adopted by democratic supramajorities . . . , [or] the perfection of the democratic process."[23]

THE COURT'S MORAL AUTHORITY IS CHALLENGED

Another line of cases proved more problematic. Even as the Court was expanding its definition of religion, it was also expanding its definition of liberty, arguing that the rights specifically enumerated in the Bill of Rights implied (although they did not explicitly state) a right to privacy, the meaning of which itself was expanded over time.

The right to privacy was first announced in *Griswold v. Connecticut*[24] in 1965, when the Court struck down a Connecticut law barring the sale and use of contraceptives. It was, however, articulated in spatial terms, referring specifically to the home and bedroom. But in a later contraceptives case, *Eisenstadt v. Baird* (1972), the concept was expanded considerably to refer to a realm of individual choice and action free of governmental interference. Justice Brennan wrote, "If the right of privacy means anything, it is the right of the individual, married or single, to be free from unwarranted governmental intrusion into matters so fundamentally affecting a person as the decision whether to bear or beget a child."[25] That articulation of the right of privacy paved the way for the Court's decision in *Roe v. Wade* the following year.

In a series of decisions concerning the constitutionality of antiabortion laws, the Court continued to refine its understanding of privacy, expanding its definition to include a right to moral autonomy. This direction became apparent in a 1992 case, *Planned Parenthood v. Casey*. In the majority opinion in that case, Justice O'Connor wrote:

> Men and women of good conscience can disagree, and we suppose always shall disagree, about the profound moral and spiritual implications of terminating a pregnancy, even in its earliest stage. Some of us as individuals find abortion offensive to our most basic principles of morality, but that cannot control our decision. Our obligation is to define the liberty of all, not to mandate our own moral code. . . . These

matters, involving the most intimate and personal choices a person may make in a lifetime, choices central to personal dignity and autonomy, are central to the liberty protected by the Fourteenth Amendment. At the heart of liberty is the right to define one's own concept of existence, of meaning, of the universe, and of the mystery of human life.[26]

In *Lawrence v. Texas*, the 2003 decision that ruled antisodomy laws unconstitutional, the Supreme Court affirmed this principle. In the preamble to the majority opinion, Justice Kennedy summarized the line of reasoning that had led the Court to recognize moral autonomy as a fundamental "liberty right" protected by the Due Process Clause:

> Liberty protects the person from unwarranted government intrusion into a dwelling or other private places. In our tradition the State is not omnipresent in the home. And there are other spheres of our lives and existence, outside the home, where the State should not be a dominant presence. Freedom extends beyond spatial bounds. Liberty presumes an autonomy of self that includes the freedom of thought, belief, expression, and certain intimate conduct.[27]

Implicit in Kennedy's statement is the notion that the Court's primary obligation is to protect freedom of conscience from unwarranted governmental interference. This is made more explicit later in the opinion where Kennedy writes:

> It must be acknowledged, of course, . . . that for centuries there have been powerful voices to condemn homosexual conduct as immoral. The condemnation has been shaped by religious beliefs, conceptions of right and acceptable behavior, and respect for the traditional family. For many persons these are not trivial concerns but profound and deep convictions accepted as ethical and moral principles to which they aspire and which thus determine the course of their lives. These considerations do not answer the specific question before us, however. The issue is whether the majority may use the power of the State to enforce these views on the whole society through operation of the criminal law.[28]

That framing of the issue had profound consequences for the debate over gay marriage. The morality of homosexual behavior, the Court was saying, was a matter of conscientious judgment, and coercive laws could not be used to sway conscience. That meant, in effect, that laws concerning homosexual behavior would have to be adjudicated in terms of the "no harm" and "no hypocrisy" rules that operate in the Civic Public Forum.[29] Later that same year the Massachusetts Supreme Judicial Court found that the state's refusal to issue marriage licenses to same-sex couples could not be justified on those terms.

It is clear that the Court's expanded understanding of privacy as a liberty right owes much to the free exercise jurisprudence described above. In fact, that free exercise jurisprudence is cited frequently in these cases. However, unlike the free exercise of religion, the democratic credentials of the right to privacy are not apparent, leading critics to charge that the Court acted autonomously in discovering the right to privacy (its recognition did not come about through the democratic process) and thus imposed (from the top down) a moral commitment that the people had not themselves voluntarily accepted (from the ground up). Nor could the decision be justified as protecting the democratic process itself. Powell puts it this way:

> The abortion statute in *Roe v. Wade* . . . was not the consequence of the exclusion of any members of the community from democratic politics (women could vote), nor did it limit or distort those politics (proponents of abortion rights remained free to take political action to overturn the statute). *Roe* therefore is a paradigm of the judicial usurpation of the community's prerogative of making moral choices.[30]

To those who object to these decisions, in other words, the Court's moral authority has become unmoored from America's Sacred Ground, and by acting autonomously may have actually undermined it.

Clearly, one's perspective on this issue is influenced by how one feels about legalized abortion and homosexuality. But the objection also rests on a failure (or refusal) to recognize that what the Court means by privacy (moral autonomy) is virtually identical to what it means by religion (conscience). The authors are not alone in making this claim.

David A. J. Richards, for instance, draws an explicit analogy between gay rights and religious freedom in his book *Identity and the Case for Gay Rights*. Indeed, from his perspective, the religion analogy is more useful than an analogy to race or gender because, like religion, homosexuality involves moral choice. He writes:

> [T]he contemporary case for gay rights is best understood as an expression of the inalienable right to conscience, and some contemporary forms of political aggression against gay rights . . . must be understood correspondingly as the expression through public law of constitutionally forbidden religious intolerance. . . . The rights-based evil of such intolerance [is] its unjust abridgment of the inalienable right to conscience, the free exercise of the moral powers of rationality and reasonableness in terms of which persons define personal and ethical meaning in living.[31]

Peter Wentz does likewise on the question of abortion in *Abortion Rights as Religious Freedom*. True enough, the question of legal abortion depends on whether or not one sees a fetus as a person—if yes, then the no-harm principle applies and abortion not only can but *should* be made illegal in accordance with the moral basis of the Civic Public Forum. However, absent better evidence of the personhood of a fetus than we now have, the determination of whether or not a fetus is a person is necessarily a matter of conscientious judgment. Wentz likens it to the question of the existence of God.[32]

Abortion, therefore, is an issue of personal conscientious judgment rather than a question of civic morality. Opponents of abortion must be satisfied, therefore, to use the means of *persuasion* available to them in the Conscientious Public Forum; they are not entitled to employ the coercive powers of the law.

Those arguments and others like them[33] have so far failed to convince critics of the Court's decisions in these areas. One suspects, indeed, that they are unlikely to be convinced in the near future that their right to condemn homosexuality rests on the right of others to celebrate it and that their right to protest legal abortion rests on the right of others to obtain one. But that is the moral foundation on which the Court's decisions in these cases now stands.

CONCLUSION

Although he objects to its activism, Gary L. McDowell aptly captures the significance of the decisions made by the Warren Court in defining the terms of the current culture of rights:

> Under Warren, the Supreme Court began teaching a generation of lawyers and law professors what Judge J. Skelly Wright called the "language of idealism." The lesson was simple: There need be "no theoretical gulf between law and morality."[34]

Under Warren's leadership, the Supreme Court established itself as the custodian of America's most fundamental values. As this chapter has shown, this was accomplished by adjudicating cases involving fundamental rights in terms consistent with America's Sacred Ground. Although the authors have acknowledged some foundation to objections to the privacy rights decisions that came down under Warren's successor, Warren Burger, those decisions can, and the authors believe should, be seen as further progress in the Court's efforts to establish the morality of law on America's Sacred Ground.

In response to these developments, some have charged the courts with hostility toward religion, specifically accusing them with denuding the public square of any shared moral values. Richard John Neuhaus, one of these critics, put it this way:

> Religion, in the court's meaning, became radically individualized and privatized. Religion became a synonym for conscience. . . . Thus religion is no longer a matter of content but of sincerity. It is no longer a matter of communal values but of individual conviction. In short, it is no longer a public reality and therefore cannot interfere with public business.[35]

Clearly, the objection here is to Protestant Christianity's loss of sovereignty that the authors have described, and, clearly, the courts have played a role in the process, although, as explained above, the courts' actions are only one of several factors that contributed to this development. From the perspective of America's Sacred Ground, however, the complaint has merit only if one fails to appreciate two points. First, in protecting freedom of conscience, including, as we have shown, public expression of conscience, the courts were preserving and expanding a realm in which religion can exert its influence unmolested by the state—the Conscientious Public Forum. Second, these constitutional deliberations provided a language for debate about matters of civic morality that persons of whatever religious stripe could use, making it possible for Catholics, Jews, Muslims, Buddhists, Hindus, and others to participate fully in the Civic Public Forum as Catholics, Jews, Muslims, Buddhist, Hindus, and so on without having to "translate" their moral convictions into Protestant Christian terms. The "loss" therefore, is not a loss of religion's public voice so much as it is a loss by the historically dominant religions to a *privileged* public voice. The complaint, as Marvin Frankel points out, reflects "mainly crabbed demands for status, authority, and petty but maddening superordination."[36]

A more serious charge, related to the first, is that the process the authors have described amounts to the establishment of secular humanism as the religion of the nation. They have argued that the culture of constitutional rights that has emerged is humanistic but decidedly *unsecular*. It presumes the existence of a transcendent order of human rights that can be known through reasoned and conscientious reflection on human experience and holds out the possibility of continued discovery through the existence and preservation of a public forum where people are free to express their views without fearing the violence of the state.

It is certainly true that, as the authors have argued above, constitutionalism provided a language of public discourse that enabled adherents of many religions to participate in civil discourse on equal terms, but does it give rise to an internal contraction? If, as argued here, America's constitutional tradition is an "unsecular humanism," then does the establishment of a constitutional culture of human rights as sovereign in the Civic Public Forum, carrying with it the full force of the law, amount to an unconstitutional establishment of religion?

McGraw would argue that the internal contradiction would occur if unsecular humanism itself becomes an overarching worldview that imposes principles on the populace beyond those within the purview of the two-tiered Public Forum of America's Sacred Ground. Then, when people are asked to live with the practical and moral implications of an unsecular constitutional culture, there is a legitimate complaint by those who disagree because the result of such overreaching is the undermining of America's Sacred Ground.[37]

In contrast, while it is true that something is "established," i.e., America's Sacred Ground, it differs fundamentally from the establishment of religion that the First Amendment was meant to address. America's Sacred Ground provides only the framework and fundamental principles of a political theology that makes the participation of everyone possible. So, although America's Sacred Ground is religiously grounded, it does not impose a whole overarching worldview on the population from the top down, which is what the First Amendment is designed to oppose, but provides the framework without which there could not be an open debate.[38]

Liberals, including the authors themselves, hold, in effect, that the unsecular humanism of America's constitutional culture is in accord with this understanding of America's Sacred Ground and, therefore, does not overreach the boundaries of the two-tiered public forum. Thus, they have found support in the Declaration of Independence, the debates surrounding passage of the Bill of Rights, and in the Ninth Amendment for the expansion of privacy and moral autonomy rights by the Court in abortion and homosexual rights cases. However, the authors are forced to admit that the evidence that has convinced them of the justice of the Court's "activism" in abortion and gay rights cases may not convince the Court's most vocal critics.

Epilogue

Issues for Further Study and Conversation

Barbara A. McGraw

INTRODUCTION

Starting a conversation on America's Sacred Ground is not easy. Participants in public debate have become so accustomed to the false religious right/secular left dichotomy and its false choice in public conversation that America's Sacred Ground has become obscured in the process. Yet the effort to begin a conversation in this book has been fruitful, bringing many insights to the public discourse, and at the same time raising questions for a continued conversation. Perhaps the conversation that has begun here will continue and, in the process, reveal ways in which America can strive toward its ideal.

ISSUES FOR FURTHER STUDY AND CONVERSATION ACROSS BOUNDARIES OF DIFFERENCE

Although one certainly may be able to identify others, three themes that cut across several chapters raise significant issues for further study and conversation across boundaries of difference. All three are related and so consequently addressing each of them in isolation is difficult. Nevertheless, an attempt will be made to do so. The issues are:

1. *Morality vs. Politics:* In what ways do the understandings of the division between the Civic and Conscientious Public Forums in the chapters differ? How does addressing those differences help to clarify the Public Forum framework and its principles?
2. *Top-Down vs. Ground-Up Approaches to Government:* How can America avoid top-down governance, while nevertheless pursuing the true and the good? In what ways do the chapters' various approaches to the doctrine of separation of church and state help to refine an understanding of what is at stake in public discourse?
3. *The Importance of Conscientious Public Forum:* Has the significance and power of participation in the Conscientious Public Forum in pursuit of the good been underestimated? How do some of the chapters help Americans recognize the importance of a vibrant conversation in the Conscientious Public Forum?

Morality vs. Politics

When are moral issues political matters? This question goes to the heart of the current debate that is challenging America's Sacred Ground. Of course, it would be much easier if the dividing line between the Civic Public Forum and the Conscientious Public Forum were always starkly clear, but as with all dividing lines, that is not the case here either. What is important for the purposes of this discussion, however, is that the arguments are made within the context of the two-tiered Public Forum framework and its principles, while keeping in mind that the whole purpose of the system is to aim for the true and the good.

The problem is, of course, that different people and their "communities of conscience" have different views about what is true and what is good. However, it was this conflict that led the founding fathers to devise a political system that did not dictate what is true and what is good, but rather to set up a system that made possible an ongoing discussion *about* the true and the good. The founders thought that this was the most government could do because the alternative—which ultimately leads to conflict and strife, abuse of power, and oppression of the people—does not produce a good society. The goal should be, then, to preserve the founders' system by ensuring that, when the discourse involves morality in politics, morality should be considered as a legitimate political issue for law and public policy in the Civic Public Forum only when it serves the principles of the Civic Public Forum.

The morality vs. politics issue is always a challenge when it involves behavior that members of prominent groups think is immoral. Often the reason these issues are so troubling is that, in effect, they are asking "who" counts as the "people" entitled to the rights of liberty and equal dignity and, therefore, the protections of the two laws of the Civic Public Forum. Two prominent examples in public discourse today are raised in some of the chapters in this book—marriage and abortion. Both topics ask the "who" question, the first primarily in terms of the question of the "consistency" principle and the second primarily in terms of the question of the "no harm" principle, although both principles apply to both issues.

The question of who is entitled to marry whom is not a new issue for the Civic Public Forum, of course. Polygamous marriage (*Reynolds v. United States* [1878]) and interracial marriage (*Loving v. Virginia* [1967]) previously challenged strongly held views of many Americans. There, what constituted moral behavior for some, for others involved abominations. With the debate about homosexual rights, marriage is once again at issue, with morality being front and center. The Buddhism, Unsecular Humanism, Confucian, and Mormon chapters have weighed in on this issue from their different perspectives. The question is complex: Do homosexuals count as a "who" to whom the consistency principle applies, or is the consistency principle applied to them appropriately already in that they can marry someone of the opposite sex, or are there other governmental interests that should prevail based on the "no harm" principle?

What is important from the perspective of this book is that debates about this issue, and others like it, take place on America's Sacred Ground. That way the conversation can move past the issue of which competing worldview will prevail and toward the question of how can Americans all live together considering that they have different views without undermining the fundamental framework and principles that make these conversations possible in the first place.

Such a conversation across boundaries of difference often can bring insights that illuminate Civic Public Forum discourse in ways that do not involve pressing one's own claims. For example, the Confucian chapter, which takes a conservative view of marriage, suggests that "both our legislators and judiciary ought to tread with utmost care here, and reassess precisely what is the Civic Public Forum interest in marriage in the first place."[1] Is not this what is really at stake in the marriage debate for the purposes of the Civic Public Forum? Once this question is answered, the question of what types of marriages honor the liberty and equal dignity core principles preserved by the two laws of the Civic Public Forum, and which marriages are matters for communities of conscience in the Conscientious Public Forum may become clearer; if not, then at least the two-tiered Public Forum framework of America's Sacred Ground will not be undermined in the process. Certainly, the marriage issue is a matter for further study and conversation across boundaries of difference as government sets Civic Public Forum policy for all of its people.

Abortion also involves an issue of behavior that is regarded by some as immoral. This is an especially difficult issue because it not only involves the liberty rights of the pregnant woman, but also involves the question of "who" counts as a person with inherent rights of liberty and equal dignity and, therefore, is entitled to the "nonharming" protections of the state. The Catholic, Buddhist, Unsecular Humanism, and Mormon chapters contribute to this debate. No doubt this will continue to be a hard-fought battle.

In the meantime, it is critical that this debate also takes place within the context of the two-tiered Public Forum, because this debate, more than any other, is undermining America's Sacred Ground. The reason is that the debate itself is framed in terms of competing worldviews vying for dominance, giving the impression that shilling for votes for the adoption of a whole worldview is a legitimate way to conduct public discourse, rather than recognizing that the issue goes to the heart of the scope of the Civic Public Forum. As a result, the debate has become full of theological justifications that do not relate in any way to the principles on which the nation stands. The issue for the state is this: At what point does the fertilized egg become a person entitled to the protection of the nonharming principle of the Civic Public Forum? Religion is an important contributor to discussions in the Civic Public Forum about this issue, but a particular tradition's theological arguments alone are not determinative of the answer for everyone. This too, of course, is a matter for further study and conversation. Perhaps reflections from traditions not heard in the current debate may help to open the discourse to a cooperative exchange of views across boundaries of difference.

The morality vs. politics issue is difficult because, as John Locke duly noted, political matters are moral matters too. America's Sacred Ground tells us that the boundary between the Civic Public Forum and the Conscientious Public Forum is decided by reference to the two principles of the Civic Public Forum. It is by reference to them that what counts as a Civic Public Forum issue and what counts as a Conscientious Public Forum issue can be discussed without undermining America's Sacred Ground in the process.

Top-Down vs. Ground-Up Government

It is interesting to note that both conservatives and liberals who participate in mainstream public debate have difficulty reorienting their contributions to place them within the context of the two-tiered Public Forum. Alternatively, those who have been more marginalized seem to grasp the significance more readily.

On the one hand, conservatives tend to assume that every issue of conscience is appropriate for government intervention and resolution. That is, they do not seem to be aware of the dangers of top-down government intervention on every issue that is important from the perspective of their own tradition. It seems they have forgotten that the pendulum of top-down dominance can swing, making no one's place secure. Consequently, their focus is to sway public opinion without due deference to the system that preserves their right, as well as everyone else's right, to conscience and its expression in the first place.

On the other hand, while liberals do see a distinction between government and conscience, they assume the line between the two is clear and precise. The reason is that generally they want to make the dividing line revolve around whether or not a view is religious—religious views being appropriate only in the Conscientious Public Forum. But this view ignores the fact that supposed "secular" views, including religious views that support a religion-free Civic Public Forum, can be every bit as adverse to the American system when they become top-down overarching worldviews, as can the conservative religious views they eschew. The interpretation (some would say misinterpretation) of Marxism promoted by the Stalinist regime in the former Soviet Union is a stark example, already referenced in chapter 1. Further, it certainly can be argued that an effort to remove religion as a contributor to public debate is itself a form of top-down governance.[2]

Both sides claim to be "right" by reference to their own perspectives. Because of this, the principles and framework of America's Sacred Ground are lost in the process of their debates. Overall, however, it is clear that the religion/secularity dichotomy that has arisen between the two is unhelpful and even confounding of the debate. All of the chapters make this abundantly clear as they work to locate the dividing line between the Civic and Conscientious Public Forums by reference to the principles of those forums. Rather than locating the dividing line by reference to religion or secularism, the appeal to governmental action should be limited to avoid domination and promote liberty, that is to appeal to the fundamental laws of "no harm" and "consistency," whether the appeal comes from Christians, Confucianists, Humanists, Jews, Muslims, Buddhists, Hindus, or anyone else. How those fundamental laws are interpreted to avoid top-down governance also are matters for further study and conversation.

The chapters on Confucianism, Judaism, Hinduism, Mormonism, Islam, the Baptists, and Catholicism all discuss a thread within their traditions, either historically or presently, that lends itself to top-down alliance of church and state. How each tradition has addressed the issue of the proper role of religion in public life in light of that thread is instructive for the debate today.

In this regard, it is interesting to note that several of the chapters reference the doctrine of the separation of church and state. Yet a close examination of those chapters reveals that the traditions' understandings of the doctrine differ. The Catholic, Mormon, and Baptist chapters are illustrative. The Catholic chapter shows that for Catholics the doctrine means that the church is to remain neutral and therefore not identify the Catholic Church with any particular political party or community. Yet it "should pass moral judgments even in matters relating to politics, whenever the fundamental rights of man or the salvation of souls requires it."[3] The Mormon chapter draws the line between church and state by reference to what it refers to as "political matters," which are matters deemed not to be appropriate for Mormons to address in the Civic Public Forum, and "moral issues," which Mormons deem to be issues that are essential to address in the Civic Public Forum.[4] Such "political matters" as urging or requiring members to vote for specific candidates or distribution of voter guides in churches are deemed inappropriate church activities. "Moral issues" are those that involve public policies that threaten the Mormon view of the family, which is central to Mormons' institutional life—that is, their understanding of the "common good." Such "moral issues" include opposition to same-sex marriage and (in most circumstances) abortion. The chapter on the traditional Baptist perspective separates church and state by reference to religion and morality. Accordingly, religion and morality are not in the purview of government in the Civic Public Forum, regardless of their content, so as to avoid "factional disputes."[5]

These three examples show that shorthand references to the "separation of church and state" do not aid the discourse, because the meaning of the doctrine varies depending on who is using it. The result is that America's Sacred Ground often is obscured in the process.

By way of example, return to the Catholic Church's conception of when its intervention in Civic Public Forum affairs is appropriate. On the one hand, the "fundamental rights of man" certainly are matters for Civic Public Forum discussion because the purpose of the political and legal system, first and foremost, is to protect the inalienable (fundamental) rights of the people. The Catholic Church, no doubt, has much to add from its rich tradition to the discussion about those fundamental rights, including freedom of conscience and its expression in the search for the true and the good.[6] On the other hand, matters having to do with the "salvation of souls" are not appropriate matters for Civic Public Forum discourse. The founding fathers, and John Locke before them, expressly left such matters to the people's individual consciences and their "communities of conscience" because the salvation of one's soul is a duty owed directly by individuals to their Creator and not to the state.[7] Any tendency toward conflating the salvation of souls and political influence misses a critical point: Religious institutions should not be concerned with getting the state to help them save souls, *but being vigilant to ensure that the state does prevent them from doing so.*

How matters that are centrally important to various religious and secular communities are addressed in the Civic Public Forum as subjects for law and governmental action is certainly a subject for further study and conversation across boundaries of difference. It is important to recognize, however, that nearly all of those traditions that are prominent in public discourse today were once the subject of severe prejudice in the United States. Consequently, it behooves their constituents to recognize today what it was about the system that eventually opened its doors to them in the past, and to extend that open door to those who have come after them. This should be done even when it is troubling to do so. After all, it was every bit as troubling to those who opened the door for them. This is important not merely for the "rights" of minorities, but for the continued revitalization of American democracy.

Recall that John Locke and the founders held that the oppressed hold a special place in the political system they devised.[8] The reason is that those in nonmainstream faiths, as well as those who are minorities in other respects, for example, race or national origin—often tend to be more sensitive to top-down trends in government, and they rise up to thwart them. They come to understand America's Sacred Ground directly as they fight for liberty within a system that proclaims that principle as its ideal. No doubt this is because the perspectives of the marginalized are closer to the original vision of the founders, and Locke before them, who sought to eliminate oppression at least in the ideal they proclaimed, if not entirely in practice.[9] The Black Churches chapter and the Islam chapter are especially instructive in this regard. Both provide what many liberationist theologians refer to as the "view from below" that is important to consider if one wishes to preserve America's Sacred Ground in the face of the dominating tendencies of others. Moreover, the Eco-Spirituality chapter brings new ways of thinking about environmental issues that might not have been considered in public discourse without conversations across boundaries that include minority perspectives.

Still, when the once marginalized gain power, there is a tendency for them to forget the "view from below," and a consequent failure to recognize the oppression of others follows. For that reason, in every era those Americans who have gained privilege must welcome new voices from the margins into public discourse on America's Sacred Ground. In this regard, the Hinduism and Buddhism chapters suggest that the nation would benefit from a "theology of pluralism." Perhaps wisdom from these regions from the east can contribute to the continued renewal of American ideals by providing an approach to accommodating the marginalized. Certainly the issue of how the privileged can locate and welcome marginalized voices into the two-tiered Public Forum discourse is a matter for further conversation across boundaries of difference.

The Importance of the Conscientious Public Forum

A number of chapters highlight the important function of the Conscientious Public Forum for the American system. For example, the Confucian chapter very much aligns with the founding fathers' charge that the development of virtue in the Conscientious Public Forum is important for the full functioning of America's Sacred Ground in the Civic Public Forum.[10] The Buddhist chapter warns of attempts to absolutize relative expressions of truth by making them matters for the Civic Public Forum when the various perspectives on such matters actually better serve as "tools" for transformation of self and society in the Conscientious Public Forum.[11]

Often those who press their perspectives in the Civic Public Forum discount the power of persuasion in the Conscientious Public Forum, which leaves the Civic Public Forum as the only avenue for their expressions of conscience. Rather than expanding their influence, however, often their views are rejected or appropriated into the language and narratives of the Civic Public Forum. The result, in either case, is that the original power of the language and stories of their traditions are lost in the debate. Perhaps the division in the Baptist Church today can be considered in this light.

The Eco-Spirituality and Mormon chapters are instructive in this regard as well. While it does seek to influence the Civic Public Forum discourse, the Eco-Spirituality chapter retains the unique voice of the Dalai Lama's Eco-Spirituality as it recognizes the important contribution that voice also can make in the Conscientious Public Forum. The Mormon community, which is based more in family and community values than in individual rights, is very strong and therefore serves as a model of how a community of conscience can serve its members outside of governmental intrusion in the Conscientious Public Forum.[12] Both chapters show how important the Conscientious Public Forum is to public life.

Moreover, Conscientious Public Forum conversations are critical for our time in that the question of the degree to which top-down government can intervene in the lives of the people is very much related to whether and how the Conscientious Public Forum remains an open public discourse beyond the purview of the state. Two topics that are especially relevant in this regard are the media and litigation.

Although no chapter raised the issue, the problem of the dominant voice of the media is one that must be addressed in the Civic Public Forum in order to preserve an open Conscientious Public Forum. The ubiquitous "screen" in American culture undermines the ability of individuals and communities of conscience to maintain and develop their own conceptions of virtue and to persuade others in the Conscientious Public Forum. The battles for top-down dominance in this arena are no less threatening to America's Sacred Ground than are such battles in the Civic Public Forum. In large part this situation is what has led to the religious/secular standoff that drowns out other potentially positive contributions. Americans must find a way to open the public airways, as well as cable and satellite television and other media, including radio, to the many voices in America so as to avoid allowing the dominant few to marginalize the many. The Internet is a hopeful open alternative, but it cannot be the only answer. This issue is certainly a matter for further discussion to ensure continued conversations across boundaries of difference.

The Confucian chapter raises the important issue of the litigious nature of American society as an affront to the Confucian virtue of reciprocity that values relationships.[13] Litigation in the Civic Public Forum, as Thomas Selover points out, undermines the potential for problems to be resolved in the Conscientious Public Forum. Surely most everyone would agree that resolving disputes in the Conscientious Public Forum would be far superior to going through the expense and trauma of litigation in the Civic Public Forum. Other cultures around the world do not appear to experience this phenomenon. What is different about America? Does a system of contingency fees and large awards to plaintiffs lead to increased litigation? Or do insurance companies that require lengthy litigation before they will settle legitimate claims produce a litigation culture? Is there another reason? What we do know is that, whatever the cause, the culture of disputation that it has produced negatively impacts both the Civic and Conscientious Public Forums. They mirror a legalistic "trial" between two "sides" whose only goal is to win, and not to work together cooperatively to build the good society from the ground up, as the founders originally intended. Certainly, further discussion is necessary from a variety of perspectives across boundaries of difference on this important issue.

CONCLUSION

These are but a few examples of the sorts of issues that are central to Civic and Conscientious Public Forum discussions. They show how a conversation on America's Sacred Ground can be enriched, but also how the two-tiered Public Forum of America's Sacred Ground and its principles can be reinforced in the process so as to preserve the system that makes all of these conversations possible in the first place.

Certainly, the founders established America's Sacred Ground in order to serve the common good. The idea was, however, that because of all of the various competing worldviews about what the common good ultimately entails, not everyone's vision of it can be made the law of the land. That is why government is limited—to leave the search for the true and the good, the common good, to the people and their communities of conscience in the Conscientious Public Forum to the greatest degree possible. The exceptions involve the fundamental principles of the Civic Public Forum that preserve freedom of conscience and its expression for the pursuit of the true and the good on America's Sacred Ground.

Notes

Chapter 1

1.   Elbridge Gerry, "Observations of the New Constitution and the Federal and State Conventions," 1788, in *Pamphlets on the Constitution of the United States*, 1–23, reprinted in Bernard Schwartz, "Commentary," in *The Bill of Rights: A Documentary History*, ed. Bernard Schwartz, 491–92 (New York: Chelsea House, 1971).

2   It should be noted here, however, that the concept of secularism as non-religious that is prominent in today's discourse actually is a distortion of the meaning of the word. Originally, "secularism" meant time bound or this-worldly. Consequently, something "secular" might be religious or not, as long as it was directed to worldly well-being. See Barbara A. McGraw, *Rediscovering America's Sacred Ground: Public Religion and Pursuit of the Good in a Pluralistic America* (Albany: State University of New York Press, 2003), 187–88.

3   "I am convinced that I am acting as the agent of our Creator. By fighting off the Jews, I am doing the Lord's work." Adolf Hitler, *Reichstag Speech*, 1936.

4   McGraw, *Rediscovering America's Sacred Ground*, 18.

5   Works of John Locke that especially influenced the American founders include *The Two Treatises of Government*, *A Letter Concerning Toleration*, and *The Reasonableness of Christianity*.

6   John Locke, *The Reasonableness of Christianity*, ed. George W. Ewing (Washington, DC: Regnery Gateway, 1965), 3–6, para. 4–6.

7   McGraw, *Rediscovering America's Sacred Ground*, 90–91.

8   "It is not the diversity of opinions (which cannot be avoided), but the refusal of toleration to those that are of different opinions (which might have been granted), that has produced all the bustles and wars that have been in the Christian world upon account of religion." John Locke, "A Letter Concerning Toleration," trans. William Popple (1685, published 1689), reprinted in *Political Writings of John Locke*, ed. David Wootton (London: Mentor, 1993), 431. See also McGraw, *Rediscovering America's Sacred Ground*, 43–44.

9   Locke, "A Letter Concerning Toleration," 409.

10   "I cannot be saved by a religion that I distrust, and by a worship that I abhor." Locke, "A Letter Concerning Toleration," 410; see also 394–95. See McGraw, *Rediscovering America's Sacred Ground*, 30–32.

11   John Locke, "Two Tracts on Government," in *The Works of John Locke*, 10 vols. (London, 1824).

12   See n. 6 above.

13   See, e.g., John Marshall, *Resistance, Religion, and Responsibility* (Cambridge: Cambridge University Press, 1994). See also references to the essential theological tendencies of Locke's philosophy in A. James Reichley, *The Values Connection* (Lanham, MD: Rowman & Littlefield, 2001); David Wootten, "Introduction," in Wootten, *Political Writings*; Mark Goldie, "Introduction," in *Political Essays*, ed. Mark Goldie (Cambridge: Cambridge University Press, 1997), xxv; and George W. Ewing, "Introduction," in *The Reasonableness of Christianity*, by John Locke, ed. George W. Ewing (Washington, DC: Regnery Gateway, 1965), xvi; John Dunn, *The Political Thought of John Locke* (Cambridge: Cambridge University Press, 1969).

14   On the term "secular," see n. 2 above.

15   John Locke, "Essay on Human Understanding," book 4, chap. 19, para. 4, in *The Works of John Locke*, 2:273; on Government, "Two Treatises of Government," chap. 9, para. 86, in *The Works of John Locke*, 4:279.

16   Locke, "A Letter Concerning Toleration," 411, 415, 417, 420, 423–24. According to Locke, "laws are valid only if they directly involve a 'political matter'—one that furthers the goals of the social contract." McGraw, *Rediscovering America's Sacred Ground*, 42, quoting Locke, "A Letter Concerning Toleration," 415.

17   Locke, on Civil Government, "Two Treatises of Government," chap. 8, para. 95–122, in *The Works of John Locke*, 4:394–411.

18   Locke, "A Letter Concerning Toleration," 420–21.

19   See, e.g., "The Rights of the Colonists and a List of Infringements and Violations of Rights," written by Samuel Adams in 1772, reprinted in Bernard Schwartz, *The Bill of Rights*, 200–211.

20   Locke, "A Letter Concerning Toleration," 401.

21   Ibid.

22   "The common good, therefore, is the end of civil government, and common consent, the foundation on which it is established." *Letters of Brutus* (1788), in Schwartz, *The Bill of Rights*, 506.

23   For a discussion of freedom of conscience and the states, see McGraw, *Rediscovering America's Sacred Ground*, 73–80.

24   Ibid., 23.

25   "[I]t appears what zeal for the Church, joined with the desire of dominion, is capable to produce; and how easily the pretence of religion, and of the care of souls, serves for a cloak to covetousness, rapine, and ambition."

John Locke, "A Letter Concerning Toleration," 417; Thomas Jefferson, "Notes on the State of Virginia," in *The Complete Jefferson: Containing His Major Writings, Published and Unpublished, Except His Letters*, ed. Saul K. Padover (New York: Duell, Sloan & Pearce, 1943), 675.

26   "[S]he [truth] is the proper and sufficient antagonist to error, and has nothing to fear from the conflict unless by human interposition [she is] disarmed of her natural weapons, free argument and debate; errors ceasing to be dangerous when it is permitted freely to contradict them." Thomas Jefferson, "A Bill for Establishing Religious Freedom" (1779), in Padover, *The Complete Jefferson*, 947.

27   See McGraw, *Rediscovering America's Sacred Ground*, 73–80. All state establishments remaining after the adoption of the Bill of Rights were abolished by 1833, when the last was abolished in Massachusetts.

28   See numerous references in ibid., 73–80.

29   See ibid., 178–79, arguing that the metaphor of the "wall of separation of church and state has been misconstrued in the discourse to imply things the founders never intended. . . ."

30   Locke, "A Letter Concerning Toleration," 431 (Protestants); 420 (Catholics); 412, 420, and 431 (Jews); 431 (Muslims); 416 (Native Americans); and 400, 417, and 431 (pagans).

31   Ibid., 431.

32   Locke, "A Letter Concerning Toleration," 402, 420.

33   Richard Henry Lee, "To James Madison," 26 November 1784, in *The Papers of James Madison*, ed. Robert A. Rutland et al., 17 vols. (Chicago: University of Chicago Press; Charlottesville: University Press of Virginia, 1961–1999), 8:149.

34   Jefferson, "Notes on Religion," October 1776, in Padover, *The Complete Jefferson*, 945 (emphasis in original).

35   Jefferson, "Autobiography, January 6–July 21, 1821," in Padover, *The Complete Jefferson*, 1150 (emphasis added).

36   See Benjamin Franklin, "To Ezra Stiles" (1790), wherein he professed a belief in one God. In *Benjamin Franklin Writings*, ed. J. A. Leo Lemay (New York: The Library of America, 1987), 1179. However, Franklin also wrote: "Morality or Virtue is the End, Faith only a Means to obtain that End: And if the End be obtained, it is no matter by what means." Benjamin Franklin, "Dialogue between Two Presbyterians" (1735), in Lemay, *Benjamin Franklin Writings*, 257.

37   See, e.g., James Madison, "A Memorial and Remonstrance against Religious Assessments," in *The Writings of James Madison*, ed. Gaillard Hunt, 9 vols. (New York: G.P. Putnam's Sons, 1900–1903), 8:185.

38   See Locke, "Essay on Human Understanding," book 4, chap. 19, para. 4, in *The Works of John Locke*, 2:273 ("Reason is natural revelation whereby the eternal Father of light and fountain of all knowledge communicates to mankind that portion of truth which He has laid within the reach of their natural faculties . . ."). See also John Locke, *Second Treatise of Government*, 438–39, equating nature and reason.

39   Jefferson, "Notes on the State of Virginia" (1782), in Padover, *The Complete Jefferson*, [Query XVII, 675].

40   Edmund S. Morgan, *Benjamin Franklin* (New Haven: Yale University Press, 2002), 19.

41   See McGraw, *Rediscovering America's Sacred Ground*, 72, arguing that, while the founders generally held to the view that the Divine is active in history

in some way, many adhered to "rational religion," which was not necessarily or generally coextensive with Christianity.

42   Madison, in a letter to Jefferson noted that "[o]ne of the objections [to the U.S. Constitution] in New England was that the Constitution, by prohibiting religious tests, opened a door for Jews Turks & infidels." James Madison, "To Thomas Jefferson" (1788), in Hunt, *The Writings of James Madison*, 5:272.

43   Jonathan Elliot, *The Debates of the Several State Conventions on the Adoption of the Federal Constitution*, 2nd ed. (1836), 4:191–92 (comments of Henry Abbot).

44   McGraw, *Rediscovering America's Sacred Ground*, 39, quoting Locke, "A Letter Concerning Toleration," 426.

45   In fact, many of the founders were adverse to oaths. See, e.g., James Madison, "To Thomas Jefferson," 24 October 1787, in Hunt, *The Writings of James Madison*, 5:30–31. "The conduct of every popular Assembly, acting on oath, the strongest of religious ties, shews that individuals join without remorse in acts agst. which their consciences would revolt, if proposed to them separately in their closets."

46   Jefferson, "Notes on Religion," October 1776, in Padover, *The Complete Jefferson*, 945.

47   "All possess alike liberty of conscience, and immunities of citizenship. It is now no more that toleration is spoken of, as if it was by the indulgence of one class of people, that another enjoyed the exercise of their inherent national right." George Washington, "Letter to the Hebrew Congregation in Newport Rhode Island," 18 August 1790, in *The Papers of George Washington, Presidential Series*, ed. Dorothy Twohig, et al., 7 vols. (Charlottesville: University Press of Virginia, 1987–2000), 6:284–85.

48   Richard Henry Lee, "Observations Leading to a Fair Examination of the System of Government," Letter 4, 12 October 1777, in *Letters from the Federal Farmer to the Republican*, ed. Walter Hartwell Bennett (Tuscaloosa: University of Alabama Press, 1978), 28.

49   See notes 43 and 44 above, and accompanying text.

50   John Locke argued that in the "state of nature" (the realm of the natural law) there is no impartial judge of disputes about whether the natural law has been violated. As a result, as disputes arise, the powerful prevail and domination of others follows. Thus, the "state of nature" becomes a "state of war." Arguing against monarchy and the doctrine of the "divine right of kings," Locke contended, in effect, that the king was merely the biggest brute (or his ancestor was the biggest brute) who rose to the top in the battle for power. Consequently, even the king himself is highly unlikely to be an impartial judge of disputes about violations of the natural law. Locke, *Second Treatise of Government*, chap. 8, para. 151–52, pp. 427–28; chap. 3, para. 16, p. 347.

51   Ibid., chap. 2, para. 6, p. 341.

52   Ibid.

53   Ibid. See also Locke, "A Letter Concerning Toleration," 417.

54   This can be derived from Locke's requirement of logical consistency in his argument. See, e.g., Locke, "A Letter Concerning Toleration," 391–92. See also generally McGraw, *Rediscovering America's Sacred Ground*, ch. 2.

55   McGraw, *Rediscovering America's Sacred Ground*, 55.

56 See, e.g., Jefferson, "A Bill for Establishing Religious Freedom," 1779, in Padover, *The Complete Jefferson*, 946; "Notes on the State of Virginia," QXVII, in Padover, *The Complete Jefferson*, 675.

57 Jefferson, "A Bill for Establishing Religious Freedom," 1779, in Padover, *The Complete Jefferson*, 946. This is especially telling in that Jefferson generally has been considered by scholars to be one of the most "deist" of the founders. But see McGraw, *Rediscovering America's Sacred Ground*, 70–72. Note in this regard that Jefferson was known to practice "private devotions." Charles B. Sanford, *Thomas Jefferson and His Library: A Study of His Literary Interests and of the Religious Attitudes Revealed by Relevant Titles in His Library* (Hamden, Conn.: Archon Books, 1977), 150, citing Henry Stephens Randall, *The Life of Thomas Jefferson*, 3 vols. (New York: Derby & Jackson, 1858), 3:407–10, quoting Jefferson's grandson.

58 McGraw, *Rediscovering America's Sacred Ground*, 100–101 and accompanying notes.

59 Ibid., 97. "The people generally ill treated, and contrary to right, will be ready upon any occasion to ease themselves of a burden that sits heavy upon them." Locke, Second Treatise, chap. 19, para. 224, p. 471. "[It is] no wonder the oppressed should rebel, and they will continue to rebel and raise disturbance until their civil rights are full[y] restored to them and all partial distinctions, exclusions and incapacitations removed." Jefferson, "Notes on Religion," October 1776, in Padover, *The Complete Jefferson*, 946.

60 See McGraw, *Rediscovering America's Sacred Ground*, 51–54 and 100.

61 Jefferson, "A Bill for Establishing Religious Freedom," 1779, in Padover, *The Complete Jefferson*, 946.

62 McGraw, *Rediscovering America's Sacred Ground*, 97–98.

63 Madison, "Memorial and Remonstrance against Religious Assessments," in Hunt, *The Writings of James Madison*, 2:184.

64 Jefferson, "To a Committee of the Danbury Baptist Association," 1 January 1802, in *The Writings of Thomas Jefferson*, memorial edition, ed. A. A. Lipscomb and Albert E. Bergh, 20 vols (Washington, D.C.: Thomas Jefferson Memorial Association, 1903–1904), 16:281–82.

65 McGraw, *Rediscovering America's Sacred Ground*, 106 (emphasis in original).

66 Ibid., 98.

67 James Madison, Speech in the Virginia Ratifying Convention, 20 June 1788, in Rutland, *The Papers of James Madison*, 11:163.

68 John Adams, "To the Officers of the First Brigade of the Third Division of the Militia of Massachusetts," 11 October 1798, in *The Works of John Adams, Second President of the United States with a life of the author, notes, and illustrations*, comp. Charles Francis Adams, 10 vols. (Boston: Charles C. Little & James Brown, 1850–1856), 9:228–29. "Statesmen . . . may plan and speculate for Liberty, but it is Religion and Morality alone, which can establish the Principles upon which Freedom can securely stand. . . ." John Adams, "To Zabdiel Adams," 21 June 1776, in *Adams Family Correspondence*, ed. Lyman H. Butterfield, 6 vols. (Cambridge: Belknap Press, 1963–1993), 2:20–21.

69 McGraw, *Rediscovering America's Sacred Ground*, 98 quoting Richard Henry Lee; see note 49.

70 See, e.g., note 27 above, quoting Jefferson.

71 For example, some Christianities, e.g., those based on the works of John Calvin, do not hold that human beings have free will.

72   For example, John Locke expressly distinguished his Christianity from the religious influences in his political works. See generally Locke, *The Reasonableness of Christianity*.

73   John Dickenson, "Letters of Fabius," 1788, in Schwartz, *The Bill of Rights*, 546.

74   McGraw, *Rediscovering America's Sacred Ground*, 184; Essex Result, 1778, in Schwartz, *The Bill of Rights*, 351.

Chapter 2

1   McGraw, *Rediscovering America's Sacred Ground*.

2   Ibid., 17.

3   Ibid., 92.

4   Of course, there are different definitions and understandings of secularism. For a useful review of the concept, see Rajeev Bhargava, *Secularism and its Critics* (Delhi, India: Oxford University Press, 1998).

5   Bernard Susser, "On the Reconstruction of Jewish Political Theory," in *Public Life in Israel and the Diaspora*, ed. Sam N. Lehman-Wilzig and Bernard Susser (Ramat Gan, Israel: Bar-Ilan University, 1981), 13.

6   Ibid., 14.

7   Yeshayahu Leibowitz, *Judaism, Human Values, and the Jewish State*, ed. and trans. Eliezer Goldman (Cambridge, Mass.: Harvard University Press, 1982), 53.

8   Ibid.

9   Ibid.

10   Susser, "On the Reconstruction," 17.

11   Daniel Judah Elazar and Stuart A. Cohen, *The Jewish Polity: Jewish Political Organization From Biblical Times to the Present* (Bloomington: Indiana University Press, 1985). For a convenient on-line compendium of Elazar's writings, see the Daniel Elazar On-Line Library at www.jcpa.org/djeindex.htm.

12   Alan L. Mittleman, *The Politics of Torah: The Jewish Political Tradition and the Founding of Agudat Israel* (Albany: State University of New York Press, 1996); David Novak, *Covenantal Rights: A Study in Jewish Political Theory* (Princeton: Princeton University Press, 2000).

13   Michael Walzer, Menachem Lorberbaum, Noam J. Zohar, and Yair Lorberman, eds., *The Jewish Political Tradition: Authority* (New Haven: Yale University Press, 2000); Michael Walzer, Menachem Lorberbaum, and Noam J. Zohar, eds., *The Jewish Political Tradition: Membership* (New Haven: Yale University Press, 2003).

14   Steven J. Brams, *Biblical Games: A Strategic Analysis of Stories in the Old Testament* (Cambridge: Massachusetts Institute of Technology Press, 1980); Ira Sharkansky, *Israel and Its Bible: A Political Analysis* (New York: Garland, 1996); and Aaron B. Wildavsky, *The Nursing Father: Moses As a Political Leader* (Tuscaloosa: University of Alabama Press, 1984).

15   Alan Dowty, *The Jewish State a Century Later* (Berkeley: University of California Press, 1998), ch. 2.

16   The tradition was not entirely supportive of democracy. With a tendency to regard the instruments of the state as the tools of a distant and hostile ruler, the Jewish experience also gave rise to a tendency to regard government as an obstacle to be overcome. Even when Jews controlled the state, the culture never enthusiastically granted legitimacy to it—hence the persistence of what Sprinzak called "illegalism" in Jewish political culture. See Ehud

Sprinzak, "Illegalism in Israeli Political Culture: Theoretical and Historical Footnotes to the Pollard Affair and the Shin Beth Cover Up," in *Israel after Begin*, ed. Gregory Mahler (Albany: State University of New York Press, 1990), 51–69.

17   Dowty, *Jewish State*, 208–15.

18   Charles S. Liebman, "Religion and Democracy in Israel," in *Israeli Judaism: The Sociology of Religion in Israel*, ed. Shlomo Deshen, Charles S. Liebman, and Moshe Skokeid (New Brunswick: Transaction, 1995), 361.

19   I follow Martin Sicker's convention by referring to Judaic tradition as the intellectual framework embraced by most Jews from antiquity to modernity. See Martin Sicker, *The Political Culture of Judaism* (Westport, Conn.: Praeger, 2001). As most streams of contemporary American Judaism claim to be the legitimate inheritors of "traditional Judaism," I have tried to avoid taking sides by using that label to describe advocates of the theocratic persuasion.

20   Ibid., 6.

21   The latter, known in Hebrew by the plural noun *mitzvot*, constitute the individual elements of the moral code. As the collective canon law, these responsibilities are codified in *halacha*. The Torah, the written version of Jewish history from which the laws are derived, is sometimes used to reference the entire corpus of Jewish law.

22   Sicker, *Political Culture*, ch. 4.

23   McGraw, *Rediscovering America's Sacred Ground*, 17.

24   Ibid., 27, emphasis in the original.

25   Ibid., 65.

26   Kenneth D. Wald and Corwin E. Smidt, "Measurement Strategies in the Study of Religion and Politics," in *Rediscovering the Religious Factor in American Politics*, ed. David C. Leege (Armonk, NY: M. E. Sharpe, 1993), 26–49.

27   As I understand it, the same would be true in principle of the more collectivist religious traditions such as Islam and Roman Catholicism.

28   Jonathan Boyarin, "Circumscribing Constitutional Identities in Kiryas Joel," *Yale Law Journal* 106 (1997): 1537–70.

29   Naomi Cohen, *Jews in Christian America* (New York: Oxford University Press, 1992), 175.

30   James Carroll, *Constantine's Sword* (Boston: Houghton Mifflin, 2001).

31   Jacob Katz, *Out of the Ghetto: The Social Background of Jewish Emancipation, 1770–1870* (New York: Schocken, 1978).

32   John K. Wilson, "Religion Under the State Constitutions, 1776–1800," *Journal of Church and State* 32 (1990): 753–73.

33   Morton Borden, *Jews, Turks and Infidels* (Chapel Hill: University of North Carolina Press, 1984).

34   Herbert McCloskey and John Zaller, *The American Ethos* (Cambridge, Mass.: Harvard University Press, 1984).

35   Cohen, *Jews in Christian America*; Marc Dollinger, *Quest for Inclusion: Jews and Liberalism in Modern America* (Princeton: Princeton University Press, 2000); Gregg Ivers, *To Build a Wall: American Jews and the Separation of Church and State* (Charlottesville: University Press of Virginia, 1995).

36   Anna Greenberg and Kenneth D. Wald, "Still Liberal After All These Years? The Contemporary Political Behavior of American Jewry," in *Jews in American Politics*, ed. Sandy Maisel and Ira N. Forman (Lanham, M.D.: Rowman & Littlefield, 2001), 167–99; Steven M. Cohen and Charles S. Liebman, "American Jewish Liberalism: Unraveling the Strands," *Public Opinion Quarterly* 61 (1997): 405–30; Kenneth D. Wald and Lee Sigelman, "Romancing

the Jews: The Christian Right in Search of Strange Bedfellows," in *Sojourners in the Wilderness: The Religious Right in Comparative Perspective*, ed. Corwin Smidt and James Penning (Lanham, M.D.: Rowman & Littlefield, 1997), 139–68.

37   Tom W. Smith, *A Survey of the Religious Right: Views on Politics, Society, Jews and Other Minorities* (New York: American Jewish Committee, 1996).

38   Not all neoconservatives shared this view. Indeed, many in the Jewish wing of the movement were uncomfortable with what they saw as the almost missionary zeal of their Christian allies and argued for a conservatism that treated religion and politics as separate spheres. See Edward Shapiro, "Right Turn? Jews and the American Conservative Movement," in Maisel and Forman, *Jews in American Politics*, 161–94. Irving Kristol's son, William, the editor of the influential *Republican Weekly Standard*, has remained guarded if not openly hostile about the evangelical capture of the GOP.

39   David G. Dalin, "Jewish Critics of Strict Separationism," in *Jews and the American Public Square: Debating Religion and Republic*, ed. Alan L. Mittleman, Jonathan D. Sarna, and Robert Licht (Lanham, Md.: Rowman & Littlefield, 2002), 291–310.

40   For evidence that popular religious insights often emerge from the lived world of ordinary practitioners in many faiths, see Richley H. Crapo, "Grass-Roots Deviance from the Official Doctrine: A Study of Latter-Day Saint (Mormon) Folk-Beliefs," *Journal for the Scientific Study of Religion* 26 (1987): 465–86.

41   Lawrence H. Fuchs, *The Political Behavior of American Jews* (Glencoe, Ill.: Free Press, 1956).

42   Jules Harlow, ed., *Siddur Sim Shalom* (New York: Rabbinical Assembly, United Synagogue of America, 1985), 415.

43   For a conspicuous exception, see *National Conference of Catholic Bishops, The Challenge of Peace: God's Promise and Our Response* (Washington, D.C.: United States Catholic Conference, 1983). In that report, the bishops recognized the difficulties inherent in extracting policies from religious thought and counseled the faithful to consider these insights as they decided about the daunting subject of nuclear war. This was a far cry from a triumphalist assertion that Mother Church knew best.

44   Reinhold Niebuhr, *The Children of Light and the Children of Darkness* (New York: Scribners, 1944).

45   John Courtney Murray, S.J., *We Hold These Truths: Catholic Reflections on the American Proposition* (New York: Sheed & Ward, 1960).

Chapter 3

1   Though there are relatively few Confucian temples, and only the occasional statue, the religious dimensions of the Confucian tradition are its primary characteristics. On this point, see T. Selover, *Hsieh Liang-tso and the Analects of Confucius: Humane Learning as a Religious Quest* (New York: Oxford University Press, 2004), 3–14, and Rodney L. Taylor, *Religious Dimensions of Confucianism* (Albany: State University of New York Press, 1990), passim.

2   One could say that the "problem of pluralism" results from the problematizing of plurality. See Wilfred Cantwell Smith, *The Meaning and End of Religion* (San Francisco: HarperSanFrancisco, 1978; repr, Augsburg Fortress, 1991), and McGraw, *Rediscovering America's Sacred Ground* 186–87.

3   See McGraw, *Rediscovering America's Sacred Ground*, 140.

4   Mencius 5A5: "This sentiment is expressed in the words of The Great Declaration,—'Heaven sees according as my people see; Heaven hears according as my people hear.'"

5   McGraw, *Rediscovering America's Sacred Ground*, 177.

6   This term is given its Chinese spelling here, but there are cognates in
Korean, Japanese, and other East Asian languages as well. The modern
word *liangxin* is composed of two characters, *liang* meaning "good" as well
as "original," and *xin* meaning both "heart" and "mind." On the suggestion
that *xin* be thought of as referring to the process of thinking and feeling, see
David L. Hall and Roger T. Ames, *Thinking through Confucius* (Albany: State
University of New York Press, 1987).

7   For an accessible account of Wang Yangming's early life and his existential
decision to dedicate himself to the realization of humanity's fullest possibility, see Tu Wei-ming, *Neo-Confucian Thought in Action: Wang Yang-ming's
Youth (1472–1509)* (Berkeley: University of California Press, 1976).

8   Discernment is a good translation for *zhi* (knowing, pronounced "jzer"),
especially in the sense of *liangzhi*, innately good knowing, or innate knowledge of the good.

9   Similarly, one of the desiderata of heavenly society according to Unification
theology is "Don't violate human rights," by which is meant not to devalue
the intrinsic worth of fellow human beings. Hyun Jin Moon explains, "It is
. . . divinity that allows us to recognize our common heritage, and that
enables us to recognize the universal qualities that tie all of us together." See
Hyun Jin Moon, *Owning the Culture of Heart* (New York: World CARP,
2003), 245.

10   The Chinese character is composed of "heart-and-mind" and "birth or life,"
so the xing can be thought of as the dispositions that we are born with, the
innate tendencies of heart and mind.

11   For a nuanced discussion of "likening-to-oneself" by a noted American
philosopher, see Herbert Fingarette, "Following the 'One Thread' of the
Analects," *Journal of the American Academy of Religion* 7, no. 3 (September
1980): 373–405.

12   "Ji suo bu yu, wu shi yu ren"; *Analects* 12.2 and 15.23.

13   Discussed in McGraw, *Rediscovering America's Sacred Ground*, 55.

14   See Jacques Gernet, *China and the Christian Impact: A Conflict of Cultures*
(Cambridge: Cambridge University Press, 1985).

15   For example, see Tu Wei-ming, "Probing the 'Three Bonds' and 'Five Rela-
tionships' in Confucian Humanism," in *Confucianism and the Family*, ed.
Walter H. Slote and George A. DeVos (Albany: State University of New York
Press, 1998), 122.

16   Moreover, the notion of "distinction" in social roles completely overlooks
the human reasons and motivations for forming couples in the first place.
Today, at a time when the virtues of the husband-wife spousal relation are
no longer taken for granted, the specific benefits of the committed marriage
relationship as a distinct sphere of love must be articulated anew.

17   This model is summarized by Stephen Post in *Spheres of Love: Toward a New
Ethics of the Family* (Dallas: Southern Methodist University Press, 1994),
and further developed by Tony Devine, Joon Ho Seuk, and Andrew Wilson
in *Cultivating Heart and Character: Educating for Life's Most Essential Goals*
(New York: Character Development Publishing, 2000).

18   The activities of the Pure Love Alliance in encouraging abstinence and fidelity, under the rubric of "absolute sex," resonate with these time-honored Confucian concerns. Pure Love Alliance is a project of the Unification movement, which is jointly led by Rev. Moon, his spouse Dr. Hak Ja Han Moon, and their immediate family members.

19   See Henry Rosemont, Jr., "Human Rights: A Bill of Worries," in *Confucianism and Human Rights*, ed. Wm. Theodore de Bary and Tu Wei-ming (New York: Columbia University Press, 1998), 54–66.

20   At the same time, it must be acknowledged (and can be celebrated) that the possibility of freely offering this critique in the public square is precisely the benefit of our shared framework.

21   Mencius does offer a justification for the overthrow of tyrants in these terms in Mencius 1B8.

22   There is an unarticulated assumption that the history of political development has ended, and that there are no new models to be discovered and implemented that might surpass our present ones in virtue. This is unlikely to be the case. Rather, we ought to continue to strive for improved systems of virtuous governance.

23   An important consequence of the commonality of *de* is that, generally speaking, religion is a friend and support of a virtuous political society. The social role of religions (and other voluntary associations that focus on personal improvement) as "schools of virtue" cannot be overlooked and ought to be supported by political leadership that aspires to "government by virtue."

24   *Analects* 2.24.

25   *Zhongyong* ("Doctrine of the Mean" or "Centrality and Commonality") 20.

26   An argument for this proposition is made in T. Selover, "Particularity, Commonality and 'Representativity' in Confucian 'Government by Virtue'" (in Chinese), in *Rujia dezhi sixiang tantao* (Exploring Confucian ideas of governing by virtue), ed. Cai Fanglu, et al. (Beijing: Xianzhuang, 2003), 87–95.

27   Zhang Zai, "Western Inscription," in *Sources of Chinese Tradition*, comp. Wm. Theodore de Bary and Irene Bloom, 2nd ed., vol. 1 (New York: Columbia University Press, 1999), 683.

28   See, for example, Tu Wei-ming's "Beyond the Enlightenment Mentality," in *Worldviews and Ecology: Religion, Philosophy, and the Environment*, ed. Mary Evelyn Tucker and John Grim (New York: Orbis Books, 1994), 19–29. As for our own environment in North America, this land was not simply a *tabula rasa*, a blank on which our Lockean forebears could write. There is sacred ground under "the Ground," and special recognition of that, by Confucians and all of us who live here, may also help us toward a more responsible ecological ethic.

29   See the articles collected in *Confucianism and Ecology: The Interrelation of Heaven, Earth, and Humans*, ed. Mary Evelyn Tucker and John Berthrong (Cambridge, MA: Distributed by Harvard University Press for the Harvard University Center for the Study of World Religions, 1998).

30   In early Unificationism, as in the early days of Confucianism, the emphasis is on fellow humans as the recipients of other-centered concern. But the seeds of a wider ecological ethic are also present, particularly in Rev. Moon's teachings on appreciation and stewardship of the oceans.

31   *Mencius* 3B9.

32   "Yi yin yi yang zhi wei dao"; from the "Great Commentary" (*Xi Cizhuan*) on the *Book of Change* (Yijing) 1/4.

33   See *Analects* 1.12.

34   Anthony J. Guerra, *Family Matters: The Role of Christianity in the Formation of the Western Family* (St. Paul, MN: Paragon House, 2002), 139. Guerra's comment that "it would be foolhardy for the churches to let these achievements slip away now" could apply equally to other religious communities, including the Confucian.

35   In East Asian languages, the word for "individualism" almost inevitably connotes selfishness rather than self-reliance, an unwillingness to recognize the mutual obligations of primordial ties. Moreover, the Confucian suspicion of such "individualism" is a legacy from Mencius's debates with one of his rivals. But this presumably is not the sort of individualism that Locke had in mind.

36   How to accomplish this is a matter for Civic Public Forum debate and decision. It is helpful to recall, though, that when America's Sacred Ground was first set up, the whole tangle of tax policy did not exist.

37   Such self-restraint as a principle in our Conscientious Public Forum would help in overcoming the shallowness and self-centeredness engendered by overstimulation in our market economy, saturated with erotic advertising.

38   McGraw, *Rediscovering America's Sacred Ground*, 55; italics in the original.

39   The Unificationist advocacy of "one God-centered human family" explicitly includes the nuances of elder/younger as well as husband/wife and parent/children. See Moon, *Owning the Culture of Heart*, 243.

40   Quoted in McGraw, *Rediscovering America's Sacred Ground*, 105.

Chapter 4

1   "Popes in the 12–18th Centuries," Web Gallery of Art, Glossary. http://gallery.euroweb.hu/database/glossary/popes/popes.html.

2   Leon Hooper, S.J., ed., *Religious Liberty: Catholic Struggles with Pluralism* (Louisville: Westminster, 1993), 25–26.

3   In fact, in 1895, Pope Leo XIII supported such a situation and wrote in his encyclical *Longinque Oceani* that "Catholics ought to prefer to associate with Catholics, a course which will be very conducive to safeguarding their faith." *The Great Encyclical Letters of Pope Leo XIII*, ed. John J. Wynne, S.J. (New York: Benzinger Brothers, 1903), 332.

4   U.S. Department of Commerce, Bureau of the Census, *Historical Statistics of the United States, Colonial Times to 1970*, 391–92.

5   *Pierce v. Society of Sisters*, 268 U.S. 501 (1925).

6   *Cochran v. Louisiana State Board of Education*, 281 U.S. 370 (1930).

7   Thomas T. McAvoy, C.S.C., *History of the Catholic Church in America* (Notre Dame: University of Notre Dame Press, 1960), 395.

8   Charles C. Marshall, "An Open Letter to the Honorable Alfred E. Smith, A Question That Needs an Answer," *Atlantic Monthly*, April 1927, 542.

9   Alfred E. Smith, "Catholic and Patriot: Governor Smith Replies," *Atlantic Monthly*, May 1927, 721.

10   Jo Renee Formicola, *The Catholic Church and Human Rights* (New York: Garland 1988). See chapter 2, which chronicles the work of U.S. Catholic Charities and Caritas in the immediate postwar period.

11   The Gallup Polls for 1950, 1953, and 1954 show Catholic support at 49 percent, 51 percent, and 58 percent respectively, but that it was never overwhelming or monolithic. Nevertheless, the statistics reflected an opposition to communism that revealed a sense of solidarity with McCarthy and his

committee. See Vincent de Santis, "American Catholics and McCarthyism," *The Catholic Historical Review* 2, April 1965, 29–31.

12   For a fuller discussion see Jo Renee Formicola, "American Catholic Political Theology," *Journal of Church and State* 29, no. 3 (1987): 457–74.

13   In *Cochran v. Louisiana State Board of Education*, 281 U.S. 370 (1930), the Supreme Court ruled that the use of state funds for textbooks for students in parochial schools did not constitute a taking of property without due process. In Everson v. Board of Education, 330 U.S. 1 (1947), the Supreme Court ruled that transportation was a student benefit and did not violate the principle of establishment in the First Amendment.

14   Among the subsequent cases that reflected this line of precedents were *Tilton v. Richardson*, 403 U.S. 679 (1971), which allowed aid to religious colleges and denied that such action was directly aiding religion. In *Widmar v. Vincent*, 454 U.S. 263 (1981), the court held that Title I funds were available to all students for remedial education. In *Mueller v. Allen*, 463 U.S. 388 (1983), the court allowed limited tax deductions for tuition to private— including religious—elementary or high schools. In *Witters v. Washington Department of Services for the Blind*, 474 U.S. 481 (1986), the Court included religious choice into programs of general benefits. In *Zobrest v. Catalina Foothills Board of Education*, 509 U.S. 1 (1993) the Court extended benefits to a broad class of citizens (including Catholics) to receive assistance with educational services for the deaf. In *Agostini v. Felton*, 117 S.Ct. (1997), the Court allowed remedial educational for those in private and parochial education. In *Mitchell v. Helms*, 530 U.S. 793 (2000), the Court allowed all types of educational materials, specifically Internet access, to be extended to private and parochial schools.

15   See, for example, John Courtney Murray, S.J., "Freedom of Religion I: The Ethical Problem," *Theological Studies* 6 (1945): 229–88; John Courtney Murray, S.J., "Contemporary Orientations of Catholic Thought on Church and State," *Theological Studies* 10 (1949): 177–234; and John Courtney Murray, S.J., "Leo XIII on Church and State: General Structure of the Controversy," *Theological Studies* 14 (1953): 1–30.

16   For a fuller explanation see Formicola, "American Catholic Political Theology," 457–74.

17   John Courtney Murray, S.J., *We Hold These Truths* (New York: Doubleday, 1964), 9–10.

18   John Courtney Murray, S.J., draft of a confidential document prepared for the National Catholic Welfare Council (NCWC) as the basis of testimony for Duggan Hearings, undated, p. 2. Available in NCWC, Church and State and Federal Aid File, Box 14, Archives of Catholic University of America.

19   Ibid., 71.

20   Murray's attempt to elevate religious pluralism to a higher order of values in effect negated traditional Catholic demands for privileged status within the United States, but it was still considered unacceptable within official Catholic circles as late as 1955. At that time, the Vatican office of orthodoxy, the Congregation for the Doctrine of the Faith, silenced Murray for supporting American pluralism and banned him from writing on the topic of religious freedom for the next seven years. Nevertheless, it was Murray whom John Kennedy consulted about church-state matters when he ran for president in 1960. It was also Murray who was brought to Rome by Francis Cardinal Spellman of New York for the General Council, known as Vatican II, that was held from 1962 to 1965.

21   On the ethical level, he argued that religious freedom was an inalienable right. On the political plane, he argued that religious freedom was a right worthy of preservation and protection by government. On the theological plane he said it was considered as the right that justified the freedom of the church. See aforementioned articles for the complete arguments.

22   "Declaration on Religious Liberty" (*Dignitatis Humanae*), chap. 1, para. 2, p. 800, in *Vatican Council II: The Conciliar and Post-Conciliar Documents*, ed. Austin Flannery, O.P. (Boston: Daughters of St. Paul, 1988).

23   "Pastoral Constitution on the Church in the Modern World" (*Gaudium et Spes*), chap. 4, para. 79, pp. 984–85, in *Vatican Council II: The Conciliar and Post-Conciliar Documents*, ed. Austin Flannery, O.P. (Boston: Daughters of St. Paul, 1988).

24   John F. Kennedy, Address to the Houston Ministerial Association, Houston, Texas, 12 June 1960. American Rhetoric, Speeches. http://www.american-rhetoric.com/speeches/johnfkennedyhoustonministerialspeech.htm.

25   This had consisted of statements, pastoral letters, and prayers. See Hugh Nolan, *Pastoral Letters of the United States Catholic Bishops*, vol. 3 (Washington, D.C.: National Conference of Catholic Bishops 1983). See the following examples: "Statement on Abortion," 17 April 1969; "Declaration on Abortion," 18 November 1970; "Ethical and Religious Directives for Catholic Health Facilities," November 1971 (revised in 1975); and "Population and the American Future: A Response," 13 April 1972.

26   Telephone conversations of the author with George Reed, National Conference of Catholic Bishops (NCCB) legal counsel at the time, on 15 and 25 February 1995.

27   John Paul II has attempted to reconcile with the Jews, establishing diplomatic relations with Israel in 1994 and publicly apologizing for the church's role in anti-Jewish behavior since its inception. Outreach has also occurred toward the Palestinians, a variety of Arab states, and Russian and officially atheistic states such as Cuba and China. For a much fuller discussion see Jo Renee Formicola, *John Paul II: Prophetic Politician* (Washington, D.C.: Georgetown University Press, 2002).

28   *Congregation for the Doctrine of the Faith*, "The Participation of Catholics in Political Life," [online] 24 November 2002. http://www.vatican.va/roman_curia/.

29   Ibid., sect. 1, para. 1.

30   Ibid.

31   Ibid.

32   Ibid., sect. 2.

33   Ibid.

34   Ibid., sect. 4, para. 7.

35   Ibid.

36   Ibid., sect. 2, para. 3.

37   For some of the writings of Pope John Paul II in these areas, see the encyclicals *Sollicitudo Rei Socialis* (*On Social Concern*) in 1987, *Centesimus Annus* (*One Hundred Years*) in 1991; and *Laborem Exercens* (*On Human Work*) in 1981. http://www.vatican.va.

38   In 1917, the American bishops formed their first national organization to deal with concerns such as education, immigration, and social action. In 1966, after Vatican II, they established the National Conference of Catholic Bishops (NCCB) and an administrative agency, the United States Catholic

Conference (USCC). The NCCB operated through committees of bishops that were assisted by its full-time staff. In July 2001, the NCCB and the USCC were combined to form the United States Conference of Catholic Bishops. The bishops' organization is a canonical, hierarchical one, composed of the 375 bishops of the dioceses in the United States. The aggregate meet twice a year to deal with matters that intersect at the juncture of morality and politics.

39   United States Conference of Catholic Bishops, "Faithful Citizenship: A Catholic Call to Political Responsibility," [online] 2003. Washington, D.C.: United States Conference of Catholic Bishops, Bishops' Statement. http://www.usccb.org/faithfulcitizenship/bishopStatement.html.

40   Ibid., sect. 5, p. 8.

41   The bishops are limited as to how they may act in the political process by the terms of their 501(c)3 status. As a tax-exempt institution, the Catholic Church may not become involved in partisan politics. However, a bill before the House, introduced by Rep. Bill Thomas (R-California), chairman of the House Ways and Means Committee, would make it easier for churches to support political candidates. An addition to a larger bill on revising corporate taxes, the Safe Harbor for Churches provision would allow religious organizations up to three political endorsements within a year, and reduce the tax penalties for such actions without jeopardizing their tax-exempt status. Such a bill could tap religious organizations for support, speaking platforms, and donations. It would benefit, for example, the actions of the Rev. Jerry Falwell, who endorsed President Bush's reelection on his e-mail newsletter, and who defended his "right to endorse political candidates in his personal capacity, even from the pulpit." See David D. Kirkpatrick, "Citing Falwell's Endorsement of Bush, Group Challenges His Tax-Exempt Status," *The New York Times*, 16 June 2004, A16.

42   United States Conference of Catholic Bishops, "Catholics in Political Life," [online] 18 June 2004. Washington, D.C.: United States Conference of Catholic Bishops. http://www.usccb.org/bishops/catholicsinpoliticallife.htm.

43   Ibid.

44   Ibid.

45   Ibid.

46   Excerpt from the Address by Archbishop Roach to the National Council of Catholic Bishops, *The New York Times*, 18 November 1981, B4.

47   See the two pastoral letters of the American Catholic Bishops: *The Challenge of Peace: God's Promise and Our Response* (Washington, D.C.: United States Conference of Catholic Bishops, 1983) and *Economic Justice for All* (Washington, D.C.: United States Conference of Catholic Bishops, 1986).

48   Governor Mario Cuomo, "Religious Belief and Public Morality: A Catholic Governor's Perspective." Remarks delivered at Notre Dame University, Indiana, 13 September 1984. http://pewforum.org/docs/print.php?DocID=14.

49   Ibid.

50   Text of Statement by Bishops on Church Role in Politics, *The New York Times*, 14 October 1984, A30.

51   Ibid.

52   Laurie Goodstein, "Bishop Would Deny Rite for Defiant Catholic Voters," *The New York Times*, 14 May 2004, A16.

53   Laurie Goodstein, "Politicians Face Bishops' Censure in Abortion Rift," *The New York Times*, 9 June 2004, A1.

54   Jodi Wilgoren, "Kerry Vows to Lift Bush Limits on Stem-Cell Research," *The New York Times*, 22 June 2004, A14.

55   Laurie Goodstein, "Communion Issue Creates Split Among U.S. Bishops," *The New York Times*, 6 June 2004, A22. She reports that only about 15 of the nation's 195 diocesan leaders have said publicly that they would deny Communion to politicians who support abortion rights.

56   Congregation for the Doctrine of the Faith, "Participation of Catholics in Political Life."

57   Goodstein, "Communion Issue," A22.

58   David D. Kirkpatrick, "Bush Sought Vatican Official's Help on Issues, Report Says," *The New York Times*, 13 June 2004, A38.

59   "Address of Pope John Paul II to the Honorable George W. Bush, President of the United States of America, 4 June 2004. http://www.vatican.va/holy_father/john_paul_ii/speeches/2004/june/documents/hf_jp-ii_spe_200 40604_president-usa_en.html.

60   Deborah Orin, "Teddy Gives the Pope Hell," *New York Post*, 18 June 2004, 22.

61   Cuomo, "Religious Belief and Public Morality."

62   As early as 1985, individuals within the church became alarmed about the number of clerical sexual abuse cases in the United States. They drafted a secret report for the bishops, defining its scope and nature as well as the potential financial and social ramifications of such actions. By 1992, the bishops established guidelines to deal with allegations of abuse, but did little to deal with its root causes. In 2001 the Congregation for the Doctrine of the Faith issued letters to bishops ordering them to report allegations of pedophilia to Rome. It was not until the Boston Globe broke the story that the Boston Archdiocese had settled fifty lawsuits against one Father Joseph Geoghan amounting to about $10 million that the crisis was recognized for what it was in the United States. For a more detailed account see Jo Renee Formicola, "The Vatican, the American Bishops, and the Church-State Ramifications of Clerical Sexual Abuse," *Journal of Church and State* 46 (2004): 479–502.

63   United States Conference of Catholic Bishops, "Effort to Combat Clergy Sexual Abuse Against Minors: A Chronology," http://www.usccb.org/comm/kit2.shtml.

64   "Society Shares Blame for Scandals, Vatican Says," *Los Angeles Times*, 26 June 1993, B5.

65   Melinda Henneberger, "Vatican to Hold Secret Trials of Priests in Pedophilia Cases," *The New York Times*, 9 January 2002, A8.

66   The United States Conference of Catholic Bishops, *The Essential Norms for Diocesan/Eparchial Policies Dealing with Allegations of Sexual Abuse of Minors by Priests Deacons or Other Church Personnel* (Washington, DC: United States Conference of Catholic Bishops, 2002), para. 10.

67   This refers to those priests who follow a way of life set down by their founders e.g., Benedictines, Franciscans, Dominicans, Jesuits etc., who live communally and receive virtually no pay. They depend on their community for housing, health benefits and retirement. They would not be turned out by their orders.

68   Sam Dillon, "Catholic Religious Orders Let Abusive Priests Stay," *The New York Times*, 10 August 2002, A8.

69   The National Review Board for the Protection of Children and Young People, "A Report on the Crisis in the Catholic Church in the United States"

(Washington, DC: United States Conference of Catholic Bishops, 2004), 61. Under church law, eight were eventually defrocked, nine were permanently suspended, and three still await canonical trials. Two others were cleared and one case was deferred. See Bruce Lambert, "17 Priests Reported Disciplined in Long Island Sex Abuse Cases," *The New York Times*, 25 January 2005, B2.

70   Pam Belluck, "Judge Denies Church's Bid to Seal Records on Priests," *The New York Times*, 20 November 2002, A18.

71   John Jay College of Criminal Justice, "The Nature and Scope of Sexual Abuse of Minors by Catholic Priests and Deacons in the U.S. 1950–2002," Research study conducted by John Jay College, 25 February 2004. www.usccb.org/nrb/johnjaystudy. In February 2005, a second Report on the Implementation of the "Charter for the Protection of Children and Young People." issued by the Office of Child and Youth Protection of the USCCB, reported that, indeed, 1,092 new accusations of abuse were made. See Neela Banerjee, "Catholic Group Receives 1,092 New Sex Abuse Reports," *The New York Times*, 19 February 2005, A12. See also http://www.nccbuscc.org/ocyp/dioceses0405-039.shtml.

72   Denise Lavoie, "Boston Archdiocese Agrees to Settle Clergy Sex Abuse Cases for $85 Million," *The Boston Globe*, 9 September 2004, A1.

73   Neela Banerjee, "Catholic Order Agrees to Pay 6.3 Million to Settle Abuse Suits," *The New York Times*, 25 December 2004, A17.

74   Ibid.

75   David Hendon and Jeremiah Russell, "Notes on Church-State Affairs," *Journal of Church and State* 46, no. 4 (2004): 926.

76   The National Review Board, "Crisis in the Catholic Church," 139–44.

77   The Survivors Network of those Abused by Priests. http://www.snapnetwork.org.

78   Dan Klepal, "Time to Take Back the Church," *The Cincinnati Enquirer*, 5 October 2003. http://www.enquirer.com.

79   See Voice of the Faithful, www.votf.org, for financial statements and membership information.

80   Laurie Goodstein, "Bishops' Leader Resists Releasing Priest's Records in His Own Diocese," *The New York Times*, 2 September 2004, A24.

81   Laurie Goodstein," Abuse Scandal Has Been Ended, Top Bishop Says," *The New York Times*, 28 February 2004, A1.

82   Since 1178 and the Third Lateran Council, clerics were to be dismissed or confined to monasteries for penance if they engaged in sexual abuse. In 1556 a papal decree stated that priests should be handed over to civil authorities for punishment. As recently as 1983, the Canon Law provided that any cleric who committed an offense against the Sixth Commandment with a minor was to be punished "with just penalties, not excluding dismissal from the clerical state if the case so warrants." See the National Review Board, "Crisis in the Catholic Church," 32.

Chapter 5

1   World Watch Institute, *Vital Signs 2002* (New York: Norton, 2002).

2   C. A. Bowers, *Educating for an Ecologically Sustainable Culture* (Albany: State University of New York Press, 1995), 19.

3   See, for example, Susan Armstrong and Richard Botzler, eds., *Environmental Ethics: Divergence and Convergence* (New York: McGraw-Hill, 1993); Richard Flotz, *Worldview, Religion, and the Environment* (Belmont, CA: Wadsworth, 2003); Roger S. Gottlieb, ed., *This Sacred Earth: Religion, Nature, Environment* (New York: Routledge, 1996); Kenneth Kraft, "The Greening of Buddhist Practice," *Cross Currents* 44, no. 2 (1994): 63–80; Joanna Macy, *World as Lover, World as Self* (Berkeley, CA: Parallax, 1991); Stan J. Row, "From Reductionism to Holism in Ecology and Deep Ecology," *The Ecologist* 27, no. 4 (1997): 147-52; and Klas Sandell, ed., *Buddhist Perspectives on the Ecocrisis* (Kandy, Sri Lanka: Buddhist Publication Society, 1987).

4   Aldous Huxley, *The Perennial Philosophy* (London: Chato & Windus, 1946).

5   His Holiness the Dalai Lama, *Ethics for the New Millennium* (New York: Riverhead, 1999), 36–37.

6   Ibid., 41.

7   Fritjof Capra, *The Web of Life: A New Scientific Understanding of Living Systems* (New York: Anchor, 1996), 22.

8   His Holiness the Dalai Lama, *Ethics for the New Millenium*, 39.

9   Ibid., 60–61.

10   E. O. Wilson, *Biophilia* (Cambridge, MA: Harvard University Press, 1984).

11   Stephen Woolpert, "Transformational Political Groups: The Political Psychology of the Green Movement," in *Transformational Politics: Theory, Study, and Practice*, ed. Stephen Woolpert, Christa Daryl Slaton, and Edwin W. Schwerin (Albany: State University of New York Press, 1998), 233–44.

12   Gregory Smith, "Creating a Public of Environmentalists," in *Ecology in Education*, ed. Monica Hale (Cambridge: Cambridge University Press, 1993), 207–27.

13   Kraft, "Greening of Buddhist Practice," 71.

14   His Holiness the Dalai Lama, *Ethics for the New Millenium*, 22.

15   Ibid., 162–63.

16   Stephen B. Sharper, *Redeeming the Time: A Political Theology of the Environment* (New York: Continuum, 1998).

17   His Holiness the Dalai Lama, *Ethics for the New Millenium*, 42.

18   C. A. Bowers, *Education, Cultural Myths, and the Environment* (Albany: State University of New York Press, 1993).

19   Stephanie Kaza and Kenneth Kraft, eds., *Dharma Rain: Sources of Buddhist Environmentalism* (Boston: Shambala, 2000), 166.

20   McGraw, *Rediscovering America's Sacred Ground*, 183.

21   Ibid., 96.

22   His Holiness the Dalai Lama, *Ethics for the New Millenium*, 174.

23   Ibid., 179.

24   Susan Griffin, *The Eros of Everyday Life* (New York: Doubleday, 1995), 29.

25   Bowers, *Education, Cultural Myths, and the Environment*.

26   His Holiness the Dalai Lama, *Ethics for the New Millenium*, 148.

27   Kraft, "The Greening of Buddhist Practice," 63–80.

28   His Holiness the Dalai Lama, *Ethics for the New Millenium*, 133.

29   Edmund O'Sullivan, *Transformative Learning* (London: Zed, 1999), 264.

30   His Holiness the Dalai Lama, *Ethics for the New Millenium*, 13–14.

Chapter 6

1   Latter-day Saints (LDS) Church official Web site figures, December 31, 2003: worldwide membership: 11,985,254; U.S. membership: 5,503,192; http://www.lds.org.

2   Jan Shipps, *Mormonism: The Story of a New Religious Tradition* (Urbana: University of Illinois Press, 1985), ix–x; cf. Terryl L. Givens, *By the Hand of Mormon: The American Scripture That Launched a New World Religion* (New York: Oxford University Press, 2002), and Edwin B. Firmage, "Restoring the Church: Zion in the Nineteenth and Twenty-first Centuries," in *The Wilderness of Faith*, ed. John Sillito (Salt Lake City: Signature Books, 1991), 1–13.

3   See, for example, John Stuart Mill's *On Liberty* (1859), Karl Marx's "Letter to Lion Philips" (1864), Leo Tolstoy's diary entries (1857) and letters to Susa Young Gates (1888–1889), and Max Weber's *The Protestant Ethic and the Spirit of Capitalism* (1904–1905).

4   Harold Bloom, *The American Religion: The Emergence of the Post-Christian Nation* (New York: Simon & Schuster, 1992), 80–84.

5   For a historical account of the development of civil society, see John Ehrenberg, *Civil Society: The Critical History of an Idea* (New York: New York University Press, 1999).

6   On various approaches to understanding the significance of civil society, see Benjamin R. Barber, "Clansmen, Consumers, and Citizens: Three Takes on Civil Society," in *Civil Society, Democracy, and Civic Renewal*, ed. Robert K. Fullinwider (Lanham, MD: Rowman & Littlefield, 1999), 9–29; Jean Cohen, "Interpreting the Notion of Civil Society," in *Toward a Global Civil Society*, ed. Michael Walzer (Providence: Berghahn Books, 1998), 35–40; and Robert Fine, "Civil Society Theory, Enlightenment and Critique," in *Civil Society: Democratic Perspectives*, ed. Robert Fine and Shirin Rai (London: Frank Cass, 1997), 7–28.

7   See, for example, Robert A. Dahl, *On Democracy* (New Haven: Yale University Press, 1998), and William A. Schambra, "Is There Civic Life beyond the Great National Community?" in Fullinwider, *Civil Society, Democracy, and Civic Renewal*, 89–125.

8   McGraw, *Rediscovering America's Sacred Ground*.

9   Ibid., 99–106.

10   Ibid., 94–99.

11   Ibid., 94–95.

12   Ibid., 93, 99.

13   Alvin Platinga, "Pluralism: A Defense of Religious Exclusivism," in *The Philosophical Challenge of Religious Pluralism*, ed. Philip L. Quinn and Kevin Meeker (New York: Oxford University Press, 2000), 174.

14   The classic Mormon treatment of this subject can be found in James E. Talmage, *Jesus the Christ: A Study of the Messiah and His Mission according to Holy Scriptures Both Ancient and Modern* (Salt Lake City: Deseret Books, 1962; originally published by the LDS Church, 1915).

15   For another classic Mormon treatment on this topic, see Le Grande Richards, *A Marvelous Work and a Wonder* (Salt Lake City: Deseret Books, 1958).

16   See, for example, John Dillenberger, "Grace and Works in Martin Luther and Joseph Smith," in *Reflections on Mormonism: Judaeo-Christian Parallels*, ed. Truman G. Madsen (Provo, UT: Brigham Young University Press, 1978), 175–86; and Davis Bitton, "The Sovereignty of God in John Calvin and Brigham Young," *Sunstone* 5 (1980): 26–30.

17   The understanding of a "public philosophy" is borrowed from Theodore J. Lowi, *The End of Liberalism*, 2nd ed. (New York: Basic Books, 1979).

18   *Pearl of Great Price, Joseph Smith–History* 1:17–18.

19   Bruce R. McConkie, *Mormon Doctrine*, 2nd ed. (Salt Lake City: Bookcraft, 1979), 200–201.

20   For an official LDS Church position on the nature of its priesthood authority, see John A. Widtsoe, *Priesthood and Church Government in the Church of Jesus Christ of Latter-day Saints* (Salt Lake City: Deseret Books, 1939).

21   In time, the LDS Church would add two more books also containing new revelations—*The Pearl of Great Price* and the *Doctrine and Covenants*—to the Mormon canon. The former contains another translation by Smith of ancient papyri from the Middle East purported to have been written by the Old Testament prophet Abraham, as well as new translations of portions of the Bible. The latter contains contemporary revelations received by Smith and some of his successors as "prophets, seers and revelators" of the newly restored church of Jesus Christ. Mormons refer to the LDS canon's four volumes of scripture as "the standard works of the church."

22   Doctrine and Covenants (hereafter D&C) 1:30.

23   In 1995 the Presbyterian Church (USA) issued a position paper containing perhaps the most thorough and objective study of the question "Are Mormons Christians?" The paper focused on whether the LDS Church accepts historical Christianity's position with regard to the following three essential areas of Christian identity: canonical scriptures, creeds, and doctrine of the trinity. For an overview, see Kent P. Jackson, "Are Mormons Christians? Presbyterians, Mormons, and the Question of Religious Definitions," *Nova Religio* 4 (2000): 54.

24   Furthermore, Joseph Smith taught that God the Father was also at one time a mortal man, as His Son had been before, and that any individual who lived an exemplary life according to the religious principles and required rituals of the restored gospel had the potential of becoming a god. On the plurality of gods, see Joseph Smith, "Funeral Sermon for King Follett," April 7, 1844, in *History of the Church of Jesus Christ of Latter-day Saints*, ed. Joseph Smith (Salt Lake City: Deseret Books, 1948), 6:303–4, 305, and *Teachings of the Prophet Joseph Smith*, ed. Joseph Fielding Smith (Salt Lake City: Deseret Books, 1976), 370–73; cf. Sterling M. McMurrin, *The Theological Foundations of the Mormon Religion* (Salt Lake City: University of Utah Press, 1965).

25   For examples of evangelical arguments that Mormonism is not Christian, see Bill McKeever and Eric Johnson, *Mormonism 101: Examining the Religion of the Latter day Saints* (Grand Rapids: Baker Books, 2000), and John R. Farkas and David A. Reed, *Mormonism: Changes, Contradictions, and Errors* (Grand Rapids: Baker Books, 1995); for an example of an apologetic view of Mormonism as Christian, see Stephen E. Robinson, *Are Mormons Christians?* (Salt Lake City: Bookcraft, 1991).

26   For an overview of this development, see Lawrence Foster, "Between Heaven and Earth: Mormon Theology of the Family in Comparative Perspective," in *Multiply and Replenish: Mormon Essays on Sex and Family*, ed. Brent Corcoran (Salt Lake City: Signature Books, 1994), 1–17; cf. William E. Berrett, *The Latter-day Saints: A Contemporary History of the Church of Jesus Christ* (Salt Lake City: Deseret Books, 1985), 175–76.

27   D&C 132.

28   For a general historical and sociological discussion, see Thomas F. O'Dea, *The Mormons* (Chicago: University of Chicago, 1957).

29   Marvin S. Hill, *Quest for Refuge: The Mormon Flight from American Pluralism* (Salt Lake City: Signature Books, 1989); Leonard J. Arrington and Davis Bitton, *The Mormon Experience: A History of the Latter-day Saints* (New York: Vintage Press, 1980); and Richard L. Bushman, *Joseph Smith and the Beginnings of Mormonism* (Urbana: University of Illinois Press, 1984).

30   In 2004, the Illinois House of Representatives passed a resolution "regretting" the forced expulsion by state government authorities of Mormons from Illinois in 1846; in 1976, the state government of Missouri issued a "revocation" of Gov. Lilburn W. Boggs's "extermination order" of 1838 regarding Mormons.

31   Kenneth H. Winn, *Exiles in a Land of Liberty: Mormons in America, 1830–1846* (Chapel Hill: University of North Carolina Press, 1989); cf. Stewart L. Udall, *The Forgotten Founders: Rethinking the History of the Old West* (Washington, DC: Island Press, 2002).

32   George M. Marsden, *Religion and American Culture* (Orlando: Harcourt Brace Javanovich, 1990), 81–82.

33   Legislation included the Anti-Bigamy Act (the Morrill law, 1862), the Poland Act (1874), the Edmunds Act (1882), and the Edmunds-Tucker Act (1887). For a brief overview of the appropriate court cases, see John Witte Jr., *Religion and the American Constitutional Experiment: Essential Rights and Liberties* (Boulder: Westview Press, 2000), 102–4.

34   John R. Pottenger, "Mormonism and the American Industrial State," *International Journal of Social Economics* 14 (1987): 25–38.

35   Richard S. Van Wagoner, *Mormon Polygamy: A History* (Salt Lake City: Signature Books, 1992).

36   For an introduction to the idea of sacred texts as a political resource, see John A. Rees, "'Really Existing' Scriptures: On the Use of Sacred Text in International Affairs," *The Brandywine Review of Faith & International Affairs* 2 (2004): 17–26.

37   In fact, the significance of the Book of Mormon in American life has recently been noted in the secular publishing world. For example, in 2003 Book magazine compiled its list of the "20 Books That Changed America," which included the Book of Mormon. According to Book magazine, "this collection of revelations, given to Joseph Smith by the angel Moroni, launched the country's biggest homegrown religion. Today, Mormonism has eleven million followers around the world; in the United States alone, its adherents outnumber Episcopalians or Presbyterians. The book provides the theological underpinnings for one of the world's most vibrant religions." "20 Books That Changed America," Book (July–August 2003). Available from World Wide Web, http://www.bookmagazine.com/issue29/twenty.html. The Book of Mormon was ranked alongside Thomas Paine's *Common Sense*; Harriet Beecher Stowe's *Uncle Tom's Cabin*; Frederick Douglass's *The Narrative of the Life of Frederick Douglass, an American Slave*; Mary Wollstonecraft's *A Vindication of the Rights of Women*; and Karl Marx's *Communist Manifesto*. Indeed, Doubleday Book Publishing, a division of Random House, has published the first commercial version of the Book of Mormon since it was originally published by Joseph Smith in 1830. According to Doubleday, "The Book of Mormon narrates the historical, religious, political, and military events that shaped and continue to inform the church's teachings. The Book of Mormon is read daily by devout Mormons and used

extensively as a tool for evangelizing converts. The publication of this trade edition offers believers and seekers the opportunity to explore one of the largest denominations in America today." Doubleday Catalogue of Books, http://www.randomhouse.com/doubleday/catalog/display.pperl?03855131 6X.

38   Book of Mormon, Alma 46–47.

39   Ibid., Alma 46:12–13.

40   D&C 88:104.

41   See, for example, Book of Mormon, 2 Nephi 1:7.

42   Joseph Smith, "The Prophet on the Constitution of the United States and the Bible—Temporal Economics," 15 October 1843, in Smith, *History of the Church*, 4:56–57.

43   Joseph Smith, "To the Church of Latter-day Saints at Quincy, Illinois, and Scattered Abroad, and to Bishop Partridge in Particular," 25 March 1839, in Smith, *History of the Church*, 3:304.

44   Brigham Young, "Celebration of the Fourth of July," 4 July 1854, in *Journal of Discourses* (London: Latter-day Saints' Book Depot, 1860), 7:14; also see Brigham Young, "The Constitution and Government of the United States—Rights and Policy of the Latter-day Saints," 18 February 1855, in *Journal of Discourses* (1855), 2:170.

45   George Q. Cannon, "The Gospel of Jesus Christ Taught by the Latter-day Saints—Celestial Marriage," 15 August 1869, in *Journal of Discourses* (1872), 14:55.

46   See, for example, the church's guide for members of the adult priesthood, which contains civics instruction: *Come unto the Father in the Name of Jesus: Melchizedek Priesthood Personal Study Guide* (Salt Lake City: The Church of Jesus Christ of Latter-day Saints, 1990), chap. 12: "On Civic Responsibilities."

47   For an explanation of this position, see Noel B. Reynolds, "The Doctrine of an Inspired Constitution," in *"By the Hands of Wise Men": Essays on the U.S. Constitution*, ed. Ray C. Hillam (Provo, UT: Brigham Young University Press, 1979), 1–28.

48   D&C 101:77.

49   D&C 58:21.

50   D&C 109:54.

51   D&C 98:10.

52   D&C 134:9.

53   D&C 134:7.

54   Lowell L. Bennion, *An Introduction to the Gospel: Course of Study for the Sunday Schools of the Church of Jesus Christ of Latter-day Saints* (Salt Lake City: Deseret Sunday School Union Board, 1955), 271.

55   Larry King, "Larry King's People," *USA Today*, 5 February 2001, D2; cf. Peggy Fletcher Stack, "TV Host Says LDS Leader's Views on Christian Charities Differ from Bush's," *Salt Lake Tribune*, 6 February 2001, A1.

56   John R. Pottenger, "Elder Dallin H. Oaks: The Mormons, Politics, and Family Values," in *Religious Leaders and Faith-Based Politics: Ten Profiles*, ed. Jo Renée Formicola and Hubert Morken (Lanham, MD: Rowman & Littlefield, 2001), 79. Oaks has served as a law clerk to the chief justice of the U.S. Supreme Court, Earl Warren; professor of law at the University of Chicago; president of Brigham Young University; and member of the Utah Supreme Court. He is now sixth in line to assume the presidency and become prophet of the LDS Church.

57   McGraw, *Rediscovering America's Sacred Ground*, 92–99.

58   Gordon B. Hinckley, *Standing for Something: Ten Neglected Virtues That Will Heal Our Hearts and Homes* (New York: Times Books, 2000), 49.

59   "Transcript: National Press Club Q&A with President Gordon B. Hinckley," *Deseret Morning News*, 9 March 2000, http://www.deseretnews.com/dn/print/1,1442,155008723,00.html.

60   R. Scott Lloyd, "Looking Forward to Congress of Families," *Deseret Morning News*, 28 November 1998, http://www.desnews.com/cgi-bin/libstory_church?dn98&9811290027.

61   World Family Policy Center, "About the World Family Policy Center" and "Mission Statement," http://www.worldfamilypolicy.org/wfpc/about.htm.

62   Ibid.

63   Dallin H. Oaks, "Introduction," in *The Wall between Church and State*, ed. Oaks (Chicago: University of Chicago Press, 1963), 2.

64   Gordon B. Hinckley, "The Family: A Proclamation to the World," *Ensign* 25 (1995): 102.

65   D. Michael Quinn, *The Mormon Hierarchy: Extensions of Power* (Salt Lake City: Signature Books, 1997), 376–402.

66   Church Educational System, *Church History in the Fullness of Times* (Salt Lake City: LDS Church, 1989), 586.

67   Quinn, *The Mormon Hierarchy*, 402–4.

68   *Ninia Baehr et al. v. Lawrence Miike*, 92 Haw. 634 (1999).

69   Dallin H. Oaks, "Same-Gender Attraction," *Ensign* 25 (1995): 8.

70   *Boy Scouts of America and Monmouth Council et al. v. James Dale*, 530 U.S. 640 (2000).

71   Terence Neilan, "Marital Rights Decreed for Gays," *Deseret Morning News*, 5 February 2004, http://deseretnews.com/dn/print/1,1442,590041026,00.html.

72   Mitt Romney, "One Man, One Woman: A Citizen's Guide to Protecting Marriage," Opinion Journal from The Wall Street Journal Editorial Page, 5 February 2004, http://www.opinionjournal.com/forms/printThis.html?id=110004647.

73   The state legislature failed to arrive at an agreement, neither on details of legislation nor on a state constitutional amendment, to restrict civil marriage to that between one man and one woman. The court's decision took effect in May 2004, permitting local magistrates to grant marriage licenses to in-state, same-sex couples.

74   Editorial board, "Amend the Constitution," *Deseret Morning News*, 26 February 2004, http://deseretnews.com/dn/print/1,1442,590045769,00.html.

75   The Church of Jesus Christ of Latter-day Saints, Press Release: "First Presidency Issues Statement on Marriage," 7 July 2004, http://www.lds.org/newsroom/showrelease/0,15503,3881-1-19733,00.html.

76   Dallin H. Oaks, "Weightier Matters," devotional address at Brigham Young University, 9 February 1999, http://speeches.byu.edu/devo/98-99/OaksW99.html.

77   In the 108th Congress, U.S. senators included Orrin G. Hatch (R-Utah), Harry Reid (D-Nevada), Robert F. Bennett (R-Utah), Mike Crapo (R-Idaho), and Gordon Smith (R-Oregon); members of the U.S. House of Representatives included Wally Herger (R-California), Ernest J. Istook (R-Oklahoma), Howard P. (Buck) McKeon (R-California), John Doolittle (R-California), Christopher Cannon (R-Utah), Mike Simpson (R-Idaho), Thomas Udall (D-New Mexico), Jeff Flake (R-Arizona), James D. Matheson (D-Utah), Rob Bishop (R-Utah), and Eni F. H. Faleomavaega (D-American Samoa).

78   Orrin G. Hatch, *Square Peg: Confessions of a Citizen Senator* (New York: Basic Books, 2002), 236; cf. Hatch's endorsement of separation of church and state, "Politics and Piety: An Interview with Senator Orrin Hatch," *Sunstone* 5 (1980): 54.
79   Hatch, *Square Peg*, 243.
80   Ibid., 246–47.
81   Ibid., 244.
82   Editorial board, "Refocusing on Stem Cells," *Deseret Morning News*, 10 June 2004, http://deseretnews.com/dn/print/1,1442,595069208,00.html.
83   For a concise and accurate overview of Mormon theology as it deals with stem-cell research, see Drew Clark, "The Mormon Stem-Cell Choir," *Slate*, 3 August 2001, http://slate.msn.com/?id=112974.
84   John A. Widstoe, "Mormonism," in *Varieties of American Religion*, ed. Charles Samuel Braden (Chicago: Willett, Clark, 1936), 130.
85   Although the LDS Church's finances are not public record, recent estimations place the church's economic assets at more than $30 billion; see, for example, Richard N. Ostling and Joan K. Ostling, *Mormon America: The Power and the Promise* (New York: HarperCollins, 1999), 115; cf. Robert Gottlieb and Peter Wiley, *America's Saints: The Rise of Mormon Power* (New York: Harcourt Brace Jovanovich, 1986), 97–102.
86   Carrie A. Moore, "Evangelical Preaches at Salt Lake Tabernacle," *Deseret Morning News*, 15 November 2004, http://deseretnews.com/dn/view/0,1249,595105580,00.html.
87   See, for example, Anthony Urti, "Battle Rages in Utah over Funding of Abortions on Disabled Babies," Center for Reclaiming America, 28 July 2004, http://www.reclaimamerica.org/Pages/News/newspageprint.asp?story=1966; cf. Amy Joi Bryson, "Rule Proposed on Abortion Funding," *Deseret Morning News*, 2 July 2004, http://deseretnews.com/dn/print/1,1442,5950 74499,00.html.
88   See, for example, Robert Booth Fowler, Allen D. Hertzke, and Laura R. Olson, *Religion and Politics in America: Faith, Culture, and Strategic Choices*, 2nd ed. (Boulder: Westview Press, 1999), 204–7, and A. James Reichly, *Faith in Politics* (Washington, DC: Brookings Institution Press, 2002), 345.

Chapter 7

I am grateful to Barbara McGraw for including me in this enlightening and exciting project. I am also especially thankful to the Center on Religion and Democracy at the University of Virginia for providing me with much-needed research support.
1   M. A. Muqtedar Khan and John L. Esposito, "The Threat of Internal Extremism," *Q-News: The Muslim Magazine*, February 2005, 16–17.
2   Dr. Fawaz Gerges made these comments in a lecture titled "Taking Stock of the War on Terror," at Adrian College on 21 February 2005.
3   See Report on Global Anti-Semitism, July 1, 2003–December 15, 2004, submitted by the Department of State to the Committee on Foreign Relations and the Committee on International Relations. Released by the Bureau of Democracy, Human Rights, and Labor, 5 January 2005, http://www.state.gov/g/drl/rls/40258.htm.
4   See the White House program on Faith-Based Initiatives, http://www.whitehouse.gov/government/fbci/.

5   The use of secret evidence on the basis of the Anti-Terrorism and Effective Death Penalty Act of 1996 and the additional provisions under the USA PATRIOT Act have disproportionately targeted Muslims. For a comprehensive analysis, see Arshad Ahmed, Umar Moghul, Farid Senzai, and Saeed Khan, *The US Patriot Act: Impact on the Arab and Muslim American Community* (Detroit: Institute for Social Policy and Understanding, 2004).

6   See M. A. Muqtedar Khan, "The Public Face of Christian Evangelical Bigotry," http://www.glocaleye.org/bigotry2.htm.

7   For historical accounts of how the American Muslim community emerged over the years, see Sulayman S. Nyang, "Islam in America: A Historical Perspective," *American Muslim Quarterly* 2, no. 1 (1998): 7–38. Also see Omar Altalib, "Muslims in America: Challenges and Prospects," *American Muslim Quarterly* 2, no. 1 (1998): 39–49.

8   Review the main themes in the works of some of the most prominent Islamic thinkers in North America—Fazlur Rahman, Ismail Farooqi, Seyyed Hossein Nasr, Taha Jabir Al-Alwani—and the desire to revive the Islamic Civilization will be the dominant theme. A recent issue of *Islamic Horizons* (March/April 1999), the main journal of the Islamic Society of North America, dedicated an entire issue to the memory and ideas of Hassan Al-Bannah, the founder of Muslim Brotherhood of Egypt and a prominent figure in the twentieth-century Islamic revivalist movements.

9   "A Forum Rebuilds: AMSS Serves as a Platform for Discussion of Issues Facing Muslims," *Islamic Horizons* (January/February 1999): 17.

10   For a review of the International Institute of Islamic Thought's (IIIT) endeavors, see Jamal Barazinji, "History of Islamization of Knowledge and Contributions of the International Institute of Islamic Thought," in *Muslims and Islamization in North America: Problems and Prospects*, ed. Amber Haque (Beltsville, MD: Amana Publications, 1999), 13–33.

11   To learn more, visit these organizations on the World Wide Web: Council on American Islamic Relations (CAIR), http://www.cair-net.org/; American Muslim Council (AMC), http://www.amconline.org/; Muslim Political Action Committee (MPAC), http://www.mpac.org; Kashmiri American Council (KAC), http://www.kashmiri.com/; American Muslim Alliance (AMA), http://www.amaweb.org/; American Muslims for Jerusalem (AMJ), http://www.amjerusalem.org/.

12   See M. A. Muqtedar Khan, "Collective Identity and Collective Action: Case of Muslim Politics in America," in Haque, *Muslims and Islamization in North America*, 147–59.

13   To learn more about the Islamic movements of North America, visit their Web sites: Islamic Society of North America (ISNA), http://www.isna.net/; Islamic Circle of North America (ICNA), http://www.icna.org/; Islamic Assembly of North America (IANA), http://www.iananet.org; Tablighi Jamaat, http://www.almadinah.org/; Naqshbandi Sufi Movement, http://www.naqshbandi.org.

14   See Jane I. Smith, *Islam in America* (New York: Columbia University Press, 1999), 65–71.

15   Defense of Islamic identity and the well-being of the Muslim world are the dominant themes in the American Muslim discourse. Examples of articles expressing these sentiments are Yvonne Haddad, "The Dynamics of Islamic Identity in North America," in *Muslims on the Americanization Path?* ed. Yvonne Haddad and John Esposito (New York: Oxford University Press, 2000), 19–46, and Fahhim Abdul Hadi, "Protecting the Future of Islam in

America," *Islamic Horizons* (March/April 1999): 30. See also Sarvath El Hassan, "Educating Women in the Muslim World," *Islamic Horizons* (March/April 1999): 54–56; "Muslims in the West Serving Muslims Worldwide," *Islamic Horizons* (January/February 1998): 47; Altaf Hussain, "Youth and the Emerging Islamic Identity," *The Message* (June/July 1999): 21–22.

16   See Edward Said, *Covering Islam: How the Media and the Experts Determine How We See the Rest of the World* (New York: Pantheon Books, 1981). See the following chapters: Ahmadullah Siddiqui, "Islam, Muslims and the American Media," 203–30; Jack Shaheen, "Hollywood's Reel Arabs and Muslims," 179–202. See also Ibrahim Hooper, "Media Relations tips for Muslim Activists," in Haque, *Muslims and Islamization in North America*, 231–56. For the most recent examples of media bias against Islam, see M. A. Muqtedar Khan, "Public Face of Bigotry," *Washington Report on Middle East Affairs* (November/December 2000): 72.

17   Read the chapter on "The Public Practice of Islam," in Smith, *Islam in America*, 173–76.

18   See Ambereen Mirza, "Muslim Women and American Choices," *Islamic Horizons* (May/June 1999): 50, and Kathleen Moore, "The Hijab and Religious Liberty: Anti-Discrimination Law and Muslim Women in the United States," in Haddad and Esposito, *Muslims on the Americanization Path?* 105–28. For more on the positive role played by Muslim women in America, see Ghazala Munir, "Muslim Women in Dialogue: Breaking Walls, Building Bridges," in Haque, *Muslims and Islamization in North America*, 337–41.

19   I am grateful to Dr. Ahmad Totonji, the secretary general of the International Institute of Islamic Thought, for filling me in on the early history of the MSA. Dr. Totonji was the general secretary and president of the national MSA in its formative years in the late 1960s. He has also played a major role in its development over the years and is still one of its major patrons.

20   See Abu Sameer, "Some Milestones in Islamic Education in North America," *The Message* (May 2000): 33–35. See Mohamed Ismail, "Islamic Education in the Weekend and Full-Time Islamic Schools," *The Message* (May 2000): 41–42, and Nassir Ali-Akbar, "Challenges Faced by Islamic Schools," *The Message* (May 2000): 29–30.

21   Details about ISNA and the ISNA convention can be accessed at their comprehensive Web site, http://www.isna.net.

22   See the editorial, "Muslims Strive with Increasing Confidence," *Islamic Horizons* (January/February 1999): 6.

23   Azam Nizamuddin, "What Muslims Can Offer America," *Islamic Horizons* (March/April 1998): 35.

24   See, for example, iViews, http://www.iviews.com/; Media Monitor, http://www.mediamonitor.com/; Ijtihad, http://www.ijtihad.org/; GlocalEye, http://www.glocaleye.org/. Some of the discussion lists that help the community explore its differences are mailto:political.islam@listbot.com, political.islam @listbot.com, and msanews: http://msanews.mynet.net.

25   Karen Leanard, "American Muslim Politics: Discourses and Practices," *Ethnicities* 3, no. 2 (2003): 147–81.

26   Julia Duin, "U.S. Muslims Use Growing Numbers to Flex Political Muscles," *Washington Times*, 11 July 2000; Michael Paulson, "Muslims Eye Role at US Polls," *Boston Globe*, 23 October 2000; John Chadwick, "American Muslims Gain a Political Voice," *The Record*, 24 September 2000; Dean E. Murphy, "For American Muslims Influence in American Politics Comes Hard," *The*

New York Times, 27 October 2000; Abu Amal Hadhrami, "Muslims Gain Political Rights," *Islamic Horizons* (January/February 1999): 24–25.

27   For a continuous estimate of Palestinian deaths, see "Palestinians killed (Shuhada) by Israeli forces," Palestine Fact Sheets, from the Palestine Monitor, http://www.palestinemonitor.org/factsheet/Palestinian_killed_fact_sheet.htm.

28   For a continuous estimate of U.S. aid to Israel, see "U.S. Financial Aid to Israel: Figures, Facts, and Impact," Washington Report on Middle East Affairs, http://www.wrmea.com/html/us_aid_to_israel.htm.

29   See Siddiqui, "Islam, Muslims and the American Media," in Said, *Covering Islam*, 203–30. Also see there Shaheen, "Hollywood's Reel Arabs and Muslims," 179–203.

30   For a comprehensive analysis, see Ahmed, Moghul, Senzai, and Khan, *The US Patriot Act*.

31   See the chapter "Refutation of Some Isolationist Arguments," in *American Muslims: Bridging Faith and Freedom*, ed. M. A. Muqtedar Khan (Beltsville, MD: Amana Publications, 2002), 32–35.

32   Leanard, "American Muslim Politics," 147–81.

33   Also see Abdul Basit's critique of the Isolationists in Abdul Basit, "How to Integrate without Losing Muslim Identity," *Islamic Horizons* (March/April 1998): 32–34.

34   Those who wish to examine Islamic sources on freedom, justice, pluralism, and tolerance in more detail should consult some of the following books: Richard K. Khuri, *Freedom, Modernity, and Islam: Towards a Creative Synthesis* (Syracuse, NY: Syracuse University Press, 1998); Abdulaziz Sachedina, *The Islamic Roots of Democratic Pluralism* (New York: Oxford University Press, 2001); and M. H. Kamali, *Freedom, Equality, and Justice in Islam* (Cambridge: Islamic Texts Society, 1999). Also see Khan, *American Muslims*.

35   See for example, a collection of essays published by the Woodrow Wilson Center from a conference on Islam in America held on June 18, 2003, on their premises in Washington, D.C: Philippa Strum and Danielle Tarantolo, *Muslims in the United States* (Washington, DC: Woodrow Wilson International Center for Scholars, 2003).

36   A good place to get a sense of the Muslim Isolationists' views is www.khilafah.com.

37   Robert Putnam, "Diplomacy and Domestic Politics: The Logic of Two-Level Games," *International Organization* 42 (1988): 427–60.

38   For an analysis of this debate, see Khan and Esposito, "The Threat of Internal Extremism." See also Enver Masud, *The War on Islam* (Arlington, VA: Madrassah Books, 2002). Also see Abid Ullah Jan, *A War on Islam?* (Pakistan: Maktabah, 2001), and Tahir Ali, "Neo-Muslims and Rand Robots," *Pakistan Link*, 24 December 2004, http://www.pakistanlink.com/Opinion/2004/Dec04/24/01.htm. See also Shayan Elahi, "Beware of Rand Robots and Muslim Neocons," *Pakistan Link*, 7 January 2005, http://www.pakistanlink.com/Opinion/2005/Jan05/07/08.htm.

39   For an example of theological debates, visit the progressive Muslim Website, www.Muslimakeup.com, and also see David Glen, "Who Owns Islamic Law?" The Chronicle of Higher Education, 25 February 2005, A14–17.

40   For example, the Institute for Social Policy and Understanding. See www.ispu.us.

41   For example, the Progressive Muslim Union. See www.pmuna.org.

42   See M. A. Muqtedar Khan, "The Manifest Destiny of American Muslims," *Washington Report on Middle East Affairs* (October/November 2000): 72. This article was published in several periodicals and Web sites. But for a fascinating accompanying discussion of American responses to this article, see the version at http://www.freerepublic.com/forum/a39f129590fe4.htm.

Chapter 8

1   Gayraud S. Wilmore, *Black Religion and Black Radicalism: An Interpretation of the Religious History of African Americans* (Maryknoll, NY: Orbis Books, 2003), 24.

2   McGraw, *Rediscovering America's Sacred Ground*, 163.

3   Phil Zuckerman, *DuBois on Religion* (Lanham, MD: Rowman & Littlefield, 2000), 16.

4   Wilmore, *Black Religion and Black Radicalism*, 24.

5   Booker T. Washington emerged in 1895, the year in which Frederick Douglass died, to dominate African American politics until his death in 1915 and may arguably constitute the first model of "secular" leadership since the collapse of Reconstruction in 1877 as a result of the Republican Rutherford B. Hayes and Samuel Tilden (Hayes-Tilden) Compromise settling the 1876 presidential contest and withdrawing federal oversight from the Confederacy. It is also plausible to interpret the "anti-Bookerite" 1905 Niagara Falls Movement challenge to Washington's power represented by his home base Tuskegee Institute as the beginning of modern civil rights. Washington's power base was known widely as the "Tuskegee Machine." *Boston Guardian Newspaper* owner William Monroe Trotter and W. E. B. DuBois were the principal opponents to Washington. Their opposition was gradual but exploded beginning in 1903 after Trotter's public attack on Washington led to his arrest. DuBois subsequently broke ties with Washington—as he would even later, with Trotter as well—and included the chapter "Of Mr. Booker T. Washington and Others," in his *The Souls of Black Folk* (New York: Bantam Books, 1903; repr., 1989). See Robert C. Smith, *We Have No Leaders: African Americans in the Post–Civil Rights Era* (Albany: State University of New York Press, 1996), 3–4.

6   Lewis Baldwin, "Revisiting the 'All-Comprehending Institution': Historical Reflections on the Public Roles of Black Churches," in *New Day Begun: African American Churches and Civic Culture in Post–Civil Rights America*, ed. R. Drew Smith (Durham, NC: Duke University Press, 2003), 32.

7   Of course there were noteworthy exceptions such as Abigail and John Adams, Gouverneur Morris of Pennsylvania, Elbridge Gerry of Massachusetts, Luther Martin of Maryland, and James Madison. Abolitionism among whites was carried out largely with convictions of antislavery that were born of the American Revolution's liberation ethos.

8   R. Drew Smith, "Black Churches within a Changing Civic Culture in America," in Smith, *New Day Begun*, 4.

9   The full title of David Walker's work is *An Appeal in Four Articles; Together with a Preamble to the Colored Citizens of the World, but in Particular, and Very Expressly, to Those of the United States*, 3rd ed. (Boston: David Walker, 1830).

10   It is expressed early in the writings, critiques, and political sermons of those individuals living or born within a generation of the American Revolution such as African Methodist Episcopal (AME) church founders Richard Allen and Absalom Jones in Philadelphia; the relatively obscure Robert Alexander

Young (of New York) and his *Ethiopian Manifesto* (1829); Boston emigrant and activist David Walker's (1785–1830) insurrectionist *Appeal* (1829); their contemporary Maria Stewart of Boston (1803–1879), who argued for insurrectionary violence in her *Productions* (1835); and radical integrationist Frederick Douglass, who supported the violence of the Civil War. See Wilson Jeremiah Moses, *Classical Black Nationalism: From the American Revolution to Marcus Garvey* (New York: New York University Press, 1996).

11   For an extended discussion, see Wilson Jeremiah Moses, *Black Messiahs and Uncle Toms* (University Park: Pennsylvania State University Press, 1993), especially chap. 3, "The Black Jeremiad and American Messianic Traditions." See also David Howard Pitney, *The Afro-American Jeremiad: Appeals for Justice in America* (Philadelphia: Temple University Press, 1990), and Moses, *Classical Black Nationalism*. The American jeremiad, defined by Sacvan Bercovitch as "a ritual designed to join social criticism to spiritual renewal, public to private identity, the shifting 'signs of the times' to certain traditional metaphors, themes, and symbols," crossed several major episodes in U.S. religious and political history. Indeed the jeremiad is derived from the name and "political sermons" of the biblical prophet Jeremiah (627–580 BCE) whose legend emanated from the record of the Old Testament narratives in the books of Jeremiah and Lamentations concerning biblical Israel's captivity in ancient Babylon. Known commonly as the "weeping prophet," Jeremiah's errand toward Babylon and captive Israel began with Jehovah-God's promise that "I have this day set thee over the nations and over the kingdoms, to root out, and pull down, and to destroy, and to throw down, to build, to plant." Subsequent generations would measure their own status in fulfilling the American mission by their ability to reform the wayward land to the original vision of "the fathers"— Jonathan Cotton, John Winthrop, Richard Mather, John Davenport—who were the first to bemoan the moral declension in their New World less than a decade after their arrival. At each chronological interval, the jeremiad presided over a self-consciously mythical people who betrayed a nationality consciousness and a sense of a providentially conceived national destiny.

12   Michael C. Dawson, *Black Visions: The Roots of Contemporary African-American Political Ideologies* (Chicago: University of Chicago Press, 2001), 5, 11–12.

13   Eugene D. Genovese, *Roll, Jordan, Roll: The World the Slaves Made* (New York: Pantheon, 1974), 166.

14   Ibid., 162.

15   Smith, *New Day Begun*, 18.

16   W. E. B. DuBois, ed. *The Souls of Black Folk* (Boston: New Bedford Books, 1997).

17   E. Franklin Frazier, *The Negro Church in America* (New York: Schocken Books, 1974), 23–25.

18   For instance, a coherent "Black consciousness" developed in Brazil only after the idea of negritude conjoined the various mulatto and Black populations in the 1930s. This was achieved gradually, after more powerful intervening forces (e.g., religion and African slave importation patterns) supplanted concerns for Brazilian national identity with larger pan-African interests.

19   Cedric Robinson, *Black Marxism: The Making of the Black Radical Tradition* (London: Zen, 1983), 174.

20   Zuckerman, *DuBois on Religion*, 14–15.

21   Dawson, *Black Visions*, 52.
22   Robinson, *Black Marxism*, 10.
23   See W. E. B. DuBois, *The World and Africa: An Inquiry into the Part which Africa Has Played in World History* (New York: International Press, 1946; repr., 1965).
24   Robinson, *Black Marxism*, 82.
25   Edmund Morgan, *American Slavery, American Freedom* (New York: Norton, 1975), 380–81; Derrick Bell, *And We Are Not Saved: The Elusive Quest for Racial Justice* (New York: Basic Books, 1987), 40–41.
26   Edmund Morgan, "Slavery and Freedom: The American Paradox," *Journal of American History* 59 (1972): 24, cited in Bell, *And We Are Not Saved*, 41.
27   Paul Finkelman, *Slavery and the Founders: Race and Liberty in the Age of Jefferson*, 2nd ed. (Armonk, NY: M. E. Sharpe, 2001), 132.
28   Charles Joyner, "'Believer I Know': The Emergence of African American Christianity," in *African American Christianity: Essays in History*, ed. Paul E. Johnson (Berkeley: University of California Press, 1994), 18.
29   John Langston Gwaltney, *Drylongso: A Self-Portrait of Black America* (New York: The New York Press, 1993), xxvi.
30   For an extended discussion, see Moses, *Black Messiahs and Uncle Toms* (1993).
31   Melville J. Herskowitz, *Myth of the Negro Past* (Boston: Beacon Press, 1941; repr., 1958).
32   E. Franklin Frazier, *The Negro in the United States* (New York: Macmillan Press, 1974).
33   The single area that Frazier concedes had a lasting African character among the slaves was the "shout songs," "the Spirituals," which were preoccupied with death and yearning for mothers, and their accompanying "holy dance[s]." See Cornel West, *Prophecy Deliverance! An Afro-American Revolutionary Christianity* (Philadelphia: Westminster Press, 1982); more extensively, historian Sterling Stuckey's research has identified the "ring dance" or "ring shout," a coordinated counterclockwise movement of a group of male and female worshipers, as an integral component of the "folk amalgam of essentially African elements," among American Black people in *Going Through the Storm: The Influence of African American Art in History* (New York: Oxford University Press, 1994), 193.
34   See Zuckerman, *DuBois on Religion*, 45.
35   Ibid., 50–51 (emphasis added).
36   Lawrence Levine, *Black Culture and Black Consciousness* (New York: Oxford University Press, 1977), p. 13.
37   Eric Lincoln and Lawrence H. Mamiya, *The Black Church in the African American Experience* (Durham, NC: Duke University Press, 1990), 2. The main elements of their brief sketch of the sacred cosmos are mostly appropriate, though not exclusively, to Black Christian adaptations. These typically find empathy in the oppression ethos of a suffering Christ who, like the race as a whole, suffered an injustice that was part of the redemptive work of God. This explains the state of nature theologies of early Christian and "Black Muslim" nationalists who attributed slavery to some Edenic offense of the race, precipitating both fall and redemption schemes or in "Yacub's history." Emphasis is also placed on the importance of human personality, where all people are universally "one in Christ" as equal "children of God." Lincoln and Mamiya point to the transduction of "freedom" in the distinct contexts of Black oppression. Freedom as a relativist expression

had certain meaning in the specific regime of subordination, though it was always "communal" rather than individualistic in nature. Finally, it includes an emotional worship or religious expressions in dance, song, music, and call-and-response preaching style.

38 Baldwin, "Revisiting the 'All-Comprehending Institution'," 18.
39 Lincoln and Mamiya, *The Black Church* (Durham, NC: Duke University Press, 1990), 194–95.
40 Henry Louis Gates, Jr. and Cornel West, *The Future of the Race* (New York: Vintage Books, 1996), 79 (emphasis in the original).
41 John Locke, *Second Treatise of Government*, 50 (emphasis in the original).
42 Ibid., 25.
43 Ibid., 63.
44 Richard K. Matthews, *The Radical Politics of Thomas Jefferson* (Lawrence: University Press of Kansas, 1984), 8.
45 Ibid., 19.
46 Like many of his eighteenth-century American students, Locke dabbled in the slave trade by virtue of his investment in the Royal Africa Company. Locke also served as a secretary to the Council of Trade and Plantations between 1673 and 1675, just five years before he began writing *Two Treatises of Government*, but apparently the experience was not integral to his political theory of the role of government. Ibid., x.
47 Ibid., 25.
48 McGraw, *Rediscovering America's Sacred Ground*, 97. Jefferson also believed in the necessity of periodic revolts (every twenty years) especially "in order to keep the Spirit of 1776 perpetually alive."
49 Thomas Jefferson, *Notes on the State of Virginia*, ed. William Peden (New York: W. W. Norton, 1972).
50 Paul Finkelman, *Slavery and the Founders: Race and Liberty in the Age of Jefferson*, 2nd ed. (Armonk, NY: M.E. Sharpe, 2001).
51 Locke, *Second Treatise of Government*, 14. Indeed he said: "to be free from such force is the only security of my preservation; and reason bids me look on him, as an enemy to my preservation, who would take away that freedom which is the fence to it; so that he who makes an attempt to enslave me, thereby puts himself into a state of war with me." And again he stated that "he who attempts to get another man into his absolute power, does thereby put himself into a state of war with him" especially where he would "make me a slave." Moreover, an individual was prevented even from selling himself into a condition of slavery as "a man, not having the power of his own life, cannot, by compact, of his own consent, enslave himself to any one, nor put himself under the absolute, arbitrary power of another, to take away his life, when he pleases."
52 Hanes Walton Jr. and Robert C. Smith, *African American Politics and the African American Quest for Universal Freedom* (New York: Longman, 2000), 6.
53 Cited in ibid., 38.
54 Cited in Moses, *Black Messiahs and Uncle Toms*, 30–31.
55 Moses, *Classical Black Nationalism*, 15.
56 The proper title of Jefferson's answer to French diplomat Marquis de Barbe'-Marbois's inquiry concerning conditions in the rebellious colonies was from Thomas Jefferson, *Notes on the State of Virginia, Written in the Year 1781, Somewhat Corrected and Enlarged in the Winter of 1782, for the Use of a Foreigner of Distinction, in Answer to Certain Queries Proposed by Him* (Paris, 1784–1785).

57   See Bell, *And We Are Not Saved*, 274 n. 28. Bell lists states that made consti-
      tutional provisions for abolition, such as Vermont (1777), Ohio (1802),
      Illinois (1818), and Indiana (1816); judicial decisions in states such as
      Massachusetts (1783); constitutional interpretation in New Hampshire
      (1857); and by gradual abolition acts in Pennsylvania (1780), Rhode Island
      (1784), Connecticut (1784 and 1797), New York (1799 and 1817), and
      New Jersey (1804).

58   Walker died in 1830 under mysterious circumstances after publishing three
      editions of his Appeal and distributing it widely throughout the slave states
      and territories with the advantage he had as an émigré to Boston; he oper-
      ated a clothing business, and he used to smuggle the Appeal in the clothes
      of white and African American travelers.

59   After all, until 1833, Garrison agreed with other white elites such as Jeffer-
      son, Harriet Beecher Stowe, and Lincoln that the best path for free and
      emancipated Blacks was expatriation to Africa, Haiti, or Mexico. The effect
      of the American Colonization Society's expatriation scheme was interpreted
      by most African American elites as an attempt to fortify the institution of
      slavery by ridding the nation of free Black antislavery agitators. It is tempt-
      ing to suggest that Black Abolitionists were torn between Garrison and
      Frederick Douglass's view on one hand, and represented earlier by David
      Walker on the other. Donald Jacobs and his colleagues (1993) view the con-
      nection between Walker and Garrison as one of reciprocity and mutual
      dependence. Garrison himself was more dependent on the appeals and
      legacy of David Walker for accessing Black Abolitionists in Boston who
      were leery of his early support for colonizationism and for the African
      American readership—which constituted the overwhelming majority of
      subscribers—and financing of Garrison's *Liberator* publication. Black Bosto-
      nians, after Walker's death in 1830, aligned more with Garrison's abolition-
      ism in the 1840s and 1850s as Garrison emerged as the central figure in
      Abolitionism. There is very little appreciation for the ideological particular-
      ities of Black Garrisonians generally and Black Bostonian antislavery propo-
      nents, in particular. Garrison employed Walker's ideas of self-reliance for
      African Americans and expressed empathy for his call to arms, and
      defended Walker's authorship of the Appeal against doubt expressed by
      many white newspaper editors, but ultimately rejected the Appeal on
      grounds of its advocacy of violence. See Donald E. Jacobs, ed. *Courage and
      Conscience: Black and White Abolitionists in Boston* (Indianapolis: Indiana
      University Press, 1993).

60   According to Wilson Jeremiah Moses, a foremost authority on the subject,
      the jeremiadic tradition of religious and social protest, as epitomized in
      Walker's *Appeal*, had as its audience both whites and Africans despite it
      being addressed to "The Coloured Citizens of the World . . . [and] Very
      Expressly, Those of The United States."

61   Herbert Aptheker, *"One Continual Cry": David Walker's Appeal to the Colored
      Citizens of the World (1829–1830)* (New York: Humanities Press, 1965), 54.

62   Ibid., 55.

63   Moses insists further that "the purpose of the black jeremiad was not sim-
      ply to provide a verbal outlet for hostilities; it was a means to demonstrat-
      ing loyalty—both to the principles of egalitarian liberalism and to the
      Anglo-Christian code of values." Moses, *Black Messiahs and Uncle Toms*, 38.

64   Aptheker, *"One Continual Cry,"* 64–65 (emphasis and exclamation in
      original).

65   Ibid., 72.
66   Ibid., 89.
67   Ibid., 137.
68   Finkelman, *Slavery and the Founders*. Finkleman notes that Jefferson "sometimes refers to 'God' in his discussion of slavery—especially a vengeful Calvinist God, which was contrary to his personal religious beliefs" (232 n. 5).
69   McGraw, *Rediscovering America's Sacred Ground*, 97.
70   Ibid., 96.
71   Ibid.
72   Ibid., 17.
73   From video excerpt of Malcolm X Speech, "FBI's War on Black America," 1964.
74   McGraw, *Rediscovering America's Sacred Ground*, 164.
75   The otherworldly orientation of African American religion was especially characteristic of the southern churches during the period of the unpolitical "Negro church," which emerged between the middle to late nineteenth century through the period just before King's monumental efforts. In turn, this makes clearer the importance of Martin Luther King Jr. in the post–World War II period as he provided temporary relief from the church's reputed antipathy for organizing politics and he accomplished reiterating its social justice orientation. Prior to King, E. Franklin Frazier identified the political orientation as being "the most important agency of social control among Negroes." See Smith, *New Day Begun*, 13–14. Political scientist Frederick Harris is a recent one of a long list of scholars who have explored the relationship between African American religious values and political participation. See Frederick C. Harris, "Something Within: Religion as a Mobilizer of African-American Political Activism," *The Journal of Politics* 56, no.1 (1994): 42–68. Harris rightly states that in the debates that have followed, "some point out how the black church catalyzed the collective involvement of African Americans in the modern civil rights movement. Others insist that black religion promotes an otherworldly orientation, functioning as an instrument of political pacification and fatalism," 42.
76   The major instrument that African American religious and political elites have employed throughout their encounter with race oppression is the Black jeremiad, and because it was reactive to this reality, it is important to give attention to the theological and political impetus which spawned the priority that African American elites from David Walker to civil-rights and post-civil-rights political elites gave to the jeremiad as a tool for dissent in the Conscientious Public Forum of persuasion.
77   Epitomizing the logic of African American religious and political strategies that preceded their own efforts, King and his contemporary Malcolm X contested over the best social strategy (integration and nationalism) and offered alternative but similar philosophies of *strategic* violence (for King, white-initiated violence was indispensable to his boycott and direct-action approaches, and for Malcolm X, the rhetoric of self-defense), and over religious philosophy (Christianity and Islam).
78   McGraw, *Rediscovering America's Sacred Ground*, 97.
79   The otherworldly orientation of African American religious life characterized a shift away from the insurrectionary sentiments of early religious dis-

sidents such as "Black Gabriel" Prosser, who attempted to lead twenty thousand whites and African American slaves in a takeover of Richmond, Virginia, in 1800; Denmark Vesey, who attempted an equally ambitious uprising in Charleston, South Carolina, in 1822—from the African Church with which David Walker had once affiliated himself—and the actual insurrection of Nat Turner of Hampton, Virginia, in 1831. These preachers, who reflect a more militant liberation-styled theology, were all motivated by religion. Intellectually, neither John Locke nor Thomas Jefferson would deny them this option.

80   For Wilmore, *Black Religion and Black Radicalism*, chaps. 6 and 7, the process by which the more radical *Christian* elements such as David Walker, Gabriel Prosser, Denmark Vesey, and Nat Turner gave way to a second and related phase he calls the "dechristianization of Black radicalism," where in the midst of the widespread perception that the Negro church was compliant with the racial status quo, large segments of disaffected African-American Christians in the northern ghettos gave audience to cult personalities and joined organizations such as Timothy "Noble" Drew Ali's Moorish Science Temple of Islam and W. D. Fard's (and later, Elijah Mohammad's) Nation of Islam. Accommodationism as practiced by Washington, who must be understood along with Marcus Garvey and Martin Luther King Jr. as preeminent in terms of their significance to African-American political life, is not related to the accommodationist orientation that McGraw rejects in *Rediscovering America's Sacred Ground* except that they share in common a "neutrality" in political questions that leaves intact the status quo of domination. Washington's position became the primary motivation for the individuals who met in 1905 at Niagara Falls to convene the Niagara Movement, out of which the NAACP was organized a few years later.

81   Gary T. Marx, *Protest and Prejudice: A Study of Belief in the Black Community* (New York: Harper Torchbooks, 1967), 104–5. The religious embodiment of the otherworldly orientation was epitomized in the protagonist of Harriet Beecher Stowe's *Uncle Tom's Cabin*, which was published during the tense period leading to the American Civil War. In short, Uncle Tom, a literary character whom Wilson Jeremiah Moses identifies as "messianic," was an embodiment of the religious long-suffering of African Americans in slavery. He suggests that "the qualities of kindliness, patience, humility, and great-hearted altruism, even in the face of abuse, were the very Christian virtues that were needed to redeem the world. Just as Christ had died for the sins of his tormentors, so had Uncle Tom been portrayed as dying for the sins of the South," 49.

82   See Robert C. Smith, *We Have No Leaders*. It is apparent that King was revenant in the middle to late 1990s among proponents of the 1960s integrationist movement, because to them, the March on Washington and the pre-1965 King represented an alternative view of national discourse on race when compared to the contents and tone offered in Louis Farrakhan's "A More Perfect Union" speech at the 1995 Million Man March.

83   Michael Dyson, *Making Malcolm: The Myth and Meaning of Malcolm X* (New York: Oxford University Press, 1995), 37.

84   Moses, *Black Messiahs and Uncle Toms*, 51.

85   McGraw, *Rediscovering America's Sacred Ground*, 98.

86   Ibid., 176.

87   Ibid., 64. Although McGraw is primarily interested in the American Revolution in this regard, Locke's "right to rebel" against arbitrary power and wanton domination could also be of use to African American religious leaders who were not committed to nonviolence.
88   Ibid., 89.

Chapter 9

1   See Diana Eck, *Encountering God: A Spiritual Journey from Bozeman to Banaras* (Boston: Beacon Press, 1993), 34–36. See also Gurinder Singh Mann, Paul David Numrich and Raymond B. Williams, *Buddhists, Hindus, and Sikhs in America* (New York: Oxford University Press, 2001), 64–66.
2   See Steven Vertovec, The Hindu Diaspora (London: Routledge, 2000), 14. Vertovec acknowledges the difficulty of arriving at an accurate number. This difficulty includes multiple meanings of the term "Hindu," which may be inclusive of ethnic, cultural, and political identities.
3   Mann, Numrich, and Williams, *Buddhists, Hindus and Sikhs in America*, 67.
4   See Harold Coward, John R. Hinnels, and Raymond Brady Williams, eds., *The South Asian Religious Diaspora in Britain, Canada, and the United States* (Albany: State University of New York Press, 2000), 213–17.
5   For a good survey of the various forms of Hinduism in the United States see Diana Eck, *A New Religious America* (New York: HarperCollins, 2001), chap. 3.
6   Ibid., 80.
7   This does not deny the reality of exclusivism in Hinduism. The point is that the predominant orientation of the tradition is pluralistic in its approach to its own internal diversity and, by extension, to other faiths.
8   See Patrick Olivelle, trans., *Upanisads* (New York: Oxford University Press, 1996).
9   While the term *ishtadeva* is theocentric, I wish to suggest that, in spirit, it can be extended in meaning to include traditions that are nontheistic. One can quite easily speak of *ishtamarga*, or the chosen way. In reality, the choice of an ishta often implies the choice of a distinct *marga*.
10   *Bhagavadgita*, trans. Winthrop Sargeant (Albany: State University of New York Press, 1984).
11   See S. S. Rama Rao Pappu, "Hindu Ethics," in *Global Hinduism*, ed. Robin Rinehart, (Santa Barbara, CA: ABC-CLIO, 2004), 157-158.
12   My translation.
13   Mahatma Gandhi, *All Men Are Brothers* (New York: Columbia University Press, 1958), 89. It is unfortunate that Gandhi still argued for the following of traditional caste-based occupation, even though he rejected birth as a criterion of caste-status. His conservative thinking is also in evidence in his call for separate and complementary roles for women and men. While he believed in spiritual equality, he also claimed that the vocations of women and men were different and that the woman's place was in the home. "The duty of motherhood," wrote Gandhi, "which the vast majority of women will always undertake, requires qualities which men need not possess. She is passive, he is active. She is essentially the mistress of the house. He is the bread-winner. She is the keeper and distributor of the bread." Ibid., 161.
14   See, for example, *Bhagavadgita* 6:29-32.
15   The author's translation.

16   "Seeing indeed the same Lord established everywhere, he does not injure the self by the self. Thereupon he goes to the supreme goal" (*Bhagavadgita* 13:28).

17   The first of the four *ashramas* is the student stage (*brahmacharya*), devoted to study and acquiring vocational skills. The second is the householder stage (*grhastya*), where the focus is on the goals of wealth, pleasure (through marriage and family satisfaction), and duty (*dharma*) through community involvement. The third is the stage of the forest-dweller (*vanaprasthya*), conceived as a semiretired stage devoted to contemplation and religious inquiry. For those so inclined, there is a fourth stage, renunciation (*sannyasa*), devoted to the pursuit of liberation (*moksha*) through a life of celibacy and simplicity.

18   Manu, *The Laws of Manu*, trans. Georg Buhler, vol. 25 of *Sacred Books of the East* (Oxford: Clarendon Press, 1886), ch. 1, vv. 87–91.

19   Ibid., 8:68.

20   Ibid., 8:111–12.

21   Louis Fischer, ed., *The Essential Gandhi* (New York: Vintage Books, 1962), 252.

22   See Diana Eck, *Encountering God: A Spiritual Journey from Bozeman to Banaras* (Boston: Beacon Press, 1993), p.205.

23   Gandhi's methods and beliefs did not have universal acceptance. For an excellent collection of essays, see Harold Coward, ed., *Indian Critiques of Gandhi* (Albany: State University of New York Press, 2003).

24   John B. Carman, "Duties and Rights in Hindu Society," in *Human Rights and the World's Religions*, ed. Leroy S. Rouner (Notre Dame: University of Notre Dame Press, 1988), 117–18.

25   See Julius Lipner, *Hindus: Their Religious Beliefs and Practices* (London: Routledge, 1994), 116–17.

26   Kancha Ilaiah, *Why I Am Not A Hindu* (Delhi: Samya, 1996), 68.

27   Carman, "Duties and Rights in Hindu Society," 120–21.

28   Kana Mitra, "Human Rights in Hinduism," in *Human Rights in Religious Traditions*, ed. Arlene Swidler (New York: Pilgrim Press, 1982), 84.

Chapter 10

Derek H. Davis gratefully acknowledges the able assistance of Aaron Tyler, doctoral student in Church-State Studies at Baylor University, for assistance in preparation of this chapter.

1   Derek H. Davis, *Religion and the Continental Congress, 1774–1789: Contributions to Original Intent* (Oxford: Oxford University Press, 2000), chap. 10.

2   Thomas Helwys, *A Short Declaration of the Mystery of Iniquity*, ed. Richard Groves (Macon, GA: Mercer University Press, 1998), 53.

3   H. Leon McBeth, *The Baptist Heritage* (Nashville: Broadman Press, 1987), 103.

4   Ibid., 128–29.

5   Joseph Martin Dawson, *Baptists and the American Republic* (Nashville: Broadman Press, 1956), 32.

6   McBeth, *The Baptist Heritage*, 129.

7   William Henry Brackney, *The Baptists* (Westport, CT: Greenwood Press, 1988), 92–93.

8   Edwin Scott Gaustad, "The Baptist Tradition of Religious Liberty in America" (Waco, TX: J. M. Dawson Institute of Church-State Studies, Baylor University, 1995), 6.

9   For an excellent biography of Roger Williams, see Edwin S. Gaustad, *Roger Williams: Prophet of Liberty* (Oxford: Oxford University Press, 2001).

10   Derek H. Davis, "The Enduring Legacy of Roger Williams: Consulting America's First Separationist on Today's Pressing Church-State Controversies," *Journal of Church and State* 41 (1999): 201.

11   John M. Mecklin, *The Story of American Dissent* (New York: Harcourt, Brace, 1934), 221. See also Dawson, *Baptists and the American Republic*, 46.

12   Mecklin. *Story of American Dissent*, 221. See also Dawson, *Baptists and the American Republic*, 47.

13   T. B. Maston, *Isaac Backus: Pioneer of Religious Liberty* (London: James Clarke, 1962), 31.

14   For an account of Backus's advocacy before the First Continental Congress, see Davis, *Religion and the Continental Congress, 1774–1789*, 125–28.

15   Ibid., 99–109.

16   Ibid., 55.

17   Letter from Backus to George Washington, 15 November 1790. See Maston, *Isaac Backus*, 69.

18   Excerpt taken from a portion of Article 2. See Matson, *Isaac Backus*, 78.

19   William G. McLoughlin, ed., *The Diary of Isaac Backus*, vol. 3, 1786–1806 (Providence: Brown University Press, 1979), 1320–21. For an older but nevertheless excellent account of the life and contributions of Isaac Backus, see Alvah Hovey, *A Memoir of the Life and Times of Isaac Backus* (1858; Harrisonburg, PA: Gano Books, 1991).

20   William G. McLoughlin, ed., *Isaac Backus on Church, State, and Calvinism* (Cambridge, MA: Harvard University Press, 1969), 422.

21   McBeth, *The Baptist Heritage*, 275. See also L. F. Greene, ed., *The Writings of John Leland* (New York: Arno Press, 1969), 179–92.

22   Gaustad, "The Baptist Tradition," 12.

23   Greene, *The Writings of John Leland*, 51. See also Dawson, *Baptists and the American Republic*, 116.

24   Dawson, *Baptists and the American Republic*, 117.

25   McBeth, *The Baptist Heritage*, 282.

26   Dawson, *Baptists and the American Republic*, 117.

27   Ibid.

28   Brackney, *The Baptists*, 274.

29   Gaustad, "The Baptist Tradition," 22.

30   George W. Truett, "The Baptist Conception of Religious Liberty," in *Proclaiming the Baptist Vision: Religious Liberty*, ed. Walter B. Shurden (Macon, GA: Smyth & Helwys, 1997), 70.

31   Ibid., 63.

32   Ibid., 67.

33   Craig Alan Sherouse, *The Social Teachings of the Baptist World Alliance, 1905–1980* (Ann Arbor: University of Michigan, Microfilms International Dissertation Services, 1982), 22–23.

34   Herbert Gezork, "Our Baptist Faith in the World Today," in *The Life of Baptists in the Life of the World*, ed. Walter B. Shurden (Nashville: Broadman Press, 1985), 180–81.

35   Ibid., 181.

36   Ibid., 181–82.

37   Brackney, *The Baptists*, 104.
38   Ibid.
39   Ibid.
40   *Everson v. Board of Education of Ewing Township*, 330 U.S. 1 (1947).
41   Baptist Joint Committee on Public Affairs (BJCPA) Minutes, 11 February 1947, 3, quoted in Stanley LeRoy Hastey, "History and Contribution of the Baptist Joint Committee on Public Affairs, 1946–1971" (Th.D. diss., Southern Baptist Theological Seminary, 1973), 73.
42   Joseph Martin Dawson, *A Thousand Months to Remember* (Waco, TX: Baylor University Press, 1964), 203.
43   Ibid.
44   Witte Jr., *Religion and the American Constitutional Experiment*, 167. See also *Engel v. Vitale*, 370 U.S. at 421, 430–32 (1962).
45   *Engel v. Vitale*, 370 U.S. at 421, 430–32 (1962).
46   "Carter Opposes School Prayer Action," *Report from the Capital* 34 (May 1979): 7.
47   See Derek H. Davis, "Baptist Approaches to Presidential Politics and Church-State Issues," *Baptist History and Heritage* 32, no. 1 (1997): 35.
48   Hastey, "History and Contribution of the Baptist Joint Committee," 196–98.
49   "Private School Aid Plan Draws Prompt Criticism," *Report from the Capital* 46 (1991): 8.
50   Oliver S. Thomas, "Views of the Wall," *Report from the Capital* 46 (1991): 6.
51   "BJCPA's Dunn Challenges Reagan on Public School Prayer Amendment," *Report from the Capital* 37 (1982): 8.
52   Daniel Martin, "Committee Supports Equal Access Bill; Affirms Opposition to School Prayer," *Report from the Capital* 39 (1984): 5.
53   "Leaders Decry Misuse of Religion in Campaigns," *Report from the Capital* 47 (1992): 9.
54   "Hatch Decides to Introduce Religious Equality Measure," *Report from the Capital* 51 (1996): 1.
55   "CLC: Let the Students Pray," *Salt* 4, no. 5 (1994): 1, 3.
56   Ibid.
57   *Oregon. v. Smith*, 484 U.S. 872 (1990).
58   Oliver Thomas, counsel for the BJC, spearheaded the effort in gathering a coalition of more than eighty different religious and civil liberty organizations to lobby for the Religious Freedom Restoration Act (RFRA).
59   Baptist Joint Committee on Public Affairs Web site. www.bjcpa.org/Pages/AboutUs/aboutus.html.
60   "Church Politics Bill Fails By Wide Margin," *Report from the Capital* 57, no. 20 (2002): 1.
61   Ibid.
62   "Building Bridges a Better Route to Securing Religious Liberty for All," *Report from the Capital* 57, no.22 (2002).
63   McGraw, *Rediscovering America's Sacred Ground*, 178.
64   Ibid.
65   James E. Wood Jr., "The New Religious Right and Its Implications for Southern Baptists," *Foundations* 25 (1982): 161. See also Brackney, *The Baptists*, 106.
66   McGraw, *Rediscovering America's Sacred Ground*, 178.
67   Brackney, *The Baptists*, 107.
68   Gaillard Hunt, ed., *The Writings of James Madison*, 9 vols. (New York: G. P. Putnam's Sons, 1900–1910), 9:100.

Chapter 11

1   Arthur Waley, *The Way and Its Power: A Study of the Tao te Ching and Its Place in Chinese Thought* (New York: Grove Press, 1958), 155.
2   See William Paden's provocative book *Religious Worlds: The Comparative Study of Religion* (Boston: Beacon, 1988).
3   This trend can be traced to the work of Masao Abe and his dialogue with Christians, whom he greatly influenced. Earlier, the work of D. T. Suzuki was also important.
4   Some of the later work of Gordon Kaufman exemplifies this tendency.
5   As a perhaps nasty aside, but one relevant to the topic under discussion, I have always been intensely irritated by the way Karl Barth and his followers illustrate this tendency. Barthians are very astute at noticing the constant tendency to make absolutes out of relatives—on the part of all other religions and most other schools within Christianity, but somehow fail to notice that, necessarily, they are doing the same thing.
6   Attributed to the historical Buddha, and quoted in Walpola Rahula, *What the Buddha Taught* (New York: Grove, 1974), 11.
7   Frances Kissling, "Is There Life after Roe? How to Think about the Fetus," *Conscience: The Newsjournal of Catholic Opinion* 25, no. 3 (Winter 2004–5): 10–18.
8   Traleg Kyabgon, *The Essence of Buddhism: An Introduction to Its Theory and Practice* (Boston: Shambhala Publications, 2001), 21.
9   William LaFleur, *Liquid Life: Abortion and Buddhism in Japan* (Princeton, NJ: Princeton University Press, 1992).
10   This is the phrase used in the Jewish Passover service to wish for the speedy arrival of the Messiah.

Chapter 12

Portions of this chapter are reprinted by permission from Phillip E. Hammond, *The Protestant Presence in Twentieth-Century America: Religion and Political Culture* (Albany: The State University of New York Press, 1992). All Rights Reserved.

1   Sanford Levinson, *Constitutional Faith* (Princeton: Princeton University Press, 1988), 27.
2   James H. Hutson, "What Are the Rights of the People?" *Wilson Quarterly* (Winter 1991): 70.
3   H. Jefferson Powell, *The Moral Tradition of American Constitutionalism: A Theological Interpretation* (Durham: Duke University Press, 1993), 152.
4   Phillip E. Hammond, David W. Machacek, and Eric Michael Mazur, *Religion on Trial: How Supreme Court Trends Threaten the Freedom of Conscience in America* (Walnut Creek, CA: AltaMira, 2004), 80.
5   Hutson, "What Are the Rights of the People?" 70.
6   Martin Marty, *Righteous Empire* (New York: Deal Press, 1970), 211.
7   David W. Machacek and Adrienne Fulco, "The Courts and Public Discourse: The Case of Gay Marriage," *Journal of Church and State* 46 (2004). The remaining responses, 35 percent of the total number, consisted of those that gave no reason for their support or opposition to the decision and were therefore uncodable.
8   Ibid., 782.
9   Ibid., 780.
10   *Lochner v. New York*, 198 U.S. 45 (1905).

11   *Gitlow v. New York*, 268 U.S. 652 (1925) at 666.
12   *Palko v. Connecticut*, 302 U.S. 319 (1937) at 324.
13   Phillip E. Hammond, *With Liberty for All: Freedom of Religion in the United States* (Louisville: Westminster John Knox Press, 1998).
14   Ibid., 51.
15   Ibid., 52.
16   *United States v. Seeger*, 380 U.S. 163 (1965) at 176.
17   *Cantwell v. Connecticut*, 310 U.S. 296 (1940).
18   *United States v. Ballard*, 322 U.S. 78 (1944).
19   In 1990, the Court reversed course, saying in *Employment Division v. Smith*, 494 U.S. 872, that as long as the law wasn't explicitly targeted at religion or a religious practice, the state did not have to justify legal burdens on the free exercise of religion.
20   *United States v. Carolene Products Co.*, 304 U.S. 144 (1938) at 153, n. 4.
21   Powell, *Moral Tradition of American Constitutionalism*, 159ff.
22   *Brown v. Board of Education*, 347 U.S. 483 (1954).
23   Powell, *Moral Tradition of American Constitutionalism*, 277.
24   *Griswold v. Connecticut*, 381 U.S. 479 (1965).
25   *Eisenstadt v. Baird*, 405 U.S. 438 (1972) at 453.
26   *Planned Parenthood of Southeastern PA v. Casey*, 505 U.S. 833 (1992) at 850.
27   *Lawrence v. Texas*, 539 U.S. 558 (2003).
28   Ibid.
29   Machacek and Fulco, "The Courts and Public Discourse," 776–77.
30   Powell, *The Moral Tradition of American Constitutionalism*, 187.
31   David A .J. Richards, *Identity and the Case for Gay Rights: Race, Gender, Religion as Analogies* (Chicago: University of Chicago Press, 1999), 86.
32   Peter S. Wenz, *Abortion Rights as Religious Freedom* (Philadelphia: Temple University Press, 1992), 168.
33   See, for instance, Ronald Dworkin, *Life's Dominion* (New York: Knopf, 1993); Hammond, Machacek, and Mazur, *Religion on Trial*, ch. 6.
34   Gary L. McDowell, "Rights without Roots," *Wilson Quarterly* (Winter 1991): 72.
35   Richard John Neuhaus, *The Naked Public Square* (Grand Rapids: Eerdmans, 1984), 80.
36   Marvin Frankel, "Religion and Public Life: Reasons for Minimal Access," *George Washington Law Review* 60 (1992): 639.
37   Private correspondence with the author, January 31, 2005. See McGraw, *Rediscovering America's Sacred Ground*, 137–66, which makes a similar point.
38   Ibid., 91–93.

Epilogue

1   See Selover in this volume.
2   See chap. 1 in this volume and McGraw, *Rediscovering America's Sacred Ground*, 119–28.
3   See Formicola in this volume.
4   See Pottenger in this volume.
5   See Davis in this volume.
6   See, e.g., "Declaration on Religious Freedom," *Dignitatis Humanae, On the Right of the Person and of Communities to Social and Civil Freedom in Matters Religious*. Promulgated by His Holiness Pope Paul VI on December 7, 1965.

7   See, e.g., Locke, *A Letter Concerning Toleration*, 433. "We have duties, for the discharge of which we are accountable to our Creator and benefactor, which no human power can cancel." *Essex Result* (1778) in Schwartz, *Bill of Rights*, 349. See also Madison, "A Memorial and Remonstrance against Religious Assessments," 2:184; Jefferson, "A Bill for Establishing Religious Freedom," 946.

8   See McGraw and also Taylor in this volume.

9   McGraw, *Rediscovering America's Sacred Ground*, 95–97; Taylor in this volume.

10   See Selover and also McGraw in this volume.

11   See Gross in this volume.

12   See Pottenger in this volume.

13   See Selover in this volume.

Bibliography

Abdul Hadi, Fahhim. "Protecting the Future of Islam in America." *Islamic Horizons* (March/April 1999): 30.

Adams, Charles Francis (from John Adams)

Adams, John. "To the Officers of the First Brigade of the Third Division of the Militia of Massachusetts." 11 October 1798. In *The Works of John Adams, Second President of the United States with a life of the author, notes, and illustrations.* Compiled by Charles Francis Adams. 10 vols. Boston: Charles C. Little & James Brown, 1850–1856.

———. John Adams to Zabdiel Adams. 21 June 1776. In *Adams Family Correspondence.* Edited by Lyman H. Butterfield, 6 vols. (Cambridge, MA: Belknap Press, 1963–1993).

Agostini v. Felton, 117 S.Ct. (1997).

Ahmed, Arshad, Umar Moghul, Farid Senzai, and Saeed Khan. *The US Patriot Act: Impact on the Arab and Muslim American Community.* Detroit: Institute for Social Policy and Understanding, 2004.

Ali, Tahir. "Neo-Muslims and Rand Robots." *Pakistan Link,* 24 December 2004. http://www.pakistanlink.com/Opinion/2004/Dec04/24/01.htm.

Ali-Akbar, Nassir. "Challenges Faced by Islamic Schools." *The Message* (May 2000): 29–30.

Altalib, Omar. "Muslims in America: Challenges and Prospects." *American Muslim Quarterly* 2, no. 1 (1998): 39–49.

American Catholic Bishops. *The Challenge of Peace: God's Promise and Our Response.* Washington, DC: USCCB, 1983.

————. *Economic Justice for All.* Washington, D.C.: USCCB, 1986.

Aptheker, Herbert. *"One Continual Cry": David Walker's Appeal to the Colored Citizens of the World (1829–1830).* New York: Humanities Press, 1965.

Armstrong, Susan, and Richard Botzler, eds. *Environmental Ethics: Divergence and Convergence.* New York: McGraw-Hill, 1993.

Arrington, Leonard J., and Davis Bitton. *The Mormon Experience: A History of the Latter-day Saints.* New York: Vintage Press, 1980.

Baldwin, Lewis. "Revisiting the 'All-Comprehending Institution': Historical Reflections on the Public Roles of Black Churches." In *New Day Begun: African American Churches and Civic Culture in Post–Civil Rights America.* Edited by R. Drew Smith. Durham: Duke University Press, 2003.

Banerjee, Neela. "Catholic Group Receives 1,092 New Sex Abuse Reports." *The New York Times,* 19 February 2005.

————. "Catholic Order Agrees to Pay $6.3 Million to Settle Abuse Suits." *The New York Times,* 25 December 2004.

Baptist Joint Committee on Public Affairs (BJCPA) Minutes, 11 February 1947. Quoted in Stanley LeRoy Hastey, "History and Contribution of the Baptist Joint Committee on Public Affairs, 1946–1971." Th.D. diss., Southern Baptist Theological Seminary, 1973.

Baptist Joint Committee on Public Affairs Web site. http://www.bjcpa.org/Pages/AboutUs/aboutus.html.

Barazinji, Jamal. "History of Islamization of Knowledge and Contributions of the International Institute of Islamic Thought." In *Muslims and Islamization in North America: Problems and Prospects.* Edited by Amber Haque. Beltsville, MD: Amana Publications, 1999.

Barber, Benjamin R. "Clansmen, Consumers, and Citizens: Three Takes on Civil Society." In *Civil Society, Democracy, and Civic Renewa.* Edited by Robert K. Fullinwider. Lanham, MD: Rowman & Littlefield, 1999.

Barna Group. General Religious Beliefs Survey, 2002. http://www.barna.org/FlexPage.aspx?Page=Topic&Topic1D=2

Basit, Abdul. "How to Integrate without Losing Muslim Identity." *Islamic Horizons* (March/April 1998): 32–34.

Becker, Carl L. *The Declaration of Independence: A Study in the History of Political Ideas.* New York: Vintage, 1922. Repr. 1942.

Bell, Derrick. *And We Are Not Saved: The Elusive Quest for Racial Justice.* New York: Basic Books, 1987.

Belluck, Pam. "Judge Denies Church's Bid to Seal Records on Priests." *The New York Times,* 20 November 2002.

Bennion, Lowell L. *An Introduction to the Gospel: Course of Study for the Sunday Schools of the Church of Jesus Christ of Latter-day Saints.* Salt Lake City: Deseret Sunday School Union Board, 1955.

Berrett, William E. *The Latter-day Saints: A Contemporary History of the Church of Jesus Christ.* Salt Lake City: Deseret Books, 1985.

The Bhagavadgita. Translated by Winthrop Sargeant. Albany: State University of New York Press, 1984.

Bhargava, Rajeev. *Secularism and Its Critics.* Delhi, India: Oxford University Press, 1998.

"BJCPA's Dunn Challenges Reagan on Public School Prayer Amendment." *Report from the Capital* 37 (1982): 8.

Bitton, Davis. "The Sovereignty of God in John Calvin and Brigham Young." *Sunstone* 5 (1980): 26–30.

Bloom, Harold. *The American Religion: The Emergence of the Post–Christian Nation*. New York: Simon & Schuster, 1992.

Borden, Morton. *Jews, Turks and Infidels*. Chapel Hill: University of North Carolina Press, 1984.

Bowers, C. A. *Educating for an Ecologically Sustainable Culture*. Albany: State University of New York Press, 1995.

———. *Education, Cultural Myths, and the Environment*. Albany: State University of New York Press, 1993.

Boy Scouts of America and Monmouth Council et al. v. James Dale, 530 U.S. 640 (2000).

Boyarin, Jonathan. "Circumscribing Constitutional Identities in Kiryas Joel." *Yale Law Journal* 106 (1997): 1537–70.

Brackney, William Henry. *The Baptists*. Westport, CT: Greenwood Press, 1988.

Brams, Steven J. *Biblical Games: A Strategic Analysis of Stories in the Old Testament*. Cambridge, MA: MIT Press, 1980.

Brown v. Board of Education, 347 U.S. 483 (1954).

Bryson, Amy Joi. "Rule Proposed on Abortion Funding." *Deseret Morning News,* 2 July 2004. http://deseretnews.com/dn/print/1,1442,595074499,00.html.

"Building Bridges: A Better Route to Securing Religious Liberty for All." *Report from the Capital* 57, no. 22 (2002).

Bushman, Richard L. *Joseph Smith and the Beginnings of Mormonism*. Urbana: University of Illinois Press, 1984.

Cannon, George Q. "The Gospel of Jesus Christ Taught by the Latter-day Saints—Celestial Marriage." 15 August 1869. *Journal of Discourses* 14 (1872): 55.

Cantwell v. Connecticut, 310 U.S. 296 (1940).

Capra, Fritjof. *The Web of Life: A New Scientific Understanding of Living Systems*. New York: Anchor, 1996.

Carroll, James. *Constantine's Sword*. Boston: Houghton Mifflin, 2001.

"Carter Opposes School Prayer Action." *Report from the Capital* 34 (1979): 7.

Chadwick, John. "American Muslims Gain a Political Voice." *The Record*, 24 September 2000.

Church Educational System. *Church History in the Fullness of Times*. Salt Lake City: LDS Church, 1989.

The Church of Jesus Christ of Latter-Day Saints. *Come unto the Father in the name of Jesus: Melchizedek Priesthood Personal Study Guide*. Salt Lake City: The Church of Jesus Christ of Latter Day Saints, 1990.

———."First Presidency Issues Statement on Marriage." Press Release, 7 July 2004. http://www.lds.org/newsroom/showrelease/0,15503,3881-1-19733,00.html.

"Church Politics Bill Fails by Wide Margin." *Report from the Capital* 57, no. 20 (2002): 1.

Clark, Drew. "The Mormon Stem-Cell Choir." Slate, 3 August 2001. http://slate.msn.com/?id=112974.

"CLC: Let the Students Pray." *Salt* 4, no .5 (1994): 1, 3.

Cochran v. Louisiana State Board of Education, 281 U.S. 370 (1930).

Cohen, Jean. "Interpreting the Notion of Civil Society." In *Toward a Global Civil Society*. Edited by Michael Walzer. Providence: Berghahn Books, 1998.

Cohen, Naomi. *Jews in Christian America*. New York: Oxford University Press, 1992.

Cohen, Steven M., and Charles S. Liebman. "American Jewish Liberalism: Unraveling the Strands." *Public Opinion Quarterly* 61 (1997): 405–30.

Commins, Saxe, ed. *Basic Writings of George Washington*. New York: Random House, 1948.

Congregation for the Doctrine of the Faith. "The Participation of Catholics in Political Life." 24 November 2002. http://www.vatican.va/roman_curia/.

Coward, Harold, ed. *Indian Critiques of Gandhi.* Albany: State University of New York Press, 2003.

Coward, Harold, John R. Hinnels, and Raymond Brady Williams, eds. *The South Asian Religious Diaspora in Britain, Canada and the United States.* Albany: State University of New York Press, 2000.

Crapo, Richley H. "Grass-Roots Deviance from the Official Doctrine: A Study of Latter-Day Saint (Mormon) Folk-Beliefs." *Journal for the Scientific Study of Religion* 26 (1987): 465–86.

Cuomo, Mario. "Religious Belief and Public Morality: A Catholic Governor's Perspective." Remarks delivered at Notre Dame University, Indiana. 13 September 1984. http://pewforum.org/docs/print.php?DocID=14.

Dahl, Robert A. *On Democracy.* New Haven: Yale University Press, 1998.

Dalin, David G. "Jewish Critics of Strict Separationism." In *Jews and the American Public Square: Debating Religion and Republic.* Edited by Alan L. Mittleman, Jonathan D. Sarna, and Robert Licht. Lanham, MD: Rowman & Littlefield, 2002.

Davis, Derek H. "Baptist Approaches to Presidential Politics and Church-State Issues." *Baptist History and Heritage* 32, no. 1 (1997): 35.

———. "The Enduring Legacy of Roger Williams: Consulting America's First Separationist on Today's Pressing Church-State Controversies." *Journal of Church and State* 41 (1999): 201.

———. *Religion and the Continental Congress, 1774–1789: Contributions to Original Intent.* Oxford: Oxford University Press, 2000.

Dawson, Joseph Martin. *Baptists and the American Republic.* Nashville: Broadman Press, 1956.

———. *A Thousand Months to Remember.* Waco, TX: Baylor University Press, 1964.

Dawson, Michael C. *Black Visions: The Roots of Contemporary African-American Political Ideologies.* Chicago: University of Chicago Press, 2001.

De Santis, Vincent. "American Catholics and McCarthyism." *The Catholic Historical Review* 2 (1965): 29–31.

Deseret Morning News. "Amend the Constitution." 26 February 2004. http://deseret news.com/dn/print/1,1442,590045769,00.html.

———. "Refocusing on Stem Cells." 10 June 10 2004. http://deseretnews.com/dn/print/1,1442,595069208,00.html.

Devine, Tony, Joon Ho Seuk, and Andrew Wilson. *Cultivating Heart and Character: Educating for Life's Most Essential Goals.* New York: Character Development Publishing, 2000.

Dickerson, John. "Letters of Fabius." 1788. In *The Bill of Rights: A Documentary History.* Edited by Bernard Schwartz. New York: Chelsea House, 1971.

Dillenberger, John. "Grace and Works in Martin Luther and Joseph Smith." In *Reflections on Mormonism: Judaeo-Christian Parallels.* Edited by Truman G. Madsen. Provo, UT: Brigham Young University Press, 1978.

Dillon, Sam. "Catholic Religious Orders Let Abusive Priests Stay." *The New York Times,* 10 August 2002.

Dollinger, Marc. *Quest for Inclusion: Jews and Liberalism in Modern America.* Princeton: Princeton University Press, 2000.

Dowty, Alan. *The Jewish State a Century Later.* Berkeley: University of California Press, 1998.

DuBois, W. E. B. *The Souls of Black Folk.* Edited by David W. Blight and Robert Gooding-Williams. Boston: New Bedford Books, 1997.

———. *The World and Africa: An Inquiry into the Part which Africa Has Played in World History.* New York: International Press, 1946. Repr. 1965.

Duin, Julia. "U.S. Muslims Use Growing Numbers to Flex Political Muscles." *Washington Times*. 11 July 2000.

Dunn, John. *The Political Thought of John Locke*. Cambridge: Cambridge University Press, 1969.

Durkheim, Emile. *The Elementary Forms of Religious Life*. Translated by Karen E. Fields. New York: Free Press, 1995.

Dworkin, Ronald. *Life's Dominion*. New York: Alfred A. Knopf, 1993.

Dyson, Michael. *Making Malcolm: The Myth and Meaning of Malcolm X*. New York: Oxford University Press, 1995.

Eck, Diana L. *A New Religious America*. New York: HarperCollins, 2001.

———. *Encountering God: A Spiritual Journey from Bozeman to Banaras*. Boston: Beacon Press, 1993.

Ehrenberg, John. *Civil Society: The Critical History of an Idea*. New York: New York University Press, 1999.

Eisenstadt v. Baird, 405 U.S. 438 (1972).

Elahi, Shayan. "Beware of Rand Robots and Muslim Neocons." *Pakistan Link*, 7 January 2005. http://www.pakistanlink.com/Opinion/2005/Jan05/07/08.htm.

Elazar, Daniel Judah, and Stuart A. Cohen. *The Jewish Polity: Jewish Political Organization from Biblical Times to the Present*. Bloomington: Indiana University Press, 1985.

El Hassan, Sarvath. "Educating Women in the Muslim World." *Islamic Horizons* (March/April 1999): 54–56.

Elliott, Jonathan. *The Debates of the Several State Conventions on the Adoption of the Federal Constitution*. 2d ed. 1836.

Engel v. Vitale, 370 U.S. 421 (1962).

Everson v. Board of Education of Ewing Township, 330 U.S. 1 (1947).

Ewing, George W. "Introduction." In *The Reasonableness of Christianity*, by John Locke. Edited by George W. Ewing. Washington, DC: Regnery Gateway, 1965.

Farkas, John R., and David A. Reed. *Mormonism: Changes, Contradictions, and Errors*. Grand Rapids: Baker Books, 1995.

Fine, Robert. "Civil Society Theory, Enlightenment and Critique." In *Civil Society: Democratic Perspectives*. Edited by Robert Fine and Shirin Rai. London: Frank Cass, 1997.

Fingarette, Herbert. "Following the 'One Thread' of the Analects." *Journal of the American Academy of Religion* 7, no. 3 (1980): 373–405.

Finkelman, Paul. *Slavery and the Founders: Race and Liberty in the Age of Jefferson*, 2d ed. Armonk, NY: M. E. Sharpe, 2001.

Firmage, Edwin B. "Restoring the Church: Zion in the Nineteenth and Twenty-first Centuries." In *The Wilderness of Faith*. Edited by John Sillito. Salt Lake City: Signature Books, 1991.

Fischer, Louis, ed. *The Essential Gandhi*. New York: Vintage Books, 1962.

Flannery, Austin, O.P., ed. *Vatican Council II: The Conciliar and Post-Conciliar Documents*. Boston: Daughters of St. Paul, 1988. *Declaration on Religious Liberty (Dignitatis Humanae)*. *Pastoral Constitution on the Church in the Modern World (Gaudium et Spes)*.

Flotz, Richard. *Worldview, Religion, and the Environment*. Belmont, CA: Wadsworth, 2003.

Formicola, Jo Renee. "American Catholic Political Theology." *Journal of Church and State* 29, no. 3 (1987): 457–74.

———. *The Catholic Church and Human Rights*. New York: Garland, 1988.

———. *John Paul II: Prophetic Politician*. Washington, DC: Georgetown University Press, 2002.

————. "The Vatican, the American Bishops, and the Church-State Ramifications of Clerical Sexual Abuse." *Journal of Church and State* 46 (2004): 479–502.

"A Forum Rebuilds: AMSS Serves as a Platform for Discussion of Issues Facing Muslims." *Islamic Horizons* (January/February 1999): 17.

Foster, Lawrence. "Between Heaven and Earth: Mormon Theology of the Family in Comparative Perspective." In *Multiply and Replenish: Mormon Essays on Sex and Family*. Edited by Brent Corcoran. Salt Lake City: Signature Books, 1994.

Fowler, Robert Booth, Allen D. Hertzke, and Laura R. Olson. *Religion and Politics in America: Faith, Culture, and Strategic Choices*. 2d ed. Boulder: Westview Press, 1999.

Frankel, Marvin. "Religion and Public Life: Reasons for Minimal Access." *George Washington Law Review* 60 (1992): 639.

Franklin, Benjamin. "Dialogue between Two Presbyterians." 1735. *Benjamin Franklin Writings*. Edited by J.A. Leo Lemay. New York: The Library of America, 1987.

————. Benjamin Franklin to Ezra Stiles. 1790. *Benjamin Franklin Writings*. Edited by J.A. Leo Lemay. New York, The Library of America, 1987.

Frazier, E. Franklin. *The Negro Church in America*. New York: Schocken, 1974.

————. The Negro in the United States. New York: Macmillan, 1974.

Fuchs, Lawrence H. *The Political Behavior of American Jews*. Glencoe, IL: Free Press, 1956.

Gandhi, Mahatma. *All Men Are Brothers*. New York: Columbia University Press, 1958.

Gates, Henry Louis, Jr., and Cornel West. *The Future of the Race*. New York: Vintage Books, 1996.

Gaustad, Edwin Scott. "The Baptist Tradition of Religious Liberty in America." Waco, TX: J. M. Dawson Institute of Church-State Studies, Baylor University, 1995.

————. *Roger Williams: Prophet of Liberty*. Oxford: Oxford University Press, 2001.

Genovese, Eugene D. Roll, *Jordan, Roll: The World the Slaves Made*. New York: Pantheon, 1974.

Gerges, Fawaz. "Taking Stock of the War on Terror." Lecture at Adrian College, 21 February 21 2005.

Gernet, Jacques. *China and the Christian Impact: A Conflict of Cultures*. Cambridge: Cambridge University Press, 1985.

Gerry, Elbridge. "Observations of the New Constitution and the Federal and State Conventions," 1788. Pamphlets on the Constitution of the United States, 1–23. Reprinted in *The Bill of Rights: A Documentary History*. Edited by Bernard Schwartz. New York: Chelsea House, 1971.

Gezork, Herbert. "Our Baptist Faith in the World Today." In *The Life of Baptists in the Life of the World*. Edited by Walter B. Shurden. Nashville: Broadman Press, 1985.

Gitlow v. New York, 268 U.S. 652 (1925).

Givens, Terryl L. *By the Hand of Mormon: The American Scripture That Launched a New World Religion*. New York: Oxford University Press, 2002.

Glen, David. "Who Owns Islamic Law?" *The Chronicle of Higher Education*, 25 February 2005, A14–17.

Goldie, Mark, ed. *Political Essays*. Cambridge: Cambridge University Press, 1997.

Goodstein, Laurie. "Abuse Scandal Has Been Ended, Top Bishop Says." *The New York Times*, 28 February 2004.

————. "Bishop Would Deny Rite for Defiant Catholic Voters." *The New York Times*, 14 May 2004.

————. "Bishops' Leader Resists Releasing Priest's Records in His Own Diocese." *The New York Times*, 2 September 2004.

————. "Communion Issue Creates Split Among U. S. Bishops." *The New York Times*, 6 June 2004.

————. "Politicians Face Bishops' Censure in Abortion Rift." *The New York Times*, 9 June 2004.

Gottlieb, Robert, and Peter Wiley. *America's Saints: The Rise of Mormon Power*. New York: Harcourt Brace Jovanovich, 1986.

Gottlieb, Roger S., ed. *This Sacred Earth: Religion, Nature, Environment*. New York: Routledge, 1996.

Greenberg, Anna, and Kenneth D. Wald. "Still Liberal After All These Years? The Contemporary Political Behavior of American Jewry." In *Jews in American Politics*. Edited by Sandy Maisel and Ira N. Forman. Lanham, MD: Rowman & Littlefield, 2001.

Greene, L. F., ed. *The Writings of John Leland*. New York: Arno Press, 1969.

Griffin, Susan. *The Eros of Everyday Life*. New York: Doubleday, 1995.

Griswold v. Connecticut, 381 U.S. 479 (1965).

Guerra, Anthony J. *Family Matters: The Role of Christianity in the Formation of the Western Family*. St. Paul, MN: Paragon House, 2002.

Gwaltney, John Langston. *Drylongso: A Self-Portrait of Black America*. New York: The New York Press, 1993.

Haddad, Yvonne. "The Dynamics of Islamic Identity in North America." In *Muslims on the Americanization Path?* Edited by Yvonne Haddad and John Esposito. New York: Oxford University Press, 2000.

Haddad, Yvonne, and John Esposito, eds. *Muslims on the Americanization Path?* New York: Oxford University Press, 2000.

Hadhrami, Abu Amal. "Muslims Gain Political Rights." *Islamic Horizons* (January/February 1999): 24–25.

Hall, David L., and Roger T. Ames. *Thinking Through Confucius*. Albany: State University of New York Press, 1987.

Hammond, Phillip E. *The Protestant Presence in Twentieth-Century America: Religion and Political Culture*. Albany: State University of New York Press, 1992.

————. *With Liberty for All: Freedom of Religion in the United States*. Louisville: Westminster John Knox Press, 1998.

Hammond, Phillip E., David W. Machacek, and Eric Michael Mazur. *Religion on Trial: How Supreme Court Trends Threaten the Freedom of Conscience in America*. Walnut Creek, CA: AltaMira, 2004.

Haque, Amber, ed. *Muslims and Islamization in North America: Problems and Prospects*. Beltsville, MD: Amana, 1999.

Harlow, Jules, ed. *Siddur Sim Shalom*. New York: Rabbinical Assembly, United Synagogue of America, 1985.

Harris, Frederick C. "Something Within: Religion as a Mobilizer of African-American Political Activism." *The Journal of Politics* 56, no. 1 (1994): 42–68.

"Hatch Decides to Introduce Religious Equality Measure." *Report from the Capital* 51 (1996): 1.

Hatch, Orrin G. *Square Peg: Confessions of a Citizen Senator*. New York: Basic Books, 2002.

Helwys, Thomas. *A Short Declaration of the Mystery of Iniquity*. Edited by Richard Groves. Macon, GA: Mercer University Press, 1998.

Hendon, David, and Jeremiah Russell. "Notes on Church-State Affairs." *Journal of Church and State* 46, no. 4 (2004): 926.

Henneberger, Melinda. "Vatican to Hold Secret Trials of Priests in Pedophilia Cases." *The New York Times*, 9 January 2002.

Herskowitz, Melville J. *Myth of the Negro Past*. Boston: Beacon Press, 1941. Repr. 1958.

Hill, Marvin S. *Quest for Refuge: The Mormon Flight from American Pluralism*. Salt Lake City: Signature Books, 1989.

Hinckley, Gordon B. "The Family: A Proclamation to the World." *Ensign* 25 (1995): 102.

———. *Standing for Something: Ten Neglected Virtues that Will Heal Our Hearts and Homes*. New York: Times Books, 2000.

His Holiness the Dalai Lama. *Ethics for the New Millennium*. New York: Riverhead, 1999.

Hitler, Adolf. Reichstag Speech, 1936.

Hooper, Ibrahim. "Media Relations Tips for Muslim Activists." In *Muslims and Islamization in North America: Problems and Prospects*. Edited by Amber Haque. Beltsville, MD: Amana, 1999.

Hooper, Leon, S.J., ed. *Religious Liberty: Catholic Struggles with Pluralism*. Louisville: Westminster Press, 1993.

Hovey, Alvah. *A Memoir of the Life and Times of Isaac Backus*. 1858. Harrisonburg: Gano Books 1991.

Hunt, Gaillard, ed. *The Writings of James Madison*. 9 vols. New York: Putnam's Sons, 1900–1910.

Hussain, Altaf. "Youth and the Emerging Islamic Identity." *The Message* (June/July 1999): 21–22.

Hutson, James H. *Religion and the Founding of the American Republic*. Washington, D.C.: Library of Congress, 1998

———. "What Are the Rights of the People?" *Wilson Quarterly* (Winter 1991), 70.

Huxley, Aldous. *The Perennial Philosophy*. London: Chato & Windus, 1946.

Huyler, Jerome. *Locke in America: The Moral Philosophy of the Founding Era*. Lawrence: University of Kansas Press, 1995.

Ilaiah, Kancha. *Why I Am Not a Hindu*. Delhi: Samya, 1996.

Ismail, Mohamed. "Islamic Education in the Weekend and Full-Time Islamic Schools." *The Message* (May 2000): 41–42.

Ivers, Gregg. *To Build a Wall: American Jews and the Separation of Church and State*. Charlottesville: University Press of Virginia, 1995.

Jackson, Kent P. "Are Mormons Christians? Presbyterians, Mormons, and the Question of Religious Definitions." *Nova Religio* 4 (2000): 54.

Jan, Abid Ullah. *A War on Islam?* Pakistan: Maktabah, 2001.

John Jay College of Criminal Justice. "The Nature and Scope of Sexual Abuse of Minors by Catholic Priests and Deacons in the U.S. 1950–2002." Research study conducted by John Jay College, 25 February 2004. United States Conference of Catholic Bishops. http://www.usccb.org/nrb/johnjaystudy.

Joyner, Charles. "'Believer I Know': The Emergence of African American Christianity." In *African American Christianity: Essays in History*. Edited by Paul E. Johnson. Berkeley: University of California Press, 1994.

Kamali, M. H. *Freedom, Equality, and Justice in Islam*. Cambridge: Islamic Texts Society, 1999.

Katz, Jacob. *Out of the Ghetto: The Social Background of Jewish Emancipation, 1770–1870*. New York: Schocken, 1978.

Kaza, Stephanie, and Kenneth Kraft, eds. *Dharma Rain: Sources of Buddhist Environmentalism*. Boston: Shambala, 2000.

Kennedy, John F. Address to the Houston Ministerial Association, Houston, Texas, 12 June 1960. http://www.americanrhetoric.com/speeches/johnfkennedyhouston-ministerialspeech.html.

Khan, M. A. Muqtedar. *American Muslims: Bridging Faith and Freedom.* Beltsville, MD: Amana, 2002.

————. "Collective Identity and Collective Action: Case of Muslim Politics in America." In *Muslims and Islamization in North America: Problems and Prospects.* Edited by Amber Haque. Beltsville, MD: Amana, 1999.

————. "The Manifest Destiny of American Muslims." *Washington Report on Middle East Affairs* (October/November 2000): 72.

————. "Public Face of Bigotry." *Washington Report on Middle East Affairs* (November/December 2000): 72.

————. The Public Face of Christian Evangelical Bigotry. http://www.glocaleye.org/bigotry2.htm.

Khan, M. A. Muqtedar, and John L. Esposito. "The Threat of Internal Extremism." *Q-News: The Muslim Magazine* (February 2005), 16–17.

Khuri, Richard K. *Freedom, Modernity, and Islam: Towards a Creative Synthesis.* Syracuse: Syracuse University Press, 1998.

King, Larry. "Larry King's People." *USA Today,* 5 February 2001.

Kirkpatrick, David D. "Bush Sought Vatican Official's Help on Issues, Report Says." *The New York Times,* 13 June 2004.

————. "Citing Falwell's Endorsement of Bush, Group Challenges His Tax-Exempt Status." *The New York Times,* 16 June 2004.

Kissling, Frances. "Is There Life after Roe? How to Think about the Fetus." *Conscience: The Newsjournal of Catholic Opinion* 25, no. 3 (2004–5): 10–18.

Klepal, Dan. "Time to Take Back the Church." *The Cincinnati Enquirer,* 5 October 2003. http://www.enquirer.com.

Kraft, Kenneth, "The Greening of Buddhist Practice." *Cross Currents* 44, no. 2 (1994): 63–80.

Kyabgon, Traleg. *The Essence of Buddhism: An Introduction to Its Theory and Practice.* Boston: Shambhala, 2001.

LaFleur, William. *Liquid Life: Abortion and Buddhism in Japan.* Princeton: Princeton University Press, 1992.

Latter-Day Saints (LDS) Church official web site figures, December 31, 2003. http://www.lds.org.

Lavoie, Denise. "Boston Archdiocese Agrees to Settle Clergy Sex Abuses Cases for $85 Million." *The Boston Globe,* 9 September 2003.

Lawrence v. Texas, 539 U.S. 558 (2003).

Leanard, Karen. "American Muslim Politics: Discourses and Practices." *Ethnicities* 3, no. 2 (2003): 147–81.

"Leaders Decry Misuse of Religion in Campaigns." *Report from the Capital* 47 (1992): 9.

Lee, Richard Henry. "Observations Leading to a Fair Examination of the System of Government." Letter 4, 12 October 1777. In *Letters from the Federal Farmer to the Republican.* Edited by Walter Hartwell Bennett. Tuscaloosa: University of Alabama Press, 1978.

————. Richard Lee to James Madison. 26 November 1784. In *The Papers of James Madison.* Edited by Robert A. Rutland, et al. 17 vols. Chicago: University of Chicago Press; Charlottesville: University Pres of Virgina, 1961–1999.

Leibowitz, Yeshayahu. Judaism, Human Values, and the Jewish State. Edited and translated by Eliezer Goldman. Cambridge, MA: Harvard University Press, 1982.

Lemay, J. A. Leo, ed. *Benjamin Franklin Writings.* New York, The Library of America, 1987.

Levine, Lawrence. *Black Culture and Black Consciousness*. New York: Oxford University Press, 1977.

Levinson, Sanford. *Constitutional Faith*. Princeton: Princeton University Press, 1988.

Liebman, Charles S. "Religion and Democracy in Israel." In *Israeli Judaism: The Sociology of Religion in Israel*. Edited by Shlomo Deshen, Charles S. Liebman and Moshe Skokeid. New Brunswick: Transaction, 1995.

Lincoln, Eric, and Lawrence H. Mamiya. *The Black Church in the African American Experience*. Durham: Duke University Press, 1990.

Lipner, Julius. *Hindus: Their Religious Beliefs and Practices*. London: Routledge, 1994.

Lipscomb, A. A., and Albert E. Bergh, eds. *The Writings of Thomas Jefferson*. Memorial edition. Vol. 16 of 20. Washington, DC: Thomas Jefferson Memorial Association, 1903–1904.

Lloyd, R. Scott. "Looking Forward to Congress of Families." *Deseret Morning News*, 28 November 1998. http://www.desnews.com/cgi-bin/libstory_church?dn98&9811290027.

Lochner v. New York, 198 U.S. 45 (1905).

Locke, John. "First Treatise." In *Political Writings of John Locke*. Edited by David Wootton, and translated by William Popple (1685, published 1689). London: Mentor, 1993.

———. *The Reasonableness of Christianity*. Edited by George W. Ewing. Washington, DC: Regnery Gateway, 1965.

———. *Second Treatise of Government*. Edited by C. B. Macpherson. Indianapolis: Hackett, 1980.

———. *The Works of John Locke*. 10 vols. London, 1824.

Lowi, Theodore J. *The End of Liberalism*. 2d ed. New York: Basic Books, 1979.

Machacek, David W., and Adrienne Fulco. "The Courts and Public Discourse: The Case of Gay Marriage," *Journal of Church and State* 46 (2004): 767–85.

Macy, Joanna. *World as Lover, World as Self*. Berkeley, CA: Parallax, 1991.

Maisel, Sandy, and Ira N. Forman, eds. *Jews in American Politics* Lanham, MD: Rowman & Littlefield, 2001.

Mann, Gurinder Singh, Paul David Numrich and Raymond B. Williams. *Buddhists, Hindus and Sikhs in America*. New York: Oxford University Press, 2001.

Manu. *The Laws of Manu*. Translated by Georg Buhler. In *Sacred Books on the East*. 25 vols. Oxford: Clarendon, 1886.

Marsden, George M. *Religion and American Culture*. Orlando: Harcourt Brace Javanovich, 1990.

Marshall, Charles C. "An Open Letter to the Honorable Alfred E. Smith, A Question that Needs an Answer." *Atlantic Monthly* (April 1927): 542.

Marshall, John. *Resistance, Religion, and Responsibility*. Cambridge: Cambridge University Press, 1994.

Martin, Daniel. "Committee Supports Equal Access Bill; Affirms Opposition to School Prayer," *Report from the Capital* 39 (1984): 5.

Marty, Martin. *Righteous Empire*. New York: Deal Press, 1970.

Marx, Gary T. *Protest and Prejudice: A Study of Belief in the Black Community*. New York: Harper Torchbooks, 1967.

Marx, Karl. "Letter to Lion Philips," 1864.

Maston, T. B. *Isaac Backus: Pioneer of Religious Liberty*. London: James Clarke, 1962.

Masud, Enver. *The War on Islam*. Arlington, VA: Madrassah Books, 2002.

Matthews, Richard K. *The Radical Politics of Thomas Jefferson*. Lawrence: University Press of Kansas, 1984.

McAvoy, Thomas T., C.S.C. *History of the Catholic Church in America*. Notre Dame: University of Notre Dame Press, 1960.

McBeth, H. Leon. *The Baptist Heritage*. Nashville: Broadman Press, 1987.

McCloskey, Herbert, and John Zaller. *The American Ethos*. Cambridge, MA: Harvard University Press, 1984.

McConkie, Bruce R. *Mormon Doctrine*. 2d ed. Salt Lake City: Bookcraft, 1979.

McDowell, Gary L. "Rights without Roots." *Wilson Quarterly* (Winter 1991): 72.

McGraw, Barbara A. *Rediscovering America's Sacred Ground: Public Religion and Pursuit of the Good in a Pluralistic America*. Albany: State University of New York Press, 2003.

McKeever, Bill, and Eric Johnson. *Mormonism 101: Examining the Religion of the Latter-day Saints*. Grand Rapids: Baker Books, 2000.

McLoughlin, William G., ed. *The Diary of Isaac Backus*. Vol. 3, *1786–1806*. Providence: Brown University Press, 1979.

———. *Isaac Backus on Church, State, and Calvinism*. Cambridge, MA: Harvard University Press, 1969.

McMurrin, Sterling M. *The Theological Foundations of the Mormon Religion*. Salt Lake City: University of Utah Press, 1965.

Mecklin, John M. *The Story of American Dissent*. New York: Harcourt, Brace, 1934.

Mill, John Stuart. *On Liberty*. London: Longman, Roberts & Green, 1869 [1859].

Mirza, Ambereen. "Muslim Women and American Choices." *Islamic Horizons* (May/June 1999): 50.

Mitchell v. Helms, 530 U.S. 793 (2000).

Mitra, Kana. "Human Rights in Hinduism." In *Human Rights in Religious Traditions*. Edited by Arlene Swidler. New York: Pilgrim Press, 1982.

Mittleman, Alan L. *The Politics of Torah: The Jewish Political Tradition and the Founding of Agudat Israel*. Albany: State University of New York Press, 1996.

Moon, Hyun Jin. *Owning the Culture of Heart*. New York: World CARP, 2003.

Moore, Carrie A. "Evangelical Preaches at Salt Lake Tabernacle." Deseret Morning News, 15 November 2004. http://deseretnews.com/dn/view/0,1249,5951055 80,00.html.

Moore, Kathleen. "The Hijab and Religious Liberty: Anti-Discrimination Law and Muslim Women in the United States." In *Muslims on the Americanization Path?* Edited by Yvonne Haddad and John Esposito. New York: Oxford University Press, 2000.

Morgan, Edmund. *American Slavery, American Freedom*. New York: Norton, 1975.

———. "Slavery and Freedom: The American Paradox." *Journal of American History* 59 (1972): 24.

———. *Benjamin Franklin*. New Haven: Yale University Press, 2002.

Moses, Wilson Jeremiah. *Black Messiahs and Uncle Toms: Social and Literary Manipulations of a Religious Myth*. University Park: Pennsylvania State University Press, 1993.

———. *Classical Black Nationalism: From the American Revolution to Marcus Garvey*. New York: New York University Press, 1996.

Mueller v. Allen, 463 U.S. 388 (1983).

Munir, Ghazala. "Muslim Women in Dialogue: Breaking Walls, Building Bridges." In *Muslims and Islamization in North America: Problems and Prospects*. Edited by Amber Haque. Beltsville, MD: Amana, 1999.

Murphy, Dean E. "For American Muslims Influence in American Politics Comes Hard." *The New York Times*, 27 October 2000.

Murray, John Courtney, S.J. "Contemporary Orientations of Catholic Thought on Church and State." *Theological Studies* 10 (1949): 177–234.

———. Draft of confidential document prepared for the National Catholic Welfare Council (NCWC) as the basis of testimony for Duggan Hearings, undated.

Available in NCWC, Church and State and Federal Aid File, Box 14, Archives of Catholic University of America.

———. "Freedom of Religion I: The Ethical Problem." *Theological Studies* 6 (1945): 229–88.

———. "Leo XIII on Church and State: General Structure of the Controversy." *Theological Studies* 14 (1953): 1–30.

———. *We Hold These Truths*. New York: Doubleday, 1964.

———. *We Hold These Truths: Catholic Reflections on the American Proposition*. New York: Sheed & Ward, 1960.

"Muslims in the West Serving Muslim's Worldwide." *Islamic Horizons* (January/February 1998): 47.

"Muslims Strive with Increasing Confidence." *Islamic Horizons* (January/February 1999): 6.

National Conference of Catholic Bishops. *The Challenge of Peace: God's Promise and Our Response*. Washington, DC: United States Catholic Conference, 1983.

The National Review Board for the Protection of Children and Young People. "A Report on the Crisis in the Catholic Church in the United States." Washington, DC: The United States Conference of Catholic Bishops, 2004.

Neilan, Terence. "Marital Rights Decreed for Gays." *Deseret Morning News*, 5 February 2004. http://deseretnews.com/dn/print/1,1442,590041026,00.html.

Neuhaus, Richard John. *The Naked Public Square*. Grand Rapids: Eerdmans, 1984.

The New York Times. Excerpt from the Address by Archbishop Roach to the national Council of Catholic Bishops. 18 November 1981.

———. Text and Statement by Bishops on Church Role in Politics. 14 October 1984.

———. Bruce Lambert, "17 Priests Reported Disciplined in Long Island Sex Abuse Cases." 25 January 2005.

Niebuhr, Reinhold. *The Children of Light and the Children of Darkness*. New York: Scribners, 1944.

Ninia Baehr et al v. Lawrence Miike, 92 Haw. 634 (1999).

Nizamuddin, Azam. "What Muslims Can Offer America." *Islamic Horizons* (March/April 1998): 35.

Nolan, Hugh. *Pastoral Letters of the United States Catholic Bishops*. Vol. 3. Washington, DC: National Conference of Catholic Bishops, 1983.

Novak, David. *Covenantal Rights: A Study in Jewish Political Theory*. Princeton: Princeton University Press, 2000.

Nyang, Sulayman S. "Islam in America: A Historical Perspective." *American Muslim Quarterly* 2, no. 1 (1998): 7–38.

Oaks, Dallin H. "Introduction." In *The Wall between Church and State*. Edited by Dallin H. Oaks. Chicago: University of Chicago Press, 1963.

———. "Same-Gender Attraction." *Ensign* 25 (1995): 8.

———. "Weightier Matters." Devotional address at Brigham Young University, February 9, 1999. http://speeches.byu.edu/devo/98-99/OaksW99.html.

Oregon v. Smith, 484 U.S. 872 (1990).

O'Dea, Thomas F. *The Mormons*. Chicago: University of Chicago, 1957.

Orin, Deborah. "Teddy Gives the Pope Hell." *New York Post*, 18 June 2004.

Ostling, Richard N., and Joan K. Ostling. *Mormon America: The Power and the Promise*. New York: HarperCollins, 1999.

O'Sullivan, Edmund. *Transformative Learning*. London: Zed, 1999.

Paden, William. *Religious Worlds: The Comparative Study of Religion*. Boston: Beacon, 1988.

Padover, Saul K., ed. *The Complete Jefferson: Containing His Major Writings, Published and Unpublished, Except His Letters*. New York: Duell, Sloan & Pearce, 1943.

"Palestinians killed (Shuhada) by Israeli forces." Palestine Fact Sheets, the Palestine Monitor. http://www.palestinemonitor.org/factsheet/Palestinian_killed_fact_sheet.htm.

Palko v. Connecticut, 302 U.S. 319 (1937).

Pappu, S. S. Rama Rao. "Hindu Ethics." In *Global Hinduism*. Edited by Robin Rinehart. Santa Barbara, CA: ABC-CLIO, 2004.

Paulson, Michael. "Muslims Eye Role at US Polls." *Boston Globe*, 23 October 2000.

Person, Carolyn W. D. "Susa Young Gates." In *Mormon Sisters: Women in Early Utah*. Edited by Claudia L. Bushman. Logan: Utah State University Press, 1997.

Pierce v. Society of Sisters, 268 U.S. 501 (1925).

Pitney, David Howard. *The Afro-American Jeremiad: Appeals for Justice in America*. Philadelphia: Temple University Press, 1990.

Planned Parenthood of Southeastern Pennsylvania v. Casey, 505 U.S. 833 (1992).

Platinga, Alvin. "Pluralism: A Defense of Religious Exclusivism." In *The Philosophical Challenge of Religious Pluralism*. Edited by Philip L. Quinn and Kevin Meeker. New York: Oxford University Press, 2000.

"Politics and Piety: An Interview with Senator Orrin Hatch." *Sunstone* 5 (1980): 54.

Pope John Paul II. Address of Pope John Paul II to the Honorable George W. Bush, President of the United States of America, 4 June 2004. The Vatican, The Holy Father, John Paul II, Speeches. http:// www.vatican.va/holy_father/john_paul_ii/speeches/2004/june/documents/hf_jp-ii_spe_20040604_president-usa_en.html.

———. *Sollicitudo Rei Socialis (On Social Concern)*, 1987; *Centesimus Annus (One Hundred Years)*, 1991; and *Laborem Exercens (On Human Work)*, 1981. The Vatican. http://www.vatican.va.

Pope Leo XIII. *Longinque Oceani*. In *The Great Encyclical Letters of Pope Leo XIII*. Edited by John J. Wynne, S.J. New York: Berzinger Brothers, 1903.

"Popes in the 12–18th Centuries." Web Gallery of Art, glossary. http://gallery.euroweb.hu/database/glossary/popes/popes.html.

Post-Stephen. *Spheres of Love: Toward a New Ethics of the Family*. Dallas: Southern Methodist University Press, 1994.

Pottenger, John R. "Elder Dallin H. Oaks: The Mormons, Politics, and Family Values." In *Religious Leaders and Faith-Based Politics: Ten Profiles*. Edited by Jo Renee Formicola and Hubert Morken. Lanham, MD: Rowman & Littlefield, 2001.

———. "Mormonism and the American Industrial State." *International Journal of Social Economics* 14 (1987): 25–38.

Powell, H. Jefferson. *The Moral Tradition of American Constitutionalism: A Theological Interpretation*. Durham: Duke University Press, 1993.

"Private School Aid Plan Draws Prompt Criticism." *Report from the Capital* 46 (1991): 8.

Putnam, Robert. "Diplomacy and Domestic Politics: The Logic of Two-Level Games." *International Organization* 42 (1988): 427–60.

Quinn, D. Michael. *The Mormon Hierarchy: Extensions of Power*. Salt Lake City: Signature Books, 1997.

Rahe, Paul A. *Republics Ancient and Modern*. Chapel Hill: University of North Carolina Press, 1992.

Rahula, Walpola. *What the Buddha Taught*. New York: Grove Press, 1974.

Randall, Henry Stephens. *The Life of Thomas Jefferson*. 3 vols. New York: Derby & Jackson, 1858.

Rawls, John. "The Idea of Public Reason Revisited." *The University of Chicago Law Review* 64, no. 3 (1997).

———. *Political Liberalism*. 1993. New York: Columbia University Press, 1996.

Rees, John A. "'Really Existing' Scriptures: On the Use of Sacred Text in International Affairs." *The Brandywine Review of Faith & International Affairs* 2 (2004): 17–26.

Reichley, A. James. *The Values Connection.* Lanham, MD: Rowman & Littlefield, 2001.

————. *Faith in Politics.* Washington, DC: Brookings Institution Press, 2002.

Reynolds, Noel B. "The Doctrine of an Inspired Constitution." In *"By the Hands of Wise Men": Essays on the U.S. Constitution.* Edited by Ray C. Hillam. Provo, UT: Brigham Young University Press, 1979.

Richards, David A. J. *Identity and the Case for Gay Rights: Race, Gender, Religion as Analogies.* Chicago: University of Chicago Press, 1999.

Richards, Le Grande. *A Marvelous Work and a Wonder.* Salt Lake City: Deseret Books 1958.

Richardson, James E., ed. *A Compilation of the Messages and Papers of the Presidents.* Vol. 1, *Prepared Under the Direction of the Joint Committee on Printing, of the House and Senate, Pursuant to an Act of the Fifty-Second Congress of the United States with Additions and Encyclopedia Index by Private Enterprise.* 20 vols. New York: Bureau of National Literature, 1911–1922.

"The Rights of the Colonists and a List of Infringements and Violations of Rights, 1772." Drafted by Samuel Adams in Massachusetts. In *The Bill of Rights: A Documentary History.* Edited by Bernard Schwartz. New York: Chelsea House, 1971.

Robinson, Cedric. *Black Marxism: The Making of the Black Radical Tradition.* London: Zen, 1983.

Robinson, Stephen E. *Are Mormons Christians?* Salt Lake City: Bookcraft, 1991.

Roe v. Wade, 410 U.S. 113 (1973).

Romney, Mitt. "One Man, One Woman: A Citizen's Guide to Protecting Marriage." Opinion Journal from The Wall Street Journal Editorial Page, Thursday, 5 February 2004. http://www.opinionjournal.com/forms/printThis.html?id=110004647).

Rosemont, Jr., Henry, Jr.. "Human Rights: A Bill of Worries." In *Confucianism and Human Rights.* Edited by Wm. Theodore de Bary and Tu Wei-ming. New York: Columbia University Press, 1998.

Rosenau, Pauline Marie. *Post-Modernism and the Social Sciences: Insights, Inroads, and Intrusions.* Princeton: Princeton University Press, 1992.

Row, Stan J. "From Reductionism to Holism in Ecology and Deep Ecology." *The Ecologist* 27, no. 4 (1997): 147–52.

Rutland, Robert A., et al, eds. *The Papers of James Madison.* 17 vols. Chicago: University of Chicago Press; Charlottesville: University Pres of Virginia, 1961–1999.

Sachedina, Abdulaziz. *The Islamic Roots of Democratic Pluralism.* New York: Oxford University Press, 2001.

Said, Edward. *Covering Islam: How the Media and the Experts Determine How We See the Rest of the World.* New York: Pantheon Books, 1981.

Sameer, Abu. "Some Milestones in Islamic Education in North America." *The Message* (May 2000): 33–35.

Sandell, Klas, ed. *Buddhist Perspectives on the Ecocrisis.* Kandy, Sri Lanka: Buddhist Publication Society, 1987.

Sanford, Charles B. *Thomas Jefferson and His Library: A Study of His Literary Interests and of the Religious Attitudes Revealed by Relevant Titles in His Library.* Hamden, CT: Archon Books, 1917.

Schambra, William A. "Is There Civic Life beyond the Great National Community?" In *Civil Society, Democracy, and Civic Renewal.* Edited by Robert K. Fullinwider. Lanham, MD: Rowman & Littlefield, 1999.

Schwartz, Bernard, ed. *The Bill of Rights: A Documentary History*. New York, Toronto, London, Sydney: Chelsea House, 1971.

Schwartz, Sally. *A Mixed Multitude*. New York: New York University Press, 1987.

Selover, T. *Hsieh Liang-tso and the Analects of Confucius: Humane Learning as a Religious Quest*. New York: Oxford University Press, 2004.

—————. "Particularity, Commonality and 'Representativity' in Confucian 'Government by Virtue'" (in Chinese). In *Rujia dezhi sixiang tantao* (Exploring Confucian ideas of governing by virtue). Edited by Cai Fanglu, et. al. Beijing: Xianzhuang, 2003.

Shaheen, Jack. "Hollywood's Reel Arabs and Muslims." In *Muslims and Islamization in North America: Problems and Prospects*. Edited by Amber Haque. Beltsville, MD: Amana, 1999.

Shapiro, Edward. "Right Turn? Jews and the American Conservative Movement." In *Jews in American Politics*. Edited by L. Sandy Maisel and Ira N. Forman. Lanham, MD: Rowman & Littlefield, 2001.

Sharkansky, Ira. *Israel and Its Bible: A Political Analysis*. New York: Garland Publishers, 1996.

Sharper, Stephen B. *Redeeming the Time: A Political Theology of the Environment*. New York: Continuum, 1998.

Sherouse, Craig Alan. *The Social Teachings of the Baptist World Alliance, 1905–1980*. Ann Arbor: University of Michigan, Microfilms International Dissertation Services, 1982.

Shipps, Jan. *Mormonism: The Story of a New Religious Tradition*. Urbana: University of Illinois Press, 1985.

Sicker, Martin. *The Political Culture of Judaism*. Westport, CT: Praeger, 2001.

Siddiqui, Ahmadullah. "Islam, Muslims and the American Media." In *Muslims and Islamization in North America: Problems and Prospects*. Edited by Amber Haque. Beltsville, MD: Amana, 1999.

Smith, Alfred E. "Catholic and Patriot: Governor Smith Replies." *Atlantic Monthly* (May 1927): 721.

Smith, Gregory. "Creating a Public of Environmentalists." In *Ecology in Education*. Edited by Monica Hale. Cambridge: Cambridge University Press, 1993.

Smith, Jane I. *Islam in America*. New York: Columbia University Press, 1999.

Smith, Joseph, ed. *Teachings of the Prophet Joseph Smith*. Salt Lake City: Deseret Books, 1976.

Smith, Joseph, ed. *History of the Church of Jesus Christ of Latter-day Saints*. 7 vols. Salt Lake City: Deseret Books, 1948.

Smith, Paul H., et al., eds. *Letters of Delegates to Congress 1774–1789*. 25 vols. Washington: Government Printing Offices, 1876–1998.

Smith, R. Drew. "Black Churches Within a Changing Civic Culture in America." In *New Day Begun: African American Churches and Civic Culture in Post-Civil Rights America*. Edited by R. Drew Smith. Durham: Duke University Press, 2003.

Smith, Robert C. *We Have No Leaders: African Americans in the Post-Civil Rights Era*. Albany: State University of New York Press, 1996.

Smith, Tom W. *A Survey of the Religious Right: Views on Politics, Society, Jews, and Other Minorities*. New York: American Jewish Committee, 1996.

Smith, Wilfred Cantwell. *The Meaning and End of Religion*. 1962. Minneapolis: Fortress Press, 1991.

Smith, Wilfred Cantwell. *The Meaning and End of Religion*. San Francisco: HarperSan Francisco, 1978. Repr. Minneapolis: Augsburg Fortress, 1991.

"Society Shares Blame for Scandals, Vatican Says." *Los Angeles Times*, 26 June 1993, B5.

Sprinzak, Ehud. "Illegalism in Israeli Political Culture: Theoretical and Historical Footnotes to the Pollard Affair and the Shin Beth Cover Up." In *Israel after Begin*. Edited by Gregory Mahler. Albany: State University of New York Press, 1990.

Stack, Peggy Fletcher. "TV Host Says LDS Leader's Views on Christian Charities Differ from Bush's." *Salt Lake Tribune*, 6 February 2001, A1.

Strum, Philippa, and Danielle Tarantolo. *Muslims in the United States*. Washington DC: Woodrow Wilson International Center for Scholars, 2003.

Stuckey, Sterling. *Going through the Storm: The Influence of African American Art in History*. New York: Oxford University Press, 1994.

The Survivors Network of Those Abused by Priests. http://www.snapnetwork.org.

Susser, Bernard. "On the Reconstruction of Jewish Political Theory." In *Public Life in Israel and the Diaspora*. Edited by Sam N. Lehman-Wilzig and Bernard Susser. Ramat Gan. Israel: Bar-Ilan University, 1981.

Talmage, James E. *Jesus the Christ: A Study of the Messiah and His Mission according to Holy Scriptures Both Ancient and Modern*. Salt Lake City: Deseret Books, 1962. Originally published by the LDS Church, 1915.

Taylor, Rodney L. *Religious Dimensions of Confucianism*. Albany: State University of New York Press, 1990.

"Text of Statement by Bishops on Church Role in Politics." *The New York Times*, 14 October 1984, A30.

Thomas, Oliver S. "Views of the Wall." *Report from the Capital* 46 (1991): 6.

Tilton v. Richardson, 403 U.S. 679 (1971).

Tolstoy, Leo. Letters to Susa Young Gates, 1888–1889. See www.ldslibrary.com.

———. *The Private Diaries of Leo Tolstoy, 1853–1857*. Edited by Louise and Aylmer Maude. Translated by Louise and Aylmer Maude. London: Heinemann, 1927. Repr. New York: Kraus 1972.

"Transcript: National Press Club Q&A with President Gordon B. Hinckley." *Deseret Morning News*, 9 March 2000. http://www.deseretnews.com/dn/print/1,1442, 155008723,00.html.

Truett, George W. "The Baptist Conception of Religious Liberty." In *Proclaiming the Baptist Vision: Religious Liberty*. Edited by Walter B. Shurden. Macon, GA: Smyth & Helwys, 1997.

Tu, Wei-ming. "Beyond the Enlightenment Mentality." In *Worldviews and Ecology: Religion, Philosophy, and the Environment*. Edited by Mary Evelyn Tucker and John Grim. New York: Orbis Books, 1994.

———. *Centrality and Commonality: An Essay on Confucian Religiousness*. Albany: State University of New York Press, 1989.

———. *Neo-Confucian Thought in Action: Wang Yang-ming's Youth (1472–1509)*. Berkeley: University of California Press, 1976.

———. "Probing the 'Three Bonds' and 'Five Relationships' in Confucian Humanism." In *Confucianism and the Family*. Edited by Walter H. Slote and George A. DeVos. Albany: State University of New York Press, 1998.

Tu, Wei-ming, and Mary Ellen Tucker, eds. *Confucian Sprituality*. 2 vols. New York: Crossroad, 2003; New York: Herder & Herder, 2003 & 2004.

Tucker, Mary Evelyn, and John Berthrong, eds. *Confucianism and Ecology: The Interrelation of Heaven, Earth, and Humans*. Cambridge, MA: Distributed by Harvard University Press for the Harvard University Center for the Study of World Religions, 1998.

"20 Books That Changed America." *Book* (July–August 2003). http://www.book-magazine.com/issue29/twenty.shtml.

Twohig, Dorothy, et al., eds. *The Papers of George Washington, Presidential Series.* 7 vols. Charlottesville: University Press of Virginia, 1987–2000.

Udall, Stewart L. *The Forgotten Founders: Rethinking the History of the Old West.* Washington, DC: Island Press, 2002.

United States Conference of Catholic Bishops. "Catholics in Political Life," 18 June 2004. http://www.usccb.org/bishops/catholicsinpoliticallife.htm.

———. "Effort to Combat Clergy Sexual Abuse Against Minors: A Chronology." U.S. Conference of Catholic Bishops, Office of Media Relations. http://www.usccb.org/comm/kit2.shtml).

———. *The Essential Norms for Diocesan/Eparchial Policies Dealing with Allegations of Sexual Abuse of Minors by Priests Deacons or Other Church Personnel.* Washington, DC: United States Conference of Catholic Bishops, 2002.

———. "Faithful Citizenship: A Catholic Call to Political Responsibility." 2003. Bishops' Statement. http://www.usccb.org/faithfulcitizenship/bishopStatement.html.

United States v. Ballard, 322 U.S. 78 (1944).

United States v. Carolene Products Co., 304 U.S. 144 (1938).

United States v. Seeger, 380 U.S. 163 (1965).

Upsanisads. Translated by Olivelle Patrick. New York: Oxford University Press, 1996.

Urti, Anthony. "Battle Rages in Utah over Funding of Abortions on Disabled Babies." Center for Reclaiming America, 28 July 2004. http://www.reclaimamerica.org/Pages/News/newspageprint.asp?story=1966.

"U.S. Financial Aid to Israel: Figures, Facts, and Impact." Washington Report on Middle East Affairs. http://www.wrmea.com/html/us_aid_ to_israel.htm.

U.S. Department of Commerce, Bureau of the Census. Historical Statistics of the United States, Colonial Times to 1970.

U.S. Department of State. Report on Global Anti-Semitism, July 1, 2003–December 15, 2004, submitted to the Committee on Foreign Relations and the Committee on International Relations. Released by the Bureau of Democracy, Human Rights, and Labor, 5 January 2005. http://www.state.gov/g/drl/rls/40258.htm.

Van Wagoner, Richard S. *Mormon Polygamy: A History.* Salt Lake City: Signature Books, 1992.

Vertovec, Steven. *The Hindu Diaspora.* London: Routledge, 2000.

Wald, Kenneth D., and Lee Sigelman. "Romancing the Jews: The Christian Right in Search of Strange Bedfellows." In *Sojourners in the Wilderness: The Religious Right in Comparative Perspective.* Edited by Corwin Smidt and James Penning. Lanham, MD: Rowman & Littlefield, 1997.

Wald, Kenneth D., and Corwin E. Smidt. "Measurement Strategies in the Study of Religion and Politics." In *Rediscovering the Religious Factor in American Politics.* Edited by David C. Leege. Armonk, NY: M. E. Sharpe, 1993.

Wald Kenneth D., and Lee Sigelman. "Romancing the Jews: The Christian Right in Search of Strange Bedfellows." In *Sojourners in the Wilderness: The Religious Right in Comparative Perspective.* Edited by Corwin Smidt and James Penning. Lanham, MD: Rowman & Littlefield, 1997.

Waley, Arthur. *The Way and Its Power: a Study of the Tao te Ching and its Place in Chinese Thought.* New York: Grove Press, 1958.

Walker, David. *An Appeal in Four Articles; Together with a Preamble to the Colored Citizens of the World, but in Particular, and Very Expressly, to Those of the United States.* 3rd ed. Boston: David Walker, 1830.

Wallis, Roy, and Steve Bruce. "Secularization: The Orthodox Model." In *Religion and Modernization: Sociologists and Historians Debate the Secularization Thesis*. Edited by Steve Bruce. Oxford: Clarendon, 1992.

Walton, Jr., Hanes, and Robert C. Smith. *African American Politics and the African American Quest for Universal Freedom*. New York: Longman, 2000.

Walzer, Michael, Menachem Lorberbaum, and Noam J. Zohar, eds. *The Jewish Political Tradition: Membership*. New Haven: Yale University Press, 2003.

Walzer, Michael, Menachem Lorberbaum, Noam J. Zohar, and Yair Lorberman, eds. *The Jewish Political Tradition: Authority*. New Haven: Yale University Press, 2000.

Weber, Max. *The Protestant Ethic and the Spirit of Capitalism*. 1904–1905. Repr. New York: Charles Scribner's 1958.

Wenz, Peter S. *Abortion Rights as Religious Freedom*. Philadelphia: Temple University Press, 1992.

West, Cornel. *Prophecy Deliverance! An Afro-American Revolutionary Christianity*. Philadelphia: Westminster Press, 1982.

White House Program on Faith-Based Initiatives. http://www.whitehouse.gov/government/fbci/.

Widmar v. Vincent, 454 U.S. 263 (1981).

Widstoe, John A. "Mormonism." In *Varieties of American Religion*. Edited by Charles Samuel Braden. Chicago: Willett, Clark, 1936.

———. *Priesthood and Church Government in the Church of Jesus Christ of Latter-day Saints*. Salt Lake City: Deseret Books, 1939

Wildavsky, Aaron B. *The Nursing Father: Moses As a Political Leader*. Tuscaloosa: University of Alabama Press, 1984.

Wilgoren, Jodi. "Kerry Vows to Lift Bush Limits on Stem-Cell Research." *The New York Times*, 22 June 2004, A14.

Wilmore, Gayraud S. *Black Religion and Black Radicalism: An Interpretation of the Religious History of African Americans*. Maryknoll, NY: Orbis Books, 2003.

Wilson, E. O. *Biophilia*. Cambridge, MA: Harvard University Press, 1984.

Wilson, John K. "Religion Under the State Constitutions, 1776–1800." *Journal of Church and State* 32 (1990): 753–73.

Winn, Kenneth H. *Exiles in a Land of Liberty: Mormons in America, 1830–1846*. Chapel Hill: University of North Carolina Press, 1989.

Winthrop, James. "Letter of Agrippa," 1788. In *The Bill of Rights: A Documentary History*. Edited by Bernard Schwartz. New York: Chelsea House, 1971.

Witte, John, Jr. *Religion and the American Constitutional Experiment: Essential Rights and Liberties*. Boulder: Westview Press, 2000.

Witters v. Washington Department of Services for the Blind, 474 U.S. 481 (1986).

Wood, James E., Jr. "The New Religious Right and Its Implications for Southern Baptists." *Foundations* 25 (1982): 161.

Woolpert, Stephen. "Transformational Political Groups: The Political Psychology of the Green Movement." In *Transformational Politics: Theory, Study, and Practice*. Edited by Stephen Woolpert, Christa Daryl Slaton, and Edwin W. Schwerin. Albany: State University of New York Press, 1998.

Wootten, David, ed. *John Locke: Political Writings*. New York: Mentor, 1993.

World Family Policy Center. "About the World Family Policy Center," and "Mission Statement." http://www.worldfamilypolicy.org/wfpc/about.htm.

World Watch Institute. *Vital Signs 2002*. New York: Norton, 2002.

Wu, Chung. *The Essentials of the Yi Jing*. St. Paul, MN: Paragon House, 2003.

Wynne, John J., S.J., ed. *The Great Encyclical Letters of Pope Leo XIII*. New York: Benzinger Brothers, 1903.

X, Malcolm. Speech. "FBI's War on Black America," 1964.

Yates, Robert. "Letters of Sydney," 1788. In *The Bill of Rights: A Documentary History*. Edited by Bernard Schwartz. New York: Chelsea House, 1971.

Young, Brigham. "Celebration of the Fourth of July," 4 July 1854. In *Journal of Discourses*. Vol. 7. London: Latter-day Saints' Book Depot, 1860.

———. "The Constitution and Government of the United States—Rights and Policy of the Latter-day Saints." 18 February 1855. *Journal of Discourses* 2 (1855): 170.

Zai, Zhang. " 'Western Inscription.' " In *Sources of Chinese Tradition*. Vol. 1. 2d ed. Compiled by William Theodore de Bary and Irene Bloom. New York: Columbia University Press, 1999.

Zobrest v. Catalina Foothills Board of Education, 509 U.S. 1 (1993).

Zuckerman, Phil. *Du Bois on Religion*. Lanham, MD: Rowman & Littlfield, 2000.

About the Contributors

DEREK H. DAVIS (B.A., M.A., J.D., Baylor University; Ph.D., University of Texas at Dallas) is director of the J.M. Dawson Institute of Church-State Studies at Baylor University, and editor of the award-winning *Journal of Church and State*. He is the author of *Original Intent: Chief Justice Rehnquist & the Course of American Church-State Relations* (1991); *Religion and the Conti nental Congress, 1774–1789: Contributions to Original Intent* (2000); and editor or coeditor of twelve additional books, including the *Legal Deskbook for Administrators of Independent Colleges and Universities* and *The Role of Religion in the Making of Public Policy*. In addition, he has published more than one hundred articles and book chapters. He serves numerous organizations given to the protection of religious freedom in national and international contexts.

JO RENEE FORMICOLA is professor of political science at Seton Hall University in South Orange, New Jersey. She is the author of *The Catholic Church and Human Rights* (1989) as well as *John Paul II: Prophetic Politician* (2002). She is the coauthor of *The Politics of School Choice* (1999) with Hubert Morken and *Faith-Based Initiatives and the Bush Administration: The Good, the Bad and the Ugly* (2003) with Mary Segers and Paul Weber. She is the senior editor and contributor to *Everson Revisited: Religion, Education, and Law at the*

Crossroads (1997) and coeditor and contributor to *Religious Leaders and Faith-Based Politics* (2001). She is currently working on a book scheduled for publication in 2006 by Rowman and Littlefield titled *The Politics of Values*. Formicola has also published a significant number of articles in the area of religion and government.

RITA M. GROSS is Professor Emerita at the University of Wisconsin, Eau Claire. She is known worldwide for her scholarship and commentary on gender and Buddhism. One of the founders of the movement for the feminist study of religion, she has many publications, of which the best known is *Buddhism after Patriarchy: A Feminist History, Analysis, and Reconstruction of Buddhism* (1992). She is also authorized as a senior *dharma* teacher who teaches Buddhism on behalf of several eminent Buddhist gurus.

PHILLIP E. HAMMOND is the D. Mackenzie Brown Professor Emeritus at the University of California, Santa Barbara. He holds the Ph.D. in sociology from Columbia University. His publications include *Religion and Personal Autonomy: The Third Disestablishment in America* (1992), *With Liberty for All: Freedom of Religion in the United States* (1998), *Soka Gakkai in America: Accommodation and Conversion* (1999) with David W. Machacek, *The Dynamics of Religious Organizations: The Extravasation of the Sacred and Other Essays* (2000), and *Religion On Trial: How Supreme Court Trends Threaten the Freedom of Conscience in America* (2004) with David W. Machacek and Eric Michael Mazur.

M. A. MUQTEDAR KHAN is assistant professor in the Department of Political Science and International Relations at the University of Delaware. He is also a nonresident fellow at the Brookings Institution. He is the author of *American Muslims: Bridging Faith and Freedom* (2002) and *Jihad for Jerusalem: Identity and Strategy in International Relations* (2004). His Web site is www.ijtihad.org.

DAVID W. MACHACEK is associate director of Humanity in Action and is a visiting assistant professor of public policy at Trinity College in Hartford, Connecticut. He holds a Ph.D. in religious studies from the University of California at Santa Barbara. He is author of *Soka Gakkai in America: Accommodation and Conversion* (1999) with Phillip E. Hammond, and *Religion on Trial: How Supreme Court Trends Threaten the Freedom of Conscience in America* (2004) with Eric Michael Mazur and Phillip E. Hammond, and editor of *Global Citizens: The Soka Gakkai Buddhist Movement in the World* (2000) with Bryan Wilson and *Sexuality and the World's Religions* (2003) with Melissa M. Wilcox.

BARBARA A. MCGRAW is professor of legal, ethical, and social environment, Saint Mary's College of California, and is an author and speaker on the role of religion in public life. As a speaker, she has addressed San Francisco's Commonwealth Club of California, as well as many other organizations. Among other things, she is the author of *Rediscovering America's Sacred Ground: Public Religion and Pursuit of the Good in a Pluralistic America* (2003) and *Many Peoples, Many Faiths: Women and Men in the World Religions* (Prentice Hall, several editions, 1999–present), with Robert S. Ellwood. In addition to her Ph.D. in religion and social ethics, she holds a Juris Doctor degree, also from the University of Southern California, and is a member of the Bar of the Supreme Court of the United States. She is currently working on a book forthcoming in 2007 by the University of Virginia Press, titled *America's Sacred Ground and the Marketplace: Rediscovering Moral Capitalism.*

JOHN R. POTTENGER, associate professor of political science at the University of Alabama in Huntsville, teaches undergraduate and graduate courses in classical and modern political philosophy, American political thought, contemporary social theory, and political ethics. His published research includes *The Political Theory of Liberation Theology: Toward a Reconvergence of Social Values and Social Science* (1989) and *Reaping the Whirlwind: Religion, the Liberal State, and Civil Society*, soon to be released by Georgetown University Press. He is also the author of numerous articles examining theoretical challenges in Platonic philosophy, modern political theory, and contemporary Christian and Islamic political theology.

ANANTANAND RAMBACHAN is professor of religion and philosophy at Saint Olaf College in Minnesota. He is the author of several books, book chapters, and articles in scholarly journals. His books include *The Limits of Scripture: Vivekananda's Reinterpretation of the Vedas* (1993); *Accomplishing the Accomplished: The Vedas as a Source of Valid Knowledge in Sankara* (1991); and *God, World and Humanity: An Inquiry into the Advaita Worldview* (New York: SUNY, forthcoming).

THOMAS SELOVER is an associate professor in the Department of Religious Studies and Anthropology at the University of Saskatchewan. He has taught at Trinity College in Hartford, as well as in China and Korea. He writes on Confucian thought, interreligious dialogue, and comparative theology. His most recent publication is *Hsieh Liang-tso and the Analects of Confucius: Humane Learning as a Religious Quest* (2005). He and his wife Grace are also involved in several congregational and small group ministries, and work with the Interreligious and International Federation for World Peace (IIFWP).

JAMES LANCE TAYLOR is an associate professor in the Department of Politics at the University of San Francisco where he teaches African-American Politics, Religion and Politics, Race and Ethnicity in the United States, and Public Policy. He has published articles and book chapters on Benjamin Chavis-Muhammed, Betty "X" Shabazz, Robert Alexander Young, and the 1995 Million Man March, which he attended. His forthcoming book with Lynne Reinner Publishers is titled *Sons of Thunder: The Post-Civil Rights Relevance of Malcolm X and Louis Farrakhan.*

KENNETH D. WALD is professor of political science at the University of Florida. A specialist on religion in American politics, his most recent books include *Religion and Politics in the United States* (4th edition, 2003) and the coauthored *Politics of Cultural Differences: Social Change and Voter Mobilization Strategies in the Post–New Deal Period* (2002) with David C. Leege, Brian S. Krueger, and Paul D. Mueller. He coedits the Cambridge University Press book series "Religion, Politics and Social Theory." Wald is currently working on a book about Jewish political behavior.

STEPHEN WOOLPERT is professor of politics and the dean of the School of Liberal Arts at Saint Mary's College of California. He is the senior editor of *Transformational Politics: Theory, Study, and Practice* (1998) and the author of numerous articles on the psychological dimensions of political life. From 1984 to 2001, he served as associate editor of the *Journal of Humanistic Psychology.*

Index

Everson v. Board of Education of Ewing Township (1947), 65, 204–5
exclusive truth claims, 216, 217, 220, 232, 233, 234
exclusivism
  of conservative Christians, 218
  in Hinduism, 294
  of Mormon Church, 107–10, 125
  versus pluralism, 177–78, 179, 216, 217, 232–33
existence (in Buddhism), 222

F
faith-based programs
  Baptist views on, 192, 211, 212
  Christian, 128
  controversy over, 208
  Jewish views on, 38
  Mormon views on, 115
Faithful Citizenship: A Catholic Call to Political Responsibility, 69, 70
false dichotomies in politics, 89, 94
false religious/secular dichotomy, 20–23, 149, 217–18, 251
Falwell, Jerry, 128, 212
family, 95, 173, 214, 229, 246, 270, 271
  and Black Church, 155, 166
  and Catholic Church, 70, 72, 76
  in Confucianism, 45, 47, 49–51, 54, 56, 57, 58
  in Hinduism, 185, 295
  and Mormonism, 104, 106, 111, 112, 115, 116, 117–19, 120, 121–24, 126, 256, 258
  and society, preserving, 51
  values, 193
Farooqi, Ismail, 129
Farrakhan, Louis, 172
Federal Council of Churches, 237
Ferraro, Geraldine, 72, 75
Finkleman, Paul, 158
First Amendment
  Baptist views on, 204, 211
  and Catholic Church, 64, 65, 66
  conscience, protection of, 243–44
  and Islam, 142
  Jewish view of, 35–36, 37
  purpose of, 9, 249, 250
  and religious pluralism, 214
  Supreme Court interpretion of, 242, 272

First Great Awakening (ca. 1730–1760), 237
five blind men and the elephant (metaphor), 178
five relations (in Confucianism), 49–50, 58
form (in Buddhism)
  and emptiness, 215, 221–26, 230, 232
  following consciousness, 91–92, 99
forms or phenomena (in Buddhism), 223–24
Foster, Augustus John, 158
founders, 2, 10–24, 28, 46, 96, 106, 149, 161–68, 169, 177, 182, 187, 192, 193, 195, 202, 207, 217, 220, 227, 231, 241, 252, 257, 259, 263, 264, 265, 269, 275
  church, 287
  hope of, 4
  ground-up approach, 10, 185, 259
  intentions of, 4, 10, 149, 167, 191, 259, 263
  of Israel, 31
  and John Locke, 5, 9, 10, 11, 13–14, 20, 21, 24, 106, 150, 163, 168, 179, 257, 261
  Puritan, 3
  project, 202
  separation of church and state, 21, 22
  vision of, 18, 28, 193, 211
founding fathers, 3, 21, 52, 100, 193, 212, 252, 257
  and Isaac Backus, 198, 212
  and John Locke, 8, 11, 191, 256
  vision of, 193
four spheres of love (in Confucianism), 50, 58
Fourteenth Amendment, 241, 242, 246
Frankel, Marvin, 249
Franklin, Benjamin, 12, 114, 162
Frazier, E. Franklin, 155, 159, 170
freedom, purpose of, 19, 20
freedom (*moksha*) in Hinduism, 174, 175, 182, 183, 184
freedom of association, 106, 108
freedom of conscience, 18, 21, 106, 246, 260, 262
  as American principle, 8–9, 10–13, 24, 106
  Baptist views on, 197, 199, 209

social sciences and religious pluralism, 238

The Souls of Black Folk (DuBois), 155, 169

Southern Baptist Convention (SBC), 202, 206, 207, 208, 211

space and silence (in Buddhism), 223, 224–25, 228, 229, 230–31, 232, 233

space/sky (metaphor), 226, 230, 232

Spiritual Enlightenment, 90

Spiritualists, 237

spiritual life, nurturing, 99–100, 101

Stanley, Charles, 212

Stanton, Elizabeth Cady, 15

stem-cell research, 74, 81, 123–24

Sulayman, Abdul Hameed Abu. *See* Abu Sulayman, Abdul Hameed

Supreme Court, 176, 235–50, 281
    and abortion, 66, 245–46, 247, 250 (*see also Roe v. Wade* [1973])
    and America's Sacred Ground, 25, 236, 242, 244, 247, 248
    civil rights and liberties focus of, 236
    and federal *versus* state power, 235
    and gay rights, 121, 239–40, 246
    moral authority of, 241–48
    and religious education, 38, 64, 204–5, 272
    and religious freedom, 112, 210
    and religious pluralism, 238
    and school prayer, 205, 206, 207

Survivors Network of those Abused by Priests (SNAP), 80

Swami Vivekananda. *See* Vivekananda, Swami

T

Tahreer (Muslim sect), 140, 144

Taliban, 138

Talmud, 41–42

Taylor, Myron C., 204

Ten Commandments, 192, 195, 212, 216, 230

Tenzin Gyatso. *See* Dalai Lama (Tenzin Gyatso)

theocracy
    definition of, 27
    and Judaism, 28, 29, 32–34, 35
    and Mormonism, 107, 110–13
    nature of, 27
    Theodosius, 213

theology of religious pluralism, 177–78, 220, 257

Thieh Nhat Hahn, 223

Thoreau, Henry David, 176–77, 189

toleration, 11, 12, 36, 201, 262, 264
    "mere," 13, 36, 192, 201
    religious, 68, 203

top-down overarching worldview
    antithetical to American's Sacred Ground 33, 38
    antidote to, 18–19, 178, 255
    in Catholic tradition, 5, 62
    Christian government aspirations, 2–3, 21, 211, 213–14, 219–20, 254–55
    in Christian history and tradition, 2–3, 15, 231, 241
    Church of England, 5
    in Confucian tradition, 46, 53
    and conscience, 254–55
    Hinduism and, 5, 185–87, 188
    Islam and, 5, 128–29, 146
    Judaism and, 39
    monarchy, 156, 162
    and Mormonism, 111–12
    opposition to, 5–6, 9
    racist, 156, 160, 168
    secularist, 2, 22, 28, 84, 255
    theocracy, 27, 28, 29, 32–34, 111–12, 213
    versus ground-up approaches to government, 5–9, 23–24, 252, 254–56
    and unsecular humanism, 249

Torah, commentaries on, 41–42

totalitarianism, 104

Transcendentalists, 176–77, 237

true and the good, seeking, 9–10, 13, 15, 19, 252, 256, 258

Truett, George W., 200–201

Truman, Harry, 37, 205

Turner, Henry McNeal, 152

Turner, Nat, 152, 167

Tu Wei-ming, 53

two-level games, 144–45

two-tiered Public Forum, 14, 17, 18, 19, 21, 59, 75, 94, 105, 107 121, 124, 149, 152, 193, 244, 250, 252, 253, 254, 257, 259
    first tier, 14
    second tier, 14, 18